RESORT TO ARMS

RESORT TO ARMS
International and Civil Wars,
1816-1980

Melvin Small   J. David Singer

With the collaboration of:
Robert Bennett, Kari Gluski, and
Susan Jones

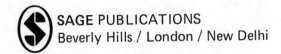
SAGE PUBLICATIONS
Beverly Hills / London / New Delhi

For information address:

SAGE Publications, Inc.
275 South Beverly Drive
Beverly Hills, California 90212

SAGE Publications India Pvt. Ltd.  SAGE Publications Ltd
C-236 Defence Colony   28 Banner Street
New Delhi 110 024, India   London EC1Y 8QE, England

Printed in the United States of America

Library of Congress Cataloging in Publication Data

Small, Melvin.
    Resort to arms.

    Rev. ed. of: The wages of war, 1816-1965 /
J. David Singer, Melvin Small. 1972.
    Bibliography: p.
    1. War. 2. War—Statistics. I. Singer, J.
David (Joel David), 1925-   II. Singer, J.
David (Joel David), 1925-   Wages of war,
1816-1965. III. Title.
U21.2.S6   1981   303.6'6   81-18518
ISBN 0-8039-1776-7   AACR2
ISBN 0-8039-1777-5 (pbk.)

FIRST PRINTING

CONTENTS

Section C: Patterns at the Systemic Level

Section D: Patterns at the National Level

Acknowledgments to the First Edition

Since books that are heavy on data and almost barren of theory are seldom written and less often published in the absence of some demand, our first acknowledgment is to the many researchers and practitioners who either urged the publication of this sort of volume or concurred in that judgment when asked for an opinion. To these few who have been working toward a scientific theory of the causes and consequences of war, and to the many more who will soon be doing so, the book is therefore appropriately dedicated.

Then there are the people responsible for getting the Correlates of War Project—of which this is an early but essential part—out of the vague idea stage and under way. First, it was our interdisciplinary colleagues at the Center for Research on Conflict Resolution and at the Mental Health Research Institute who encouraged and prodded when the project looked more intractable than attractive. Second, the Carnegie Corporation, then willing to support high-risk research in international politics, financed the first phase of the project as well as a number of related studies at the University of Michigan.

We have benefited greatly from the frequent advice of Karl Deutsch during his monthly visits to Ann Arbor, and that of Bruce Russett, who was always available during the critical year 1965-1966. We are equally grateful to that army of historians who alternately delighted us with their painstakingly gathered military statistics, and infuriated us with their Olympian disdain for the comparative and the nomothetic. All are identified, if not classified, in the References section and in the several Appendices.

We thank those who carried out the day-to-day work involved in an enterprise of this nature. In the early data-gathering stage, George

Kraft and Bernard Mennis helped us to screen the hundreds of primary and secondary sources that we used. Responsible for data management and conversion during the long road from raw facts to scientifically useful tables were Marcia Feingold, Vilma Ungerson, Warren Phillips, Michael Wallace, Larry Arnold, Tim Pasich, Urs Luterbacher, John Stuckey, Hugh Wheeler, and Stuart A. Bremer; the latter four were particularly helpful in analyzing the trend and periodicity data. Perhaps more than anyone else, the person who made many of the compilations, prepared most of the draft tables, generally coordinated the entire operation, and repeatedly picked up the loose ends was Susan Jones; along with Ann Clawson and Marsha Stuckey, she also prepared most of the typescript and tabular layouts. Among those who have read parts or all of the manuscript and have given us their suggestions were Bruce Russett, Samuel Huntington, Karl Deutsch, Philip Chase, and Raymond Tanter.

Finally, our gratitude must go to those two pioneers whose intelligence, commitment, and vision are largely responsible for the fact that war is well on the way to becoming an object of scientific inquiry: Lewis Richardson and Quincy Wright.

J. David Singer
Melvin Small
Ann Arbor, 1970

Acknowledgments to the Second Edition

During the time that has passed since the publication of the first edition, many colleagues have contributed to the revision and updating of our data set. Karl Deutsch again played a central role during the early stages, especially in his support for our civil war project. Robert Bennett and Susan Jones launched that project, worked up suitable coding rules, and ultimately collected most of the data. Moreover, the methodological and theoretical comments in Chapter 12 reflect their approach to the problem. Among those who assisted with our data collection efforts were Mike Champion, Charles Gochmann, Tom Kselman, Russell Leng, Zeev Maoz, Brad Martin, Alden Mullins, Judy Nowack, Mark Small, Richard Stoll, John Thomas, Michael Wallace, and Peter Wallensteen.

Kari Gluski prepared all of the tables for the new volume and helped to interpret them. Virginia Corbin gave her usual virtuoso performance at the typewriter. Sarajane Miller Small helped edit and inspire. Mary Macknick tidied the final loose ends.

During this phase of our work, the project was supported by the Mental Health Research Institute, the National Science Foundation, and the Harry Frank Guggenheim Foundation. Wayne State University was especially generous with computer time. And, of course, we again thank our readers and colleagues for their many useful suggestions concerning ways to improve upon the first edition.

Melvin Small
J. David Singer

Detroit, 1981

Preface

In the opening chapter of Quincy Wright's *Study of War,* completed on the eve of World War II, we are reminded that war has many meanings.

> To some it is a plague which ought to be eliminated; to others, a crime which ought to be punished; to still others, it is an anachronism which no longer serves any purpose. On the other hand, there are some who take a more receptive attitude toward war, and regard it as an adventure which may be interesting, an instrument which may be legitimate and appropriate, or a condition of existence for which one must be prepared [1942:I, 3].

Regardless of how we conceive of war, we have made but modest progress in understanding this most complex and recurring social phenomenon—in terms of either its causes or its consequences. The speculation has been endless and the verbiage overwhelming, yet anything close to full explanation has eluded us.

Without belittling the efforts of earlier generations, it is only within the past several decades that any intellectual assault of promise has been launched against this organized tribal slaughter. That is, until war has been systematically described, it cannot be adequately *understood,* and with such understanding comes the first meaningful possibility of controlling it, eliminating it, or finding less reprehensible substitutes for it. In our judgment, the important turning point is marked by the rise of scientific (and therefore quantitative) analyses of war, manifested primarily in the work of Quincy Wright and Lewis Richardson beginning in the 1930s.

Inspired by the efforts of these scholars, and encouraged by their limited successes, we launched a project in 1963 designed to identify the variables most frequently associated with the onset of war during the century and a half since the Congress of Vienna. More specifically, we committed ourselves to a research program that might help to ascertain which factors characterize those conflicts that terminate in war, and which accompany those that find a less violent resolution. One of the first requirements in such a study was to discover the trends and fluctuations in the frequency, magnitude, severity, and intensity of war during that period; once our data were gathered for these variables, a systematic search for the most potent explanatory variables could begin.

The purpose of this volume is to bring to our colleagues and students in the war/peace field a report on our progress in this very limited, but essential, first task. As we have emphasized more than once, it is all very well to speculate about the causes and correlates of war, or even to spell out our speculation in formal mathematical terms, but until we have carefully described the spatial and temporal distribution of war, there is absolutely no way to know whether or not we are on the right track. To put it even more bluntly, there is no way to choose among rival *explanations* of a phenomenon until we have *described* that phenomenon. And we mean "describe" in the strictest sense: using explicit criteria and reproducible procedures to sort through the bewildering array of facts, non-facts, impressions, and recollections from all corners of the world and from many national, ethnic, and ideological perspectives, and thus generate a data set of high reliability and validity. With such a data set, we and others can then pursue the elusive causes-of-war question in a systematic fashion, following a wide variety of theoretical predilections in the context of rigorous and cumulative empirical research. Later we will return to the question of research strategy and theoretical orientation, but we need first say a bit more about the volume at hand.

This is, of course a revised, updated, and expanded version of the original *Wages of War* handbook, published by John Wiley and Sons in 1972. The purpose of that first edition was to make our data on international war for the period 1816-1965 available to a wider circle of researchers, students, and practitioners. While we had already made that data set available to a fair number of our colleagues in America and Europe via computer printout and magnetic tape, it seemed important to make it available to those other than close colleagues, former students, and those with experience in and access to computerized data analysis. The assumption, of course, was that more people of diverse orientations might be stimulated to think about the causes of war in a creative and systematic way if they could just "look at" this large array of information. Since that first edition, reports indicate that thousands of students and hundreds of colleagues here and abroad have indeed questioned the criteria, pondered the procedures, mulled over the data, and speculated on the causes and consequences of those 93 wars that are described in so detached and objective a manner. Perhaps more gratifying has been the response of the research community. While no effort has been made to keep close track, well over a hundred scholars around the world have written for and received the magnetic tape or punch card versions of the data set for research and teaching purposes. And we have seen approximately three dozen dissertations, books, and articles relying in part or whole on the *Wages of War* data base, as well as other sets from the Correlates of War Project. In any event, there has been more than enough of an affirmative response to that effort to persuade us that a new and revised edition is definitely in order.

Wherein do the two volumes differ? First, we have extended the temporal domain another 15 years, from 1965 to 1980, leading to the inclusion of events that are all too predictable—more international wars. Second, by ourselves and with the advice of others, we "found" nine more episodes of sustained combat that were not classified as international wars in the first edition. Third, in a handful of cases we have found additional evidence such that a few war dates have been changed and several battle death levels re-estimated. Fourth, and perhaps most important, we have combined the extension and revision work on international war with a wholly new enterprise: identifying all major *civil wars* that have occurred within any of the state members of the international system since the Congress of Vienna. The second half of the volume is devoted to a description of the 106 civil wars that met our criteria for inclusion. (The number of civil wars is remarkably close to the 118 international wars that occurred within the same spatial and temporal domain.) Finally, in order to keep this edition to a manageable size (and price), some pruning was essential. This took two forms.

First, we present markedly fewer descriptive analyses of the interstate and extra-systemic war distributions than in the first edition. These exclusions seem justified not only on the grounds that some of these analyses produced little of theoretical interest, but also because those results that *were* most interesting are largely replicated in the new and enlarged data set. Given the alarmingly slow pace at which politicians and citizens seem to learn from history, it is no surprise that the patterns in international war of 1965-1980 are quite similar to those of the previous 150 years.

The second mode—reflecting the fact that international war remains our major concern, and its explication our dominant commitment—led us to devote less space to descriptive analyses of the civil war data set. This is not to downgrade the importance of civil war or our effort to describe its incidence over the past 165 years; our procedures have been as rigorous and our sifting of the historical materials as complete as in the case of the international wars. But as eager as we are to see a research assault on civil war that is as rigorous as that now under way vis-à-vis international war, it is clearly a task better left to others. Thus, our effort in this connection is essentially a response to the exigencies of today's world, an acknowledgment of the excellent work already initiated by several scholars of internal war and an invitation to them and others to both improve upon and exploit this rich lode of historical material.

Returning to our preoccupation with the elimination of international war and the possible role of solid explanatory knowledge in that enterprise, let us close here with a brief overview of the way we hope to generate that knowledge. How, in fact, have we gone about the effort to account for the incidence of war reported here, and what are our next steps? In the Correlates of War Project Bibliography, one finds a fairly complete listing of the books and articles that have emanated from the project, and in these we spell out our assumptions, hypotheses, findings, and interpretations, as well as (with some frequency) our epistemology and research strategies. The general outlines of our particular strategy were laid down about 15 years ago as the project went through that incremental metamorphosis from casual speculation to serious commitment. While certain elements have been refined along the way, we have found no reason—either in the many findings to date or in the comments of our colleagues—to make any fundamental changes in our basic design. Therefore, we summarize it here briefly in order to put the present volume into proper context and to suggest one possible approach to those who may pick up the challenge that these war data pose.

Beginning with the key epistemological arguments, it is obvious that we believe strongly in the need for an inductive, empirical approach. Our frequent and systematic examination of both the data-based work (Singer, 1981) and the extensive speculative work persuades us of two things in this regard. First, there are many plausible hunches and models regarding the causes of war, some of which are logically incompatible with one another. Second, outside of the more trivial ones, few of these models or hunches—whether concerned with all wars, a particular subset of them, or even those few that are bounded by a given time-space frame—have yet been successfully confirmed or disconfirmed. This is not to say that we find all of the contending notions equally plausible; rather, we merely emphasize the importance of distinguishing between the a priori plausibility and post-investigative comparison of the models with the evidence. From this it follows that we must indeed be tentative enough to begin with a search for the *correlates* of war; hence the name of the project. In other words, we began with a systematic "fishing expedition" during the earlier phase of the enterprise.

Such an approach need not, however, be either mindless or atheoretical. We, like others of this persuasion, have some clear ideas as to which potentially "causal" variables ought to be examined first and rather definite views as to the methods by which their explanatory power may eventually be appraised. Regarding the latter, our investment continues to be heaviest in the multivariate statistical analysis approach. Our immediate objective has been to discover which particular clusters of variables, singly and in combination, show the consistently strongest association with fluctuations in the incidence of war over the 165 years under study. To put it simply, we want first to discover what kinds of conditions and events are most regularly associated with periods and places characterized by the highest and lowest incidence of such violence. Once those patterns have been satisfactorily ascertained, we can move on to the more fundamental question: What events and conditions most sharply differentiate between those international conflicts of the past 165 years that terminated in war and those that found another and less violent resolution?

Of course, the social sciences are already well equipped to begin such an inquiry. We have utilized such simple techniques as the scatter diagram, rank order and product moment correlations, and the multiple regression type of data analysis. But we also used more complex and powerful techniques, including a variety of causal inference types of longitudinal analysis. The generic name for such techniques already indicates that the line between the search for correlation and for causality is far from sharp and clear. Thus, as the statistical regularities become increasingly apparent, the mode of inquiry becomes increasingly theoretical, and the search for causal patterns and sequences becomes more intense.

Moreover, as the more causal models were systematically tested against our data, and those that give the best fit were more clearly identified, the use of a further analytical tool became appropriate. Reference is to computerized dynamic modeling, permitting us not only to discover which historical configurations best account for the incidence of war, but also to deal with a range of "what if" questions. One of the more frequent criticisms of the longitudinal, ex post facto, experimental type of study under way here is that it can handle only events and conditions that *did* appear in the referent world and must therefore be forever inadequate in dealing with what *might have* occurred. This criticism loses much of its salience when one can move back and forth between ideas and evidence, gradually improving one's models. As these explanatory schemes, based on configurations that *could have* obtained as well as those which we have indeed observed, become more refined and subtle, the relevance of this strategy becomes increasingly apparent. That is, we are no longer restricted to accounting for wars that erupted in the past, but are in an increasingly strong position to search for configurations that could well erupt into war in the future.

So much for the tools and techniques we employ. What types of evidence are to be evaluated? There are four basic sets of data in which we find our independent and intervening (or, less rigidly put, our predictor) variables. First, there are the physical, structural, and cultural attributes of the international system itself. Using operational observations taken on an annual or other regular basis, we can describe the state of the system (or any of its sub-systems) at a given point in time and can also measure and record the directions and rates of change therein over time. These particular data will permit us both to identify the systemic patterns that are most strongly associated with fluctuations in the incidence of war under varying time-lag conditions and to control for the ecological constraints and opportunities that are at work as the specific international conflicts unfold.

Second, there are the attributes of the nations themselves. Using a variety of indicators by which their physical, structural, and cultural characteristics may be operationally measured, we can go on to ascertain which particular types of nations, at which particular stages in their history, have been most and least war prone. In Chapters 10 and 17 of this volume, we merely identify which specific nations have been most war prone during their entire tenure in the system, but with the above indicators we will be able to generalize about *classes* of nations and *stages* in their military, economic, and political history. When we use our systemic and national attribute data together, our analyses reveal which types of nations in which particular ecological contexts have been—and might be—most likely to go to war, either by initiative or response, or, more likely, by some combination of the two.

A third set of predictor variables are those that describe the fluctuating relationships between and among specific pairs and clusters of

nations over time. Reflecting the strength and types of interdependence that characterize all dyads and groups of system members,
these measures get at the diplomatic, military, political, economic,
and cultural links between and among them.

The fourth and final set of variables is at once the most intriguing
and the most elusive of those that help us identify the causes of war.
Reference is to the behavioral and interactional sequences that characterize each inter-nation conflict process. In the complex stages by
which pairs and groups of nations move from modest competition
through sustained rivalry into conflict and crisis, there will be certain modes of behavior that regularly lead to war and others that lead
to a less violent outcome. When we use a feedback type of scheme,
these data permit us to identify the national decisions and moves that
are most often self-aggravating in their effects and those that tend to
be self-correcting. Controlling for the state of the larger system, the
types of nations engaged in the conflict, and their preconflict relationships, we should be able to discover which strategies and resulting interaction patterns have been—and may continue to be—most
likely to lead to large-scale international violence.

PART I

INTERNATIONAL WAR

CHAPTER 1

Introduction

For more than a decade, we at the Correlates of War Project have been generating and analyzing systematic data on the incidence of international war and on those factors that might account best for the distribution of such war. And, as indicated in the preface, the research task is of such magnitude that we have no expectation of ever completing it by ourselves. We may privately hope that the important discoveries and major breakthroughs will be our own, but the stakes —scientifically and socially—are much too high for us to rely on a single team, be it ours or another, to produce these discoveries. Thus, we continue our long-established practice of making all our data available to the rest of the research community as soon as it is in reasonably clean condition. Sometimes we merely send out tapes, cards, or printouts along with the coder's manual, but when feasible we also try to publish the information in a more generally accessible form.

Our purpose here, then, is to make our war data as generally and quickly available as possible, and in a maximally useful format. But two additional motives were also at work. First, as data on international and civil wars are not easy to come by, we have occasionally had to rely upon relatively weak evidence. Thus, despite herculean efforts at maximum accuracy and precision, errors will inevitably have crept in, and we trust that any such errors of fact—as well as objections to coding rules—will be brought promptly to our attention. Indeed, since the original publication in 1972, colleagues have offered us a variety of useful additions and corrections. A second and more minor consideration is that publication of our data and the rather elaborate procedures by which they were generated spares us the need for lengthy reiteration in the more analytical books and articles that rest upon these data.

Thus, our intent is to supply the kind of evidence that will accelerate and strengthen the trend toward rigorous historical research into the causes of international war. This is not, however, the only use to which this report may be put. After all, war is more than just a dependent variable or an outcome in most formulations of international politics. Its onset and its termination play an important role at many other points in the feedback loops that characterize the processes of international politics. War often brings in its train a dramatic range of phenomena, and the memory or expectation of war is also not without its effects. To illustrate, several of our studies examine the extent to which the recency and magnitude of given wars predict such subsequent changes in the international system as the distribution of power and diplomatic status, alliance configurations and polarization, and lateral and vertical mobility rates. Likewise, war experience affects a nation's internal politics, social structure, and economy, its alliance and trading propensities, and the way in which it handles subsequent diplomatic and military problems.

Carrying this approach a step further, we are not unaware of the interest other social scientists might have in data such as these. The sociologist might use them to examine, in addition to the phenomena noted above, the effect of war on crime, health, suicide, divorce, social organization, and the like; the economist might investigate the correlations between our data and such conditions as unemployment, distribution practices, collective bargaining procedures, and economic growth; and the anthropologist or psychologist might use these data to analyze the impact of war on national character, ethical norms, child-rearing practices, mental illness, or alcoholism. In sum, war may be viewed as a dependent, independent, or intervening variable, and we therefore see this volume as contributing not only to peace research but to a great many other theoretical concerns in all the social sciences.

It is one thing to hope that a compendium such as this will be well received and widely used and quite another to assume that it will escape its share of criticism, constructive and otherwise. In order to spare certain of our readers the need to point out those obvious pitfalls of which we are already aware, we thought it might be useful to say a pre-emptive word or two in anticipation of the inevitable phrases stressing "the authors' hopeless näiveté" and related themes. Four of these criticisms come readily to mind.

First, it will undoubtedly be argued that no two wars are the same and that any such effort at accumulation and comparison will founder on the rocks of apparent, but unreal, similarity. The point is well taken, and as our many alternative categories of war make clear, we are not oblivious to the problem. No two social events ever *are* quite the same, and as a matter of fact, neither are any two physical events; at the very least, they must occur at different points in time or space. But depending on the scientific interests of the researcher, they often are sufficiently similar to permit meaningful generalization. Clearly, this report, and the project of which it is a part, is not intended to stifle detailed inquiry into each or any of the wars we describe statistically; instead, its purpose is to provide the kind of hard evidence that would make such an inquiry that much more productive. Thus, even as we generalize across all or some of these international wars, we are painfully aware of the inconsistencies and dissimilarities that made the original data-making operations a source of such agony and frustration.

A second and somewhat related criticism is likely to arise over the point that, even if there is sufficient comparability within or between the various classes of wars, the settings in which they occurred and the factors that preceded or caused them will have been appreciably different over the time span covered. This observation is undoubtedly true but not particularly interesting. The scientifically interesting point concerns the specific dimensions along which the settings and situations *do* differ and by how much. That, of course, is an empirical question and one to which we have directed a great deal of attention.

Another criticism to be anticipated concerns the data themselves. Many will no doubt argue, and not without reason, that it is impossible to find military statistics of sufficient authenticity and accuracy to be worth assembling. They will remind us that not only do field commanders and foreign ministries have personal or institutional axes to grind, but that scholars may also have been less than dedicated in *their* search for all the facts. This is true enough, but it is largely beside the point. First, if we were to refrain from doing historical analyses because of the relative paucity or unreliability of the available evidence, some of the most important work in archaeology, zoology, and astronomy—not to mention history, philosophy, and political science—would also come to a halt. The job of the scientist is to sift, evaluate, and collate by procedures that are *sufficiently rigorous* to satisfy her or his own skepticisms, and *sufficiently replicable* to satisfy the skepticism of her or his fellow scholars. This we believe we have done, but as we noted earlier, there is no ironclad guarantee that we have utilized only the best sources or drawn our data from them by the best methods.

Finally, as readers come to one after another of our combinations, aggregations, and analyses, they may wonder why *other* computations and analyses have not been provided. All we can say is that we have tried to strike the most intelligent balance we could, weighing the possible needs of the research community on the one hand and the extent to which excessive or redundant tabulations might make the volume less useful, less readable, less compelling, and more expensive on the other.

Closely related to this is the matter of summarizing a wide variety of indicators in economical form. This is a subject of considerable controversy in the social sciences today. In these techniques, the objective is to reduce one's data by ascertaining the presence and strength of a few underlying dimensions or factors. One point of view is that one should gather the maximum amount of data or generate the maximum number of measures, and then go on to combine, compress, or reduce them to their dominant and "natural" underlying dimensions. Thus, we might take every one of the indicators presented in the chapters that follow, compute the product moment correlations between and among them, and then factor-analyze the resulting matrix. Such an exercise would probably produce a number of factors that might be labeled "amount of war begun," "amount of war under way," and "amount of war terminated." But it could just as likely produce a rather different set of factors, such as "amount of central system war" and "amount of peripheral system war"; this because there is inevitably a high correlation among the amounts of war begun, under way, and terminated for given subsets of the world's nations.

Others hold that most data reduction or compression procedures tend to blur and conceal many important differences, merging and combining information that is of greater scientific value when left isolated and identifiable. We have not only discussed and debated the merits of these arguments, but we have also subjected much of these data to such reduction processes as "construct mapping" (Jones, 1966). The results were essentially as we predicted and are not sufficiently interesting or useful to report here.

Our own approach involves posing a few of the general questions regarding the incidence of war, and then applying only such analyses as seem most relevant to those particular concerns. Our data might suggest or provide answers to many more descriptive questions than we have asked, and there are many more modes of analysis than we have utilized.

In the chapters that follow, we will summarize prior efforts (serious and otherwise) to put together quantitative evidence on the recurrence of war, compare our results with these earlier and incomplete attempts, describe our data-making procedures in detail, present a wide range of figures in a variety of forms, develop a number of frequency distributions, and suggest some of the ways in which these data might be used by others who agree with us that war is important enough to warrant the most thorough and rigorous analysis known to modern social science.

PRIOR QUANTITATIVE COMPILATIONS

There is probably not a single scholar in the field who is not at least partly familiar with Quincy Wright's *A Study of War* (1942, revised in 1965), and those having more than a passing acquaintance with this monumental study will know that in Appendix XX of Volume 1, the author presents a list of 278 "Wars of Modern Civilization" covering the period from 1480 to 1940. For most of these wars, he provides the opening and closing dates; the name of the peace treaty that terminated it; the nations that participated and their dates of entry; his classification of the initiating and defending sides; the number of participants vis-à-vis the number of states in the system at the time; the number of important battles; and his classification as to whether it was a balance of power, civil, defensive, or imperialistic war. While he does not provide casualty figures for the specific nations in the *specific* wars, he moves in that direction in Appendix XXI, showing estimates of war casualties and number of combatants for the leading powers over various periods since the seventeenth century, as well as figures on the proportions of various populations that were killed during those periods and in World War I. Most of these estimates were

gathered by James C. King, one of Wright's students and collabora-
tors in the project, and were compared with figures compiled by
Pitirim Sorokin for *Social and Cultural Dynamics* (1937). In the revised edition (1965), Wright updated his list to cover the post-World
War II period and included battle death estimates for each of these
more recent wars.

As familiar as Wright's work may be, that of the other researcher
whose pioneering efforts we follow, until recently, was relatively unknown: Lewis Richardson's *Statistics of Deadly Quarrels* (1960a). As
early as 1919, this British physicist-meteorologist had written (and
run off 300 copies, since, "there was no learned society to which I
dared offer so unconventional a work") a paper on the "Mathematical
Psychology of War"; and during the 1930s he continued to employ
statistical techniques in a variety of papers on war and peace. This
serious avocation of Richardson's culminated, due largely to the efforts of Quincy Wright as well as Anatol Rapoport, Nicholas
Rashevsky, Ernest Trucco, and Carl Lienau, in the *Statistics of
Deadly Quarrels* and *Arms and Insecurity* (1960b), both published
seven years after his death. Only a portion of the first of these volumes will concern us here—those chapters in which he sought to uncover and list all wars that terminated between 1820 and 1949 and
that resulted in battle-associated deaths of 317 or more (Rapoport,
1957). Also included in his tabulation are the protagonists, the initial
and terminal dates for each pair of them, the number of deaths, and
his evaluations of the protagonists' objectives and the conditions associated with the pre-war conflict.

While these two scholars have done the most valuable work to date,
the work of several others should be mentioned. A third important
figure is the aforementioned sociologist, Pitirim A. Sorokin, whose
Social and Cultural Dynamics (1937) also presents a wide range of
figures on the frequency and severity of war. But while his time span
began with antiquity, he was concerned with only the most diplomati-
cally active nations and their wars. Moreover, his theoretical purposes required much less precision than do ours; instead of conduct-
ing one more exhaustive search in a project that had already led to
many such empirical expeditions, he devised an ingenious, but
highly approximate, set of estimation procedures. Taking rough account of the military tactics and technology of the time, and introducing a range of intuitively reasonable weighting factors, he produced a
number of war lists that were quite satisfactory for the "order of magnitude" requirements demanded by his *Fluctuations of Social Relationships, War, and Revolution: Arms and Security* (1937) study. A

valuable by-product of that investigation is his most penetrating discussion (in Chapter Nine) on the uses and limits of precision in longitudinal social science research.

A fourth scholar who attempted a fairly exhaustive compendium is the Russian historian Boris T. Urlanis. His *Wars and the Population of Europe* (1960), however, was not as useful as the first three sources. In addition to an ideological preoccupation with the differential class suffering imposed by "imperialist wars," his volume also suffers from certain methodological difficulties. Its casualty categories were not always comparable from war to war and analysis to analysis; estimates for a given war did not always include some of the most active combatant nations, and compilations were often for periods embracing a number of wars that were not specified. In addition, since Urlanis and we relied on many of the same sources, it was more feasible to apply our own explicit criteria to those sources than to rely on his less visible coding rules.

A fifth and extremely valuable series of studies is that inaugurated in 1911 by the Division of Economics and History of the Carnegie Endowment for International Peace. Two of the volumes in the series, which was established "to promote a thorough and scientific investigation of the causes and results of war," were especially useful: Gaston Bodart's *Losses of Life in Modern Wars* (1916), and Samuel Dumas and Knud Otto Vedel-Peterson's *Losses of Life Caused by War* (1923). Bodart examined the wars of France and Austria-Hungary from the seventeenth to the twentieth century, and since these two nations participated in many of the major wars in that period, his results are quite valuable. For their part, Dumas and Vedel-Peterson examined most of the "important" wars from the Seven Years War through World War I. Both studies were concerned with civilian deaths, ratios between officer and enlisted battle deaths, disease and prisoner of war figures, and treatments of separate battles and separate campaigns. In many ways, these two volumes served as our most valuable point of departure, and without them the enterprise would have been more costly and our results less reliable.

A sixth effort along these lines was that undertaken by Frank Klingberg (1945 and 1966), an associate of Wright's in the Study of War Project. Toward the closing days of World War II, with Allied speculation running high as to when and under what conditions the Japanese might surrender, a consultant to Secretary of War Henry L. Stimson (William Shockley, later the joint winner of a Nobel Prize for the development of transistors) suggested that a historical survey of casualties might help ascertain under what conditions Japan might capitulate. At Wright's urging, the study was soon begun, but it was not completed in time to exercise any impact on strategic planning. Klingberg did, however, gather a large number of casualty estimates, and while they were subjected to a most insightful analysis, they were seldom in a form we could use directly. Most often, the estimates (largely based on Bodart, 1916) were for given battles rather than total wars, and when a war's figures were presented, they generally included civilian casualties as well. This suggestive study, which had remained virtually unknown for 20 years, was finally resurrected at our urging and subsequently published by Klingberg in abbreviated form in the *Journal of Conflict Resolution* (1966). We will allude to it further in Chapter 11, where we analyze the victor-vanquished ratios in terms of the magnitude of their war experiences and the severity of their losses.

More recently (1976), Bouthoul and Carrère put together a list of 366 major wars and revolutions from 1740 to 1974. Incorporating most of the wars and violent actions cited by Richardson, Wright, and ourselves, and bringing the compendium up through the early 1970s, Bouthoul and Carrère were interested in wars and revolutions that met *any* of six criteria—"involved more than one state, took place beyond a province or a capital, lasted more than one year, resulted in more than 1,000 deaths, had important internal consequences, had important international consequences." While these French polemologists are less concerned with precise dating and battle death figures than are we, and while their criteria are sometimes vague, their list is valuable, as is their analysis of trends. Kende (1971, 1978) is a widely cited source for the post-1945 wars, revolutions, and interventions. While a good deal of care and effort has gone into his studies, this Hungarian scholar is not very concerned about precise battle death figures or onset and termination dates. Moreover, he labels as wars actions we consider covert interventions that do not lead directly to 1,000 deaths.

Less useful than Bouthoul and Carrère and Kende is the *Annual of Power and Conflict* that has been published since 1971 by London's Institute for the Study of Conflict. Each year, editor Brian Crozier offers narrative accounts of the year's violent events in most of the countries of the world. This synopsis may serve as a starting point for those seeking to catalogue violent manifestations, especially internal violence, since the early 1970s, but it is of little value for those in search of hard data.

Then there were a number of statistical studies that dealt with either a single war or a few at most and usually for only a handful of nations or battles. Among the most useful to us were Perce (1858), Berndt (1897), Harbottle (1904), Bodart (1908), Beebe and de Bakey (1952), and Eggenberger (1967). These and the others that served to provide, corroborate, or correct our battle death and duration estimates for each specific war are listed in Appendix A and are cited in the references.

Another investigation, motivated by many of the considerations that entered into our own study, was Woods and Baltzly's *Is War Diminishing?* (1915). They tell us that it was their "wholesome disgust at the unscientific nature" of existing work that led them to "collect these humble facts" on trends in the incidence of war. Covering the war experiences of about a dozen nations for the period 1450-1900, the study was nevertheless of marginal value. Even though the authors turned up a number of general patterns, their coding rules and measuring procedures were much too vague and imprecise to permit our use of their figures.

SUMMARY

The basic arrangement of Parts I and II of the volume is as follows. After outlining our rationale and general procedure (Section A), we divide each part into three major sections, depending on the unit of analysis. In Section B, the individual wars represent our unit of analysis; there we describe each of them in terms of their magnitude, severity, and intensity, after which we go on to rank them according to each of these measures. In Section C, we aggregate the separate wars in order to generalize about the incidence of war in the international system across time. Here, the system is our unit of analysis, and our concern is to identify the amount of war that began, was under way, or that terminated each year in the total system and in its several regional and functional sub-systems. Finally, in Section D, we shift to the individual nation as our unit of analysis, indicating the total amount of war experienced by each during its tenure in the system and comparing and ranking the nations (and regions) according to a variety of raw and normalized measures of war experience. This final part also presents the data by which certain systematic comparisons might be made between the battle losses of the victors and the vanquished, and by which one might discover whether the termination of wars can be predicted on the basis of such fatality figures.

In sum, we believe these results represent a significant advance in accuracy and comparability over any prior compilation, and hope that they will not only be useful to those scholars already engaged in research on the causes, characteristics, and consequences of war but will, by their mere availability, encourage rapid acceleration in such research in the years ahead.

CHAPTER 2

Identifying the International Wars
The Inclusion and Exclusion Problem

We now turn to the task at hand and try to explain the procedures we used in arriving at the results that are reported in Chapter 4 and those following. Here, of course, is where we part company with many of our colleagues in political science and history. If we look at the international scene over the 1816-1980 period, we find at first glance a bewildering array of events. And for our concerns, there seem to be many periods and places characterized by war, others characterized by peace, and others that appear to represent neither war nor peace. But can we generalize on the basis of these impressions? Can we honestly do any more than say that there has indeed been a "great deal" of war among nations over these 165 years? Given the haziness of the line between war and peace and the elusiveness of these boundaries in time and space, some will contend that any sharp delineations are either impossible or so arbitrary as to be politically meaningless. Others will urge that the exercise is hardly necessary in the first place. So be it. All we can do is advise readers who are so persuaded to skip Chapters 2 and 3 and turn immediately to the results that emerge.

But for those who recognize that the quality of a product is often determined by the procedures by which it is created, and that creativity devoid of rigor may be aesthetically pleasing but scientifically dubious, our preoccupation with method will be seen as essential.

Here, and at appropriate places later on, we will spell out our data-making steps in considerable detail. What we intend to do is articulate the procedures and criteria employed in our conversion of the vast, buzzing confusion of military history so that users of the results can do two things. First, this description will permit them to apply the same coding and classifying criteria to the same period and come up with (almost) exactly the same results. Few, if any, will actually do this, but it is a cardinal rule in scientific investigations that such replication be possible; if it is not, there is no way of knowing whether the resulting figures are indeed reliable enough for the analyst and theorizer to use with any confidence. The second, and equally important, consequence of this self-conscious delineation of procedures is that others will be able to discover easily not only *how* we arrived at our descriptions but *why* their intuitive expectations differ from our results, if any surprises do indeed turn up.

Given this set of considerations, and seeking to discover the frequency, magnitude, severity, and intensity of war in the international system since the end of the Napoleonic Wars, it behooves us to begin with a delineation and justification of the spatial-temporal domain to which the study is confined.

THE SPATIAL-TEMPORAL DOMAIN

In order to generalize, it is imperative first to specify the spatial-temporal domain to which one's generalizations apply. As obvious as this dictum may be, it is violated frequently in the study of international politics. It is an easy matter to find contemporary as well as relatively ancient writings in which authors either fail to specify the boundaries in time and space to which their generalizations should be confined or, worse yet, generalize to a broad domain on the basis of evidence drawn from a limited number of years or a few political entities. Only by a very explicit specification of one's domain can this type of sin be avoided, and it is to that specification which we now turn.

The Temporal Boundaries

As the movement toward greater quantification in international politics research has accelerated, there seems to have been a decreasing emphasis on the long, historical view. While this apparent correlation is understandable, in our judgment it is most unfortunate. It is understandable because there clearly are less and less hard data available on many variables as we go back in time. That is, the post-World War II period is characterized by a rapid increase in the availability and reliability of comparative and cumulative cross-national data, thanks largely to the United Nations, OECD, and many other international governmental organizations. Likewise, while both the quantity and quality of such data for the inter-war period are lower than for the post-1945 era, the statistical compilations of the League of Nations and the International Labor Organization, for example, represent an impressive advance over what was available prior to World War I.

But it can be argued that such compilations, despite their great value for social science (and social policy) may well be ignoring the variables that are most critical for an understanding of international politics. One might even agree with the charge that, to some extent, the social sciences have tended to lose in relevance what they have gained in precision. Or, to use a familiar metaphor, we may—like the drunk on a dark street—be looking under the lamp post for things that were lost further down the block. Moreover if the socio-economic variables that are most widely measured and reported are not the ones that will best explain the phenomena that concern us (and this remains an empirical question), and if we must eventually get back to the traditional variables of diplomacy, strategy, decision making, and the like, then there is an additional argument in favor of taking the longer view. That is, if most of the information from which such diplomatic data might be generated is found in the collections of documents and communications of the relevant foreign and defense ministries, and these archives are withheld from public scrutiny for periods of from two to five decades or longer, there is no way to acquire a full and accurate picture of the immediate past.

In addition to these two considerations, there is a third and perhaps more important reason for not restricting one's research to a brief (and usually quite contemporary) time span. This is our conviction that no social phenomena are comprehensible except in the context of the historical flow in which they are embedded. Prior events and conditions, along with the direction and rate of change in them, must be taken into account if we hope to explain the present or predict the future.

Finally, the long view is essential just because anti-scientific critics are correct in one of their assertions: as conditions change, the relationships among variables will change, and regularities that hold in the early nineteenth century will often not hold in the late twentieth, or perhaps even the mid-nineteenth century. This is not exactly news to the social scientist; we are perfectly aware that correlational, and thus causal, associations will seldom apply over very long historical periods. But it is one thing to make this vague assertion and quite another to ascertain which patterns change when, how much, and in which directions. With that sort of empirical evidence, we actually move closer to explanatory theory, because we are compelled to address the question as to *why* this or that set of regularities will hold from 1848 through 1908, for example, but disappear and be replaced by a rather different set of regularities during the 1914-1939 period. In other words, there is too much vague talk about not only the inconstancy of history, but just as foolishly, the "fact" that we have a "completely different" system after 1848 (or any other date). Our point is that the international system is a relatively fluid one, with certain of its attributes changing slowly and others rapidly, some rapidly at one time and slowly at another, some cyclically and some secularly. The same holds for the relationships among these attributes, or between them and the behavior pattern of the nations. But these are not only interesting theoretical issues; they are also highly researchable *empirical* questions. Thus, for both accurate description and compelling explanation, it is essential that we cover a relatively long historical period.

As to how far back in time one might go, the considerations are myriad, and we have no intention of going into all of them here. But it does seem that the burden of proof should rest on those who argue for the briefer time span (usually on the grounds that "things" are radically different now than they were then), rather than on those who urge the longer span. By and large, there is insufficient evidence behind most assertions of radical change, and often there is not even a specification of which variables have so changed as to make earlier and later periods incomparable. We certainly recognize the problem, and one of the by-products of the Correlates of War Project is a set of longitudinal observations for a wide variety of phenomena on the basis of which one might be able to ascertain precisely which attributes of the global system—or behavioral regularities of its constituent parts—did indeed change, and to what degree, at any particular point in time.

With these often incompatible considerations in mind, we finally decided to look for the correlates (and causes) of war within a time span that runs from January 1, 1816 to December 31, 1980.

Social System Levels

While the selection of chronological cutting points is essentially a matter of data availability and research strategy, the delineation of one's spatial domain raises a host of awkward and controversial definitional issues. If we hope to describe and analyze the amount of international war every year, it is essential to identify either the locale within which such war occurred or the specific political entities that participated in these recurrent exercises in legitimized homicide. The *geographical* loci are, from our point of view, of limited interest. Our major concern is with the *political* systems within which, and among which, international war occurs, and it is to their specification that we now turn.

To begin, we consider the concept of system a useful one and take the view that a system exists largely in the eye of the beholder. However, we believe that the construct should be applied only to social entities and aggregations, not to the behavior, interaction, or relationships in which such entities become involved. Thus, we define a social system as any aggregation of individuals or groups which manifests a modest (and for the moment, undefined) degree of interdependence, similarity, or common destiny, and whose treatment as a single unit is scientifically useful to the researcher. Combined with this relatively loose set of requirements, however, is our conviction that it is not scientifically useful to treat as *separate* and successive systems those interdependent aggregates made up of a given class of component units (individuals or groups) merely because some or many of that system's attributes change in magnitude over time. As indicated earlier, we reject the notion that there have been many different and successive international systems in the world since 1648 or 1713 or 1815, if the same general territorial area and the same class of social entities (that is, nations) are embraced during the period under examination.

On the other hand, we fully agree that, at any given moment, there exist several different systems (or, more precisely, systems and subsystems) embracing ever smaller aggregations of units at lower and lower levels of analysis. Thus, at the highest level of analysis for our purposes we postulate the existence of a *global* system, comprising all of humankind and any of the worldwide groupings that humans have formed and are of interest to the scientific enterprise at hand. At the next lower, and more restricted, level is the *international* system, comprised of all the national political units in existence at a given time, all of the people who live in these nations, and any of the many existing sub-national and extra-national groups of interest to the researcher. Somewhat more restricted is the *interstate* system, embracing all those national entities that satisfy certain criteria of statehood (discussed below) along with the individuals and the sub-national and extra-national groupings found within or among these national states. Our primary focus in this enterprise is on this interstate system, and whenever the word "system" is used without a modifier, we refer to the interstate system. We also focus, but to a lesser extent, on those nations which, while not meeting our criteria for inclusion in the interstate system, combine with those that do to form the larger international system. In principle, depending on the era under investigation and the criteria employed, all national entities may qualify as states, making the interstate and the international systems identical and coterminous.

Within the interstate system are two sub-systems of a more restricted nature. One is called the *central* system, and it embraces all those states that are particularly interdependent and that play especially vigorous parts in interstate politics. The specific criteria for inclusion in this system, a system essentially identical to the European state system, plus a handful of other states, are described below. Finally, at the lowest of our five main levels of analysis (global, international, interstate, and central are the first four) is the *major power* system, or once again and more precisely, the major power sub-system. We will turn in a moment to the criteria by which we define these five nested system levels, but a preliminary step is to discuss the general benchmarks that permit us to identify the several types of war that concern us here.

CRITERIA FOR INCLUSION

Having specified our temporal boundaries fully and our spatial ones less completely, we can now discuss the criteria by which one might differentiate between and among those numerous instances of armed violence that qualify as wars of one type or another and those that do not. We begin with a description and critique of the criteria used by the two pioneers in the field and then revert to those system levels outlined above, as the major basis for selection—and subsequent classification—of those wars included in the present enterprise.

At the outset, we find in Wright's *Study of War* an effort to distinguish among four different types of war: "(a) balance of power war, in the sense of a war *among* state members of the modern family of nations; (b) civil war, in the sense of war *within* a state member of the modern family of nations; (c) defensive war, in the sense of a war to *defend* modern civilization against an alien culture; and (d) imperial war, in the sense of a war to *expand* modern civilization at the expense of an alien culture" (1942: 641; italics added). In the *Statistics of*

Deadly Quarrels, however, Richardson eschews any effort to establish such a typology. As his editors (one of whom was Wright) remind us, he sought to avoid "conventional and legal distinctions difficult to quantify." Rather, he chose to classify strictly on the basis of casualties, in order to put them into a single series, "whether they occurred in Europe, America, Asia, or Africa, whether between recognized states, between revolutionary groups within a state, between primitive tribes, or between a government and rebels, insurgents, or colonials" (1960a: vii).

Since our concern in this section of the volume is only to describe various attributes of *international* wars, and since we are ignoring civil wars for the time being, it might make perfect sense to proceed to a delineation of our population by (a) ignoring Richardson's undifferentiated list and (b) merely including Wright's balance of power, defensive, and imperial wars, excluding those wars he classifies as civil. However reasonable such a procedure would be in the abstract, it turns out in practice to be insufficient. As the following paragraphs indicate, Wright goes on to introduce additional criteria that lead to the omission of certain wars that *do* seem relevant, and to include several that appear to be irrelevant in establishing a consistent and complete population of such events. Thus it might be useful to examine both his and Richardson's criteria in more detail, and the classificatory effects of each, before articulating the ones employed here.

Among the criteria that might reasonably be used in determining how a given sequence of military combat should be classified are (a) the objectives of the participants, (b) the political consequences, (c) the legal status of the hostilities, (d) the political attributes or status of the participants, (e) the duration of hostilities, (f) the number of troops involved, and (g) the casualties arising from the hostilities. Although Richardson rejects all but the last of these criteria, Wright uses four of them in determining whether the event qualified for his list of 278 wars between 1480 and 1940. Thus, he ignores the participants' objectives but goes on to indicate that "the legal recognition of the warlike action, the scale of such action, and the importance of its legal and political consequences . . . all have been taken into consideration in deciding whether a given incident was sufficiently important to include in a list of wars." More specifically, Wright includes "all hostilities involving members of the family of nations, whether international, civil, colonial, or imperial, which were recognized as states of war in the legal sense or which involved over 50,000 troops." Also included are "some other incidents . . . in which hostilities of considerable but lesser magnitude, not recognized as legal states of war, led to important legal results such as the creation or extinction of states, territorial transfers, or changes of government" (1942: 636).

Richardson, though recognizing that Wright's criteria are "probably more objective" than those employed by earlier experts, concludes that they are "hardly satisfactory for statistical purposes: because the *importance* of results is surely a matter of opinion; because opposing belligerents have often differed about what was *legal*; and because important legal and political effects, such as the separation of Norway from Sweden, have been arranged *without* war" (1960a: 5). Although these criticisms may not be fully justified, one may nevertheless be slightly uncomfortable with Wright's mixture of coding rules. First, he does not specify the criteria used for determining whether a participant is in fact a "member of the family of nations"; second, he apparently discards all his other criteria if over 50,000 troops were involved. This observation brings us, then, to Richardson's almost sole emphasis on the casualties—what he calls the magnitude—of the belligerent action. He insists often that no other criteria are worth considering, but this is so only because of his prime interest in all deadly quarrels in which casualties reached a magnitude of 317 or greater.

Given these valuable but inconsistent precedents, we decided to employ somewhat more discriminating—as well as more complex— coding procedures in preparing our tabulation of wars. The opening step was to identify and list, in chronological order, all deadly quarrels between 1816 and 1980 that had been identified as wars by Wright or Richardson, by the standard diplomatic and military histories, or by the many other sources noted in the references and the appendices. Once this (we hope) exhaustive tabulation was completed, the elimination process began, during which we screened out those quarrels that failed of inclusion because of (a) the inadequate political status of their participants, or (b) their failure to meet a minimum threshold of battle-connected casualties or troops in combat. Let us describe these exclusion criteria in some detail.

POLITICAL STATUS OF WAR PARTICIPANTS

For a war to be classified as international, it is quite reasonable to require that it occur within the international system of the moment and that it involve at least one national entity on each side. Of course, neither the practitioners of global politics nor the scholars who study their behavior have ever agreed on a set of hard and fast rules by which membership in the system could be unambiguously ascertained, and it was therefore incumbent on us to offer such a set of criteria. Through three prior papers we have moved partly toward that goal.

In the most inclusive of these papers (Russett, Singer, and Small, 1968), we attempt to list all national or quasi-national political entities that have existed since 1900 and that have a population of at least 10,000 (For an update, see Wyckoff, 1980.) We further categorize the degree of each entity's independence—that is, the extent to which it has effective control over its foreign policy—as (a) an independent nation; (b) a colony or dependency; (c) a mandate or trust territory, as established by the League or the United Nations; and (d) militarily occupied. We go on to specify the periods during which each such status was in effect for each entity. Each of these entities is also assigned a geographically determined three-digit code number, to maximize the efficient exchange of machine-readable cross-national data among researchers in comparative and international politics. The more restricted listings (Singer and Small, 1966, 1973) go further back in time (to 1816) but only include the entities that met our criteria for inclusion in the inter*state* system. There we did not make the interstate-international distinction followed here, and thus applied the label of international system to what is really the more restricted interstate system; one effect of that label was to treat as outside the international system the many national entities (colonies, mandates, annexed or occupied regions, and so on) that, while clearly not in the sovereign state category, definitely are constituent units of that larger inter*national* system. The distinction will become clear in the following paragraphs as we summarize the classification procedures used for inter*state* system membership in the 1816-1919 and 1920-1980 periods. The criteria established in the 1968 article thus constitute an operational definition of the *international system*.

Interstate System Membership Criteria, 1816-1919

Whether or not a national political entity qualifies as a member of the interstate system should be a function of two factors. First, was it large enough in population or other resources to play a moderately active role in world politics, to be a player more than a pawn, and to generate more signal than noise in the system? Several criteria other than population come to mind (for example, territory, unity, self-sufficiency, and armed might), but it would be premature to screen out nations deficient on such grounds, even assuming the availability of reasonably accurate evidence. Some minimum population, on the

other hand, is always a basic requirement of national survival; moreover, it frequently correlates highly with a number of other criteria of
national power. Finally, it is one of the variables for which adequate
data have existed over a long period of time.

Thus, our first criterion for treating a nation—no matter what its
legal status—as an active member of the interstate system was gross
population; and the threshold decided on was a minimum of 500,000
as opposed to only 10,000 for inclusion in our "national entity" list.
This figure precluded the need to deal with such minor entities as the
smaller of the pre-unification Italian or German states and, more recently, Monaco, Andorra, Liechtenstein, San Marino, or the like. An
indication of the sensitivity of that particular threshold may be seen
in the fact that if it had been raised to one million, the following
would have been excluded during the specified period: Baden, 1816-
1820; Greece, 1830-1845; Argentina, 1841-1850; Chile, 1839-1850;
Ecuador, 1854-1860; El Salvador, 1875-1900; Guatemala, 1849-1862;
and Haiti, 1859-1897. Excluded during the entire 1816-1919 period
would be Albania, Hanover, Hesse Electoral, Hesse Grand Ducal,
Mecklenburg-Schwerin, Modena, Parma, Dominican Republic, Honduras, Nicaragua, Paraguay, and Uruguay.

The second criterion for membership in the interstate system involves whether the entity was sufficiently unencumbered by legal,
military, economic, or political constraints to exercise a fair degree of
sovereignty and independence. The apparent pre-operational nature
of this criterion is largely compensated for by the great consistency of
diplomatic practice, such that almost all national governments
tended to agree on the status of another national entity, at least prior
to World War I. That agreement was manifested in a most operational
fashion via the granting or withholding of diplomatic recognition,
and it will be remembered that this was rarely used as a political
weapon until after World War I. Such decisions were not based on one
government's approval or disapproval of another, but strictly on the
judgment as to whether it could and would effectively assume its international obligations.

At first our criterion was to ask whether the nation in question was
extended such recognition by the majority of the international community, but it soon became evident that so thorough an investigation
was not necessary. For the period up to World War I, dominated as the
system was by the major European powers, we found that as Britain
and France went, so went the majority. Thus, we designated them our
"legitimizers," and once both of these major powers had established
diplomatic missions at or above the rank of chargé d'affaires in the

capital of any nation with the requisite half-million population, that nation was classed as a member of the interstate system. We used the establishment of the mission rather than the granting of recognition, since there were occasions on which one government might "recognize" another but delay sending its representative for long periods. For example, during the 1820s most of the newly independent Latin American states were recognized by European powers, but few permanent missions were dispatched for several decades. This, then, provided us with a highly operational pair of criteria by which we could identify the composition of the interstate system from the Congress of Vienna to the Versailles Conference after World War I.

Interstate System Membership Criteria, 1920-1980

For the post-Versailles era, however, the problem was not solved quite so easily. France and England may have emerged victorious from the war, but they found their supremacy somewhat less secure. Their capacity to extend or withhold legitimacy became increasingly a perquisite to be shared with other nations directly, as well as through international organizations. In this later period, then, a nation was classified as a system member if it either (a) was a member of the League or the United Nations at any time during its existence, or (b) met the half-million population minimum and received diplomatic missions from *any two* (rather than the *specific* two) major powers; membership in the latter oligarchy is defined below. We could no longer find two specific legitimizers to replace France and Britain, and even if we could, the norms of recognition had so changed that too many obviously qualified states would have been excluded; hence the reliance on *any* two major powers. Moreover, with the appearance of the League and then the United Nations, we were provided with an institutionalized legitimation procedure by which the comity of nations told us, in effect, which national entities satisfied the requirements for inclusion in the interstate system and which did not. (While the principle of universality of membership was neither explicitly stated in the League Covenant nor practiced in effect, the United Nations Charter not only asserts the fundamental aim, but has moved increasingly toward its realization.) Thus, the post-World War I period is one in which we utilize either of two different sets of criteria. Even though the results of either set would be quite similar, it is worth noting that if we had not used international organization membership as an alternative route to inclusion in our interstate system, such low population nations as Panama, Costa Rica, Iceland,

Malta, Kuwait, Gambia, and the Maldives would have been excluded. In our judgment, it would be wrong to exclude from the interstate system any nation that belonged to the League or its successor.

Despite their apparent reasonableness, however, these rules nevertheless required us to make several exceptions. First, among those
entities which qualified by one or both of the above criteria but which
we excluded were India, Slovakia, and Manchukuo. India did not
qualify for system membership during the 1920s and 1930s because it
did not control its own foreign policy. India's membership in the
League, as well as its representation at Versailles, was a concession
to the British, in much the same way that the inclusion of the
Ukraine and Byelorussia (two exceptions for the post-1945 period) in
the United Nations was a concession to the Russians.

Both Manchukuo and Slovakia were puppet states that also did not
control their own foreign policies in any meaningful sense. Established by Japan and ruled by Emperor Henry Pu Yi from 1932 to
1945, Manchukuo never achieved League membership (not surprising, considering the ramifications of the Lytton Report), although it
did receive its requisite second major power mission in 1937. Slovakia, on the other hand, posed a more difficult problem. More than 25
states recognized it, including three major powers before the start of
World War II. Yet a careful analysis of the sources suggests that when
Monseigneur Tiso placed his country under the protection of Germany some days after Germany took over Bohemia and Moravia,
Slovakia signed over its freedom of action in foreign policy (Mikus,
1963; Lettrich, 1955). In other words, Slovakia resembled occupied
Poland more than Rumania or Bulgaria, two of Germany's "independent" allies.

As for the states that we *included* even though they did not meet
our admission rules, Outer Mongolia, Nepal, Saudi Arabia, and
Yemen are the outliers. We have treated Outer Mongolia as an independent system member from 1921 to the present, despite the fact
that it was not a League member and enjoyed recognition from only
one major power, the Soviet Union. Our inquiries have led us to conclude that the remote republic was at least as independent as Panama and Nicaragua during the interwar period, for example. For conflicting interpretations, see Friters (1949), Tang (1959), and Rupen
(1964). Nepal, even more remote than Outer Mongolia in terms of
relationship to the system, and thus without major power recognition, was nevertheless considered independent by almost all observers. Both Saudi Arabia and Yemen existed as independent entities
prior to Versailles but were not treated as system members until they

were recognized by Italy and Britain in "legitimizing" treaties of the mid-1920s.

In the post-1945 period, aside from the aforementioned cases of the Ukraine and Byelorussia, China posed a problem. While not represented in the United Nations until 1971, the mainland regime was recognized promptly by both the USSR and England; Taiwan, conversely, qualified via UN membership. Thus, we classify China as a continuing system member and successor state to the nationalist regime after 1949, at which time Taiwan was added to the list as a new member.

An additional consideration in determining whether or not a political entity qualified as a system member in either of the periods—and, therefore, as a war participant—was that of governments that may have been forced by war into exile or into a small salient of their own national territory. The rule we adopted here was that as long as a government could field, and maintain in active combat, an independent fighting force of 100,000 or more, it continued to exist as a system member and war participant and therefore to contribute to our computations of the war's magnitude, severity, and intensity. For example, Belgium and Serbia were almost completely overrun and occupied in 1914 and 1915, respectively, but each managed to keep relatively large forces fighting against the Central Powers. On the other hand, in World War II, even though contingents identified with their home countries were maintained by the Dutch, the Poles, and the French, neither the Dutch nor the Polish air, ground, and naval forces met the 100,000 threshold, and the Free French did not meet it until De Gaulle and his troops helped to liberate Paris in 1944.

Central System Membership Criteria, 1816-1919

Once the basic list of the nations that qualified for membership in the interstate system was compiled, a further coding procedure seemed necessary. For a number of purposes, mere identification of the members of the system as of any given year may not be adequate. Much of the theorizing in international politics focuses on the most active or influential nations and quite legitimately ignores or depreciates the others. Recognizing this need, we have gone a step further and differentiated between national states that played a fairly vigorous part in global diplomacy and those whose role was much more peripheral. The former constitute a sub-system that we have labeled the *central* system, and it will be seen that it is almost identical to that more intuitive grouping known to diplomatic history as the European state system. We are persuaded, however, that our dichotomy makes sense only up through World War I, after which the total system seems to have become sufficiently interdependent to justify this sharp distinction no longer. Thus, from 1920 on, the central and peripheral systems are treated as a single, interdependent one. How, then, do we differentiate between central and peripheral system membership during the 1816-1919 period?

Here is the point at which our criteria become somewhat softer and more intuitive. Basically, our classification required that a central system member be active and influential in European-centered diplomacy. Thus, we follow the scholarly consensus and exclude and include as follows. First, there were some European nations that did not qualify for central system membership during part or all of the 1816-1919 period. Although several of the German states met both the population and recognition criteria, all but Austria and Prussia are relegated to the peripheral system. The major reason is that their 1815 treaty of confederation prohibited entrance into any alliance directed against other members of the confederation and thus markedly restricted their freedom of activity. Likewise, the Italian states other than Sardinia-Piedmont enjoyed limited independence prior to their unification in the 1860s. Linked in an intimate fashion to Austria by dynastic ties, Modena, Parma, Tuscany, and the Two Sicilies became little more than satellites of Vienna. In the same vein, the Papal States were effectively precluded from any significant diplomatic activity by French and Austrian guarantees.

On the other hand, certain non-European nations moved into positions of influence and activity during the period under consideration. Following the Sino-Japanese War and the Treaty of Shimoneseki in 1895, both the victor and the vanquished became increasingly involved in European affairs and are therefore included in the central system. The other extra-continental nation to be included in the central system was the United States, which qualified following its easy victory over Spain in 1898.

Major Power System Membership Criteria, 1816-1980

One last point must be considered in completing our hierarchical scheme. At one end of the status or power spectrum, a political entity may have most of the earmarks of statehood but not qualify for system membership, or it may merit inclusion in the system but remain peripheral enough in activity, power, or importance to fail of inclusion in the central system prior to 1920. At the other end of the spectrum, all students of world politics use, or appreciate the relevance of, the concept of "major power." Sharing that appreciation and recognizing its relevance for establishing a wide range of war data categories, we add this smallest sub-system to our classification scheme.

Although the criteria for differentiation between major powers and others are not as operational as we might wish, we do achieve a fair degree of reliability on the basis of intercoder agreement. That is, for the period up to World War II, there is high scholarly consensus on the composition of this oligarchy. As we interpret this consensus, the major powers and the period during which that august status was maintained seem to be as follows: Austria-Hungary from 1816 to defeat and dismemberment in 1918; Prussia from 1816 to 1870, and its successor state of Germany from 1871 to 1918 and 1925 to 1945; Russia from 1816 to 1917 and the USSR from 1922 on; France from 1816 to its defeat and occupation in 1940; England from 1816 on; Italy from its unification in 1860 to its defeat in 1943; Japan from its victory over China in 1895 to its surrender in 1945; and the United States from its victories over Spain in 1898 to the final defeat of the Axis.

For the post-World War II period through the mid-1960s, there is somewhat less consensus, but it would seem difficult to disagree with the continuation of major power status for the USSR and the United States, as well as for England, despite the dramatic gap between the latter and the two superpowers. And bearing in mind their ultimate possession of limited nuclear capabilities and permanent seats on the UN Security Council, it seems reasonable to include France as of the Allied victory in 1945 and China as of the Communist victory in 1949.

Since we completed the first version of this study, we have become even less confident of our major power classifications, especially for the period since 1965. In economic terms, West Germany and Japan have indeed become major powers, but we are reluctant to include them as major *military* actors because of the several constitutional provisions that preclude them—through the 1970s—from exercising a global military presence. Similarly, one might also argue that the age of the major power is over, that even the mightiest cannot control a handful of poorly organized Iranians in Teheran. Or perhaps we have entered a period dominated by major *regional* powers with, in 1980, for example, India, South Africa, Brazil, and even Cuba exercising the dominant influence in their own bailiwicks. Despite these alternatives, as well as a variety of others that might be suggested, we decided to stay, through 1980, with our "Big Five" as the best of a number of imperfect solutions to this problem.

Composition of the Several Systems

Given this range of considerations and the decisions we adopted, we hope that we have defined a number of populations and sub-populations by criteria that satisfy the requirements of not only reliability and reproducibility but validity and reasonableness as well. Throughout this volume, the reader will note the often conflicting pulls of these two sets of requirements. Our conviction is that scientific work on theoretically and socially significant problems cannot go forward unless we are willing to engage in these tradeoffs and to try to come up with the best (or least bad) of both worlds.

The ultimate results of these necessarily complex coding and classifying procedures are shown in 2.1, where we provide a list of all those entities (N = 176) that met our criteria for inclusion in the interstate system at any point during the period under study, along with the year in which it first qualified for, and (occasionally) later lost, membership. This list also shows which states qualified for inclusion in the 1816-1919 central system and when; no state in the central system lost membership in it unless it also lost membership in the overall system. It further identifies the major powers by the years during which that status was enjoyed, according to our criteria. In addition, note that the states are arranged in order of approximate geographical propinquity within each of the major continental regions and are identified by the standardized (Russett et al., 1968) code numbers discussed above. Finally, it should be reiterated that entities that are in the larger international system, but not in the more restricted interstate system, are not listed here.

TYPES OF WAR

We have now, admittedly at some length, defined the criteria by which national entities are assigned to the international, interstate, central, and major power systems, and presented the populations that emerge from these classification procedures. And since, as mentioned earlier in the chapter, the political status (that is, system or sub-system membership) of the combatant nations serves as our major basis for categorizing each war, we can now move on to a summary of the war types that emerge therefrom. We should note in passing, however, that an additional set of criteria—the level of military participation at which a nation may be said to have been sufficiently involved in a given war—needs to be considered, and we will return to that matter in the next section. For the moment, however, we can say

2.1 Nation Members of the Interstate System, 1816–1980

Nat# Abb Nation	Inclusive Years in Interstate System	Inclusive Years in Central System	Inclusive Years a Major Power
WESTERN HEMISPHERE			
2 USA UNITED STATES OF AMERICA	1816-1980	1899-1919	1899-1980
20 CAN CANADA	1920-1980		
31 BHM BAHAMAS	1973-1980		
40 CUB CUBA	1902-1906		
	1909-1980		
41 HAI HAITI	1859-1915		
	1934-1980		
42 DOM DOMINICAN REPUBLIC	1887-1888		
	1892-1916		
	1925-1980		
51 JAM JAMAICA	1962-1980		
52 TRI TRINIDAD	1962-1980		
53 BAR BARBADOS	1966-1980		
54 DMA DOMINICA	1978-1980		
55 GRN GRENADA	1974-1980		
56 SLU SAINT LUCIA	1979-1980		
70 MEX MEXICO	1831-1980		
90 GUA GUATEMALA	1849-1980		
91 HON HONDURAS	1899-1980		
92 SAL EL SALVADOR	1875-1980		
93 NIC NICARAGUA	1900-1980		
94 COS COSTA RICA	1920-1980		
95 PAN PANAMA	1920-1980		
100 COL COLOMBIA	1831-1980		
101 VEN VENEZUELA	1841-1980		
110 GUY GUYANA	1966-1980		
115 SUR SURINAM	1975-1980		
130 ECU ECUADOR	1854-1980		
135 PER PERU	1838-1880		
	1883-1980		
140 BRA BRAZIL	1826-1980		
145 BOL BOLIVIA	1848-1980		
150 PAR PARAGUAY	1846-1870		
	1876-1980		
155 CHL CHILE	1839-1980		
160 ARG ARGENTINA	1841-1980		
165 URU URUGUAY	1882-1980		
EUROPE			
200 UK UNITED KINGDOM	1816-1980	1816-1919	1816-1980
205 IRE IRELAND	1922-1980		
210 NTH NETHERLANDS	1816-1940		
	1945-1980	1816-1919	
211 BEL BELGIUM	1830-1940		
	1945-1980	1831-1919	
212 LUX LUXEMBURG	1920-1940		
	1944-1980		
220 FRN FRANCE	1816-1942	1816-1919	1816-1940
	1944-1980		1945-1980

(continued)

2.1 (Continued)

```
225 SWZ SWITZERLAND               1816-1980 1816-1919
230 SPN SPAIN                     1816-1980 1816-1919
235 POR PORTUGAL                  1816-1980 1816-1919
240 HAN HANOVER                   1838-1866
245 BAV BAVARIA                   1816-1871
255 GMY GERMANY/PRUSSIA           1816-1945 1816-1919 1816-1918
                                                      1925-1945

260 GFR GERMAN FEDERAL REPUBLIC   1955-1980
265 GDR GERMAN DEMOCRATIC REP.    1954-1980
267 BAD BADEN                     1816-1870
269 SAX SAXONY                    1816-1867
271 WRT WUERTTEMBURG              1816-1870
273 HSE HESSE ELECTORAL           1816-1866
275 HSG HESSE GRAND DUCAL         1816-1867
280 MEC MECKLENBURG SCHWERIN      1843-1867
290 POL POLAND                    1919-1939
                                  1945-1980 1919-1919

300 AUH AUSTRIA-HUNGARY           1816-1918 1816-1918 1816-1918
305 AUS AUSTRIA                   1919-1938 1919-1919
                                  1955-1980
310 HUN HUNGARY                   1919-1980 1919-1919
315 CZE CZECHOSLOVAKIA            1918-1939
                                  1945-1980
325 ITA ITALY/SARDINIA            1816-1980 1816-1919 1860-1943
327 PAP PAPAL STATES              1816-1860
329 SIC TWO SICILIES              1816-1861
332 MOD MODENA                    1842-1860
335 PMA PARMA                     1851-1860
337 TUS TUSCANY                   1816-1860
338 MLT MALTA                     1964-1980
339 ALB ALBANIA                   1914-1939 1914-1919
                                  1944-1980
345 YUG YUGOSLAVIA/SERBIA         1878-1941 1878-1919
                                  1944-1980
350 GRC GREECE                    1828-1941 1828-1919
                                  1945-1980
352 CYP CYPRUS                    1960-1980
355 BUL BULGARIA                  1908-1980 1908-1919
360 RUM RUMANIA                   1878-1980 1878-1919
365 USR USSR (RUSSIA)             1816-1980 1816-1919 1816-1917
                                                      1922-1980
366 EST ESTONIA                   1918-1940 1918-1919
367 LAT LATVIA                    1918-1940 1918-1919
368 LIT LITHUANIA                 1918-1940 1918-1919
375 FIN FINLAND                   1919-1980
380 SWD SWEDEN                    1816-1980 1816-1919
385 NOR NORWAY                    1905-1940 1905-1919
                                  1945-1980
390 DEN DENMARK                   1816-1940 1816-1919
                                  1945-1980
395 ICE ICELAND                   1944-1980
```

AFRICA

```
402 CAP CAPE VERDE               1975-1980
403 STP SAO TOME PRINCIPE        1975-1980
404 GNB GUINEA-BISSAU            1974-1980
411 EQG EQUATORIAL GUINEA        1968-1980
420 GAM GAMBIA                   1965-1980
432 MLI MALI                     1960-1980
```

2.1 (Continued)

```
433 SEN SENEGAL                    1960-1980
434 BEN BENIN/DAHOMEY              1960-1980
435 MAA MAURITANIA                 1960-1980
436 NIR NIGER                      1960-1980
437 IVO IVORY COAST                1960-1980
438 GUI GUINEA                     1958-1980
439 UPP UPPER VOLTA                1960-1980
450 LBR LIBERIA                    1920-1980
451 SIE SIERRA LEONE               1961-1980
452 GHA GHANA                      1957-1980
461 TOG TOGO                       1960-1980
471 CAO CAMEROUN                   1960-1980
475 NIG NIGERIA                    1960-1980
481 GAB GABON                      1960-1980
482 CEN CENTRAL AFRICAN REPUBLIC   1960-1980
483 CHA CHAD                       1960-1980
484 CON CONGO                      1960-1980
490 ZAI ZAIRE (CONGO,KINSHASA)     1960-1980
500 UGA UGANDA                     1962-1980
501 KEN KENYA                      1963-1980
510 TAZ TANZANIA/TANGANYIKA        1961-1980
511 ZAN ZANZIBAR                   1963-1964
516 BUI BURUNDI                    1962-1980
517 RWA RWANDA                     1962-1980
520 SOM SOMALIA                    1960-1980
522 DJI DJIBOUTI                   1977-1980
530 ETH ETHIOPIA                   1898-1936
                                   1941-1980
540 ANG ANGOLA                     1975-1980
541 MZM MOZAMBIQUE                 1975-1980
551 ZAM ZAMBIA                     1964-1980
552 RHO ZIMBABWE (RHODESIA)        1966-1980
553 MAW MALAWI                     1964-1980
560 SAF SOUTH AFRICA               1920-1980
570 LES LESOTHO                    1966-1980
571 BOT BOTSWANA                   1966-1980
572 SWA SWAZILAND                  1968-1980
580 MAG MALAGASY                   1960-1980
581 COM COMOROS                    1975-1980
590 MAS MAURITIUS                  1968-1980
591 SEY SEYCHELLES                 1976-1980
```

MIDDLE EAST

```
600 MOR MOROCCO                    1847-1911
                                   1956-1980
615 ALG ALGERIA                    1962-1980
616 TUN TUNISIA                    1825-1881
                                   1956-1980
620 LIB LIBYA                      1952-1980
625 SUD SUDAN                      1956-1980
630 IRN IRAN (PERSIA)              1855-1980
640 TUR TURKEY/OTTOMAN EMPIRE      1816-1980    1816-1919
645 IRQ IRAQ                       1932-1980
651 EGY EGYPT/UAR                  1855-1882
                                   1937-1980
652 SYR SYRIA                      1946-1958
                                   1961-1980
660 LEB LEBANON                    1946-1980
663 JOR JORDAN                     1946-1980
666 ISR ISRAEL                     1948-1980
```

(continued)

2.1 (Continued)

670 SAU SAUDI ARABIA	1927-1980		
678 YAR YEMEN ARAB REPUBLIC	1926-1980		
680 YPR YEMEN PEOPLES REPUBLIC	1967-1980		
690 KUW KUWAIT	1961-1980		
692 BAH BAHREIN	1971-1980		
694 QAT QATAR	1971-1980		
696 UAE UNITED ARAB EMIRATES	1971-1980		
698 OMA OMAN	1971-1980		

ASIA

700 AFG AFGHANISTAN	1920-1980		
710 CHN CHINA	1860-1980	1895-1919	1950-1980
712 MON MONGOLIA	1921-1980		
713 TAW TAIWAN	1949-1980		
730 KOR KOREA	1888-1905		
731 PRK KOREA, DEM. PEOPLE'S REP.	1948-1980		
732 ROK KOREA, REPUBLIC OF	1949-1980		
740 JPN JAPAN	1860-1945		
	1952-1980	1895-1919	1895-1945
750 IND INDIA	1947-1980		
760 BHU BHUTAN	1971-1980		
770 PAK PAKISTAN	1947-1980		
771 BNG BANGLADESH	1973-1980		
775 BUR BURMA	1948-1980		
780 SRI SRI LANKA (CEYLON)	1948-1980		
781 MAD MALDIVE ISLANDS	1965-1980		
790 NEP NEPAL	1920-1980		
800 THI THAILAND	1887-1980		
811 KHM KAMPUCHEA (CAMBODIA)	1953-1980		
812 LAO LAOS	1954-1980		
816 DRV VIETNAM, DEMOCRATIC REP.	1954-1980		
817 RVN VIETNAM, REPUBLIC OF	1954-1975		
820 MAL MALAYSIA	1957-1980		
830 SIN SINGAPORE	1965-1980		
840 PHI PHILIPPINES	1946-1980		
850 INS INDONESIA	1949-1980		
900 AUL AUSTRALIA	1920-1980		
910 PNG PAPUA NEW GUINEA	1975-1980		
920 NEW NEW ZEALAND	1920-1980		
940 SOL SOLOMON ISLANDS	1978-1980		
950 FIJ FIJI	1970-1980		
990 WSM WESTERN SAMOA	1976-1980		

that our general rule was to exclude any war that did not lead to at least 1,000 battle fatalities among all participating system members.

It will be recalled that Wright differentiated among balance of power, defensive, imperial, and civil wars, and we expressed certain reservations then in regard to his coding procedures. We would also question the basic conceptualization. In our judgment, his definition of defensive and imperial wars in terms of whether "modern civilization" was defending against, or expanding at the expense of, "an alien culture" is risky, in that it requires us to ascertain the motives of decision makers and to distinguish between initiator and defender. It also calls for indefensible and invidious distinctions between civi-

lized and alien cultures. As a matter of fact, our non-Western colleagues may detect the degree of embarrassment we feel because of
the relatively ethnocentric criteria that we already have—in our
judgment, unavoidably—been obliged to employ. Thus, even while
adhering to Wright's general categories, we propose and utilize a typology that is not only more operational but more neutral in the normative sense. Using the political status and system memberships of
the participants as our dominant classificatory benchmark, we began
by differentiating between two basic types of international war: *intra*-systemic, or interstate war, and *extra*-systemic, or imperial and
colonial war. (A third basic type—civil war—is of concern to us here
only if it becomes "internationalized," and will be discussed in Part II
of the volume.) Let us now examine each of these types and their subtypes in turn.

Intra-Systemic (Interstate) Wars

Our primary focus in this section is on fluctuations in the frequency, magnitude, severity, and intensity of interstate war between
1816 and 1980. Since the bulk of this handbook is devoted to the measurement and reportage of these phenomena, we will be returning to
intra-systemic or interstate wars in considerable detail, and need
only give the summary definitions here. An interstate war is defined
as one in which at least one sufficiently active participant on each
side is a qualified nation member of the interstate system; hence the
interchangeable use of the "intra-systemic" and "interstate" labels.
Since the criteria for "sufficiently active" participation are discussed
in the next section, it will suffice to say here that the number of battle
fatalities and the size of the combatant forces constitute the key dimensions.

Central System and Major Power Wars

Even though our dominant preoccupation is with the interstate
system as a whole, there will certainly be occasions on which we (or
other users of this volume) may want to limit our attention to more
restricted empirical domains. In order to do this, it would be useful to
offer tabulations that separate out from the larger setting the wars
that occur entirely or primarily within the central or major power
sub-systems. Moreover, some types of analysis may best be restricted
to the war experience of nations within these two smaller domains

even though the wars themselves may have involved nations that fall outside of them. Thus, in several places we will compute and present data restricted to these two sub-systems.

Extra-Systemic (Imperial and Colonial) Wars

Although our chief theoretical interest is in wars between and among state members of the international system, it is evident that any understanding of international war in general cannot rest on interstate wars alone; we must also consider other international wars in which one or more system members have been engaged. Reference is, of course, to wars in which the system member's forces fought against those (however irregular and disorganized) of a political entity that was *not* a system member, but in which the member nevertheless sustained a minimum of 1,000 battle-connected fatalities. Within this category there are three sub-types, depending once more on the political status of the adversary. The adversary might be an independent political entity that did not qualify for membership because of serious limitations on its independence, a population insufficiency, or a failure of other states to recognize it as a legitimate member. These are classed as *imperial* wars (indicated by the letter I after the dates in 2.2) and would include the British-Zulu War of 1879 and the Franco-Madagascan War of 1896, for example.

If, on the other hand, the adversary were a colony, dependency, or protectorate composed of ethnically different people and located at some geographical distance from the given system member, or at least peripheral to its center of government, the war is classed as colonial (indicated by the letter C in 2.2). Among these were the Greek War for Independence of 1821-1828, the Texan War of 1835-1836, the Polish rebellions of 1831 and 1863, and the French-Indochinese War of 1945-1954.

The third type of extra-systemic war is one in which the adversary was a rebellious group located within the territory of *another* system member and in which the first system member intervened on the side of the regime against the insurgents. This is an *internationalized civil war* that has become internationalized by virtue of the military intervention of the outside state's forces. The question of civil wars is dealt with in Part II. In closing, it should be noted that what gives these three types of war their identity and similarity is that they involve a system member's active participation in a war beyond its own metropolitan territory, against the forces of a political entity that is not a recognized member of the system.

Ambiguities and Exclusions

Most of the wars that fall into one of the above categories cause us some (but relatively little) difficulty in coding. The political status criterion plus the military participation threshold (described in the next section) seem to solve most of our selection and classification problems. There are, however, certain kinds of wars that pose awkward problems, and even though these are all excluded from this section, it seems worthwhile to say a few words about them. In the process, the boundaries between the wars that are *included* and those that are *excluded* should be sharpened, thus further clarifying our coding rules and reassuring the reader that our criteria are neither capricious nor inconsistent.

One major source of ambiguity arises out of those cases in which the political status of a participant undergoes change either during or just before the war in question. This problem falls, in turn, into two classes. First, there is the possible conversion of a sufficiently severe imperial or colonial war into an interstate war; second, there is the possible internationalization of a civil war, through either outside intervention or the changing status of the rebel forces. Since the latter are more complicated and account for most of the exclusions from our compilation, we will deal first with the former, and simpler, set of cases.

Our rules for dealing with imperial and colonial wars are quite straightforward. It will be recalled that these are wars in which a nation member of the interstate system is engaged against either a national entity that fails of system inclusion on grounds of population or recognition, or against an entity that is a colony, dependency, or mandate, and therefore fails of system inclusion on grounds of non-independence. Taking the latter class first, the mere proclamation of independence by a colonial entity fighting against its former mother country would not be sufficient to convert the colonial war into an interstate war. The rebellious faction or self-proclaimed independent entity must have satisfied our criteria of system membership six months *prior to the onset of hostilities* to merit participation in an interstate war. Thus, the battles of the Baltic peoples against Soviet Russia from 1918 to 1920 were not classified as interstate wars despite their 1918 declarations of independence; these remained in the colonial war category. By way of a contrary example, Finland's "second war for independence" in 1939-1940, fought some 20 years after the initial and successful colonial war, *is* treated as an interstate one because the ex-dependency's independent political status had by then been established.

As to the imperial wars, it might appear at first glance that a similar kind of rule should apply to these as well. There is, however, an important difference. In the case of colonies, as distinct from independent but non-member entities, system membership depends not only on diplomatic recognition and population but, most important, on the establishment of de facto independence. For the entity that engages a system member in an imperial war, this is no problem at all, since it is by definition already an independent entity.

Turning now to civil wars, there are in principle two ways by which they may become internationalized and thereby ultimately qualify for inclusion in this investigation. As should be evident by now, even though a standard civil war between a member government and its domestic insurgents might be classified technically as an international war (since it involves at least one system member), it differs substantially in its nature, and usually in its political implications, from those that we call internationalized. Among the civil wars that become internationalized, however, an important distinction must be made. When the intervening system member comes into a civil war *alongside another member government* and against the insurgents and comes to play the dominant role on the government's side, the war becomes an interstate war. In most cases of such interventions, as we will see in the second part of this volume, the intervener does not come to play such a role. One rare case is the Soviet assistance to the government of Afghanistan in December 1979. The authorities in Kabul had been fighting a civil war against Moslem insurgents since 1978. When the Red Army crossed the border to assist its ally, it clearly came to play the dominant role in the war. The status of that war thus changed from civil to interstate.

Civil wars can and do, however, become internationalized interstate wars through an alternative process. We refer, of course, to those that involve the armed forces and the insurgents of a single nation at the outset but in which there is subsequent intervention by an outside system member's forces on the side of the insurgents and *against* the existing regime. The war India fought against Pakistan in December 1971, a war that grew out of the *civil* war between East and West Pakistan, is such a war.

LEVEL OF MILITARY PARTICIPATION

As we suggested above, the political status and system or sub-system membership of the participants do not themselves suffice for the inclusion of a deadly quarrel in a rigorously defined population of international or interstate wars. Nor does a simple declaration of war, or the dispatch of personnel, supplies, or equipment, necessarily mean that the concerned system member has participated in the war in a meaningful way. We have therefore imposed the additional requirement of active participation, measured in terms of battle-connected fatalities and/or size of armed forces engaged in active combat. In Chapter 3, we spell out in considerable detail the measurement procedures we used, but let us summarize the general criteria here.

Interstate Wars

Very simply, no hostility involving one or more system members qualified as an interstate war unless it led to a minimum of 1,000 battle fatalities among all of the system members involved. Any *individual* member nation could qualify as a participant through either of two alternative criteria. The threshold used most frequently was a minimum of 100 fatalities, and this sufficed in all but the most ambiguous cases. There were, however, a few cases in which a member not only declared war but sent combat units into the war theater, without sustaining even this low number of casualties. The problem was to differentiate between a nation that committed many troops but fortunately sustained few casualties, and one that sent only limited numbers of troops, many of whom were killed. That is, if only battle deaths are used as the basis for a system member's inclusion, one which dispatches 2,000 troops but uses them so skillfully or cautiously as to lose only 50 would not qualify, whereas one that sent 200 and lost half would be included. In such cases, an alternative route to qualified participation was necessary: a minimum of 1,000 armed personnel engaged in active combat within the war theater.

We found only five cases in which it was necessary to invoke this consideration as a basis for *including* certain nations: England in the Second Syrian War of 1839-1840; England, France and the United States in the Boxer Rebellion; the Philippines in the Korean War; France and England in the Sinai War of 1956; and Jordan in the Yom Kippur War. On the other hand, there were eight cases in which marginal participants were ultimately *excluded* on the grounds that they neither sustained the necessary 100 battle deaths nor committed 1,000 troops to *active* combat: England and France in the La Plata wars of the 1830s and 1840s; Austria in the Second Syrian War of 1839-1840; Mexico and Thailand in World War II; South Africa and New Zealand in the Korean War; and New Zealand in the Vietnam War.

A third criterion was considered, but as our data began to come in, it was apparent that the battle death threshold itself would cover most cases and the 1,000 combat troops would cover the remaining few. Thus, we might have required that the system member's forces be involved in active combat for some minimum period in order to exclude brief skirmishes and isolated engagements. But rarely in the past has an extremely brief conflict had a sufficiently large number of combat units and battle fatalities. (Of course, nuclear war could easily produce a fantastic number of fatalities in a matter of minutes.)

Imperial and Colonial Wars

Turning to wars involving a system member against extra-systemic polities or dependencies, we found it necessary to use slightly different threshold criteria. Whereas an interstate war that qualified on the basis of battle deaths would be included if the total fatality figure for the protagonists on each side reached 1,000, the member *itself* (including system member allies, if any) had to sustain 1,000 battle fatalities *per year* in order for the extra-systemic war to be included.

In other words, we do not consider the fatalities sustained by non-member forces in ascertaining whether an extra-systemic war is to be included in our tabulations. Thus, even though the net battle death requirement for inclusion is similar for the intra- and extra-systemic wars (at least 1,000 for all participating system members), it is incumbent on us to justify our failure to account for non-member fatalities in the imperial and colonial wars. While such deaths did not go unmourned, they often went uncounted or unrecorded. And given the dubious authenticity of the figures they produce, it is doubtful whether the earlier institution of the contemporary "body count" would have made the task any easier.

On the other hand, we did impose an additional requirement on the system member's fatalities in order to have the war included; if the war lasted more than a year, its battle deaths had to reach an *annual* average of 1,000. This coding rule also requires some justification. One of our measures of international war is its frequency, meaning that we must be able to count the *number* of wars, extra-systemic as well as interstate, and here we were faced with what would otherwise have been a serious coding problem. A great many colonial and imperial struggles tended to drag on for quite a few years—a decade's duration was by no means infrequent—but they seldom generated the same amount of combat year after year. Generally, the European governments (who account for most of these wars) were quite content to permit these conflicts to continue at length, providing the casualty levels were not too high; several hundred fatalities a year were often accepted as the price of empire. But if the tempo of the struggle quickened, the familiar cry of "win or get out!" was often raised—and heeded. Usually, when more than a thousand of its soldiers were killed in a given year, the system member either escalated to a degree sufficient for victory or withdrew.

Thus, even though our coding rules in principle could have led to the exclusion of an extra-systemic war that killed several thousand system member troops over a number of years, in fact it did not. A representative case is that of the Spanish struggle for control of parts of Morocco from 1909 into the mid-1930s. In 1909 and 1910, it fought a full-scale war against the independent state of Morocco, but from 1910 to 1921, it engaged in mopping-up campaigns against paramilitary, semi-organized bands that resisted Spanish rule. These engagements were limited both in terms of the amount of troops committed and the casualty rate. Then, in 1921, Abd-el-Krim rallied many of the rebels around him and raised an organized insurrection against the Spanish and, later, the French. After his capture in 1926, the rebels continued desultory warfare similar to that waged from 1910 through 1921. We have treated this sequence as follows: (a) the Spanish-Moroccan War of 1909-1910 was included as an interstate war, with Morocco losing its independence in 1910; (b) the Spanish pacification campaign of 1910-1921 was excluded because the Spanish did not suffer anything near the requisite average annual 1,000 battle deaths over the 11-year period; (c) the rebellion of Abd-el-Krim of 1921-1926 was included as a colonial war; and (d) the pacification effort from 1926 to the mid-1930s was excluded because the annual death rate again was not satisfied. In another, more recent case, Portuguese efforts to subdue Angola, Mozambique, and Guinea-Bissau fail of inclusion because of the relatively low levels of system member battle deaths over a lengthy period.

THE POPULATION IDENTIFIED

We have now specified, in as clear and operational terms as we can, the criteria that must be satisfied in order for a sequence of military hostilities to be classified as an international war. To summarize, we first had to decide whether a political entity was a member nation of the interstate system; then we had to decide whether it had been sufficiently involved in the war to count as a participant; third, on the basis of which entities participated in the hostilities, and whether a minimum of 1,000 fatalities were sustained by these participants, we decided on whether the event was an interstate war or not; finally, if it did not qualify for the category of interstate war, we classified it as imperial or colonial, depending on the status of the entities that participated. The results of this series of screening procedures appear in 2.2.

Alterations in the Original List

Since the publication of our first volume, we have uncovered new data sources and have had several errors called to our attention by helpful colleagues and reviewers. Although we have added nine new wars to our 1816-1965 list and have dropped one of the original wars, the basic trends and patterns first described in 1972 still obtain, as will be seen below.

As for the wars added, the French conquest of Algeria, 1839-1847, the Spanish attempt to reconquer Santo Domingo from 1863 to 1865, the Ilinden insurrection of Macedonians against Turkey in 1903, the Sino-Soviet clash in Manchuria in 1929, the Chankufeng incident between Russia and Japan in 1938, the Franco-Thai border skirmishes of 1940-1941, and the Indian takeover of Hyderabad of 1948—all rather small conflicts—now appear to meet our minimum battle death threshold. The Boxer Rebellion was added because of evidence that Chinese regulars officially participated in much of the fighting in 1900. The Russo-Polish War of 1919-1920, originally subsumed in our Russian Nationalities War, is now considered an interstate war because of the establishment of Polish independence for six months prior to the onset of formal hostilities. Interestingly, of the nine wars added, none was suggested by scholars *outside* our project. The one-day Battle of Navarino Bay of 1827 was dropped as a "war" and is now classified as an incident in the Greek War for Independence.

We have slightly altered certain war dates as follows: the termination of the Mexican-American War from February 12 to February 2, 1848; the elimination of the one day of combat between France and Rome on April 30, 1849 from the Roman Republic War; the termination of the Spanish-Moroccan War from March 26 to March 25, 1860; the entry of Italy into the Seven Weeks War from June 15 to June 20, 1866; the beginning of the Sino-French War from June 15 to August 23, 1884; the entry of Bulgaria into World War II from December 8 to December 13, 1941; the entry of England and France into the Suez

2.2   Simple List of Interstate and Extra-Systemic Wars, 1816–1980

Interstate Wars (N = 67)

Franco-Spanish (1823)
Russo-Turkish (1828–1829)
Mexican-American (1846–1848)
Austro-Sardinian (1848–1849)
First Schleswig-Holstein (1848–1849)
Roman Republic (1849)
La Plata (1851–1852)
Crimean (1853–1856)
Anglo-Persian (1856–1857)
Italian Unification (1859)
Spanish-Moroccan (1859–1860)
Italo-Roman (1860)
Italo-Sicilian (1860–1861)
Franco-Mexican (1862–1867)
Ecuadorian-Colombian (1863)
Second Schleswig-Holstein (1864)
Lopez (1864–1870)
Spanish-Chilean (1865–1866)
Seven Weeks (1866)
Franco-Prussian (1870–1871)
Russo-Turkish (1877–1878)
Pacific (1879–1883)
Sino-French (1884–1885)
Central American (1885)
Sino-Japanese (1894–1895)
Greco-Turkish (1897)
Spanish-American (1898)
Boxer Rebellion (1900)
Russo-Japanese (1904–1905)
Central American (1906)
Central American (1907)
Spanish-Moroccan (1909–1910)
Italo-Turkish (1911–1912)
First Balkan (1912–1913)

Second Balkan (1913)
World War I (1914–1918)
Russo-Polish (1919–1920)
Hungarian-Allies (1919)
Greco-Turkish (1919–1922)
Sino-Soviet (1929)
Manchurian (1931–1933)
Chaco (1932–1935)
Italo-Ethiopian (1935–1936)
Sino-Japanese (1937–1941)
Changkufeng (1938)
Nomohan (1939)
World War II (1939–1945)
Russo-Finnish (1939–1940)
Franco-Thai (1940–1941)
Palestine (1948–1949)
Korean (1950–1953)
Russo-Hungarian (1956)
Sinai (1956)
Sino-Indian (1962)
Vietnamese (1965–1975)
Second Kashmir (1965)
Six Day (1967)
Israeli-Egyptian (1969–1970)
Football (1969)
Bangladesh (1971)
Yom Kippur (1973)
Turco-Cypriot (1974)
Vietnamese-Cambodian (1975—)
Ugandan-Tanzanian (1978–1979)
Sino-Vietnamese (1979)
Russo-Afghan (1979—)
Irani-Iraqi (1980—)

Extra-Systemic Wars (N = 51)

British-Maharattan (1817–1818) I
Greek (1821–1828) C
First Anglo-Burmese (1823–1826) I
Javanese (1825–1830) C
Russo-Persian (1826–1828) I
First Polish (1831) C
First Syrian (1831–1832) C
Texan (1835–1836) C

First British-Afghan (1838–1842) I
Second Syrian (1839–1840) C
Franco-Algerian (1839–1847) I
Peruvian-Bolivian (1841) I
First British-Sikh (1845–1846) I
Hungarian (1848–1849) C
Second British-Sikh (1848–1849) I
First Turco-Montenegran (1852–1853) I

(continued)

2.2   (Continued)

Sepoy (1857–1859) C	Boer (1899–1902) C
Second Turco-Montenegran (1858–1859) I	Ilinden (1903) C
Second Polish (1863–1864) C	Russian Nationalities (1917–1921) C
Spanish-Santo Dominican (1863–1865) I	Riffian (1921–1926) C
Ten Years (1868–1878) C	Druze (1925–1927) C
Dutch-Achinese (1873–1878) C	Indonesian (1945–1946) C
Balkan (1875–1877) C	Indochinese (1945–1954) C
Bosnian (1878) C	Madagascan (1947–1948) C
Second British-Afghan (1878–1880) I	First Kashmir (1947–1949) I
British-Zulu (1879) I	Hyderabad (1948) I
Franco-Indochinese (1882–1884) I	Algerian (1954–1962) C
Mahdist (1882–1885) C	Tibetan (1956–1959) C
Serbo-Bulgarian (1885) I	Philippine-MNLF (1972–) C
Franco-Madagascan (1894–1895) I	Ethiopian-Eritrean (1974–) C
Cuban (1895–1898) C	Timor (1975–) C
Italo-Ethiopian (1895–1896) I	Saharan (1975–) C
First Philippine (1896–1898) C	Ogaden (1976–) C
Second Philippine (1899–1902) C	

War from November 2 to October 31, 1956, and the beginning of that war from October 31 to October 29.

We have also made the following changes: Modena and Tuscany were added as participants in the Austro-Sardinian War of 1848-1849; the Lopez War of 1864-1870 was changed from the extra-systemic category to the interstate because Paraguay was deemed to have reached the 500,000 population threshold by 1846, Mecklenberg-Schwerin was switched from Austria's side to Prussia's in the Seven Weeks War in 1866; France was added as a combatant on the German side in World War II when the Vichy government fought the British in Syria from July 1940 to July 1941; and France's battle deaths in Algeria were changed from 15,000 to 18,000. We hope that these changes have not inconvenienced our users. Most of them were made during the first few years after publication of the *Wages of War* and are already incorporated in analyses done by ourselves and our correspondents.

SUMMARY

The above coding rules, of course, not only produced the table of wars for inclusion in the book but also served to *exclude* a good many that might, intuitively, be expected to appear in such a compilation. For the more ambiguous and debatable exclusions, we have provided an explanation in Appendix B, accompanied, where critical, by the sources from which our information was derived.

The detailed discussion above was necessary on two grounds. First, there is the complex question of whether each of a multitude of military conflicts does or does not qualify for inclusion in a list of wars whose compilation is theoretically defensible and methodologically operational. Needless to say, few of our coding criteria were completely a priori, and most were determined after we had proceeded well into the examination of a good many cases. Once these rules had been applied and our population had been defined and then subdivided into interstate and extra-systemic categories, our second set of problems came to the fore. Reference is to the matter of scaling these wars and their various attributes.

International wars may be classified and differentiated along any number of dimensions, depending on one's theoretical needs. Among the possible criteria might be location; time; the issues; the types or number of nations involved; the size, strength, military organization, technologies, strategies, or ideologies of the participants; number of major battles; duration; casualties; and political results. The concern may be with the war's effect on the demography, industrial base, transport net, internal stability, or power of each participant; on the strength and direction of a given relationship between any two protagonists and/or non-belligerents; or on the structure, status ordering, centralization, or rate of change in the international system, for example. We will be looking primarily for more general indicators of the war's impact on both the belligerents and on the system; that is, we are looking not only for measures that reflect the destructive and disruptive effects of the war but for those that could also be used as predictor variables in the examination of the political, social, or economic *consequences* of any given wars. Given these requirements, and persuaded of the need to establish such measures, we proceeded to develop three sets of indicators, which we define in detail in Chapter 3.

CHAPTER 3

Quantifying International War
Three Sets of Indicators

In the previous chapter we dealt with the first of the steps necessary to convert qualitative phenomena into quantitative, scientifically useful data. That is the step that differentiates between the cases to be examined later and those in which we are *not* interested; with the application of these inclusion-exclusion criteria, we are able to *enumerate*. And while the criteria leading to enumeration need not be quantitative in nature—or, as in the case here, may be a mixture of the logical and the quantitative—the *results* are definitely quantitative. Once we have identified and counted the cases that interest us, we are free to go on to the second step and to differentiate among those that remained in the population of cases that satisfied our screening criteria. Measurement, then, must be preceded by identification and enumeration.

With that step taken, we proceed to make explicit the dimensions along which such differentiation should be made, in light of the theoretical purposes to which the data will later be put. Our major goal here is simple: to ascertain the "amount" of war that began, or was under way, or ended, in any given time-place domain. Measures or indicators reflecting the amount of war that began in each such domain would normally serve as the outcome (or dependent) variable in most studies, and those reflecting the amount that ended would usually serve as the predictor (independent or intervening) variable. The amount of war under way, in turn, might be used either as the predictor or the outcome variable, depending on one's theoretical focus and the resulting research design. To put it another way, when war is the "effect," we may want to use a different measure of its amount than is the case when war is the putative "cause" of some subsequent set of events or conditions. Since the major concern of the Correlates of War Project is with the amount of war as the *consequence* of certain prior phenomena, we will be more interested in measuring the amount that *began* within certain specified spatial-temporal domains. But since we are also using feedback models, we require measures of the amount of war that *ended* within such domains. Moreover, others who will be using our data may be more interested in treating war as a predictor than as an outcome variable, and it thus behooves us to generate indicators reflecting the amount of war under way and ending, as well as beginning. We call these onset, underway, and termination measures and will return to them in Chapter 6.

Turning, then, to the construction of these measures, we note immediately that nothing can be said about the amount of war that occurred within a given spatial-temporal domain until we have measured each separate war that falls into our population of cases. Only then can we aggregate the separate and single war amounts into a combined onset (or under way or termination) amount for a given region and time period. How, then, do we differentiate among the wars that met our criteria for inclusion, and how do we compare them to one another in a quantitative fashion?

Given the above considerations, we settled on three sets of indicators, one reflecting the *magnitude* of a given war, another its *severity,* and a third its *intensity.* The magnitude indicator is intended to get at the spatial and temporal extent of the war—how many nations participated in it and how long it lasted; we measure this in "nation months." Severity is intended to get at the human destructiveness of the war, and is measured in battle-connected deaths. Intensity is supposed to reflect the ratio between battle deaths and nation months.

A word or two in defense of our verbal labels is in order. On the one hand, we were most reluctant to part company with Richardson, who labels his battle fatalities "magnitude." On the other hand, magnitude connotes *size,* and the reader is more likely to associate size and magnitude with the spatial—and, to a lesser extent, temporal— attributes of the event or condition being measured than with its destructiveness. Second, since our coding rules differ from Richardson's, the use of identical labels might obscure that difference in our measures. Third, when one thinks of the wounds and bloody deaths of battle, the word "severity" comes to mind well before magnitude. Fourth, since we develop these two rather different measures of the "amount" of war, it would be confusing to assign the same label—such as magnitude—to both. To do so would require constant use of the distinguishing phrase: magnitude in battle deaths or magnitude in nation months. Finally, since intensity almost invariably connotes some kind of ratio, the use of this label to identify battle deaths per nation month or per capita seemed quite obvious.

MAGNITUDE: NATION MONTHS

Addressing ourselves first to the measurement of war's magnitude, it seemed reasonable to develop one index that reflected space and time in the broadest sense. The "spatial" dimension could be represented by square mileage (or, more recently, even cubic mileage) of the combat zone, the number or territorial area of the participants, their population size, industrial acreage, and so forth. The "temporal" dimension, or duration, could be in any "real time" measure (days, weeks, months) or in some such artificial measure as diplomatic, communication, or military "time," so as to permit meaningful comparisons between wars fought in differing technological settings. In addition, the sheer number of battles might offer a sensitive measure of magnitude.

The magnitude of war indicator we decided to use for getting at the time-space dimension is an extremely simple one, characterized by high reliability and face validity. Labeled "nation months," this measure is nothing more than the sum of all the participating nations' separate months of active involvement in each war.

This measure, of course, has certain liabilities. For example, it does not differentiate between a British war month and a Peruvian war month, nor does it differentiate between an early nineteenth-century war month and a mid-twentieth-century one. These factors could, without too much difficulty, be taken into account were certain types of data available. One could, for example, weight each nation's war month by its diplomatic importance score, various indicators of its industrial or military capability, domestic cohesion or stability scores, and so forth. Likewise, one might weight months as a function of the technological period in which the war was fought, on the assumption that such technology might well compress the amount and scale of combat and perhaps the fatality rates accompanying wars of different epochs. However, as the calculations in Chapter 7 show, there seems to be almost no secular trend toward a greater number of battle deaths per month over the 165 years covered here, despite radical developments in weapons technology.

In partial response to the need for differentiation among various classes of nation month, however, we have gone on to distinguish among those experienced by peripheral system nations, those of the central system members, and those experienced by major powers, thus providing a first approximation to some more sophisticated weighting scheme. In addition, so that the user of our data will be able to distinguish between the nation months of those engaged in savage fighting and those whose participation is less bloody, we present in Chapter 10 a possible criterion by which certain nations might reasonably be omitted, even though they satisfied our criteria. There we compute one index of the intensity of each nation's participation by dividing its fatalities in all of its wars by the length of its participation in all wars. Other researchers will thus have an operational threshold by which to eliminate certain low-level participants from their own computations.

Measuring Duration

How do we convert the nation month concept into hard numbers with which one aspect of a war's magnitude may be measured? Once the participants in any given war have been identified, the next step is to ascertain, as precisely as possible, the dates on which each qualified participant entered and left the war. This, in turn, raises the problem of measuring the duration of the war itself.

Richardson and Wright recognized the pitfalls involved in adhering strictly to legal documents as time boundaries. Among the possible sources of confusion, Richardson suggested the following: (a) provocative incidents prior to the formal declaration; (b) prolonged hostilities without a declaration of war; (c) pauses between battles which are not armistices, and are therefore included in the total duration; (d) irregular warfare which continued after the main defeat or after the declaration of peace; and (e) the cessation of hostilities without a declaration of peace. As a consequence, he accepted the conventional dates if the historical authorities agreed, but where they differed, he preferred "common sense to legalism; that is to say, I have been guided by actual warlike alertness rather than by formal declarations of war or peace" (1960a: 15-16).

Likewise, Wright encountered "no small difficulty ... in determining when a given war began and ended." Thus, "the date of beginning is generally taken as the first important hostilities," since "formal declarations of war have been rare and, when they have occurred, have often *followed* active hostilities." But when it comes to terminal dates, Wright reverted to legal criteria again and used "the date of signature of a treaty of peace, or the date of its going into effect if that is different." In a good many cases, however, he recognized that there was no formal treaty; then "the date of armistice, capitulation, or actual ending of active hostilities is given" (1965: 638).

Given the ambiguities and inconsistencies of these and other previously used rules, in addition to the fact that precise duration figures are more important to us than to our predecessors, we developed the following procedures. Each war's *opening date* is that of the formal declaration, but only if it is followed immediately by sustained military combat. If hostilities precede the formal declaration and continue in a sustained fashion up to and beyond that latter date, the first day of combat is used. Even in the absence of a declaration, the sustained continuation of military incidents or battle, producing the requisite number of battle deaths, is treated as a war, with the first day of combat again used for computing duration.

Turning to *termination,* we again rely on a combination of legal and military events, with the latter more dominant. That is, the war's duration continues as long as there is sustained military action. If such combat comes to an end on the same day as an armistice is signed and does not resume after the armistice, there is no problem. But if there is a delay between the cessation of military action and the armistice (which is very rare), or if the armistice fails to bring combat to an end, we use the day that most clearly demarcates the close of sustained military conflict. Similarly, the date of the peace treaty would not be used unless it coincided with the end of combat.

Temporary Interruptions

In addition to the identification of a war's onset and termination dates, there is the complication arising out of truces, temporary cease-fires, and armistice agreements. In general, a cessation of hostilities that endured for less than 30 days is not treated as an interruption of the war, whereas a longer break is so treated and would lead to a reduction in the war's overall duration measure equal to the exact length of the interruption. To illustrate, the three-week truce (December 19, 1933 to January 8, 1934) arranged by the League of Nations during the Chaco War is not counted as a break, and the war is treated as if it had run continuously for the three years from June 15, 1932 through June 12, 1935, for a duration of 35.9 months. On the other hand, because a formal truce lasted for two of the total six months between the onset and termination of the Second Schleswig-Holstein War (February 1, through August 20, 1864), that war is treated as having a duration of only 3.6 months.

Measuring Each Nation's Participation

Once the problem of defining a given war's duration is resolved, we can go on to the measurement of its magnitude, counted in nation months. To do so, we must face two separate questions: (a) What constitutes "participation" in a war by a given nation? (b) What are the opening and closing dates of such participation? As to participation, the criteria outlined in Chapter 2 may be summarized as follows. First, the nation must be a qualified member of the interstate system. Second, it must have had regular, uniformed, national military personnel in sustained combat. Third, no matter how brief or lengthy that combat, those forces must have either numbered at least 1,000 or sustained at least 100 battle-connected deaths. Fourth, a nation need not have been, either formally or physically, at war with *all* of the nations on the opposing side in order to be classed as an active participant. Its forces need only have been in sustained combat with those of any *one* adversary in order to qualify, providing that the first three requirements were satisfied.

As to the total duration of each single nation's participation in a given war—and hence its contribution to that war's magnitude—there are 17 interstate and 5 extra-systemic wars in which some participants either did not become involved on the opening day of hostilities or did not continue fighting until the end of the war. In those cases, as we noted in Chapter 2, the active participation period is that marked by the beginning and end of their forces' involvement in sustained military combat. In addition, there is the logical extension of our rule that only qualified members of the interstate system are included as participants. Even if a nation participated in a given war for its total duration, only that period during which it was a system member is counted when we compute the war's magnitude or that nation's war months. An example is the Franco-Prussian War of 1870-1871; even though Baden, Bavaria, and Wuerttemberg had troops in active combat during the entire war, they were not qualified system members after November 1870, when they became integrated into the new German empire. Thus their participation after that date did not contribute to the magnitude of the war as a systemic event. Similarly, in the Russo-Turkish War of 1877-1878, the military participation of Serbia, Rumania, and Montenegro did not contribute to the nation months of that war because they were not qualified system members during any part of the war.

Computation and Levels of Confidence

Before closing our description of the ways we measured nation months of war, a word regarding the precision and accuracy of our data is in order. First, and despite thorough investigations, we were

unable to pin down the *exact* dates for the termination of the Second
Turco-Montenegran War of 1858-1859, the Dutch-Achinese War of
1873-1878, the Bosnian revolt of 1878, and the Druze rebellion of
1925-1927. In all cases we have treated the ending date as the first of
the month.

One scholar (Weiss, 1963a: 103-104) found a certain pattern in the
relative accuracy of Richardson's data. When he dichotomized those
duration figures (on the basis of Richardson's judgments, discussed in
the next section) into either the "accurate" or the "approximate"
category, he found that the fewer the fatalities produced by the war,
the less likely were the precise dates to be known. In tabular form, the
estimates were distributed as follows:

Fatality Range	No. of Accurate Figures	No. of Approximate Figures	Total in Range	% Accurate
2.5–3.5	65	144	209	31
3.5–4.5	53	18	71	75
4.5–5.5	19	7	26	73

In other words, when the fatalities from a war are fewer, there
appears to be less detailed reporting and less thorough research on
that war.

Our experience was not quite the same, in that we generally found
as high a percentage of uncertain dates for high-fatality wars as for
those that produced relatively few battle deaths. This discrepancy,
however, is not surprising, since we had the advantage of looking at
fewer deadly quarrels, especially at the lower end of the fatality
range. Another point to keep in mind is that whether we speak of
dates or of fatalities, the accuracy—or even the availability—of that
data is largely a function of the industrial and educational level of the
nation involved, with the nation months and battle deaths of many of
the non-Western nations much more a matter of intelligent estimate
than retrieval of authentic information.

Second, there is the question of how precise we want our duration
and magnitude measures to be, given some of the problems we
encountered. In order to avoid conveying greater precision than was
possible, we considered rounding only to the nearest half-month for
both duration and magnitude. However, that rounding procedure not
only led to inconsistencies between our war duration score and the
separate national war month figures but seemed to discard too much
accurate information unnecessarily. Thus, we ended up by computing

simple duration, the combat time of the individual national participants, and the nation month war magnitudes in months and tenths of
months. One year was standardized as 365.25 days (taking into
account the extra day in leap years), and one month was set equal to
one-twelfth of one year, or 30.44 days. Then we counted the total
number of days of each combat experience, including the first and last
days, and divided by 30.44, with the resulting figures given to one
decimal place—that is, to the nearest tenth of a month.

To summarize this section, then, our ultimate objective is to measure the magnitude of war which began, was under way, or terminated in a given time-space domain. But in order to do this, we must
first ascertain the magnitude of *each war* that began, was under way,
or ended in that domain. And in order to measure each war's magnitude, we must, in turn, begin by measuring the war's duration and
then the number of months that each qualified nation spent as a
participant in that war. Let us now shift from the measurement of
magnitude to that of severity.

SEVERITY: BATTLE-CONNECTED DEATHS

The second of our basic measures is that of severity, operationalized
in terms of battle-connected deaths. Let us begin by recapitulating
Richardson's procedures, since his is the only study comparable in
this regard.

In computing his figures, he first listed *all possible* war-connected
death categories, which we rearrange and paraphrase as follows: (a)
belligerent military personnel killed in fighting or drowned in action
at sea, or who died from wounds or from poison or from starvation in a
siege or from other malicious acts of their enemies; (b) belligerent
military personnel who died from disease or exposure; (c) civilians
belonging to the belligerent nations who died from malicious acts of
their enemies; (d) members of neutral populations (civilian or military) accidentally killed in the war; (e) neutral or belligerent civilians who died from exposure and disease; and (f) the additional number of babies that would presumably have been born if war had not
occurred. In Richardson's estimates, the military and civilian deaths
resulting from enemy action were included "because they were inten-
tionally inflicted," and military deaths due to disease and exposure
were included "because they were accepted as a risk contingent to
planned operations" (1960a: 9). In sum, he included military *and* civilian deaths that could be attributed to the hostile actions of the
participants (a, b, and c), but excluded those that could not reasonably be so explained (d, e, and f).

Inclusion Criteria

Although we found ourselves in general agreement with Richardson's line of reasoning in trying to develop a valid and reliable indicator of a war's severity, we finally decided to restrict our figures to combat-connected deaths of military personnel only. Our reasons for excluding civilian casualties are twofold. First, there is the concern for validity. In seeking a measure of the severity of wars that occur as much as a century and a half apart, it was essential to minimize the effects of the tremendous technological changes that have taken place during this period. In the early nineteenth century, there was not only little military incentive for inflicting civilian casualties but little technological capacity for doing so. Wars were won by the destruction and disorganization of enemy armies (and navies) and by the successful occupation of territory. But as industrial production and civilian support became more critical to military success, the incentive to destroy them increased markedly, as did, of course, the capability. At the same time, despite great advances in weaponry, there was little increase in the efficiency with which combat personnel could be killed; even the availability of tactical nuclear weapons, given the political as well as military costs associated with their use, has had little impact so far on battle-connected deaths. Thus, by restricting ourselves to military casualties only, we maximize the comparability of our indices over the entire period. To support this contention, we can note (7.7) the absence of any strong upward secular trend in the various war *intensity* measures.

It might also be added that, as a quantitative matter, the inclusion of civilian deaths in our severity measure would not have done much for validity via a somewhat broader index. That is, we soon discovered that civilian deaths were quantitatively negligible in most of the international (as distinguished from civil) wars during our time span, except for the world wars; and given the fact that the approximately 9 and 15 million battle-connected *military* deaths in those wars so overshadowed all other wars, there seemed no good analytical and comparative reason to include civilian casualties. On the other hand, no study of civil or guerrilla war could afford to exclude non-military deaths; we thus include such deaths in our civil war tabulations.

This brings us to considerations of reliability. First, as difficult as it might be to gather and evaluate military fatality estimates over so wide a domain in space and time, the problem of doing this for civilian fatalities is more difficult still. Even for World War II, civilian death estimates range from 20 to 35 million. The second consideration was the fact that civilians could have died in so wide a variety of situations and at so many different sets of hands that no reasonable and operational criteria could be developed. Third, our investigations revealed that few of the sources on whom we would be relying had included civilian fatalities in their analyses.

Given this range of considerations, then, we settled on *battle-connected fatalities among military personnel only* as our measure of war's severity. This was defined to include not only those personnel killed in combat but those who subsequently died from combat wounds or from diseases contracted in the war theater. It should also be noted that these figures include not only personnel of the system member but native troops from the colonies, protectorates, and dominions who fought alongside them.

Estimating Procedures

Shifting from classificatory schemes to the straightforward matter of ascertaining the casualty figures within each category, Richardson again provides us with a valuable point of departure. In addition to perusing Harbottle (1904), Bodart (1916), Dumas and Vedel-Peterson (1923), and Sorokin (1937), he conducted "long searches in the pages of literary history." That the search was frustrating as well as long is reflected in his comment that such histories were

> deplorably vague on the subject of casualties. We look for numbers but find instead phrases such as "many fell in the battle" or "routed their enemies" or "suffered heavy loss."...The number killed in one or two outstanding battles may be mentioned, but these melancholy statistics are seldom totaled for the whole war. Military historians . . . sometimes give precise casualties for their own forces, but only very vague statements about their enemies.

Thus his pique at "those historians who prefer rhetoric to numbers" (1960a: 9-10).

Given the absence or unreliability of many wartime casualty figures, Richardson introduced a procedure designed to both indicate the level of reliability and reduce the effects of low reliability. This is the logarithmic (to the base 10) scale mentioned earlier, and he illustrates its applicability by reference to three different sources of Union death statistics in the American Civil War. The estimates are 359,528; 279,376; and 166,623, and "each, if seen alone [is] apparently accurate to a man." Although the first is over twice the size of the third estimate, the assumption is that on a casualty scale that ranges from 317 to 20,000,000 (World War II), all three estimates cluster very closely together. This clustering is seen when the three absolute figures are converted to their logarithmic scale equivalents: 5.6, 5.4, and 5.2.

In order to indicate the degree of confidence in the final digits of his figures, Richardson utilized a standard notational form. The ladder of diminishing confidence in a battle death estimate of magnitude 4 (that is, 10,000) is reflected in the following forms: 4.00, 4.0, $4._0$, 4, and $4?$. When he was willing to include a final digit, but not with complete confidence, he printed it below the line, or dropped it entirely, depending on his confidence level; and if he was even uncertain as to the reliability of the gross magnitude class, he followed it with a question mark.

It should now be evident that, despite the solid foundation laid by Richardson's explorations, his estimates were unsatisfactory for our purposes. Interested as he was in almost all of the casualty statistics of almost all deadly quarrels, his sample is much larger and less discriminating than ours: too many wars and too many categories of casualty. We did, however, often begin with his estimates and then go on to revise them for differences in duration, participants, and casualty types.

Our procedure was first to prepare our list of wars, participants, and their dates of involvement in the hostilities as described in the previous sections. Next, we entered all available estimates from earlier general studies under separate columns, indicating whether they were for the entire war or some geographical or chronological part, and which nation months and casualty classes were included. Whether a ready concurrence among them could be established or not, we next turned to the specialized treatises and monographs that so frustrated Richardson. The assumption here was that such high agreement could often be traced to the fact that some or all of the general studies had found their original figures in the same sources or in ones based on the same source. What this return to the monographs often involved was wading through such literary accounts as Hozier's (1878) massive two volumes on the Russo-Turkish War of 1877-1878, recording his estimates of battle deaths for every engagement, and finally adding up the hundreds of figures. While it would have been simpler to accept Richardson's estimates, in retracing his steps we discovered not only a failure to explore all available sources but a distressing propensity to base his final count on mere guesswork or intuition.

Once all the available estimates were in for a given war and adjustments were made of the varying classificatory criteria, the semi-operational estimating began. Among the considerations affecting our final figure were army size, weapons and medical technology available, number of major battles, others' estimates of the wounded-to-killed ratio (Bodart, 1916, seems to have discovered a constant of about 3.5 to 1), and historians' appraisals of the war's intensity. A final "reality test" required us to compare victorious and defeated, major and minor, central and peripheral, and active and passive nations across a number of wars. As Klingberg (1966) discovered, in wars of a given duration among nations of given strength there tend to be some rough but fairly constant ratios among population size and casualties, for both victor and vanquished.

Confidence Levels

Despite these multiple cross-checks and a large dose of skepticism at every turn, we must reemphasize the fact that our battle death figures are only estimates. It is worth bearing in mind the possible sources of erroneous data. First, not all armed forces have been consistent in differentiating among dead, captured, missing, wounded, and deserting. As Dumas (*Losses of Life Caused by War*, 1923: 21) reminds us, the field commander "attaches no importance to the cause of the absences ... for him it is all the same." Second, there is the simple matter of accurate estimates, compounded by the fact that the size of a force may not be known with any accuracy even by its commanders. Third, there are the tactical reasons for exaggerating the enemy's losses and minimizing one's own. Finally, the archivists and historians who eventually sift through the reports and provide our basic sources of data may well suffer not only from a lack of statistical sophistication but even occasionally from personal and national biases of their own.

To make more explicit our own relative sense of confidence in the battle fatality figures, we classify them as follows, but without using the conventional percentage error ranges, which would themselves be little more than educated guesses. Among the interstate wars, we have *high confidence* in our estimates for the following cases:

1823 Franco-Spanish	1849 Roman Republic
1846-1848 Mexican-American	1853-1856 Crimean
1848-1849 Austro-Sardinian	1859 Italian Unification
1848-1849 First Schleswig-Holstein	1860 Italo-Roman
	1860-1861 Italo-Sicilian

1863 Ecuadorian-Colombian
1864 Second Schleswig-Holstein
1865-1866 Spanish-Chilean
1866 Seven Weeks
1870-1871 Franco-Prussian
1885 Central American
1897 Greco-Turkish
1898 Spanish-American
1906 Central American
1907 Central American

1932-1935 Chaco
1935-1936 Italo-Ethiopian
1938 Changkufeng
1939 Nomohan
1956 Sinai
1967 Six Day
1969-1970 Israeli-Egyptian
1969 Football
1971 Bangladesh
1973 Yom Kippur

The interstate wars for which our confidence level is somewhat lower (if only certain participants' figures proved elusive, they are italicized) are:

1828-1829 Russo-*Turkish*
1851-1852 La Plata
1856-1857 Anglo-*Persian*
1859-1860 Spanish-*Moroccan*
1862-1867 Franco-*Mexican*
1864-1870 Lopez
1877-1878 Russo-*Turkish*
1879-1883 Pacific
1884-1885 *Sino*-French
1894-1895 Sino-Japanese
1900 Boxer Rebellion *(China)*
1904-1905 Russo-*Japanese*
1909-1910 Spanish-*Moroccan*
1911-1912 Italo-*Turkish*
1912-1913 First Balkan
1913 Second Balkan
1914-1918 World War I
1919 Hungarian-Allies
1919-1920 Russo-Polish
1919-1922 Greco-Turkish

1929 Sino-Russian
1931-1933 Manchurian
1937-1941 Sino-Japanese
1939-1945 World War II
1939 Russo-Finnish
1940-1941 Franco-Thai
1948-1949 Palestine [*Arabs*]
1950-1953 Korean [*China,
   N. Korea*]
1956 Russo-Hungarian
1962 Sino-Indian
1965 Second Kashmir
1965-1975 Vietnamese
1974 Turco-Cypriot
1975— Vietnamese-Cambodian
1978-1979 Ugandan-Tanzanian
1979 Sino-Vietnamese
1979— Russo-Afghan
1980— Irani-Iraqi

Ironically enough, as the above lists indicate, the post-1945 period gave us more difficulty than the earlier period.

As for extra-systemic wars, we are confident in our estimates of system member battle deaths for the following:

1817 British-Maharattan

1823-1826 First Anglo-Burmese

1825-1830 Javanese

1835-1836 Texan

1838-1842 First British-Afghan

1839-1847 Franco-Algerian

1841 Peruvian-Bolivian

1845-1846 First British-Sikh

1848-1849 Hungarian

1848-1849 Second British-Sikh

1857-1859 Sepoy

1863-1865 Spanish-Santo Dominican

1873-1878 Dutch-Achinese

1878-1880 Second British-Afghan

1879 British-Zulu

1882-1884 Franco-Indochinese

1885 Serbo-Bulgarian

1894-1895 Franco-Madagascan

1895-1896 Italo-Ethiopian

1899-1902 Second Philippine

1899-1902 Boer

1921-1926 Riffian

1925-1927 Druze

1945-1947 Indonesian

1945-1954 Indochinese

1947-1948 Madagascan

1948 Hyderabad

1954-1962 Algerian

We are somewhat less confident in the system member fatality estimates for the following extra-systemic wars:

1821-1828 Greek

1826-1828 Russo-Persian

1831 First Polish

1831-1832 First Syrian

1839-1840 Second Syrian

1852-1853 First Turco-Montenegran

1858-1859 Second Turco-Montenegran

1863-1864 Second Polish

1868-1878 Ten Years

1875-1877 Balkan

1875-1877 Bosnian

1882-1884 Mahdist

1895-1898 Cuban

1896-1898 First Philippine

1903 Ilinden

1917-1921 Russian Nationalities

1947-1949 First Kashmir

1956-1959 Tibetan

1972— Philippine-MNLF

1974— Ethiopean-Eritrean

1975— Timor

1975— Saharan

1976— Ogaden

It should also be noted here—in accordance with the discussion of
the accuracy of our battle death estimates—that we have rounded off
the *total* battle death figures for the three bloodiest wars (World
War I, World War II, and Korean) to the nearest million. While the
figure given for *each nation* in each war is the most accurate possible
estimate, the range of precision varies considerably; sometimes this
accuracy is expressed only to the nearest 100,000 (as is the case of
such major protagonists as Russia and Germany in World War II and

China in the Korean conflict); but in the case of several of the less active participants (such as Belgium and South Africa in World War II), our estimates are expressed to the nearest 100 deaths, or even to the nearest 10 (for some UN nations fighting in Korea). Given this range of precision, it would be misleading to assume that the exact sum of each nation's fatalities in those three wars is indeed a precise reflection of their severity. Thus, in 4.2 we have rounded off these severity figures as follows: World War I, from 8,555,800 to 9,000,000; World War II, from 15,164,300 to 15,000,000; and the Korean War, from 1,892,100 to 2,000,000. These changes were made by hand to emphasize the fact that they were rounded off *after* summing the nations' battle deaths. In subsequent chapters, however, all war totals will be based on the summation of the national totals and so reflected in the computerized data decks. Our purpose here, then, is merely to alert the reader and user to the dangers of misplaced precision.

INTENSITY: FATALITY RATIOS

Whereas the magnitude and severity measures outlined above may be quite useful in describing the *extensiveness* of the wars included here, they tell us nothing about their *intensiveness*. One might want to know, for example, whether a particular war was brief but bloody, whether it exacted a higher relative toll in bloodshed than another, whether it was receiving a high concentration of attention or resources, or whether the rate at which deaths were being sustained might predict to its termination. Several such indicators are readily calculated once the data have been gathered for a number of base lines.

In earlier studies, we used three indicators of intensity. All of them proceeded from the estimate of battle-connected deaths, with base lines reflecting (a) nation months, (b) the total size of the pre-war armed forces of all member nations which participated, and (c) the total pre-war population of all of the member nations that participated. In each case, the war's intensity index was computed by dividing the base line figure into the total number of fatalities that the war produced. In this volume, we have simplified our analyses so as to include *only* the BD/NM and BD/POP indicators to measure intensity.

SUMMARY

In this chapter, then, we have gone beyond the steps of merely identifying and classifying the international wars since the Congress of

Vienna. That is, as useful as frequency counts may be, they permit only the most primitive kind of theorizing and hypothesis testing; to the extent that we can go beyond such enumeration and develop measures of an ordinal, interval, or ratio scale nature, more subtle inquiry becomes possible. Moreover, we must be able not only to describe any particular war, but to compare many wars, many nations or regions, and many time periods as well. In the chapters that follow, we present the various measures and transformations by which such comparisons might be made, along with detailed descriptions of the procedures by which such indices have been generated.

CHAPTER 4

The Qualifying Wars and Their Quantitative Attributes

In the preceding two chapters, we described in detail the way we —as well as our predecessors—defined our population of wars and estimated the duration, participation, and human destructiveness of each. This chapter presents the quantitative results arising out of those data-making and scaling procedures.

A simple chronological listing of all 118 international wars that met our inclusion criteria is shown in 4.1, along with the dates and the wars' code numbers. Because many analyses will deal with inter-state and extra-systemic wars separately, they are numbered in two different series; interstate wars run from 1 through 199, and colonial and imperial wars are combined in the series 301 through 451.

INTERSTATE WARS

In 4.2, we single out the interstate wars, list them chronologically, and then present the following basic information for each. On the left is the war number and name and the number and name of the participants, followed by the opening and closing dates of the war; and for those nations that participated in only part of the war, the dates of such participation are indicated below. Then come the three basic indicators for each war: duration in months, magnitude in nation months, and severity in battle-connected deaths among military personnel. Under the gross magnitude and severity figures, we show the nation months and battle deaths for each qualifying participant.

These data are followed by a variable that is needed to compute one of our intensity ratios: the total combined pre-war populations of all

4.1 All Interstate and Extra-Systemic Wars Listed Chronologically (N = 118)

301	BRITISH-MAHARATTAN (1817-1818)I		49	LOPEZ (1864-1870)
304	GREEK (1821-1828)C		52	SPANISH-CHILEAN (1865-1866)
1	FRANCO-SPANISH (1823)		55	SEVEN WEEKS (1866)
307	FIRST ANGLO-BURMESE (1823-1826)I		361	TEN YEARS (1868-1878)C
310	JAVANESE (1825-1830)C		58	FRANCO-PRUSSIAN (1870-1871)
313	RUSSO-PERSIAN (1826-1828)I		364	DUTCH-ACHINESE (1873-1878)I
4	RUSSO-TURKISH (1828-1829)		367	BALKAN (1875-1877)C
316	FIRST POLISH (1831)C		61	RUSSO-TURKISH (1877-1878)
319	FIRST SYRIAN (1831-1832)C		370	BOSNIAN (1878)C
322	TEXAN (1835-1836)C		373	SECOND BRITISH-AFGHAN (1878-1880)I
325	FIRST BRITISH-AFGHAN (1838-1842)I		64	PACIFIC (1879-1883)
328	SECOND SYRIAN (1839-1840)C		376	BRITISH-ZULU (1879)I
331	FRANCO-ALGERIAN (1839-1847)I		379	FRANCO-INDOCHINESE (1882-1884)I
334	PERUVIAN-BOLIVIAN (1841)I		382	MAHDIST (1882-1885)C
337	FIRST BRITISH-SIKH (1845-1846)I		67	SINO-FRENCH (1884-1885)
7	MEXICAN-AMERICAN (1846-1848)		70	CENTRAL AMERICAN (1885)
10	AUSTRO-SARDINIAN (1848-1849)		385	SERBO-BULGARIAN (1885)I
13	FIRST SCHLESWIG-HOLSTEIN (1848-1849)		73	SINO-JAPANESE (1894-1895)
340	HUNGARIAN (1848-1849)C		388	FRANCO-MADAGASCAN (1894-1895)I
343	SECOND BRITISH-SIKH (1848-1849)I		391	CUBAN (1895-1898)C
16	ROMAN REPUBLIC (1849)		394	ITALO-ETHIOPIAN (1895-1896)I
19	LA PLATA (1851-1852)		397	FIRST PHILIPPINE (1896-1898)C
346	FIRST TURCO-MONTENEGRAN (1852-1853)I		76	GRECO-TURKISH (1897)
22	CRIMEAN (1853-1856)		79	SPANISH-AMERICAN (1898)
25	ANGLO-PERSIAN (1856-1857)		400	SECOND PHILIPPINE (1899-1902)C
349	SEPOY (1857-1859)C		403	BOER (1899-1902)C
352	SECOND TURCO-MONTENEGRAN (1858-1859)I		82	BOXER REBELLION (1900)
28	ITALIAN UNIFICATION (1859)		406	ILINDEN (1903)C
31	SPANISH-MOROCCAN (1859-1860)		85	RUSSO-JAPANESE (1904-1905)
34	ITALO-ROMAN (1860)		88	CENTRAL AMERICAN (1906)
37	ITALO-SICILIAN (1860-1861)		91	CENTRAL AMERICAN (1907)
40	FRANCO-MEXICAN (1862-1867)		94	SPANISH-MOROCCAN (1909-1910)
43	ECUADORIAN-COLOMBIAN (1863)		97	ITALO-TURKISH (1911-1912)
355	SECOND POLISH (1863-1864)C		100	FIRST BALKAN (1912-1913)
358	SPANISH-SANTO DOMINICAN (1863-1865)I		103	SECOND BALKAN (1913)
46	SECOND SCHLESWIG-HOLSTEIN (1864)		106	WORLD WAR I (1914-1918)

(continued)

4.1 (Continued)

409	RUSSIAN NATIONALITIES (1917-1921)C	433	ALGERIAN (1954-1962)C
109	RUSSO-POLISH (1919-1920)	154	RUSSO-HUNGARIAN (1956)
112	HUNGARIAN-ALLIES (1919)	157	SINAI (1956)
115	GRECO-TURKISH (1919-1922)	436	TIBETAN (1956-1959)C
412	RIFFIAN (1921-1926)C	160	SINO-INDIAN (1962)
415	DRUZE (1925-1927)C	163	VIETNAMESE (1965-1975)
118	SINO-SOVIET (1929)	166	SECOND KASHMIR (1965)
121	MANCHURIAN (1931-1933)	169	SIX DAY (1967)
124	CHACO (1932-1935)	172	ISRAELI-EGYPTIAN (1969-1970)
127	ITALO-ETHIOPIAN (1935-1936)	175	FOOTBALL (1969)
130	SINO-JAPANESE (1937-1941)	178	BANGLADESH (1971)
133	CHANGKUFENG (1938)	439	PHILIPPINE-MNLF (1972---)C
136	NOMOHAN (1939)	181	YOM KIPPUR (1973)
139	WORLD WAR II (1939-1945)	184	TURCO-CYPRIOT (1974)
142	RUSSO-FINNISH (1939-1940)	442	ETHIOPIAN-ERITREAN (1974---)C
145	FRANCO-THAI (1940-1941)	187	VIETNAMESE-CAMBODIAN (1975---)
418	INDONESIAN (1945-1946)C	445	TIMOR (1975---)C
421	INDOCHINESE (1945-1954)C	448	SAHARAN (1975---)C
424	MADAGASCAN (1947-1948)C	451	OGADEN (1976---)C
427	FIRST KASHMIR (1947-1949)I	190	UGANDAN-TANZANIAN (1978-1979)
148	PALESTINE (1948-1949)	193	SINO-VIETNAMESE (1979)
430	HYDERABAD (1948)I	196	RUSSO-AFGHAN (1979---)
151	KOREAN (1950-1953)	199	IRANI-IRAQI (1980---)

NOTE: War numbers 1-199 are interstate wars; 301-451 are extra-systemic wars. I indicates an imperial war; C indicates a colonial war.

system members actively participating in the war. Next are shown two intensity ratios for the wars and for each participant: battle deaths per nation month and battle deaths per capita based on total population.

Additional information relevant for analyses done in later chapters is provided in 4.2. Since all but two of the interstate wars that concluded by December 31, 1980 resulted in clear-cut victory for one side (Korean and Israeli-Egyptian of 1969-1970, with the criteria spelled out in Chapter 11), we have shown this by placing the victor or victors first in the list of participants. For wars that had more than one participant on a side, a space has been left between the victorious side and the vanquished. As a final refinement of this table, we have indicated with an asterisk those participating nations which, from 1816 through 1919, were members of the peripheral subset only and did not qualify for the more restricted central system membership.

EXTRA-SYSTEMIC WARS

Turning to the extra-systemic wars—those in which the adversary is not a member of the interstate system but is an independent nonmember of the system or a non-independent national entity—we present 4.3 in a format similar to 4.2. But this table presents data *only for the system members* involved and not for their extra-systemic adversaries. Furthermore, since only 6 of the 51 extra-systemic wars actively involved more than a single system member, the war totals are usually the same as the individual *national* totals.

As before, we have identified the peripheral system participants by an asterisk, revealing that all but two of these imperial and colonial wars were fought by members of the central sub-system. It is noteworthy that more than half of this limited group's experience in extra-systemic wars is accounted for by an even more limited group—the major powers—with 29 of these 51 wars fought by majors.

Finally, since the extra-systemic listing presents only the system members' experiences, we could not indicate the victorious side as we did in 4.2. Instead, we refer the reader to 11.3, in which we list the system members who won and those who lost in extra-systemic combat, along with certain pertinent data from those engagements.

These, then, constitute our two basic bodies of data, and all of the subsequent compilations will represent little more than a wide variety of rearrangements and new combinations of the data shown in this chapter.

4.2 List of Interstate Wars, with Participants, Duration, Magnitude, Severity, and Intensity

Number and Name of War / Participants and Code Number	Dates of War / National Dates When Different	Duration in Months	Magnitude in Nation Months	Severity in Battle Deaths	Population (millions pre-war)	Battle Deaths per Nation Month	Battle Deaths per 10000 Population
1 FRANCO-SPANISH	4/7/1823-11/13/1823	7.3	14.6	1000	42.6	68.5	.2
220 FRANCE			7.3	400	30.9	54.8	.1
230 SPAIN			7.3	600	11.7	82.2	.5
4 RUSSO-TURKISH	4/26/1828-9/14/1829	16.7	33.4	130000	80.5	3892.2	16.1
365 USSR (RUSSIA)			16.7	50000	56.6	2994.0	8.8
640 TURKEY/OTTOMAN EMPIRE			16.7	80000	23.9	4790.4	33.5
7 MEXICAN-AMERICAN	5/12/1846-2/2/1848	20.7	41.4	17000	28.0	410.6	6.1
2 *UNITED STATES OF AMERICA			20.7	11000	20.5	531.4	5.4
70 *MEXICO			20.7	6000	7.5	289.9	8.0
10 AUSTRO-SARDINIAN	3/24/1848-8/9/1848	4.7	17.9	9200	43.3	514.0	2.1
300 AUSTRIA-HUNGARY	3/20/1849-3/23/1849		4.7	5600	36.3	1191.5	1.5
337 *TUSCANY	3/29/1848-8/9/1848		4.4	100	1.5	22.7	.7
325 ITALY/SARDINIA	4/9/1848-8/9/1848		4.7	3400	4.9	723.4	6.9
332 *MODENA	4/9/1848-8/9/1848		4.1	100	.6	24.4	1.7
13 FIRST SCHLESWIG-HOLSTEIN	4/10/1848-8/26/1848	8.1	16.2	6000	18.5	370.4	3.2
255 GERMANY/PRUSSIA	3/25/1849-7/10/1849		8.1	2500	16.2	308.6	1.5
390 DENMARK			8.1	3500	2.3	432.1	15.2
16 ROMAN REPUBLIC	5/8/1849-7/1/1849	1.8	6.5	1900	83.8	292.3	.2
329 *TWO SICILIES			1.8	100	8.8	55.6	.1
220 FRANCE	6/3/1849-7/1/1849		1.1	300	35.6	272.7	.1
300 AUSTRIA-HUNGARY			1.8	100	36.4	55.6	.0
327 *PAPAL STATES			1.8	1400	3.0	777.8	4.7
19 LA PLATA	7/19/1851-2/3/1852	6.6	13.2	1300	8.4	98.5	1.5
140 *BRAZIL			6.6	500	7.4	75.8	.7
160 *ARGENTINA			6.6	800	1.0	121.2	8.0

Number and Name of War / Participants and Code Number	Dates of War / National Dates When Different	Duration in Months	Magnitude in Nation Months	Severity in Battle Deaths	Population (mil) pre-war	Battle Deaths per Nation Month	Battle Deaths per 10000 Population
22. CRIMEAN	10/23/1853-3/1/1856	28.3	116.5	264200	167.3	2267.8	15.8
200 UNITED KINGDOM	3/31/1854-3/1/1856		23.1	22000	27.7	952.4	7.9
325 ITALY/SARDINIA	1/10/1855-3/1/1856		13.7	2200	5.0	160.6	4.4
220 FRANCE	3/31/1854-3/1/1856		23.1	95000	36.2	4112.6	26.2
640 TURKEY/OTTOMAN EMPIRE			28.3	45000	29.0	1590.1	15.5
365 USSR (RUSSIA)			28.3	100000	69.4	3533.6	14.4
25. ANGLO-PERSIAN	10/25/1856-3/14/1857	4.6	9.2	2000	29.0	217.4	.7
200 UNITED KINGDOM			4.6	500	28.0	108.7	.2
630 *IRAN (PERSIA)			4.6	1500	1.0	326.1	15.0
28. ITALIAN UNIFICATION	4/29/1859-7/12/1859	2.5	7.3	22500	79.2	3082.2	2.8
325 ITALY/SARDINIA			2.5	2500	5.1	1000.0	4.9
220 FRANCE	5/3/1859-7/12/1859		2.3	7500	36.5	3260.9	2.1
300 AUSTRIA-HUNGARY			2.5	12500	37.6	5000.0	3.3
31. SPANISH-MOROCCAN	10/22/1859-3/25/1860	5.2	10.4	10000	22.5	961.5	4.4
230 SPAIN			5.2	4000	15.3	769.2	2.6
600 *MOROCCO			5.2	6000	7.2	1153.8	8.3
34. ITALO-ROMAN	9/11/1860-9/29/1860	.6	1.2	1000	24.1	833.3	.4
325 ITALY/SARDINIA			.6	300	20.9	500.0	.1
327 *PAPAL STATES			.6	700	3.2	1166.7	2.2
37. ITALO-SICILIAN	10/15/1860-1/19/1861	3.2	6.4	1000	30.3	156.3	.3
325 ITALY/SARDINIA			3.2	600	20.9	187.5	.3
329 *TWO SICILIES			3.2	400	9.4	125.0	.4

4.2 (Continued)

Number and Name of War — Participants and Code Number	Dates of War — National Dates When Different	Duration in Months	Magnitude in Nation Months	Severity in Battle Deaths	Population (millions pre-war)	Battle Deaths per Nation Month	Battle Deaths per 10000 Population
40.FRANCO-MEXICAN	4/16/1862-2/5/1867	57.7	115.4	20000	46.5	173.3	4.3
70 *MEXICO			57.7	12000	8.8	208.0	13.6
220 FRANCE			57.7	8000	37.7	138.6	2.1
43.ECUADORIAN-COLOMBIAN	11/22/1863-12/6/1863	.6	1.2	1000	3.6	833.3	2.8
100 *COLOMBIA			.6	300	2.6	500.0	1.2
130 *ECUADOR			.6	700	1.0	1166.7	7.0
46.SECOND SCHLESWIG-HOLSTEIN	2/1/1864-4/25/1864	3.6	10.8	4500	55.4	416.7	.8
255 GERMANY/PRUSSIA	6/25/1864-7/20/1864		3.6	1000	19.0	277.8	.5
300 AUSTRIA-HUNGARY			3.6	500	33.7	138.9	.1
390 DENMARK			3.6	3000	2.7	833.3	11.1
49.LOPEZ	11/12/1864-3/1/1870	63.6	187.1	310000	11.4	1656.9	271.9
160 *ARGENTINA	3/5/1865-3/1/1870		59.9	10000	1.7	166.9	58.8
140 *BRAZIL			63.6	100000	9.2	1572.3	108.7
150 *PARAGUAY			63.6	200000	.5	3144.7	4000.0
52.SPANISH-CHILEAN	10/25/1865-5/9/1866	6.5	16.8	1000	20.1	59.5	.5
155 *CHILE	1/14/1866-5/9/1866		6.5	100	1.8	15.4	.6
135 *PERU			3.8	600	2.3	157.9	2.6
230 SPAIN			6.5	300	16.0	46.2	.2

Number and Name of War / Participants and Code Number	Dates of War / National Dates When Different	Duration in Months	Magnitude in Nation Months	Severity in Battle Deaths	Population (millions pre-war)	Battle Deaths per Nation Month	Battle Deaths per 10000 Population
55.SEVEN WEEKS	6/15/1866-7/26/1866	1.4	14.5	36100	94.6	2489.7	3.8
325 ITALY/SARDINIA			1.4	4000	23.7	2857.1	1.7
255 GERMANY/PRUSSIA	6/20/1866-7/26/1866		1.4	10000	22.1	7142.9	4.5
280 *MECKLENBURG SCHWERIN			1.4	100	.6	71.4	1.7
269 *SAXONY			1.4	600	2.4	428.6	2.5
300 AUSTRIA-HUNGARY			1.4	20000	34.4	14285.7	5.8
273 *HESSE ELECTORAL			1.4	100	.7	71.4	1.4
245 *BAVARIA			1.4	500	4.8	357.1	1.0
271 *WUERTTEMBURG			1.4	100	1.8	71.4	.6
275 *HESSE GRAND DUCAL			1.4	100	.8	71.4	1.3
240 *HANOVER	6/15/1866-6/29/1866		.5	500	1.9	1000.0	2.6
267 *BADEN			1.4	100	1.4	71.4	.7
58.FRANCO-PRUSSIAN	7/19/1870-2/26/1871	7.3	27.0	187500	81.1	6944.4	23.1
271 *WUERTTEMBURG			4.3	1000	1.8	232.6	5.6
255 GERMANY/PRUSSIA	7/19/1870-11/25/1870		7.3	40000	34.6	5479.5	11.6
245 *BAVARIA	7/19/1870-11/15/1870		3.9	5500	4.8	1410.3	11.5
267 *BADEN	7/19/1870-11/22/1870		4.2	1000	1.4	238.1	7.1
220 FRANCE			7.3	140000	38.5	19178.1	36.4
61.RUSSO-TURKISH	4/12/1877-1/3/1878	8.8	17.6	285000	123.3	16193.2	23.1
365 USSR (RUSSIA)			8.8	120000	95.1	13636.4	12.6
640 TURKEY/OTTOMAN EMPIRE			8.8	165000	28.2	18750.0	58.5

(continued)

4.2 (Continued)

Number and Name of War / Participants and Code Number	Dates of War / National Dates When Different	Duration in Months	Magnitude in Nation Months	Severity in Battle Deaths	Population (millions pre-war)	Battle Deaths per Nation Month	Battle Deaths per 10000 Population
64. PACIFIC	2/14/1879-12/11/1883	57.8	170.1	14000	65.0	82.3	215.4
155. *CHILE			57.8	3000	22.0	51.9	136.4
145. *BOLIVIA	4/5/1879-10/20/1883		57.8	1000	15.0	17.3	66.7
135. *PERU			54.5	10000	28.0	183.5	357.1
67. SINO-FRENCH	8/23/1884-6/9/1885	9.5	19.0	12100	5017.0	636.8	2.4
220. FRANCE			9.5	2100	380.0	221.1	5.5
710. *CHINA			9.5	10000	4637.0	1052.6	2.2
70. CENTRAL AMERICAN	3/28/1885-4/15/1885	.5	1.0	1000	20.0	1000.0	50.0
92. *EL SALVADOR			.5	200	7.0	400.0	28.6
90. *GUATEMALA			.5	800	13.0	1600.0	61.5
73. SINO-JAPANESE	8/1/1894-3/30/1895	8.0	16.0	15000	5163.0	937.5	2.9
740. *JAPAN			8.0	5000	411.0	625.0	12.2
710. *CHINA			8.0	10000	4752.0	1250.0	2.1
76. GRECO-TURKISH	2/15/1897-5/19/1897	3.0	6.0	2000	263.0	333.3	7.6
640. TURKEY/OTTOMAN EMPIRE			3.0	1400	238.0	466.7	5.9
350. GREECE			3.0	600	25.0	200.0	24.0

Number and Name of War / Participants and Code Number	Dates of War / National Dates When Different	Duration in Months	Magnitude in Nation Months	Severity in Battle Deaths	Population (millions pre-war)	Battle Deaths per Nation Month	Battle Deaths per 1000 Population
79.SPANISH-AMERICAN	4/21/1898-8/12/1898	3.7	7.4	10000	91.5	1351.4	1.1
2 *UNITED STATES OF AMERICA			3.7	5000	73.1	1351.4	.7
230 SPAIN			3.7	5000	18.4	1351.4	2.7
82.BOXER REBELLION	6/17/1900-8/14/1900	1.9	11.4	3003	817.8	263.4	.0
740 JAPAN			1.9	622	43.8	327.4	.1
200 UNITED KINGDOM			1.9	34	41.2	17.9	.0
365 USSR (RUSSIA)			1.9	302	135.7	158.9	.0
220 FRANCE			1.9	24	38.9	12.6	.0
2 UNITED STATES OF AMERICA			1.9	21	76.0	11.1	.0
710 CHINA			1.9	2000	482.2	1052.6	.0
85.RUSSO-JAPANESE	2/8/1904-9/15/1905	19.3	38.6	130000	191.4	3367.9	6.8
740 JAPAN			19.3	85000	46.6	4404.1	18.2
365 USSR (RUSSIA)			19.3	45000	144.8	2331.6	3.1
88.CENTRAL AMERICAN	5/27/1906-7/20/1906	1.8	5.4	1000	3.1	185.2	3.2
90 *GUATEMALA			1.8	400	1.6	222.2	2.5
91 *HONDURAS			1.8	300	.5	166.7	6.0
92 *EL SALVADOR			1.8	300	1.0	166.7	3.0
91.CENTRAL AMERICAN	2/19/1907-4/23/1907	2.1	6.3	1000	2.3	158.7	4.3
93 *NICARAGUA			2.1	400	.8	190.5	5.0
92 *EL SALVADOR			2.1	300	1.0	142.9	3.0
91 *HONDURAS			2.1	300	.5	142.9	6.0

(continued)

4.2 (Continued)

Number and Name of War / Participants and Code Number	Dates of War / National Dates When Different	Duration in Months	Magnitude in Nation Months	Severity in Battle Deaths	Population (millions pre-war)	Battle Deaths per Nation Month	Battle Deaths per 10000 Population
94. SPANISH-MOROCCAN							
230 SPAIN	7/7/1909-3/23/1910	8.5	17.0	10000	24.2	588.2	4.1
			8.5	2000	19.7	235.3	1.0
600 *MOROCCO			8.5	8000	4.5	941.2	17.8
97. ITALO-TURKISH							
325 ITALY/SARDINIA	9/29/1911-10/18/1912	12.7	25.4	20000	59.5	787.4	3.4
			12.7	6000	34.7	472.4	1.7
640 TURKEY/OTTOMAN EMPIRE			12.7	14000	24.8	1102.4	5.6
100 FIRST BALKAN	10/17/1912-4/19/1913	6.1	20.4	82000	32.1	4019.6	25.5
350 GREECE	10/17/1912-4/19/1913		6.1	5000	2.7	819.7	18.5
345 YUGOSLAVIA/SERBIA	10/17/1912-12/3/1912 2/3/1913-4/19/1913		4.1	15000	3.0	3658.5	50.0
355 BULGARIA	10/17/1912-12/3/1912 2/3/1913-4/19/1913		4.1	32000	4.4	7804.9	72.7
640 TURKEY/OTTOMAN EMPIRE	10/17/1912-4/19/1913		6.1	30000	22.0	4918.0	13.6
103 SECOND BALKAN	6/30/1913-7/30/1913	1.0	4.2	60500	38.9	14404.8	15.6
640 TURKEY/OTTOMAN EMPIRE	7/15/1913-7/30/1913		4.5	20000	21.3	40000.0	9.4
350 GREECE			1.0	2500	2.7	2500.0	9.3
345 YUGOSLAVIA/SERBIA			1.0	18500	3.0	18500.0	61.7
360 RUMANIA	7/11/1913-7/30/1913		.7	1500	7.4	2142.9	2.0
355 BULGARIA			1.0	18000	4.5	18000.0	40.0

Number and Name of War / Participants and Code Number	Dates of War / National Dates When Different	Duration in Months	Magnitude in Nation Months	Severity in Battle Deaths	Population (millions pre-war)	Battle Deaths per Nation Month	Battle Deaths per 10000 Population
106. WORLD WAR I	7/29/1914-11/11/1918	51.6	607.9	9 000 000	604.6	14074.4	141.5
740 JAPAN	8/23/1914-11/11/1918		50.7	300	53.4	5.9	0.1
211 BELGIUM	8/4/1914-11/11/1918		51.3	87500	7.6	1705.7	115.1
2 UNITED STATES OF AMERICA	4/17/1917-11/11/1918		18.9	126000	96.0	6666.7	13.1
345 YUGOSLAVIA/SERBIA			51.6	48000	4.5	930.2	106.7
200 UNITED KINGDOM	8/5/1914-11/11/1918		51.2	908000	46.2	17734.4	196.5
235 PORTUGAL	3/1/1916-11/11/1918		32.4	7000	6.0	216.0	11.7
360 RUMANIA	8/27/1916-12/9/1917		15.4	335000	7.1	21753.2	471.8
220 FRANCE	8/3/1914-11/11/1918		51.3	1350000	41.0	26315.8	329.3
350 GREECE	6/29/1917-11/11/1918		16.5	5000	2.7	303.0	18.5
325 ITALY/SARDINIA	5/23/1915-11/11/1918		41.7	650000	35.2	15587.5	184.7
365 USSR (RUSSIA)	8/1/1914-12/5/1917		40.2	1700000	162.0	42288.6	104.9
640 TURKEY/OTTOMAN EMPIRE	10/28/1914-11/11/1918		48.5	325000	18.5	6701.0	175.7
300 AUSTRIA-HUNGARY	7/29/1914-11/3/1918		51.2	1200000	52.6	23437.5	228.1
255 GERMANY/PRUSSIA	8/1/1914-11/11/1918		51.4	1800000	67.0	35019.5	268.7
355 BULGARIA	10/12/1915-9/29/1918		35.6	14000	4.8	393.3	29.2
109. RUSSO-POLISH	2/14/1919-10/18/1920	20.1	40.2	100000	149.8	2487.6	6.7
290 POLAND			20.1	40000	25.8	1990.0	15.5
365 USSR (RUSSIA)			20.1	60000	124.0	2985.1	4.8
112. HUNGARIAN-ALLIES	4/16/1919-8/4/1919	3.6	10.8	11000	30.7	1018.5	3.6
360 RUMANIA			3.6	3000	9.7	833.3	3.1
315 CZECHOSLOVAKIA			3.6	2000	13.1	555.6	1.5
310 HUNGARY			3.6	6000	7.9	1666.7	7.6
115. GRECO-TURKISH	5/5/1919-10/11/1922	41.3	82.6	50000	15.7	605.3	31.8
640 TURKEY/OTTOMAN EMPIRE			41.3	20000	11.0	484.3	18.2
350 GREECE			41.3	30000	4.7	726.4	63.8

(continued)

4.2 (Continued)

Number and Name of War / Participants and Code Number	Dates of War / National Dates When Different	Duration in Months	Magnitude in Nation Months	Severity in Battle Deaths	Population (millions pre-war)	Battle Deaths per Nation Month	Battle Deaths per 10000 Population
118. SINO-SOVIET	8/17/1929-12/3/1929	3.6	7.2	3200	614.1	444.4	.1
365 USSR (RUSSIA)			3.6	200	135.7	55.6	.0
710 CHINA			3.6	3000	478.4	833.3	.1
121. MANCHURIAN	12/19/1931-5/6/1933	16.6	33.2	60000	551.1	1807.2	1.1
740 JAPAN			16.6	10000	65.4	602.4	1.5
710 CHINA			16.6	50000	485.7	3012.0	1.0
124. CHACO	6/15/1932-6/12/1935	35.9	71.8	130000	3.4	1810.6	382.4
150 PARAGUAY			35.9	50000	.9	1392.8	555.6
145 BOLIVIA			35.9	80000	2.5	2228.4	320.0
127. ITALO-ETHIOPIAN	10/3/1935-5/9/1936	7.2	14.4	20000	55.0	1388.9	3.6
325 ITALY/SARDINIA			7.2	4000	42.8	555.6	.9
530 ETHIOPIA			7.2	16000	12.2	2222.2	13.1
130. SINO-JAPANESE	7/7/1937-12/7/1941	53.1	106.2	1000000	536.5	9416.2	18.6
740 JAPAN			53.1	250000	71.3	4708.1	35.1
710 CHINA			53.1	750000	465.2	14124.3	16.1
133. CHANGKUFENG	7/29/1938-8/11/1938	.6	1.2	1726	252.8	1438.3	.1
740 JAPAN			.6	526	72.2	876.7	.1
365 USSR (RUSSIA)			.6	1200	180.6	2000.0	.1
136. NOMOHAN	5/11/1939-9/16/1939	4.2	12.6	28000	241.7	2222.2	1.2
365 USSR (RUSSIA)			4.2	5000	170.5	1190.5	.3
712 MONGOLIA			4.2	3000	.6	714.3	50.0
740 JAPAN			4.2	20000	70.6	4761.9	2.8

90

139. WORLD WAR II

Number/Code & Name	National Dates When Different	Duration in Months	Magnitude in Nation Months	Severity in Battle Deaths	Population (millions pre-war)	Battle Deaths per Nation Month	Battle Deaths per 10000 Population
139. WORLD WAR II	9/1/1939-8/14/1945	71.4	887.9	15 000 000	1427.3	17086.6	106.3
355 BULGARIA	9/9/1944-5/7/1945		7.9	1000	6.3	126.6	1.6
200 UNITED KINGDOM	9/3/1939-8/14/1945		71.4	270000	47.5	3781.5	56.8
900 AUSTRALIA	9/3/1939-8/14/1945		71.4	33826	6.8	473.8	49.7
20 CANADA	9/10/1939-8/14/1945		71.2	39300	11.4	552.0	34.5
530 ETHIOPIA	1/24/1941-7/3/1941		5.3	5000	13.4	943.4	3.7
290 POLAND	9/1/1939-9/27/1939		.9	320000	34.9	355555.6	91.7
2 UNITED STATES OF AMERICA	12/7/1941-8/14/1945		44.3	408300	130.0	9216.7	31.4
365 USSR (RUSSIA)	6/22/1941-5/7/1945 / 8/8/1945-8/14/1945		46.7	7500000	172.0	160599.6	436.0
211 BELGIUM	5/10/1940-5/28/1940		.6	9600	8.4	16000.0	11.4
140 BRAZIL	7/6/1944-5/7/1945		10.1	1000	39.5	99.0	.3
710 CHINA	12/7/1941-8/14/1945		44.3	1350000	541.0	30474.0	25.0
345 YUGOSLAVIA/SERBIA	4/6/1941-4/17/1941		.4	5000	15.4	12500.0	3.2
210 NETHERLANDS	5/10/1940-5/14/1940		.2	6200	8.8	31000.0	7.0
360 RUMANIA	9/9/1944-5/7/1945		7.9	10000	20.0	1265.8	5.0
325 ITALY/SARDINIA	10/18/1943-5/7/1945		18.7	17500	43.6	935.8	4.0
920 NEW ZEALAND	9/3/1939-8/14/1945		71.4	17300	1.6	242.3	108.1
220 FRANCE	9/3/1939-6/22/1940		19.4	210000	41.1	10824.7	51.1
560 SOUTH AFRICA	10/23/1944-8/14/1945 / 9/6/1939-8/14/1945		71.3	8700	10.2	122.0	8.5
350 GREECE	10/25/1940-4/23/1941		5.9	10000	7.1	1694.9	14.1
385 NORWAY	4/9/1940-6/9/1940		2.0	2000	2.9	1000.0	6.9
712 MONGOLIA	8/10/1945-8/14/1945		.2	3000		15000.0	50.0
740 JAPAN	12/7/1941-8/14/1945		44.3	1000000	70.6	22573.4	141.6
220 FRANCE	7/7/1940-7/14/1941		12.4	2500	41.2	201.6	.6
325 ITALY/SARDINIA	6/10/1940-9/2/1943		38.8	60000	43.9	1546.4	13.7
255 GERMANY/PRUSSIA	9/1/1939-5/7/1945		68.2	3500000	69.7	51319.6	502.2
360 RUMANIA	6/22/1941-8/23/1944		38.1	290000	20.0	7611.5	145.0
355 BULGARIA	12/13/1941-9/8/1944		32.9	9000	6.3	273.6	14.3
310 HUNGARY	6/27/1941-1/20/1945		42.8	40000	9.2	934.6	43.5
375 FINLAND	6/25/1941-9/19/1944		38.9	42000	3.9	1079.7	107.7

(continued)

4.2 (Continued)

Number and Name of War / Participants and Code Number	Dates of War / National Dates When Different	Duration in Months	Magnitude in Nation Months	Severity in Battle Deaths	Population (millions prewar)	Battle Deaths per Nation Month	Battle Deaths per 10000 Population
142 RUSSO-FINNISH							
365 USSR (RUSSIA)	11/30/1939-3/12/1940	3.4	6.8 / 3.4	90000 / 50000	174.4 / 170.5	13235.3 / 14705.9	5.2 / 2.9
375 FINLAND			3.4	40000	3.9	11764.7	102.6
145 FRANCO-THAI							
800 THAILAND	12/1/1940-1/22/1941	1.7	3.4 / 1.7	1400 / 700	56.1 / 15.0	411.8 / 411.8	.2 / .5
220 FRANCE			1.7	700	41.1	411.8	.2
148 PALESTINE							
666 ISRAEL	5/15/1948-7/18/1948	4.7	19.4 / 4.7	8000 / 3000	31.2 / 1.4	412.4 / 638.3	2.6 / 21.4
663 JORDAN	5/15/1948-7/18/1948 / 10/22/1948-10/31/1948		2.5	1000	1.3	400.0	7.7
645 IRAQ	5/15/1948-7/18/1948 / 10/22/1948-10/31/1948		2.5	500	5.0	200.0	1.0
652 SYRIA	5/15/1948-7/18/1948 / 10/22/1948-10/31/1948		2.5 / 4.7	1000 / 2000	3.1 / 19.2	400.0 / 425.5	3.2 / 1.0
651 EGYPT/UAR	5/15/1948-7/18/1948						
660 LEBANON	10/22/1948-10/31/1948		2.5	500	1.2	200.0	4.2
151 KOREAN+	6/24/1950-7/27/1953	37.1	514.1	*2 000 000*	958.8	3680.4	19.7
350 GREECE	1/20/1951-7/27/1953		30.2	170	7.6	5.6	.2
200 UNITED KINGDOM	8/29/1950-7/27/1953		35.0	670	50.8	19.1	.1
20 CANADA	12/29/1950-7/27/1953		31.3	310	13.7	9.9	.2
800 THAILAND	1/20/1951-7/27/1953		30.2	110	20.2	3.6	.1
211 BELGIUM	1/20/1951-7/27/1953		30.2	100	20.7	3.6	.1
640 TURKEY/OTTOMAN EMPIRE	10/18/1950-7/27/1953		33.0	720	20.9	21.6	.3
2 UNITED STATES OF AMERICA	6/27/1950-7/27/1953		37.0	54000	150.7	1459.5	3.6
900 AUSTRALIA	12/10/1950-7/27/1953		31.6	281	8.2	34.3	.3
210 NETHERLANDS	1/20/1951-7/27/1953		30.2	110	10.3	3.6	.1
530 ETHIOPIA	5/1/1951-7/27/1953		26.9	120	15.8	4.5	
100 COLOMBIA	6/6/1951-7/27/1953		25.7	140	11.6	5.4	.1
840 PHILIPPINES	9/16/1950-7/27/1953		34.4	90	20.3	2.6	.0
220 FRANCE	1/1/1951-7/27/1953		30.8	290	43.0	9.4	.1
732 KOREA, REPUBLIC OF			37.1	415000	20.5	11186.0	202.4
731 KOREA, DEM. PEOPLE'S REP	10/27/1950-7/27/1953		37.1	520000	9.7	14016.2	536.1
710 CHINA			33.1	900000	546.8	27190.3	16.5

Number and Name of War / Participants and Code Number	Dates of War / National Dates When Different	Dura-tion in Months	Magni-tude in Nation Months	Severity in Battle Deaths	Popula-tion (mil-lions pre-war)	Battle Deaths per Nation Month	Battle Deaths per 10000 Popula-tion
154 RUSSO-HUNGARIAN	10/23/1956-11/14/1956	.8	1.6	10000	210.1	6250.0	.5
365 USSR (RUSSIA)			.8	7500	200.2	9375.0	.4
310 HUNGARY			.8	2500	9.9	3125.0	2.5
157 SINAI		.3	1.0	3230	121.6	3230.0	.3
220 FRANCE	10/29/1956-11/6/1956		.2	10	44.6	50.0	.0
200 UNITED KINGDOM	10/31/1956-11/6/1956		.2	20	51.6	100.0	.0
666 ISRAEL	10/31/1956-11/6/1956		.3	200	1.8	666.7	1.1
651 EGYPT/UAR			.3	3000	23.6	10000.0	1.3
160 SINO-INDIAN	10/20/1962-11/22/1962	1.1	2.2	1000	1119.3	454.5	.0
710 CHINA			1.1	500	670.1	454.5	.0
750 INDIA			1.1	500	449.2	454.5	.0
163 VIETNAMESE	2/7/1965-4/30/1975	122.7	729.7	1215992	342.1	1666.4	35.5
816 VIETNAM DEMOCRATIC REP			122.7	500000	19.9	4075.0	251.3
800 THAILAND	10/1/1967-1/28/1973		63.9	1000	32.7	15.6	.3
817 VIETNAM REPUBLIC OF	2/7/1965-1/27/1973		122.7	650000	16.1	5297.5	403.7
2 UNITED STATES OF AMERICA	3/1/1970-4/17/1975		95.6	56000	194.2	585.8	2.9
811 KAMPUCHEA (CAMBODIA)	5/1/1965-1/28/1973		61.6	2500	6.7	40.6	3.7
732 KOREA, REPUBLIC OF	2/7/1965-12/20/1972		92.9	5000	28.4	53.8	1.8
900 AUSTRALIA	10/1/1966-1/28/1973		94.4	492	11.4	5.2	.3
840 PHILIPPINES			75.9	1000	32.7	13.2	.3
166 SECOND KASHMIR	8/5/1965-9/23/1965	1.6	3.2	6800	588.8	2125.0	.1
770 PAKISTAN			1.6	3800	113.9	2375.0	.3
750 INDIA			1.6	3000	474.9	1875.0	.1
169 SIX DAY	6/5/1967-6/10/1967	.2	.8	19600	41.4	24500.0	4.7
666 ISRAEL			.2	1000	2.7	5000.0	3.7
651 EGYPT/UAR			.2	10000	30.9	50000.0	3.2
663 JORDAN			.2	6100	2.1	30500.0	29.0
652 SYRIA			.2	2500	5.7	12500.0	4.4

(continued)

93

4.2 (Continued)

Number and Name of War / Participants and Code Number	Dates of War / National Dates When Different	Duration in Months	Magnitude in Nation Months	Severity in Battle Deaths	Population (millions pre-war)	Battle Deaths per Nation Month	Battle Deaths per 10000 Population
172. ISRAELI-EGYPTIAN+	3/6/1969-8/7/1970	17.3	34.6	5368	35.4	155.1	1.5
666 ISRAEL			17.3	368	2.9	21.3	1.3
651 EGYPT/UAR			17.3	5000	32.5	289.0	1.5
175 FOOTBALL	7/14/1969-7/18/1969	.2	.4	1900	4.4	4750.0	4.3
92 EL SALVADOR			.2	700	2.5	3500.0	2.8
91 HONDURAS			.2	1200	1.9	6000.0	6.3
178. BANGLADESH	12/3/1971-12/17/1971	.6	1.2	11000	666.9	9166.7	.2
750 INDIA			.6	8000	550.3	13333.3	.1
770 PAKISTAN			.6	3000	116.6	5000.0	.3
181. YOM KIPPUR	10/6/1973-10/24/1973	.6	3.6	16401	67.0	4555.8	2.4
666 ISRAEL			.6	3000	3.2	5000.0	9.4
651 EGYPT/UAR			.6	5000	35.7	8333.3	1.4
645 IRAQ			.6	278	10.4	463.3	.3
652 SYRIA			.6	8000	7.0	13333.3	11.4
663 JORDAN	10/10/1973-10/24/1973		.6	23	2.5	38.3	.1
670 SAUDI ARABIA	10/10/1973-10/24/1973		.6	100	8.2	166.7	.1
184. TURCO-CYPRIOT	7/20/1974-7/29/1974	.4	.8	1500	38.9	1875.0	.4
640 TURKEY/OTTOMAN EMPIRE	8/14/1974-8/16/1974		.4	1000	38.3	2500.0	.3
352 CYPRUS			.4	500	.6	1250.0	8.3

Number and Name of War / Participants and Code Number	Dates of War / National Dates When Different	Duration in Months	Magnitude in Nation Months	Severity in Battle Deaths	Population (millions pre-war)	Battle Deaths per Nation Month	Battle Deaths per 10000 Population
187. VIETNAMESE-CAMBODIAN (ONGOING)	5/1/1975-12/31/1980	68.0	136.0	8000	31.7	58.8	2.5
816 VIETNAM DEMOCRATIC REP.			68.0	3000	23.6	44.1	1.3
811 KAMPUCHEA (CAMBODIA)			68.0	5000	8.1	73.5	6.2
190. UGANDAN-TANZANIAN	10/30/1978-4/12/1979	5.5	16.5	3000	31.4	181.8	1.0
510 TANZANIA/TANGANYIKA			5.5	1000	16.3	181.8	.6
500 UGANDA			5.5	1500	12.5	272.7	1.2
620 LIBYA			5.5	500	2.6	90.9	1.9
193. SINO-VIETNAMESE	2/17/1979-3/10/1979	.9	1.8	21000	1013.2	11666.7	.2
710 CHINA			.9	13000	964.0	14444.4	.1
816 VIETNAM DEMOCRATIC REP.			.9	8000	49.2	8888.9	1.6
196. RUSSO-AFGHAN (ONGOING)	12/22/1979-12/31/1980	12.4	24.8	10500	282.7	423.4	.4
700 AFGHANISTAN			12.4	8000	21.4	645.2	3.7
365 USSR (RUSSIA)			12.4	2500	261.3	201.6	.1
199. IRANI-IRAQI (ONGOING)	9/22/1980-12/31/1980	3.4	6.8	7000	51.2	1029.4	1.4
630 IRAN (PERSIA)			3.4	4000	38.1	1176.5	1.0
645 IRAQ			3.4	3000	13.1	882.4	2.3

* indicates that the nation was not a member of the central sub-system (1816-1919) at the time war began.
+ after the war name indicates no clear-cut victor.
ONGOING figures are provisional through December 31, 1980.

4.3 Extra-Systematic Wars with System Member Participants, Duration, Magnitude, Severity, and Intensity

Number and Name of War / Participants and Code Number	Dates of War / National Dates When Different	Duration in Months	Magnitude in Nation Months	Severity in Battle Deaths	Population (millions pre-war)	Battle Deaths per Nation Month	Battle Deaths per 10000 Population
301 BRITISH-MAHARATTAN	11/6/1817-6/3/1818	6.9	6.9	2000	19.8	289.9	1.0
200 UNITED KINGDOM			6.9	2000	19.8	289.9	1.0
304 GREEK	3/25/1821-4/25/1828	85.1	85.1	15000	24.7	176.3	6.1
610 TURKEY/OTTOMAN EMPIRE			85.1	15000	24.7	176.3	6.1
307 FIRST ANGLO-BURMESE	9/24/1823-2/24/1826	29.1	29.1	15000	21.7	515.5	6.9
200 UNITED KINGDOM			29.1	15000	21.7	515.5	6.9
310 JAVANESE	7/23/1825-3/28/1830	56.2	56.2	15000	6.0	266.9	25.0
210 NETHERLANDS			56.2	15000	6.0	266.9	25.0
313 RUSSO-PERSIAN	9/28/1826-2/28/1828	17.0	17.0	5000	55.7	294.1	.9
365 USSR (RUSSIA)			17.0	5000	55.7	294.1	.9
316 FIRST POLISH	2/7/1831-10/18/1831	8.3	8.3	15000	58.0	1807.2	2.6
365 USSR (RUSSIA)			8.3	15000	58.0	1807.2	2.6
319 FIRST SYRIAN	11/1/1831-12/21/1832	13.7	13.7	10000	23.1	729.9	4.3
610 TURKEY/OTTOMAN EMPIRE			13.7	10000	23.1	729.9	4.3
322 TEXAN	10/1/1835-4/22/1836	6.7	6.7	1000	6.7	149.3	1.5
70 • MEXICO			6.7	1000	6.7	149.3	1.5
325 FIRST BRITISH-AFGHAN	10/1/1838-10/12/1842	48.4	48.4	20000	25.9	413.2	7.7
200 UNITED KINGDOM			48.4	20000	25.9	413.2	7.7
328 SECOND SYRIAN	6/10/1839-6/24/1839 9/9/1840-11/27/1840	3.1	5.7	10010	50.5	1756.1	2.0
200 UNITED KINGDOM	6/10/1839-6/24/1839		2.6	10	26.5	3.8	.0
610 TURKEY/OTTOMAN EMPIRE	9/9/1840-11/27/1840		3.1	10000	24.0	3225.8	4.2
331 FRANCO-ALGERIAN	11/1/1839-12/23/1847	97.9	97.9	15000	33.9	153.2	4.4
220 FRANCE			97.9	15000	33.9	153.2	4.4
334 PERUVIAN-BOLIVIAN	10/19/1841-11/18/1841	1.0	1.0	1000	1.7	1000.0	5.9
135 • PERU			1.0	1000	1.7	1000.0	5.9
337 FIRST BRITISH-SIKH	12/13/1845-3/9/1846	2.9	2.9	1500	27.8	517.2	.5
200 UNITED KINGDOM			2.9	1500	27.8	517.2	.5
340 HUNGARIAN	9/9/1848-8/13/1849	11.1	12.2	59500	102.7	4877.0	5.8
300 AUSTRIA-HUNGARY			11.1	45000	36.3	4054.1	12.4
365 USSR (RUSSIA)	7/16/1849-8/13/1849		1.1	14500	66.4	13181.8	2.2

Number and Name of War Participants and Code Number	Dates of War National Dates When Different	Duration in Months	Magnitude in Nation Months	Severity in Battle Deaths	Population (millions pre-war)	Battle Deaths per Nation Month	Battle Deaths per 10000 Population
343. SECOND BRITISH-SIKH 200 UNITED KINGDOM	10/10/1848-3/12/1849	5.1	5.1	1500 1500	27.2 27.2	294.1 294.1	.6 .6
346. FIRST TURCO-MONTENEGRAN 640 TURKEY/OTTOMAN EMPIRE	12/2/1852-3/13/1853	3.4	3.4	5000 5000	28.8 28.8	1470.6 1470.6	1.7 1.7
349. SEPOY 200 UNITED KINGDOM	5/10/1857-4/7/1859	22.9	22.9	3500 3500	28.2 28.2	152.8 152.8	1.2 1.2
352. SECOND TURCO-MONTENEGRAN 640 TURKEY/OTTOMAN EMPIRE	5/4/1858-6/1/1859	12.9	12.9	3000 3000	26.1 26.1	232.6 232.6	1.1 1.1
355. SECOND POLISH 365 USSR (RUSSIA)	1/22/1863-4/19/1864	14.9	14.9	5000 5000	78.4 78.4	335.6 335.6	.6 .6
358. SPANISH-SANTO DOMINICAN 230 SPAIN	11/2/1863-1/27/1865	15.1	15.1	7000 7000	15.7 15.7	463.6 463.6	4.5 4.5
361. TEN YEARS 230 SPAIN	10/10/1868-2/10/1878	112.1	112.1	100000 100000	16.4 16.4	892.1 892.1	61.0 61.0
364. DUTCH-ACHINESE 210 NETHERLANDS	3/26/1873-9/1/1878	65.2	65.2	6000 6000	3.7 3.7	92.0 92.0	16.2 16.2
367. BALKAN 640 TURKEY/OTTOMAN EMPIRE	7/3/1875-4/12/1877	21.4	21.4	10000 10000	28.2 28.2	467.3 467.3	3.5 3.5
370. BOSNIAN 300 AUSTRIA-HUNGARY	7/29/1878-10/1/1878	2.1	2.1	3500 3500	37.2 37.2	1666.7 1666.7	.9 .9
373. SECOND BRITISH-AFGHAN 200 UNITED KINGDOM	11/20/1878-5/26/1879 9/3/1879-9/2/1880	18.2	18.2	4000 4000	33.9 33.9	219.8 219.8	1.2 1.2
376. BRITISH-ZULU 200 UNITED KINGDOM	1/11/1879-7/4/1879	5.7	5.7	3500 3500	34.3 34.3	614.0 614.0	1.0 1.0
379. FRANCO-INDOCHINESE 220 FRANCE	4/25/1882-6/14/1884	25.7	25.7	4500 4500	37.7 37.7	175.1 175.1	1.2 1.2
382. MAHDIST 200 UNITED KINGDOM	9/13/1882-12/30/1885	39.6	39.6	20000 20000	35.2 35.2	505.1 505.1	5.7 5.7

(continued)

4.3 (Continued)

Number and Name of War / Participants and Code Number	Dates of War / National Dates When Different	Dura- tion in Months	Magni- tude in Nation Months	Severity in Battle Deaths	Popula- tion (mil- lions pre-war)	Battle Deaths per Nation Month	Battle Deaths per 10000 Nation Popula- tion
385 SERBO-BULGARIAN 345 YUGOSLAVIA/SERBIA	11/2/1885-12/7/1885	1 2	1 2 1 2	2000 2000	1 9 1 9	1666 7 1666 7	10 5 10 5
388 FRANCO-MADAGASCAN 220 FRANCE	12/12/1894-10/1/1895	9 7	9 7 9 7	6000 6000	38 4 38 4	618 6 618 6	1 6 1 6
391 CUBAN 230 SPAIN	2/24/1895-4/20/1898	37 3	37 3 37 3	50000 50000	18 2 18 2	1340 5 1340 5	27 5 27 5
394 ITALO-ETHIOPIAN 325 ITALY/SARDINIA	12/7/1895-10/21/1896	10 5	10 5 10 5	9000 9000	31 1 31 1	857 1 857 1	2 9 2 9
397 FIRST PHILIPPINE 230 SPAIN	5/30/1896-5/1/1898	23 1	23 1 23 1	2000 2000	18 2 18 2	86 6 86 6	1 1 1 1
400 SECOND PHILIPPINE 2 UNITED STATES OF AMERICA	2/4/1899-7/4/1902	40 9	40 9 40 9	4500 4500	74 5 74 5	110 0 110 0	6 6
403 BOER 200 UNITED KINGDOM	10/11/1899-5/31/1902	31 6	71 6 31 6	22000 22000	40 8 40 8	696 2 696 2	5 4 5 4
406 ILLINDEN 640 TURKEY/OTTOMAN EMPIRE	8/2/1903-11/2/1903	3 1	3 1 3 1	2000 2000	24 0 24 0	645 2 645 2	8 8
409 RUSSIAN NATIONALITIES 365 USSR (RUSSIA)	12/9/1917-3/18/1921	39 3	39 3 39 3	50000 50000	162 0 162 0	1272 3 1272 3	3 1 3 1
412 RIFFIAN 230 SPAIN 220 FRANCE	7/18/1921-5/27/1926	58 3	71 9 58 3 13 6	29000 25000 4000	62 0 21 4 40 6	403 3 428 8 294 1	4 7 11 7 1 0
415 DRUZE 220 FRANCE	7/18/1925-6/1/1927	22 4	22 4 22 4	4000 4000	40 6 40 6	178 6 178 6	1 0 1 0
418 INDONESIAN 200 UNITED KINGDOM 210 NETHERLANDS	11/10/1945 10/15/1946	11 2	22 4 11 2 11 2	1400 1000 400	57 0 48 3 8 7	62 5 89 3 35.7	2 2 2 2 5
421 INDOCHINESE 220 FRANCE	12/1/1945-6/1/1954	102 0	102 0 102 0	95000 95000	41 9 41 9	931 4 931 4	22 7 22 7
424 MADAGASCAN 220 FRANCE	3/29/1947-12/1/1948	20 2	20 2 20 2	1800 1800	41 6 41 6	89 1 89 1	4 4

Number and Name of War / Participants and Code Number	Dates of War / National Dates When Different	Duration in Months	Magnitude in Nation Months	Severity in Battle Deaths	Population (millions pre-war)	Battle Deaths per Nation Month	Battle Deaths per 10000 Population
427 FIRST KASHMIR 750 INDIA	10/26/1947-1/1/1949	14.3	14.3	1500 1500	342.3 342.3	104.9 104.9	.0 .0
430 HYDERABAD 750 INDIA	9/13/1948-9/17/1948	.2	.2	1000 1000	348.0 348.0	5000.0 5000.0	.0 .0
433 ALGERIAN 220 FRANCE	11/1/1954-3/17/1962	88.5	88.5 88.5	18000 18000	43.9 43.9	203.4 203.4	4.1 4.1
436 TIBETAN 710 CHINA	3/1/1956-3/22/1959	36.7	36.7 36.7	40000 40000	617.5 617.5	1089.9 1089.9	.6 .6
439 PHILIPPINE MNLF (ONGOING) 840 PHILIPPINES	1/1/1972-12/31/1980	108.0	108.0 108.0	10000 10000	39.8 39.8	92.6 92.6	2.5 2.5
442 ETHIOPIAN-ERITREAN (ONGOING) 530 ETHIOPIA	1/1/1974-12/31/1980	84.0	84.0 84.0	25000 25000	27.2 27.2	297.6 297.6	9.2 9.2
445 TIMOR (ONGOING) 850 INDONESIA	12/7/1975-12/31/1980	60.8	60.8 60.8	10000 10000	136.0 136.0	164.5 164.5	.7 .7
448 SAHARAN (ONGOING) 600 MOROCCO	12/11/1975-12/31/1980	60.7	104.5 60.7	7000 5000	30.2 17.1	67.0 82.4	2.3 2.9
435 MAURITANIA	12/11/1975-8/5/1979		43.8	2000	13.1	45.7	1.5
451 OGADEN (ONGOING) 530 ETHIOPIA 40 CUBA	7/1/1976-12/31/1980 1/30/1977-12/31/1980	20.5	41.6 20.5 13.6	21000 15000 1000	41.0 28.2 9.5	504.8 731.7 73.5	5.1 5.3 1.1
520 SOMALIA	8/1/1977-3/14/1978		7.5	5000	3.3	666.7	15.2

* next to the nation number indicates that it was not a member of the central sub-system (1816-1919) at the time war began.
ONGOING figures are provisional through December 31, 1980.

CHAPTER 5

Ranking the Wars by Severity, Magnitude, and Intensity

In Chapter 4, we identified all of the wars that satisfied our criteria for inclusion, and then went on to present our estimates of their duration, magnitude, severity, and intensity. For certain purposes such a format is quite useful, but it does not readily lend itself to the needs of those with more restricted interests. Some scholars, for example, may want to analyze only wars of a particular type (interstate or extra-systemic, central interstate, or major power). Others may be primarily interested in those that fall above or below a certain threshold on one or more of our measures. Therefore, we devote the present chapter to a computation and presentation of the wars' ranking on five different dimensions: battle-connected deaths, nation months, total population of the system members involved, battle deaths per nation month, and battle deaths per capita.

RANKING ALL INTERNATIONAL WARS

Although there might be some limited usefulness in presenting a separate rank order tabulation for each of the five dimensions, it does not seem to merit the space required. Thus, we present only one such tabulation, but include additional rank position data in each. To illustrate, 5.1 lists all 118 international wars ranked according to battle deaths, but following the column showing each war's rank position on that dimension are separate columns indicating its rank on the four other dimensions.

One new measure appears here for the first time: a ranking based on the total population of all of the system members that participated in each of the wars. It is probably best thought of as an additional measure of magnitude, since it reflects both the number and the size of the states involved in the war. The population rankings are also introduced because the figures on which they are based serve as the denominator in computing one of the intensity measures: battle deaths per capita.

A word of justification is in order as to why we selected severity rather than one of the other indicators as the primary basis for ranking the wars. As was suggested earlier, we share Richardson's implied view that the single most valid and sensitive indicator of the "amount of war" experienced by the system is that of battle deaths or severity. To illustrate its advantage over the nation month (magnitude) measure, compare the rank position of the Russo-Turkish War of 1877-1878 as shown in 5.1. This is considered by most historians one of the most important and "great" conflicts of the epoch under study. Because it involved only two powers and lasted less than 9 months, its magnitude is a relatively low 17.6 nation months, for a rank position of 48. But the ferocity with which it was fought and the human resources allocated to it are dramatically revealed in its 285,000 battle deaths, giving it the more representative seventh position in the severity rankings.

It should be noted, of course, that interstate wars dominate these rankings, not only because they tended to be of higher severity, magnitude, and intensity than the extra-systemic wars, but also because of the limits of our data. That is, since our major theoretical concern is with the interstate system, we have gathered severity and magnitude data only for the entities that were qualified system members. Moreover, even if we *were* interested in the additional data, the problems of availability and reliability would have been far more formidable than for the interstate wars. Thus, the extra-systemic wars reflect only the severity, magnitude, and intensity figures for the national members of the system and therefore understate the *total* range and destructiveness of the hostilities. To illustrate, the Ten Years War of 1868-1878 between Spain and Cuba is ranked 13.5 in the severity column, even though the battle deaths sustained by the Cuban forces (as a non-member of the system) are not included in the total; our estimate is that this war might have been in seventh position on that dimension if Cuban military fatalities had been included.

RANK ORDER CORRELATIONS

As will be evident from visual inspection of 5.1, there tends to be a fairly strong and positive correlation between the rank orderings of

5.1　Rank Order of All International Wars by Severity

War No.	Name of War	Battle Deaths 1	Nation Months 2	Popula- tion 3	Battle Deaths per Nation Month 4	Battle Deaths per Capita 5
139	WORLD WAR II	1.0	1.0	1.0	2.0	4.0
106	WORLD WAR I	2.0	3.0	9.0	5.0	3.0
151	KOREAN	3.0	4.0	4.0	19.0	15.0
163	VIETNAMESE	4.0	2.0	16.0	35.0	6.0
130	SINO-JAPANESE	5.0	10.0	12.0	11.0	16.0
49	LOPEZ	6.0	5.0	97.0	36.0	2.0
61	RUSSO-TURKISH	7.0	48.0	26.0	3.0	12.0
22	CRIMEAN	8.0	7.0	23.0	25.0	19.0
58	FRANCO-PRUSSIAN	9.0	34.0	32.0	13.0	11.0
4	RUSSO-TURKISH	11.0	26.0	21.0	20.0	24.0
85	RUSSO-JAPANESE	11.0	26.0	21.0	20.0	24.0
124	CHACO	11.0	17.0	105.0	32.0	1.0
109	RUSSO-POLISH	13.5	23.0	25.0	24.0	25.0
361	TEN YEARS	13.5	9.0	94.0	51.0	5.0
421	INDOCHINESE	15.0	11.0	51.0	50.0	13.0
142	RUSSO-FINNISH	16.0	79.0	22.0	6.0	32.0
100	FIRST BALKAN	17.0	43.0	66.0	17.0	9.0
103	SECOND BALKAN	18.0	88.0	56.5	4.0	20.0
121	MANCHURIAN	19.0	31.0	11.0	31.0	73.0
340	HUNGARIAN	20.0	65.0	28.0	16.0	29.0
115	GRECO-TURKISH	22.0	15.0	92.5	60.0	7.0
391	CUBAN	22.0	27.0	24.5	40.0	8.0
409	RUSSIAN NATIONALITIES	22.0	25.0	24.0	41.0	52.0
436	TIBETAN	24.0	28.0	7.0	42.0	84.0
55	SEVEN WEEKS	25.0	61.0	29.0	22.0	45.0
412	RIFFIAN	26.0	16.0	38.0	75.0	35.0
136	NOMOHAN	27.0	64.0	19.0	26.0	69.0
28	ITALIAN UNIFICATION	28.0	74.0	34.0	21.0	54.0
403	BOER	29.0	32.0	54.0	55.0	31.0
193	SINO-VIETNAMESE	30.0	97.0	3.0	7.0	102.0
40	FRANCO-MEXICAN	33.0	8.0	47.0	94.0	42.0
97	ITALO-TURKISH	33.0	36.0	39.0	53.0	49.0
127	ITALO-ETHIOPIAN	33.0	59.0	45.0	38.0	46.0
325	FIRST BRITISH-AFGHAN	33.0	20.0	81.0	73.0	22.0
382	MAHDIST	33.0	24.0	62.0	65.0	30.0
169	SIX DAY	36.0	108.0	53.0	1.0	34.0
433	ALGERIAN	37.0	13.0	48.0	88.0	44.0
7	MEXICAN-AMERICAN	38.0	21.0	76.0	74.0	27.0
181	YOM KIPPUR	39.0	92.0	37.0	14.0	58.0
73	SINO-JAPANESE	42.5	53.5	13.0	49.0	95.0
304	GREEK	42.5	14.0	82.0	92.0	26.0
307	FIRST ANGLO-BURMESE	42.5	33.0	88.0	64.0	23.0
310	JAVANESE	42.5	19.0	101.0	84.0	10.0
316	FIRST POLISH	42.5	73.0	40.0	28.0	56.0
331	FRANCO-ALGERIAN	42.5	12.0	64.5	99.0	38.0
64	PACIFIC	46.0	6.0	100.0	107.0	14.0
67	SINO-FRENCH	47.0	45.0	14.0	57.0	99.0
112	HUNGARIAN-ALLIES	48.5	68.0	70.0	43.0	47.0
178	BANGLADESH	48.5	102.5	6.0	8.0	103.0
328	SECOND SYRIAN	50.0	85.0	46.0	29.0	60.0
31	SPANISH-MOROCCAN	53.5	70.0	87.0	48.0	37.0
79	SPANISH-AMERICAN	53.5	75.0	30.0	39.0	72.0
94	SPANISH-MOROCCAN	53.5	49.5	83.0	61.0	43.0
154	RUSSO-HUNGARIAN	53.5	98.0	20.0	12.0	90.0
319	FIRST SYRIAN	53.5	60.0	86.0	54.0	40.0
367	BALKAN	53.5	41.0	74.5	67.0	48.0
10	AUSTRO-SARDINIAN	57.0	47.0	49.0	63.0	59.0
394	ITALO-ETHIOPIAN	58.0	68.0	69.0	52.0	53.0
148	PALESTINE	59.0	44.0	68.0	72.0	57.0
358	SPANISH-SANTO DOMINICAN	60.0	55.0	95.5	68.0	36.0
166	SECOND KASHMIR	61.0	92.0	10.0	27.0	104.0
13	FIRST SCHLESWIG-HOLSTEIN	63.0	53.5	91.0	76.0	50.0
364	DUTCH-ACHINESE	63.0	18.0	103.0	104.0	17.0
388	FRANCO-MADAGASCAN	63.0	71.0	58.0	58.5	62.0
172	ISRAELI-EGYPTIAN	65.0	29.0	61.0	97.0	64.0
313	RUSSO-PERSIAN	67.0	49.5	43.0	82.0	79.0
346	FIRST TURCO-MONTENEGRAN	67.0	89.0	73.0	37.0	61.0
355	SECOND POLISH	67.0	56.0	35.0	77.0	85.0
46	SECOND SCHLESWIG-HOLSTEIN	70.0	68.0	44.0	71.0	81.0
379	FRANCO-INDOCHINESE	70.0	35.0	59.0	93.0	67.0
400	SECOND PHILIPPINE	70.0	22.0	36.0	101.0	86.0
373	SECOND BRITISH-AFGHAN	72.5	46.0	64.5	87.0	68.0
415	DRUZE	72.5	39.0	55.0	91.0	76.0
349	SEPOY	75.0	38.0	74.5	98.0	66.0
370	BOSNIAN	75.0	95.5	60.0	33.0	78.0
376	BRITISH-ZULU	75.0	84.0	63.0	58.5	74.0
157	SINAI	77.0	106.5	27.0	15.0	96.0
118	SINO-SOVIET	78.0	76.0	8.0	69.0	106.0
82	BOXER REBELLION	79.0	66.0	5.0	83.0	108.0
190	UGANDAN-TANZANIAN	80.5	52.0	67.0	90.0	77.0
352	SECOND TURCO-MONTENEGRAN	80.5	63.0	80.0	85.0	70.0
25	ANGLO-PERSIAN	84.5	72.0	72.0	86.0	83.0
76	GRECO-TURKISH	84.5	82.5	79.0	78.0	82.0
301	BRITISH-MAHARATTAN	84.5	77.0	90.0	81.0	75.0
385	SERBO-BULGARIAN	84.5	99.0	109.0	30.0	21.0
397	FIRST PHILIPPINE	84.5	37.0	92.5	106.0	71.0
406	ILINDEN	84.5	92.0	85.0	56.0	80.0
16	ROMAN REPUBLIC	88.5	81.0	31.0	79.0	101.0
175	FOOTBALL	88.5	109.0	102.0	10.0	41.0
424	MADAGASCAN	90.0	42.0	52.0	105.0	91.0
133	CHANGKUFENG	91.0	102.5	18.0	34.0	105.0
184	TURCO-CYPRIOT	93.5	106.5	56.5	23.0	93.0

5.1   (Continued)

War No	Name of War	Battle Deaths 1	Nation Months 2	Population 3	Battle Deaths per Nation Month 4	Battle Deaths per Capita 5
337	FIRST BRITISH-SIKH	93.5	94.0	77.0	62.0	88.0
343	SECOND BRITISH-SIKH	93.5	87.0	78.0	80.0	87.0
427	FIRST KASHMIR	93.5	58.0	15.0	102.0	107.0
145	FRANCO-THAI	96.5	90.0	42.0	70.0	97.0
418	INDONESIAN	96.5	40.0	41.0	109.0	98.0
19	LA PLATA	98.0	62.0	98.0	103.0	63.0
1	FRANCO-SPANISH	104.5	57.0	50.0	108.0	100.0
34	ITALO-ROMAN	104.5	102.5	84.0	45.5	92.0
37	ITALO-SICILIAN	104.5	80.0	71.0	96.0	94.0
43	ECUADORIAN-COLOMBIAN	104.5	102.5	104.0	45.5	55.0
52	SPANISH-CHILEAN	104.5	51.0	89.0	110.0	89.0
70	CENTRAL AMERICAN	104.5	102.5	108.0	45.5	33.0
88	CENTRAL AMERICAN	104.5	86.0	106.0	89.0	51.0
91	CENTRAL AMERICAN	104.5	82.5	107.0	95.0	39.0
160	SINO-INDIAN	104.5	95.5	2.0	66.0	110.0
322	TEXAN	104.5	78.0	99.0	100.0	65.0
334	PERUVIAN-BOLIVIAN	104.5	102.5	110.0	45.5	28.0
430	HYDERABAD	104.5	110.0	17.0	9.0	109.0

all types of war based on severity and those based on magnitude. But when we look at the two intensity indicators and the population base line, the picture is much less clear. This should not be surprising, since any war that is low on battle deaths and relatively high on nation months (such as the War of the Pacific of 1879-1883) will inevitably have a low battle deaths per nation month intensity rank, and one that ranks high on battle deaths and low on total population (such as the Chaco War of 1932-1935) will inevitably have a high battle deaths per capita intensity rank, and so on.

If we think of the three delineators used for ranking these international wars as falling into two rather distinct groupings, we can then examine a rank order correlation matrix and make some sense of it. That is, if we had no information at all, it would be reasonable to expect that (a) wars that lead to a great many battle death are those involving quite a few nations and/or enduring for many months; and (b) wars that were very intense in terms of battle deaths per nation month would also rank high on battle deaths per capita. In 5.2 we see the extent to which such expectations are borne out. Given the number of tied scores, we used Kendall's tau (B statistic).

As we suggested earlier, there are just enough cases that deviate from the näively expected to make some of the correlations fairly low. That is, the battle death rank positions tend to correlate strongly and positively with those of the other four ranking criteria, but we find that population rankings are less closely associated with battle deaths than are the others. This stems from the low (.14) correlation between these two variables in the extra-systemic wars; and even in the interstate wars, the relationship is not as strong as the others. Additional correlations of a fairly strong and positive character are those between rankings on nation months and battle deaths per capita, and (at least for interstate wars) between population and battle deaths per nation month. The only notable correlation in the *negative*

5.2 Rank Order Correlations Among Several War Indicators, by Type of War

	Pop	Nat-Mos	B-Dths	B-Dths/NM	B-Dths/Cap
Population (All Wars)	1.00				
Interstate Wars	1.00				
Extra-Systemic Wars	1.00				
Nation-Months (All Wars)	.03	1.00			
Interstate Wars	.07	1.00			
Extra-Systemic Wars	.04	1.00			
Battle Deaths (All Wars)	.27	.46	1.00		
Interstate Wars	.31	.49	1.00		
Extra-Systemic Wars	.14	.48	1.00		
B-Dths per Nation-Month (All Wars)	.28	-.16	.39	1.00	
Interstate Wars	.31	-.05	.47	1.00	
Extra-Systemic Wars	.07	-.27	.25	1.00	
B-Dths per Capita (All Wars)	-.22	.41	.51	.19	1.00
Interstate Wars	-.18	.45	.52	.25	1.00
Extra-Systemic Wars	-.33	.33	.55	.18	1.00

direction is that between population and battle deaths per capita, and this is, of course, fully expected. We can conclude, therefore, that the statistical relationships predicted above are generally what we find.

FREQUENCY DISTRIBUTIONS

Having now identified the various types of war, described them in terms of several quantitative indicators, and ranked them according to those indicators, we are in a position to attempt a summary of the results. What kinds of patterns emerge? How many large wars are there? Are many of them particularly bloody? What fraction of them are quite short in duration? Through the computation of frequency distributions, we can efficiently answer these and other questions. Such distribution matrices not only make these simple descriptive statements possible, but they answer that question so dear to the heart of statistically oriented scholars: Are these events randomly distributed, or is there some underlying pattern and regularity? The corollary question, of course, is whether these distributions fit one or more well-known equations: Poisson, polynomial, binomial, log normal, and so on.

Our general view is that this latter "curve fitting" operation is better conducted in the context of a theoretical inquiry, where one is explicitly trying to discover relationships among variables and testing alternative hypotheses that might account for the observed distributions. And since this volume is expressly limited to the presentation and systematic arrangement of our war data only, with no attention to the factors that account for them, there are good reasons for not going beyond the descriptive statements mentioned above. But in order to emphasize the regularity of some of our distributions, and to compare them with the work of others, we have computed the goodness of fit in a few places.

First, we looked at all 110 international wars (omitting the eight still under way) and determined the number that fell into each of five different groupings along the *severity* (battle death) dimension. As 5.3 makes clear, if we use Richardson's log breakdown (and the numerical equivalents in battle deaths), there are a good many wars of low severity, somewhat more of moderate severity, and very few in the upper ranges. Moreover, the same pattern seems to hold for all classes of war. And even though Richardson (1960a: 147) uses different criteria and includes more wars, it turns out that his observed frequencies would not be sharply different from ours if they did not embrace so many of those wars in which only a few hundred were

5.3   Frequencies of International War by Severity

Log_{10} range	2.5–3.0	3.5–4.5	4.5–5.5	5.5–6.5	6.5–7.5	
Absolute battle death range	1000–3,100	3,100–31,000	31,000–310,000	310,000–3,100,000	3,100,000–31,000,000	N
All Wars	32	53	20	3	2	110
Interstate Wars	19	26	14	3	2	64
Extra-systemic Wars	13	27	6	0	0	46
Central System Wars	25	50	19	3	2	99
Major Power Wars	1	2	4	1	2	10

killed. But it should also be noted that, in regard to any variable, appreciably different distributions can be obtained with different scale intervals.

Shifting now to the *magnitude* measure, we may again summarize the distributions in the same fashion. By treating all wars of 12 nation months or less as the smallest range and those of 193-960 nation months (16-80 nation years) as the largest, we find a pattern similar to that of the severity distributions (5.4).

Here, perhaps, we might profitably succumb to the temptation of curve fitting, since the range in magnitude of wars is fairly manageable. We hypothesize that our distribution is very close to a natural logarithmic curve (skewed to the right); one way of testing this is to transform the actual values to more nearly approximate normal curve (bell-shaped) values, and then test the transformed values for normality via the chi-square.

First, we transformed our raw magnitude scores to natural log (log_e) values in order to collapse the extreme high scores; we had to add .9 nation months to the actual magnitude of each war so that no log_e scores were negative. Then we calculated the mean and standard deviation of the transformed scores, from which point we could determine what percentage of our observed cases could be expected to fall within a given distance from the mean. With a normal curve distribu-

5.4 Frequencies of International War by Magnitude

Nation months Nation years	12 or less 1 or less	13-48 1-4	49-96 4-8	97-192 8-16	193-960 16-80
All International Wars	46	44	8	8	4
Interstate Wars	30	23	2	5	4
Central System Wars	40	41	8	6	4
Major Power Wars	2	4	0	1	3
Extrasystemic Wars	16	21	6	3	0

tion, 50 percent of the cases occur on each side of the mean, and approximately two-thirds of all events fall within one standard deviation from the mean on both sides. We chose to divide the area under the normal curve into 10 interval ranges, each of which was expected to contain 10 percent of the total (transformed) cases; we used a normal curve areas table, employing the standard score (z) formula: $z = x - \bar{x}/s.d$, solving for x at the percentage intercepts (10, 20, 30, and so on) of the area under a normal curve.

In 5.5 the $\log_e$ intervals for 110 international wars (the eight ongoing wars are excluded) are presented, along with the actual, untransformed values for each interval division. The "expected" values—10 percent of the total number of wars of each type in each interval—and the "observed" number of wars whose transformed magnitudes fell into each interval are reported, along with the means and standard deviations used to compute the interval ranges.

With the values in 5.5 we could compute the similarity between the expected and observed frequencies for each type of war. We used the chi-square $\Sigma (f_{observed} - f_{expected})^2/f_{expected})$, which would be equal to zero if all expected and observed values were identical and increasingly higher as the differences between the values were greater.

We present in 5.6 a visual representation of the observed and expected frequencies in the form of a cumulative probability graph. The broken line represents the expected frequency at each percentage level given on the horizontal axis; the $\log_e$ scale is given as the vertical axis. The line connecting the heavy dots represents the observed number of wars, each dot showing the actual percentage of wars included in each successive $\log_e$ range. The distribution thus tested fit the expected distribution at a .05 level of significance, which permits us to say that the distribution of war magnitude scores can be described as natural logarithmic curves.

Finally, the wars embraced in this study may be grouped according to their *intensity* ranges, as measured by battle deaths per nation month (5.7). Here we note, not too surprisingly, that the distribution frequencies of the extra-systemic wars differ somewhat from those of the other classes of war. To some extent, this is probably a statistical artifact arising from the fact that the non-members' battle deaths are not included. But it also may be accounted for by the fact that the colonial powers seldom allocated as much in material and manpower per year to these wars as to those fought against other system members.

5.5 Observed and Expected Frequencies of International War by Magnitude, Natural Logarithmic Transformation

ALL WARS

Interval range- logE	Interval range- nation months	Observed frequencies	Expected frequencies
0- .94	0- 2.6	14	11.0
.95- 1.56	2.7- 4.7	8	11.0
1.57- 2.01	4.8- 7.5	11	11.0
2.02- 2.43	7.6- 11.5	11	11.0
2.44- 2.76	11.6- 15.8	12	11.0
2.77- 3.09	15.9- 22.1	13	11.0
3.10- 3.50	22.2- 33.4	10	11.0
3.51- 3.95	33.5- 52.4	12	11.0
3.96- 4.57	52.5- 97.4	7	11.0
4.58+	97.5+	12	11.0

mean = 2.77   standard deviation = 1.42

INTERSTATE WARS

Interval range- logE	Interval range- nation months	Observed frequencies	Expected frequencies
0- .66	0- 1.9	9	6.4
.67- 1.36	2.0- 3.9	3	6.4
1.37- 1.86	4.0- 6.4	5	6.4
1.87- 2.32	6.5- 10.2	9	6.4
2.33- 2.70	10.3- 14.8	7	6.4
2.71- 3.07	14.9- 21.5	12	6.4
3.08- 3.53	21.6- 34.3	4	6.4
3.54- 4.04	34.4- 56.9	4	6.4
4.05- 4.74	57.0- 114.4	3	6.4
4.75+	114.5+	8	6.4

mean = 2.70   standard deviation = 1.59

(continued)

5.5 (Continued)

110

EXTRASYSTEMIC WARS

Interval range-logE	0-1.39	1.40-1.89	1.90-2.25	2.26-2.59	2.60-2.86	2.87-3.12	3.13-3.46	3.47-3.82	3.83-4.32	4.33+
Interval range-nation months	0-4.0	4.1-6.6	6.7-9.5	9.6-13.3	13.4-17.4	17.5-22.6	22.7-31.8	31.9-45.8	45.9-75.7	75.8+
Observed frequencies	6	4	3	3	5	4	6	6	4	5
Expected frequencies	4.6	4.6	4.6	4.6	4.6	4.6	4.6	4.6	4.6	4.6

mean = 2.86   standard deviation = 1.15

5.6 Cumulative Probability, Expected and Observed, of International War Magnitudes

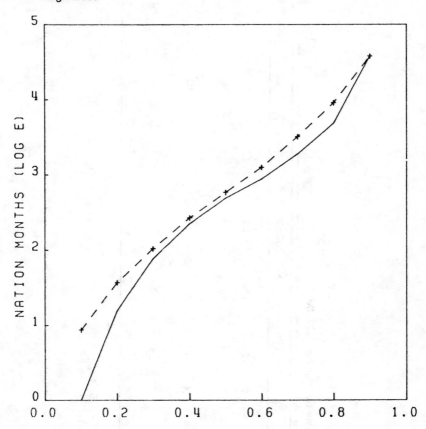

SUMMARY

Having already summarized the way these wars rank on a variety of dimensions, there is little to add here. Not surprisingly, the world

5.7 Frequencies of International War by Intensity (BD/NM)

Intensity Ratio	0-66	66-286	286-1000	1000-3000	3000-8000	8000-22000	22000-60000
All Wars	2	26	39	22	10	10	1
Interstate Wars	1	11	19	14	9	9	1
Central System Wars (includes Extrasystemics)	2	21	34	21	10	10	1
Major Power Wars (Major vs. Major only)	0	0	0	4	4	2	0
Extrasystemic Wars	1	15	20	8	1	1	0

wars rank at the very top on severity and magnitude, and within the first five on intensity; the Korean War ranks third on severity and fourth on magnitude, but it is in positions 19 and 15 on the two intensity dimensions. The Vietnam War ranks second in magnitude, fourth in severity, sixth in battle deaths per capita, and thirty-fifth in battle deaths per nation month. In general, the wars that rank high on severity also tend to rank high on magnitude and intensity, and those which are low on one tend to be low on the others. We also found that the interstate wars that engaged more nations (and/or the more populous ones) were also those that saw more battle deaths per nation month but fewer battle deaths per capita. Finally, there seems to be a rather close fit between the frequencies observed and those predicted by the log normal distribution.

This chapter marks the end of our concern with the wars themselves. In the next chapter, we shift our object of analysis to the system and to the way the wars are distributed throughout the system across time.

CHAPTER 6

Annual Amounts of War Begun and Under Way

Up to this juncture, we have focused exclusively on wars as separate, discrete events occurring at different points in time and space within our empirical domain. For those who want to examine a given war in isolation or do a comparative analysis of several (or many) such cases, this type of presentation is perfectly satisfactory. That is, one may generalize about all of the wars included in our compilation, or a specified subset of them, on the basis of these original presentations.

One cannot, however, discover very much about the international system (or its interstate, central, and major power sub-systems) on the basis of such raw data. In order to generalize about the role of war in these settings, it is necessary to rearrange and recombine our figures and convert them from a war-by-war basis to a period-by-period (for example, year or decade) basis. Furthermore, to the extent that we care to ascertain the strength of the correlation between war and a variety of other conditions or events in the international system, some such recombination is absolutely essential. The literature abounds with hypotheses (and, all too often, assertions) about the way certain discrete or cyclical phenomena constitute the necessary and/or sufficient preconditions of war. Some scholars argue, for example, that wars are unlikely until a sufficient interval has elapsed such that the relevant nations can recover from (or forget) the previous carnage, or until a new generation has come to power. Others suggest that the onset of war is intimately related to cyclical processes of an economic, demographic, or even a meteorological nature. Then there are the frequent but undocumented allusions to increases and decreases in the frequency, severity, or magnitude of war over the past century or two. But outside of the partial figures assembled by our predecessors, no sufficient data base exists by which these and other propositions of a bivariate or multivariate nature might be put to the test; hence the need for a reordering of our compilations along some kind of time scale.

As to the particular unit of time that best serves this need for a chronological breakdown of our war data, one might select the microsecond, hour, day, week, month, quarter, year, half-decade, decade, generation, or century, depending on the independent or intervening variables to be used and the types of analyses contemplated. We have selected the year as our unit here; it is not only the most widely used unit in longitudinal societal science research, but it appears to be most practical as well. Many political, economic, and social data are traditionally presented on a year-by-year basis, and annual figures may readily be combined to make for longer periods. And if units of less than a year are needed—as when we shift from structural and cultural phenomena to behavioral ones, or when we do case studies— we can always go back to the raw data and compute our onset, underway, and termination figures for a shorter period.

Nor can we leave this subject without a brief allusion to the distinction between "real" (that is, chronological) time and diplomatic, military, technological, or political time. Depending on the variables under consideration, there is always the possibility that certain environmental factors may change sufficiently over the years and centuries to make one's measurements not quite comparable from one epoch to another. This is particularly true when factors that show definite secular trends (such as technology, demography, or system size) are at work. One may partially solve the comparability problem by controlling for these environmental factors via the use of an artificial and shifting unit of time.

TWO TYPES OF ANNUAL INDICATOR

With the above considerations in mind, we can now turn to the types of annual indicator that are used in this book. At first glance, the most obvious description of annual systemic war experience would appear to be the amount of war going on, or *under way*, during that year. Here we would report the number of nations engaged in given types of wars during the year, the number of wars under way, and the number of nation months and battle deaths experienced during that year. But it should be clear that this particular form, while meriting attention, is not entirely useful for our purposes. For certain descriptive or comparative purposes, or for use as an *independent* or predictor variable, measures of the amount of war under way during a given year may be quite appropriate, but as a *dependent* or outcome variable, a different form of aggregation is mandatory. Given our theoretical predilections, we are most interested in the period immediately *preceding the outbreak* of war and the circumstances that resulted in some conflicts being settled peacefully while others terminated in war. In other words, if the causes of war are understood best by studying the configurations of variables on the eve of that war, we might well prefer to know how much war *began* in a given year rather than how much war was *under way*. Although some of our wars begin and end in the same year, and would therefore show the same figures whether we look at onset or under way data, the majority begin in one year and end in another and thus produce appreciable differences between the onset and underway figures for a given year.

To take one example—in 1870 and in 1914—the number of nation months *under way* is exactly the same (41.3), but, whereas the 1870 figure for nation months *begun* was 27, it was 607.9 for 1914. All things being equal, the latter year would appear to be much bloodier than the former, despite the fact that the system experienced the same amount of war *during* those two 12-month periods. Consequently, although we are also concerned with how much war is going on each year, we emphasize the amount of war begun in each year— the total nation months and battle deaths resulting from wars begun in that year, whether those wars terminated during that year or a subsequent one. By adopting this approach, we may ascertain the extent to which the frequency, magnitude, and severity of war might be associated with the state of the system or the properties or behavior of the actors during any defined preceding period.

In our first edition, we also examined the amount of war *terminated*. While those interested in the *consequences* of war might find these data useful, we have chosen to eliminate them here because of space considerations and because earlier analyses proved theoretically uninteresting.

FORMAT AND EXPLANATION

The tables in this chapter, then, will include the two different types of measure outlined above. And in addition to the distinctions among onset and underway figures, a further breakdown might also specify the particular domain that is embraced by each set of figures: the international, interstate, central, or major power system. Here, however, we begin with a table showing only the annual amounts of international war that began and were under way and then move on to rank order those years along both dimensions.

Amount of War Begun

For each year, from 1816 through 1980, we will first show in 6.1 (column 1) the number of nations in the international system as of the close of that year; even if a nation did not qualify for membership until December (and the exact day or month is often difficult to ascertain), it is treated as if it were a member during the entire year.

Then (column 2) we show the number of wars that began during that year; this is the factor from which all other indicators in the tables will flow. Next (column 3), we indicate the number of nations that participated in all qualifying wars begun within the system, regardless of when they entered those wars.

From there we move on to the more refined indicators of magnitude and severity; the first (column 4) is the number of battle deaths (in thousands) of war resulting from those wars that began each year. Again, let us emphasize that we are not interested here in the years in which these wars ended, only in the total battle deaths arising out of war begun during any given year. Next (column 5) is the number of nation months resulting from all qualifying wars that began in the system during that year. Then, with that figure, we can proceed to the compilation of two intensity measures: battle deaths per nation month of war begun (column 6) and battle deaths per capita based on the total prewar population of all the nations participating in wars begun that year (columns 7 and 8). The last ratio is presented in natural logarithmic form, as well as in raw figures, since the raw, nontransformed figure offers only a moderately useful index. Because the denominator is so large and the numerator so small, it is sometimes difficult to make an intelligent interpretation of the ratio. And while the raw ratio is based on 100 for total population and therefore results in a percentage figure, the transformed $\log_e$ figure for battle deaths is based on one million population in order to avoid negative $\log_e$ values.

Amount of War Under Way

Shifting now from the annual onset data to data on the amount of war under way, we find somewhat less detailed presentations. We list (column 9) the number of qualifying wars that were under way at any time during the year, regardless of when they began or ended. Following this is the number of nations that were at war at any time during the year (column 10). This figure is then normalized by computing (column 11) the percentage of nations in the system that were at war

(text continued page 123)

6.1 Annual Amounts of International War

		WAR BEGUN							WAR UNDER WAY				
Year	No. in System	No. of Wars Begun	No. of Particpants	Battle Deaths 000's	Battle Deaths 000's per Nation Months	Battle Deaths 000's per Nation Month	Battle Deaths per Hundred Million Population	Log of Battle Deaths per Million Population	No. of Wars Under way	No. of Nations in War	% of Nations in War	Nation Months Under way	% of Nation Months Exhausted
	1	2	3	4	5	6	7	8	9	10	11	12	13
1816	23	0	0	0.	0.	0.	0.	0.	0	0	0.	0.	0.
1817	23	1	1	2.00	6.9	.29	.01	4.62	1	1	4.35	1.8	.66
1818	23	0	0	0.	0.	0.	0.	0.	1	1	4.35	5.1	1.85
1819	23	0	0	0.	0.	0.	0.	0.	0	0	0.	0.	0.
1820	23	0	0	0.	0.	0.	0.	0.	0	0	0.	0.	0.
1821	23	1	1	15.00	85.1	.18	.06	6.41	1	1	4.35	9.2	3.34
1822	23	0	3	0.	0.	0.	0.	0.	1	1	4.35	12.0	4.35
1823	23	2	3	16.00	43.7	.37	.02	5.52	3	4	17.39	29.7	10.76
1824	24	0	0	0.	0.	0.	0.	0.	2	2	8.70	24.0	8.70
1825	25	1	1	15.00	56.2	.27	.25	7.82	3	3	12.50	29.3	10.17
1826	25	1	1	5.00	17.0	.29	.01	4.50	3	4	16.00	29.0	9.65
1827	25	0	0	0.	0.	0.	0.	0.	1	3	12.00	36.0	12.00
1828	26	1	2	130.00	33.4	3.89	.16	7.39	2	5	19.23	34.2	10.95
1829	26	0	0	0.	0.	0.	0.	0.	1	3	11.54	28.9	9.27
1830	27	0	0	0.	0.	0.	0.	0.	1	1	3.70	2.9	.90
1831	29	2	2	25.00	22.0	1.14	.03	5.73	2	2	6.90	10.4	2.98
1832	29	0	0	0.	0.	0.	0.	0.	1	1	3.45	11.7	3.36
1833	29	0	0	0.	0.	0.	0.	0.	0	0	0.	0.	0.
1834	29	0	0	0.	0.	0.	0.	0.	0	0	0.	0.	0.
1835	29	1	1	1.00	6.7	.15	.01	5.01	1	1	3.45	3.0	.86
1836	29	0	0	0.	0.	0.	0.	0.	1	1	3.45	3.7	1.07
1837	29	0	0	0.	0.	0.	0.	0.	0	0	0.	0.	0.
1838	31	1	3	20.00	48.4	.41	.08	6.65	1	1	3.23	3.0	.81
1839	32	2	3	25.01	103.6	.24	.03	5.69	3	3	9.38	14.5	3.78
1840	32	0	0	0.	0.	0.	0.	0.	3	3	9.38	29.3	7.62
1841	34	1	1	1.00	1.0	1.00	.06	6.38	3	3	8.82	25.0	6.13
1842	35	0	0	0.	0.	0.	0.	0.	2	2	5.71	21.4	5.09
1843	36	0	0	0.	0.	0.	0.	0.	1	1	2.78	12.0	2.78
1844	36	0	0	0.	0.	0.	0.	0.	1	1	2.78	12.0	2.78
1845	36	1	2	1.50	2.9	.52	.01	3.99	2	2	5.56	12.6	2.92
1846	36	2	9	17.00	41.4	.41	.06	6.41	4	4	10.81	29.6	6.66
1847	37	0	4	0.	0.	0.	0.	0.	3	3	7.89	35.7	7.84
1848	38	4	9	76.20	51.4	1.48	.04	5.99	5	10	25.64	35.2	7.51
1849	39	1	4	1.90	6.5	.29	.00	3.12	5	7	17.50	24.5	5.10
1850	40	0	0	0.	0.	0.	0.	0.	0	0	0.	0.	0.
1851	41	1	2	1.30	13.2	.10	.02	5.04	1	2	4.88	10.8	2.20
1852	41	1	1	5.00	3.4	1.47	.02	5.16	2	3	7.32	3.2	.65
1853	41	1	5	264.20	116.5	2.27	.16	7.36	2	3	7.32	7.0	1.42
1854	42	0	0	0.	0.	0.	0.	0.	1	4	9.52	42.1	8.35

	WAR BEGUN							WAR UNDER WAY				
Year No. in System 1	No. of Wars Begun 2	No. of Partic-ipants 3	Battle Deaths 000's 4	Battle Deaths per Nation Months 5	Battle Deaths 000's per Nation Month 6	Battle Deaths per Hundred Nation Population 7	Log of Battle Deaths per Million Population 8	No. of Wars Under way 9	No. of Nations in War 10	% of Nations in War 11	Nation Months Under way 12	% of Nation Months Exhausted 13
1855 44	0	0	0.	0.	0.	0.	0.	1	5	11.36	59.7	11.31
1856 44	1	2	2.00	9.2	.22	.01	4.23	2	7	15.91	14.6	2.77
1857 44	1	1	3.50	22.9	.15	.01	4.82	2	3	6.82	12.6	2.39
1858 44	1	1	3.00	12.9	.23	.01	4.74	2	2	4.55	19.9	3.77
1859 45	2	5	32.50	17.7	1.84	.03	5.77	2	7	15.56	20.1	3.73
1860 47	2	2	2.00	7.6	.26	.00	3.60	4	6	12.77	12.0	2.12
1861 43	0	0	0.	0.	0.	.00	0.	3	2	4.65	1.2	.24
1862 42	1	2	20.00	115.4	.17	.04	6.06	1	2	4.76	17.0	3.37
1863 42	3	4	13.00	31.2	.42	.01	4.89	4	6	14.29	38.3	7.60
1864 42	2	6	314.50	197.9	1.59	.47	8.46	5	9	21.43	53.9	10.70
1865 42	1	3	1.00	16.8	.06	.00	3.91	4	8	19.05	63.2	12.54
1866 42	1	11	36.10	14.5	2.49	.04	5.94	4	19	45.24	86.5	17.16
1867 40	0	0	0.	0.	0.	0.	0.	2	5	12.50	38.4	7.99
1868 37	1	0	100.00	112.1	.89	.61	8.72	2	4	10.81	38.7	8.72
1869 37	0	0	0.	0.	0.	0.	0.	2	4	10.81	48.0	10.81
1870 37	1	5	187.50	27.0	6.94	.23	7.75	3	9	24.32	41.3	9.29
1871 34	0	0	0.	0.	0.	0.	0.	3	3	8.82	15.9	3.89
1872 33	0	0	0.	0.	0.	0.	0.	1	1	3.03	12.0	3.03
1873 33	1	1	6.00	65.2	.09	.16	7.39	2	2	6.06	21.2	5.35
1874 33	0	0	0.	0.	0.	0.	0.	2	2	6.06	24.0	6.06
1875 34	1	1	10.00	21.4	.47	.04	5.87	3	3	8.82	29.9	7.34
1876 35	0	0	0.	0.	0.	0.	0.	3	3	8.57	36.0	8.57
1877 35	1	2	285.00	17.6	16.19	.23	7.75	4	6	14.29	44.7	10.64
1878 37	2	2	7.50	20.3	.37	.01	4.66	5	6	16.22	13.1	2.95
1879 37	2	4	17.50	176.0	.10	.04	6.06	3	5	13.51	44.5	10.03
1880 37	0	0	0.	0.	0.	0.	0.	2	3	8.11	44.1	9.93
1881 36	0	0	0.	0.	0.	0.	0.	1	3	8.33	36.0	8.33
1882 36	2	2	24.50	65.3	.38	.03	5.82	3	5	13.89	47.8	11.06
1883 36	0	0	0.	0.	0.	0.	0.	3	5	13.89	56.3	13.04
1884 36	1	2	12.10	19.2	.63	.00	3.18	3	4	11.11	26.0	6.03
1885 36	2	3	3.00	2.4	1.25	.08	6.65	4	6	16.67	25.0	5.79
1886 36	0	0	0.	0.	0.	0.	0.	0	0	0.	0.	0.
1887 38	0	0	0.	0.	0.	0.	0.	0	0	0.	0.	0.
1888 39	0	0	0.	0.	0.	0.	0.	0	0	0.	0.	0.
1889 38	0	0	0.	0.	0.	0.	0.	0	0	0.	0.	0.
1890 38	0	0	0.	0.	0.	0.	0.	0	0	0.	0.	0.
1891 38	0	0	0.	0.	0.	0.	0.	0	0	0.	0.	0.
1892 39	0	0	0.	0.	0.	0.	0.	0	0	0.	0.	0.
1893 39	0	0	0.	0.	0.	0.	0.	0	0	0.	0.	0.

(continued)

6.1 (Continued)

		WAR BEGUN							WAR UNDER WAY				
Year No. in System	No. of Wars Begun	No. of Partic-ipants	Battle Deaths 000's	Battle Deaths Nation Months 000's	Battle Deaths 000's per Nation Month	Battle Deaths per Hundred Million Population	Log of Battle Deaths per Million Population	No. of Wars Under way	No. of Nations in War	% of Nations in War	Nation Months Under way	% of Nation Months Exhausted
1	2	3	4	5	6	7	8	9	10	11	12	13
1894 39	2	3	21.00	25.7	.82	.00	3.63	2	3	7.69	10.6	2.28
1895 39	2	2	59.00	47.8	1.23	.12	7.09	4	5	12.82	25.9	5.54
1896 39	1	1	2.00	23.1	.09	.01	4.70	3	3	7.69	28.7	6.14
1897 39	1	2	2.00	6.2	.32	.01	4.33	3	4	10.26	30.2	6.46
1898 40	2	2	10.00	7.4	1.35	.01	4.69	3	4	10.00	15.1	3.15
1899 41	2	2	26.50	72.5	.37	.02	5.44	2	2	4.88	13.6	2.76
1900 41		6	3.00	11.4	.26	.00	1.30	3	8	19.05	35.5	7.05
1901 42	0	0	0.	0.	0.	0.	0.	2	2	4.76	24.0	4.76
1902 42	0	0	0.	0.	0.	0.	0.	2	2	4.65	11.1	2.16
1903 43			2.00	3.1	.65	.01	4.42	1	1	2.33	3.0	.59
1904 43	1	2	130.00	38.6	3.37	.07	6.52	1	2	4.65	21.5	4.17
1905 43	0	0	0.	0.	0.	0.	0.	1	2	4.55	17.0	3.22
1906 44		3	1.00	5.4	.19	.03	5.78	1	3	6.98	5.4	1.05
1907 42	0	3	1.00	6.3	.16	.04	6.07	1	3	7.14	6.	1.26
1908 43	0	0	0.	0.	0.	0.	0.	0	0	0.	0.	0.
1909 44	0	2	10.00	17.0	.59	.04	6.02	1	2	4.55	11.6	2.20
1910 44	0	2	0.	0.	0.	0.	0.	1	2	4.55	5.5	1.04
1911 44	1	4	20.00	25.4	.79	.03	5.82	2	6	13.95	6.1	1.16
1912 43	1	5	82.00	20.4	4.02	.26	7.85	2	7	16.28	27.3	5.29
1913 44	1	15	60.50	4.2	14.40	.16	7.35	2	9	20.45	16.5	3.21
1914 43	1	15	8555.0	607.9	14.07	1.42	9.56	1	11	25.00	41.3	7.83
1915 43		0	0.	0.	0.	0.	0.	2	13	30.23	117.9	22.34
1916 42	0	0	0.	0.	0.	0.	0.	2	16	38.10	146.2	28.33
1917 46	1	1	50.00	39.3	1.27	.03	5.73	2	14	30.43	169.7	33.68
1918 49	0	0	0.	0.	0.	0.	0.	4	8	16.33	145.1	26.29
1919 59	3	7	161.00	133.6	1.21	.08	6.71	3	5	8.47	59.7	10.15
1920 60	0		0.	0.	0.	0.	0.	3	4	6.67	55.2	7.79
1921 61	1	2	29.00	71.9	.40	.05	6.15	2	3	4.92	32.0	4.45
1922 61	0	0	0.	0.	0.	0.	0.	1	1	1.64	30.7	4.20
1923 61	0	0	0.	0.	0.	0.	0.	1	1	1.64	12.0	1.64
1924 62	0	0	0.	0.	0.	0.	0.	1	1	1.64	12.0	1.64
1925 63	1	1	4.00	22.4	.18	.01	4.59	3	3	4.84	26.1	3.51
1926 64	0	0	0.	0.	0.	0.	0.	2	3	4.76	21.7	2.88
1927 64	0	0	0.	0.	0.	0.	0.	1	1	1.56	5.0	.65
1928 64	0	0	0.	0.	0.	0.	0.	0	0	0.	0.	0.
1929 64	1	2	3.20	7.2	.44	.00	1.65	2	2	3.13	7.2	.93
1930 64	0	0	0.	0.	0.	0.	0.	0	0	0.	0.	0.
1931 64	1	2	60.00	33.2	1.81	.01	4.69	1	2	3.13	.8	.11
1932 65	1	2	130.00	71.8	1.81	3.82	10.55	2	4	6.15	37.1	4.75

		WAR BEGUN							WAR UNDER WAY				
Year	No. in System	No. of Wars Begun	No. of Participants	Battle Deaths 000's	Battle Deaths Nation Months	Battle Deaths 000's per Nation Month	Battle Deaths per Hundred Million Population	Log of Battle Deaths per Million Population	No. of Wars Under way	No. of Nations in War	% of Nations in War	Nation Months Under way	% of Nation Months Exhausted
1		2	3	4	5	6	7	8	9	10	11	12	13
1933	65	0	0	0.	0.	0.	0.	0.	2	4	6.15	32.4	4.15
1934	66	0	0						1	2	3.03	24.0	3.03
1935	66	1	2	20.00	14.4	1.39	.04	5.90	2	4	6.06	16.7	2.10
1936	66	0	0	1000.00	106.2	9.42	.19	7.53	1	2	3.03	8.6	1.08
1937	66	1	2	1.73	1.2	1.44	.00	1.92	1	2	3.03	11.6	1.47
1938	66	1	2	15289.22	907.3	16.85	.83	9.02	2	4	6.06	24.9	3.14
1939	65	3	34	1.40	3.4	.41	.00	3.22	4	15	23.08	66.0	8.57
1940	62	1	2						4	19	30.65	126.0	16.94
1941	55	0	0						3	23	41.82	151.8	23.00
1942	53	0	0						1	15	28.30	180.0	28.30
1943	52	0	0						1	16	30.77	178.5	28.61
1944	57	0	0	96.40	124.4	.77	.10	6.88	1	18	31.58	184.2	26.94
1945	64	2	3						3	19	29.69	97.8	12.74
1946	66	0	0	3.30	34.5	.10	.00	2.04	3	3	4.55	31.0	3.91
1947	68	2	2	9.00	19.6	.46	.00	3.19	3	3	4.41	23.3	2.85
1948	72	2	7						5	10	13.89	53.9	6.24
1949	75	0	0						3	2	2.67	12.5	1.39
1950	75	1	16	1892.11	514.1	3.68	.20	7.59	2	10	13.33	43.9	4.88
1951	75	0	0						2	17	22.67	192.4	21.38
1952	77	0	0						2	17	22.08	204.0	22.08
1953	78	0	0						2	17	21.79	121.9	13.03
1954	82	0	1	18.00	88.5	.20	.04	6.02	1	2	2.44	7.0	.71
1955	84	1	7						4	1	1.19	12.0	1.19
1956	87	3	7	53.23	39.3	1.35	.01	4.03	2	8	9.20	24.6	2.35
1957	89	0	0						2	2	2.25	24.0	2.25
1958	90	0	0						2	2	2.22	24.7	2.22
1959	89	0	0						1	2	2.25	14.7	1.38
1960	107	0	0						1	1	.93	12.0	.93
1961	111	0	0	1.00	2.2	.45	.00	-.11	2	1	.90	12.0	.90
1962	117	1	2						1	3	2.56	4.8	.34
1963	119	0	0						0	0	0.	0.	0.
1964	122	2	10	1222.79	732.9	1.67	.13	7.18	0	0	0.	0.	0.
1965	124	2	2	19.60	.8		.00		2	7	5.65	54.4	3.66
1966	129	0	0						1	6	4.65	63.0	4.07
1967	130	1	4						2	11	8.46	75.8	4.86
1968	133	0	0	19.60	.8		.00		1	7	5.26	84.0	5.26
1969	133	2	4	7.27	35.0	.21	.02	5.21	3	11	8.27	104.0	6.52

(continued)

6.1 (Continued)

			WAR BEGUN						WAR UNDER WAY				
Year	No. of Wars Begun	No. of Partic- ipants	Battle Deaths 000's	Nation Months	Battle Deaths 000's per Nation Month	Battle Deaths per Hundred Million Popu- lation	Log of Battle Deaths per Million Popu- lation	No. of Wars Under way	No. of Nations in War	% of Nations in War	Nation Months Under way	% of Nation Months Exhaust- ed
No. in System												
1	2	3	4	5	6	7	8	9	10	11	12	13
1970 134	0	0		0.	0.	.00	0	2	10	7.46	108.4	6.74
1971 139	1	2	11.00	1.2	9.17	.00	2.80	2	10	7.19	97.0	5.81
1972 139	1	1	10.00	108.0	.09	.03	5.53	2	9	6.47	107.6	6.45
1973 141	1	6	16.40	3.6	4.56	.02	5.50	3	14	9.93	55.0	3.25
1974 143	2	3	26.50	84.8	.31	.04	5.99	4	7	4.90	60.8	3.55
1975 150	3	5	25.00	301.3	.08	.01	4.84	6	10	6.67	53.7	2.98
1976 151	1	3	21.00	41.6	.50	.05	6.24	6	8	5.30	90.0	4.97
1977 152	0	0	0.	0.	0.	.01	0.	6	10	6.58	112.1	6.14
1978 154	3	3	3.00	16.5	.18	.01	4.56	7	13	8.44	116.6	6.31
1979 155	2	4	31.50	26.6	1.18	.00	3.19	9	16	10.32	115.5	6.21
1980 155	1	2	7.00	6.8	1.03	.01	4.92	8	12	7.74	126.6	6.81

during each year. Then in column 12 is the more sensitive underway magnitude, measured in nation months. Finally (column 13), there is perhaps the most sensitive and generally useful of the underway indicators: the percentage of *possible* nation months of war that were exhausted during the year. This is computed by multiplying the number of nations in the system by 12 (months in a year) and dividing that figure into the total number of nation months under way during the year. The virtue of this measure is that we are able to make meaningful comparisons between years in which the system size differed drastically; one possible drawback of this indicator is that a nation can have more than 12 nation months of war per year via participation in more than one war simultaneously. Therefore, our posited "maximum" number of nation months per year is incorrect in principle, but in fact it reflects the situation accurately most of the time.

As to battle deaths sustained by system members during each year, we recognize that such infomation might be useful for some researchers, but we finally decided against any effort to gather these estimates. To do so would require us to ascertain the approximate date on which these fatalities occurred, and, like those "body counts" prepared by others, they would necessarily be extremely rough. For most theoretical purposes the figures are just not sufficiently useful to merit the research time that would be required.

RANKING THE YEARS

With the data now in on the annual amounts of war begun and under way, we can readily move on to additional analyses and summaries. But in order to look for chronological patterns such as secular trends, it is often necessary to convert these figures from a mere chronological ordering to a variety of rank orderings. Thus, we close this chapter with the presentation of several such listings, showing each year's rank position and its value on several of the most useful and revealing measures.

The first of these (6.2) shows the rank position of those 85 of our 165 years in which *any* international war began; they are ranked according to the number of battle deaths that resulted from all qualifying international wars that began in that year. In addition to the rank position score, we show the estimated number of these battle deaths, as well as the rank position and value for nation months of war that began in that year.

Next (6.3), we rank all of the 145 years in which any international war was under way, according to two measures. First is the number of

6.2   Rank Order of Years by Amount of War Begun

Year	Battle Deaths from Wars Begun (000's)	Rank	Nation Months of War Begun	Rank	Year	Battle Deaths from Wars Begun (000's)	Rank	Nation Months of War Begun	Rank
1939	15289.2	1.0	907.3	1.0	1962	1.0	82.5	2.2	81.0
1914	8555.8	2.0	607.9	3.0	1816	0.	125.5	0.	125.5
1950	1892.1	3.0	514.1	4.0	1818	0.	125.5	0.	125.5
1965	1222.8	4.0	732.9	2.0	1819	0.	125.5	0.	125.5
1937	1000.0	5.0	106.2	14.0	1820	0.	125.5	0.	125.5
1864	314.5	6.0	197.9	6.0	1822	0.	125.5	0.	125.5
1877	285.0	7.0	17.6	53.0	1824	0.	125.5	0.	125.5
1853	264.2	8.0	116.5	10.0	1827	0.	125.5	0.	125.5
1870	187.5	9.0	27.0	39.0	1829	0.	125.5	0.	125.5
1919	161.0	10.0	133.6	8.0	1830	0.	125.5	0.	125.5
1828	130.0	12.0	33.4	36.0	1832	0.	125.5	0.	125.5
1904	130.0	12.0	38.6	33.0	1833	0.	125.5	0.	125.5
1932	130.0	12.0	71.8	21.0	1834	0.	125.5	0.	125.5
1868	100.0	14.0	112.1	12.0	1836	0.	125.5	0.	125.5
1945	96.4	15.0	124.4	9.0	1837	0.	125.5	0.	125.5
1912	82.0	16.0	20.4	48.0	1840	0.	125.5	0.	125.5
1848	76.2	17.0	51.4	25.0	1842	0.	125.5	0.	125.5
1913	60.5	18.0	4.2	74.0	1843	0.	125.5	0.	125.5
1931	60.0	19.0	33.2	37.0	1844	0.	125.5	0.	125.5
1895	59.0	20.0	47.8	27.0	1847	0.	125.5	0.	125.5
1956	53.2	21.0	39.3	31.5	1850	0.	125.5	0.	125.5
1917	50.0	22.0	39.3	31.5	1854	0.	125.5	0.	125.5
1866	36.1	23.0	14.5	58.0	1855	0.	125.5	0.	125.5
1859	32.5	24.0	17.7	52.0	1861	0.	125.5	0.	125.5
1979	31.5	25.0	26.6	40.0	1867	0.	125.5	0.	125.5
1921	29.0	26.0	71.9	20.0	1869	0.	125.5	0.	125.5
1899	26.5	27.5	72.5	19.0	1871	0.	125.5	0.	125.5
1974	26.5	27.5	84.8	18.0	1872	0.	125.5	0.	125.5
1839	25.0	29.0	103.6	15.0	1874	0.	125.5	0.	125.5
1831	25.0	30.5	22.0	46.0	1876	0.	125.5	0.	125.5
1975	25.0	30.5	301.3	5.0	1880	0.	125.5	0.	125.5
1882	24.5	32.0	65.3	22.0	1881	0.	125.5	0.	125.5
1894	21.0	33.5	25.7	41.0	1883	0.	125.5	0.	125.5
1976	21.0	33.5	41.6	29.0	1886	0.	125.5	0.	125.5
1838	20.0	36.5	48.4	26.0	1887	0.	125.5	0.	125.5
1862	20.0	36.5	115.4	11.0	1888	0.	125.5	0.	125.5
1911	20.0	36.5	25.4	42.0	1889	0.	125.5	0.	125.5
1935	20.0	36.5	14.4	59.0	1890	0.	125.5	0.	125.5
1967	19.6	39.0	.8	85.0	1891	0.	125.5	0.	125.5
1954	18.0	40.0	88.5	16.0	1892	0.	125.5	0.	125.5
1879	17.5	41.0	176.0	7.0	1893	0.	125.5	0.	125.5
1846	17.0	42.0	41.4	30.0	1901	0.	125.5	0.	125.5
1973	16.4	43.0	3.6	75.0	1902	0.	125.5	0.	125.5
1823	16.0	44.0	43.7	28.0	1905	0.	125.5	0.	125.5
1821	15.0	45.5	85.1	17.0	1908	0.	125.5	0.	125.5
1825	15.0	45.5	56.2	24.0	1910	0.	125.5	0.	125.5
1863	13.0	47.0	31.2	38.0	1915	0.	125.5	0.	125.5
1884	12.1	48.0	19.2	51.0	1916	0.	125.5	0.	125.5
1971	11.0	49.0	1.2	82.5	1918	0.	125.5	0.	125.5
1875	10.0	51.5	21.4	47.0	1920	0.	125.5	0.	125.5
1898	10.0	51.5	7.4	65.0	1922	0.	125.5	0.	125.5
1909	10.0	51.5	17.0	54.5	1923	0.	125.5	0.	125.5
1972	10.0	51.5	108.0	13.0	1924	0.	125.5	0.	125.5
1948	9.0	54.0	19.6	50.0	1926	0.	125.5	0.	125.5
1878	7.5	55.0	20.3	49.0	1927	0.	125.5	0.	125.5
1969	7.3	56.0	35.0	34.0	1928	0.	125.5	0.	125.5
1980	7.0	57.0	6.8	68.0	1930	0.	125.5	0.	125.5
1873	6.0	58.0	65.2	23.0	1933	0.	125.5	0.	125.5
1826	5.0	59.5	17.0	54.5	1934	0.	125.5	0.	125.5
1852	5.0	59.5	3.4	76.5	1936	0.	125.5	0.	125.5
1925	4.0	61.0	22.4	45.0	1941	0.	125.5	0.	125.5
1857	3.5	62.0	22.9	44.0	1942	0.	125.5	0.	125.5
1947	3.3	63.0	34.5	35.0	1943	0.	125.5	0.	125.5
1929	3.2	64.0	7.2	66.0	1944	0.	125.5	0.	125.5
1858	3.0	66.5	12.9	61.0	1946	0.	125.5	0.	125.5
1885	3.0	66.5	2.4	80.0	1949	0.	125.5	0.	125.5
1900	3.0	66.5	11.4	62.0	1951	0.	125.5	0.	125.5
1978	3.0	66.5	16.5	57.0	1952	0.	125.5	0.	125.5
1817	2.0	71.5	6.9	67.0	1953	0.	125.5	0.	125.5
1856	2.0	71.5	9.2	63.0	1955	0.	125.5	0.	125.5
1860	2.0	71.5	7.6	64.0	1957	0.	125.5	0.	125.5
1896	2.0	71.5	23.1	43.0	1958	0.	125.5	0.	125.5
1897	2.0	71.5	6.2	72.0	1959	0.	125.5	0.	125.5
1903	2.0	71.5	3.1	78.0	1960	0.	125.5	0.	125.5
1849	1.9	75.0	6.5	70.0	1961	0.	125.5	0.	125.5
1938	1.7	76.0	1.2	82.5	1963	0.	125.5	0.	125.5
1845	1.5	77.0	2.9	79.0	1964	0.	125.5	0.	125.5
1940	1.4	78.0	3.4	76.5	1966	0.	125.5	0.	125.5
1851	1.3	79.0	13.2	60.0	1968	0.	125.5	0.	125.5
1835	1.0	82.5	6.7	69.0	1970	0.	125.5	0.	125.5
1841	1.0	82.5	1.0	84.0	1977	0.	125.5	0.	125.5
1865	1.0	82.5	16.8	56.0					
1906	1.0	82.5	5.4	73.0					
1907	1.0	82.5	6.3	71.0					

nation months of war that were under way during that year, along with the year's rank position on that measure; then, in order to permit comparisons over time, we normalize this figure by controlling for system size. This gives us the percentage of possible nation months (12 x N) that were indeed devoted to war, along with the year's rank position on this normalized figure. Worth reiterating here is that while there were only 85 years in which any war began, 145 of a possible 165 years saw at least some international war under way, given our inclusion criteria.

SUMMARY

For most theoretical purposes, the war data as presented in this chapter are the most important in the volume. First, they permit us to enter into empirical investigations on the basis of which we might generalize about the "causes" and "consequences" of international war over the period since the Napoleonic Wars. Second, and of more immediate interest, they provide us with the basis for a number of descriptive and analytic inquiries in the chapters that follow. Thus, we now turn to a consideration of trends (Chapter 7) and cycles (Chapter 8) in international war since 1816.

6.3 Rank Order of Years by Amount of War Under Way

Year	Nation Months of War Underway	Rank	% of Possible Nation Months Exhausted	Rank	Year	Nation Months of War Underway	Rank	% of Possible Nation Months Exhausted	Rank	Year	Nation Months of War Underway	Rank	% of Possible Nation Months Exhausted	Rank
1952	204.0	1.0	22.1	9.0	1864	53.9	36.0	10.7	23.0	1896	28.7	71.0	6.1	56.5
1951	192.4	2.0	21.4	10.0	1948	53.9	37.0	6.2	54.0	1912	27.3	72.0	5.3	65.0
1944	184.2	3.0	26.9	5.0	1975	53.7	38.0	3.0	98.5	1925	26.1	73.0	3.5	87.0
1942	180.0	4.0	28.3	4.0	1869	48.0	39.0	10.8	21.0	1884	26.0	74.0	6.0	60.0
1943	178.5	5.0	28.6	2.0	1882	47.8	40.0	11.1	19.0	1895	25.9	75.0	5.5	63.0
1917	169.7	6.0	33.7	1.0	1877	44.7	41.0	10.6	24.0	1841	25.0	76.5	6.1	58.0
1941	151.8	7.0	23.0	7.0	1872	44.5	42.0	10.0	27.0	1885	25.0	76.5	5.8	62.0
1916	146.2	8.0	28.3	3.0	1880	44.1	43.0	9.9	28.0	1938	24.9	78.0	3.1	95.0
1918	145.1	9.0	26.3	6.0	1950	43.9	44.0	4.9	70.0	1956	24.6	79.0	2.3	109.0
1980	126.6	10.0	6.8	47.0	1854	42.1	45.0	8.3	36.0	1849	24.5	80.0	5.1	67.0
1940	126.0	11.0	16.9	12.0	1914	41.3	46.0	7.8	40.0	1824	24.0	83.5	8.7	33.0
1953	121.9	12.0	13.0	14.0	1870	41.3	47.0	9.3	30.0	1874	24.0	83.5	6.1	59.0
1915	117.9	13.0	22.3	8.0	1868	38.7	48.0	8.7	32.0	1901	24.0	83.5	4.8	72.0
1978	116.6	14.0	6.3	53.0	1867	38.4	49.0	8.0	38.0	1934	24.0	83.5	3.0	96.5
1979	115.5	15.0	6.2	55.0	1863	38.3	50.0	7.6	43.0	1957	24.0	83.5	2.3	111.0
1977	112.1	16.0	6.1	56.5	1932	37.1	51.0	4.8	73.0	1958	24.0	83.5	2.2	112.0
1970	108.4	17.0	6.7	48.0	1827	36.0	53.0	12.0	17.0	1947	23.3	87.0	2.8	103.0
1972	107.6	18.0	6.4	52.0	1876	36.0	53.0	8.6	34.5	1926	21.7	88.0	2.9	102.0
1969	104.0	19.0	6.5	50.0	1881	36.0	53.0	8.3	37.0	1904	21.5	89.0	4.2	77.0
1945	97.8	20.0	12.7	15.0	1847	35.7	55.0	7.8	39.0	1842	21.4	90.0	5.1	68.0
1971	97.0	21.0	5.8	61.0	1900	35.5	56.0	7.0	46.0	1873	21.2	91.0	5.3	64.0
1976	90.0	22.0	5.0	69.0	1848	35.2	57.0	7.5	44.0	1859	20.1	92.0	3.7	84.0
1866	86.5	23.0	17.2	11.0	1828	34.2	58.0	10.9	20.0	1858	19.9	93.0	3.8	83.0
1968	84.0	24.0	5.3	66.0	1933	32.4	59.0	4.1	78.0	1862	17.0	94.5	3.4	88.0
1967	75.8	25.0	4.9	71.0	1921	32.0	60.0	4.4	74.0	1905	17.0	94.5	3.2	92.0
1939	66.9	26.0	8.6	34.5	1946	31.0	61.0	3.9	80.0	1935	16.7	96.0	2.1	117.0
1865	63.2	27.0	12.5	16.0	1922	30.7	62.0	4.2	76.0	1913	16.5	97.0	3.2	93.0
1966	63.0	28.0	4.1	79.0	1897	30.2	63.0	6.5	51.0	1871	15.9	98.0	3.9	81.0
1974	60.8	29.0	3.5	86.0	1875	29.9	64.0	7.3	45.0	1898	15.1	99.0	3.1	94.0
1855	59.7	30.0	11.3	18.0	1823	29.7	65.0	10.8	22.0	1959	14.7	100.0	1.4	124.0
1919	59.7	31.0	10.1	26.0	1846	29.6	66.0	6.7	49.0	1856	14.5	101.0	2.8	106.0
1883	56.3	32.0	13.0	13.0	1825	29.3	67.0	10.2	25.0	1839	14.5	102.0	3.8	82.0
1920	55.2	33.0	7.8	41.0	1840	29.3	68.0	7.6	42.0	1899	13.6	103.0	2.8	107.0
1973	55.0	34.0	3.3	91.0	1826	29.0	69.0	9.6	29.0	1878	13.1	104.0	2.9	100.0
1965	54.4	35.0	3.7	85.0	1829	28.9	70.0	9.3	31.0	1845	12.6	105.5	2.9	101.0

(continued)

6.3 (Continued)

Year	Nation Months of War Underway	Rank	% of Possible Nation Months Exhausted	Rank	Year	Nation Months of War Underway	Rank	% of Possible Nation Months Exhausted	Rank	Year	Nation Months of War Underway	Rank	% of Possible Nation Months Exhausted	Rank
1857	12.6	105.5	2.4	108.0	1936	8.6	126.0	1.1	128.0	1816	0.	155.5	0.	155.5
1949	12.5	107.0	1.4	123.0	1929	7.2	127.0	.9	132.5	1819	0.	155.5	0.	155.5
1822	12.0	112.0	4.3	75.0	1954	7.0	128.0	.7	138.0	1820	0.	155.5	0.	155.5
1843	12.0	112.0	2.8	104.5	1853	7.0	129.0	1.4	122.0	1833	0.	155.5	0.	155.5
1844	12.0	112.0	2.8	104.5	1907	6.4	130.0	1.3	125.0	1834	0.	155.5	0.	155.5
1872	12.0	112.0	3.0	96.5	1911	6.1	131.0	1.2	127.0	1837	0.	155.5	0.	155.5
1923	12.0	112.0	1.6	119.5	1910	5.5	132.0	1.0	131.0	1850	0.	155.5	0.	155.5
1924	12.0	112.0	1.6	119.5	1906	5.4	133.0	1.0	130.0	1886	0.	155.5	0.	155.5
1955	12.0	112.0	1.2	126.0	1818	5.1	134.0	1.8	118.0	1887	0.	155.5	0.	155.5
1960	12.0	112.0	.9	132.5	1927	5.0	135.0	.6	140.5	1888	0.	155.5	0.	155.5
1961	12.0	112.0	.9	134.5	1962	4.8	136.0	.3	143.0	1889	0.	155.5	0.	155.5
1860	12.0	117.0	2.1	116.0	1836	3.7	137.0	1.1	129.0	1890	0.	155.5	0.	155.5
1832	11.7	118.0	3.4	89.0	1852	3.2	138.0	.6	140.5	1891	0.	155.5	0.	155.5
1909	11.6	119.5	2.2	113.5	1903	3.0	139.0	.6	142.0	1892	0.	155.5	0.	155.5
1937	11.6	119.5	1.5	121.0	1835	3.0	140.5	.9	136.0	1893	0.	155.5	0.	155.5
1902	11.1	121.0	2.2	115.0	1838	3.0	140.5	.8	137.0	1908	0.	155.5	0.	155.5
1851	10.8	122.0	2.2	113.5	1830	2.9	142.0	.9	134.5	1928	0.	155.5	0.	155.5
1894	10.6	123.0	2.3	110.0	1817	1.8	143.0	.7	139.0	1930	0.	155.5	0.	155.5
1831	10.4	124.0	3.0	98.5	1861	1.2	144.0	.2	144.0	1963	0.	155.5	0.	155.5
1821	9.2	125.0	3.3	90.0	1931	.8	145.0	.1	145.0	1964	0.	155.5	0.	155.5

CHAPTER 7

Secular Trends in the Incidence of War

In the previous chapter we converted our data on the separate and particular wars into a form that permitted us to describe the amount of war in the system year by year. This shift of our unit of analysis from individual *wars* to the *system* as a whole produced 165 annual observations for a variety of measures on the incidence of war and their fluctuations over time. Now we want to see whether these fluctuations reveal any regular patterns in our historic period.

Those patterns may be of two basic types: (a) steady upward or downward trends and (b) recurrent cyclical fluctuations. In any historical process we may find one, or both, or neither; furthermore, one may be sufficiently strong and the other sufficiently weak that only the stronger one is readily apparent. Hence, it is desirable (for example, as economists have discovered) to try to disentangle them from one another, and this is what we undertake here. We begin with a search for secular trends in this chapter and then go on in the following one to look for any recurrent periodicities that may be concealed in the unanalyzed maze of annual figures.

PRIOR INVESTIGATIONS

One of the most frequently voiced notions in the international politics literature is that the system is undergoing constant change, and that as we move from decade to decade or generation to generation, things become so radically different that no legitimate comparisons may be made across time. This seems to be a major premise of those, for example, who hold that there can be no serious science of international politics.

When we shift from statements about "all" of international politics to those concerning the constancy of war alone, the problem becomes more manageable. Would we expect its incidence to rise or fall over the period since Waterloo? If so, why? Among the factors that might be expected to produce an *increase* in the frequency, severity, or magnitude of international war are increases in the lethality and range of offensive weapons, increases in the politicization of diplomacy, and the simple increase in the number of people and nations in the system. Among those that might produce a *diminishing* effect could be improvements in defensive weapons, technology, and military medicine, more sophisticated modes of national behavior, the increasing efficacy of such intergovernmental organizations as the League of Nations and the United Nations, and an increasing reluctance to see the more modern and destructive weapons used. The mere listing of such factors makes evident the need to discriminate among the several measures of the incidence of war, since it is quite possible, for example, for wars to increase in frequency over time but not in severity.

COMPARING SUCCESSIVE PERIODS FOR AMOUNT OF WAR IN THE SYSTEMS

In searching for an upward or downward secular trend, there are many computational approaches open to us. Each one can, depending on the number of categories and cutting points used, produce a somewhat different impression. At the simplest, we can divide our entire time span into two roughly equal periods, indicate the total scores on our several measures, and then ask whether the differences in the two periods' scores, if any, are large enough to have occurred by sheer chance. This we do in 7.1, which is calculated as follows.

First, since the amounts of war under way and the amount begun in any period will be equal if the period is long enough and if the breaks do not come during any war, we need use only one set of measures; for our purposes, the onset data are as useful as any. Second, in order to cope with the strong upward trend in the system's size, we compute several of the measures in normalized as well as in absolute form.

As to the *number of wars* in each period, we normalize by dividing that figure by N (which, in this case, is the average size of the system during each period). A more refined measure might have been achieved by dividing by $N(N-1)/2$, but that would be appropriate only if all or most of the wars in any class were bilateral; while this is largely true of the extra-systemic wars, it is only true of 63 percent of the interstate wars. Shifting from the *frequency* of war in a particular

7.1 Comparing the Amount of War Begun in Two Successive Periods

Type of War	Onset Measure	1816-1897	1898-1980	Totals	Means
ALL INTERNATIONAL	Avg. No of Nations (N)	34.8	78.5		59.0
	Number of Wars	59	59	118	
	Wars/N	1.69	.75	2.45	1.22
	Nation Months	1734.7	4413.2	6147.9	3073.9
	Nation Months/N	49.8	56.2	106.1	53.0
	Battle Deaths (000's)	1786.8	29125.4	30912.3	15456.1
INTERSTATE ONLY	Number of Wars	26	41	67	33.5
	Wars/N	.75	.52	1.27	.63
	Nation Months	890.7	3502.2	4392.9	2196.4
	Nation Months/N	25.6	44.6	70.2	35.1
	Battle Deaths (000's)	1356.3	28782.2	30138.5	15069.3
EXTRA-SYSTEMIC ONLY	Number of Wars	33	18	51	25.5
	Wars/N	.95	.23	1.18	.59
	Nation Months	834.0	890.3	1724.3	862.1
	Nation Months/N	24.0	11.3	35.3	17.7
	Battle Deaths (000's)	430.5	343.2	773.7	386.9

period to the total *magnitude* in nation months begun, we again normalize by the number of nations in the relevant system or sub-system during the "average" year of the period. As to *battle deaths,* although we know the total combined population of all the nations in each of the systems examined, we have chosen not to use these data. A case can be made for including some measures that are not normalized, since the latter procedure will certainly help to suppress any upward secular trend pattern.

What kind of visual pattern emerges from these computations? Or, to put it another way, how strong is the deviation, if it exists at all, from the null model that predicts that the five individual measures for each of the three types of war should be approximately the same magnitude for each of the two periods? The picture is mixed. Although the number of wars of all types is exactly the same in each period, there were more interstate and fewer extra-systemic wars in the period since 1898. Controlling for system size, however, does produce a sharp decline in all wars for the second period. The reverse holds true for magnitude and severity. That is, the number of nation months and battle deaths rises sharply for both the raw and the normalized figures. But this holds only for all international wars and for the interstate war subset; extra-systemic wars, conversely, decline not only in frequency but in the total number of normalized nation months and battle deaths arising from these wars.

In looking at these *extra-systemic* wars from the secular trend point of view, even though we compute normalized scores, they should not be taken seriously, for as the size of the international system *increases,* the number of non-systemic entities *decreases.* That is, as more and more national units become qualified state members of the system, the opportunity for extra-systemic wars must inevitably diminish, especially those of the imperial variety.

Returning to the distributions of war in our successive time periods, we next ask whether the same general impressions emerge when we use a more discriminating set of time periods. In 7.2, we divide our 165 years into five periods of roughly 32 years each, and it is apparent that the pattern is equally mixed. The number of wars fluctuates slightly around the mean, and when we control for system size, the general frequency trend is downward. As for total nation months and battle deaths sustained during these five periods, there is again (despite the fluctuations) a general upward trend for all wars and interstate wars, normalized or not. Once more, the extra-systemic war tendency is roughly a downward one—at least until the most recent period, 1945-1980, where the normalized figures reveal a downward

7.2 Comparing the Amount of War Begun in Five Successive Periods

Type of War	Onset Measure	1816-1848	1849-1881	1882-1914	1915-1944	1945-1980	Totals	Means
	Avg. No. of Nations (N)	28.8	39.4	40.4	59.8	115.5		
ALL INTERNATIONAL	Number of Wars	20	28	24	20	26	118	23.6
	Wars/N	.70	.71	.59	.33	.23	2.56	.51
	Nation Months	519.7	1025.3	1009.3	1570.8	2022.8	6147.9	1229.6
	Nation Months/N	18.1	26.0	25.0	26.3	17.5	112.9	22.6
	Battle Deaths	349.7	1313.5	9025.4	16849.2	3374.4	30912.3	6182.5
INTERSTATE ONLY	Number of Wars	5	17	14	13	18	67	13.4
	Wars/N	.17	.43	.35	.22	.16	1.32	.26
	Nation Months	122.3	726.4	782.4	1272.9	1488.9	4392.9	878.6
	Nation Months/N	4.3	18.4	19.4	21.3	12.9	76.2	15.2
	Battle Deaths	163.2	1163.0	8903.4	16666.5	3242.4	30138.5	6027.7
EXTRASYSTEMIC ONLY	Number of Wars	15	11	10	7	8	51	10.2
	Wars/N	.52	.28	.25	.12	.07	1.23	.25
	Nation Months	394.7	292.8	221.8	291.7	523.3	1724.3	344.9
	Nation Months/N	13.7	7.4	5.5	4.9	4.5	36.1	7.2
	Battle Deaths	186.5	150.5	122.0	182.7	132.0	773.7	154.7

trend only in battle deaths and normalized nation months, but upward in terms of absolute nation months.

Does a more consistent pattern emerge when we shift from five periods of 30 years each to 15 periods of 11 each? Hardly. What we see (7.3) is an accentuation of the fluctuating pattern that was present, but less evident, in the earlier breakdown. The muting effect of using ever smaller time periods that we saw in the shift from two to five periods is further emphasized when the number of observation periods is raised to 15; even the downward trend in the extra-systemic war indicators is less evident here. More distressing, perhaps, is evidence of an increase in the frequency of martial activity for the 1970s as compared to the 1960s, especially in the extra-systemic category.

As we have seen, the length of the time limit used can exercise an appreciable impact on the patterns that emerge. Indian mathematician P.C. Mahalanobis reminds us of a similar pattern when one correlates rainfall and temperature. With the month as the unit of analysis, there is a strong *positive* correlation; with the day as the unit, there is a strong *negative* correlation; and with the week, there is *no* correlation. The explanation, of course, is that rainfall occurs on the cool days of the hotter months. Even if we were to compute the deviations from the mean (that is, no trend) for each of the cells of our data, it is clear that no obvious trends, up or down, would emerge. All of this suggests, then, that our first impression may well have been misleading and that an alternative mode of analysis is called for.

REGRESSION LINES AS TREND INDICATORS

A second approach we use in examining the long-range trends in the incidence of war is that of linear regression. The idea here is to plot each set of measures along the vertical axis of a scattergram on which the longitudinal axis represents the successive years. By fitting a straight line that minimizes the square of the distance between that line and all of the data points on the scattergram, we can ascertain how much it departs from the horizontal (no trend) line over the 165 annual observations. Thus, if there *is* any clear upward or downward trend in a particular measure of war, it will become immediately apparent.

In 7.4, we do this with what is perhaps the best all-around indicator for these purposes: the amount of war under way, measured by normalized nation months. Visual inspection makes clear that the line that best fits the data shows only a slight departure from the horizontal, suggesting the absence of any clear trend. The slope of this line

7.3 Comparing the Amount of War Begun in Fifteen Successive Periods

Type of War	Onset Measure	1816–1826	1827–1837	1838–1848	1849–1859	1860–1870	1871–1881	1882–1892
	Avg. No. of Nations (N)	23.3	27.9	35.1	42.4	41.0	34.9	37.3
ALL INTERNATIONAL	Number of Wars	6	4	10	9	12	7	5
	Wars/N	.26	.14	.28	.21	.29	.20	.13
	Nation Months	208.9	62.1	248.7	202.3	522.5	300.5	86.9
	Nation Months /N	9.0	2.2	7.1	4.8	12.7	8.6	2.3
	Battle Deaths	53.0	156.0	140.7	313.4	674.1	326.0	39.6
INTERSTATE ONLY	Number of Wars	1	1	3	6	9	2	2
	Wars/N	.04	.04	.09	.14	.22	.06	.05
	Nation Months	14.4	33.2	74.7	161.5	377.4	187.5	20.0
	Nation Months /N	.6	1.2	2.1	3.8	9.2	5.4	.5
	Battle Deaths	1.0	130.0	32.2	301.9	562.1	299.0	13.1
EXTRASYSTEMIC ONLY	Number of Wars	5	3	7	3	3	5	3
	Wars/N	.21	.11	.20	.07	.07	.14	.08
	Nation Months	193.9	28.4	172.4	38.9	141.8	112.1	66.2
	Nation Months /N	8.3	1.0	4.9	.9	3.5	3.2	1.8
	Battle Deaths	52.0	26.0	108.5	11.5	112.0	27.0	26.5

(continued)

7.3 (Continued)

Type of War	Onset Measure	1893-1903	1904-1914	1915-1925	1926-1936	1937-1947	1948-1958	1959-1969	1970-1980	Totals	Means
	Avg. No. of Nations (N)	40.5	43.4	53.5	64.6	61.3	80.4	119.5	146.6		
ALL INTERNATIONAL	Number of Wars	11	8	6	4	10	7	6	13	118	7.9
	Wars/N	.27	.18	.11	.06	.16	.09	.05	.09	2.55	.17
	Nation Months	197.2	725.2	267.2	126.6	1177.0	661.5	770.9	590.4	6147.9	409.9
	Nation Months /N	4.9	16.7	5.0	2.0	19.2	8.2	6.5	4.0	113.2	7.5
	Battle Deaths	125.5	8860.3	244.0	213.2	16392.0	1972.3	1250.7	151.4	30912.3	2060.8
INTERSTATE ONLY	Number of Wars	4	8	3	4	6	4	6	8	67	4.5
	Wars/N	.10	.18	.06	.06	.10	.05	.05	.05	1.29	.09
	Nation Months	40.0	722.4	132.9	125.8	1014.2	533.9	768.9	186.1	4392.9	292.9
	Nation Months /N	1.0	16.7	2.5	1.9	16.6	6.6	6.4	1.3	75.8	5.1
	Battle Deaths	30.0	8860.3	161.0	213.2	16292.3	1913.3	1250.7	78.4	30138.5	2009.2
EXTRASYSTEMIC ONLY	Number of Wars	7	0	3	0	4	3	0	5	51	3.4
	Wars/N	.17	0.	.06	0.	.07	.04	0.	.03	1.25	.08
	Nation Months	155.6	0.	133.2	0.	158.5	125.2	0.	398.1	1724.3	115.0
	Nation Months /N	3.8	0.	2.5	0.	2.6	1.6	0.	2.7	36.8	2.5
	Battle Deaths	95.5	0.	83.0	0.	99.7	59.0	0.	73.0	773.7	51.6

may also be expressed statistically via the linear regression coefficients; for nation months under way (normalized for system size) the coefficient of determination (r^2) of the regression line, predicting from year of observation, is .01, which is so low as to have easily occurred by chance alone. When the period is divided by century (7.4a and 7.4b), the absence of a trend is seen again in both cases.

What happens when we do the same thing for a number of other measures of the incidence of war? In 7.5, we show the coefficients for a number of onset and underway measures. It is readily apparent that no clear trend, either upward or downward, is found for all wars or for the several types of interstate wars. Even the very modest upward (positive correlation) trends almost completely disappear when we normalize nation months of war for the number of nations in the system at hand.

WAR RANK CORRELATIONS AS TREND INDICATORS

So far we have, quite reasonably, used the year or other time span as our unit of analysis, and no discernible trends seem to be evident. But it occurs to us that one reason for the prevalent belief that war is on the increase is that the *wars* themselves may have become longer,

7.4 Regression Lines for Normalized Nation Months of War Under Way, 1816-1980

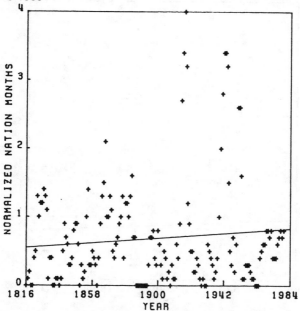

7.4a   Regression Lines for Normalized Nation Months of War Under Way,
       Nineteenth Century

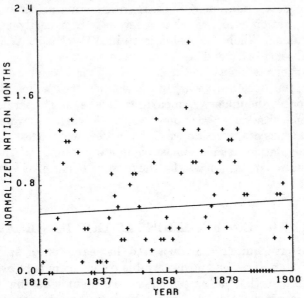

7.4b   Regression Lines for Normalized Nation Months of War Under Way,
       Twentieth Century

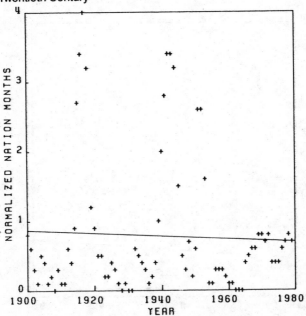

7.5 Linear Trend Statistics for Annual Amounts of War Begun and Under Way, 1816-1980 (N = 165 Annual Observations)

Type of Measure	Variable	Correlation Coefficient With Time (r)	Coefficient of Determination (r²)	Regression Coefficient (b)
BEGUN	Nation months of international war	.151	.023	.358
	Nation months of international war/no. of nations in interstate system	.018	.000	.001
	Nation months of international war/no. of combatant nations	.030	.001	.016
	Battle deaths in international war	.089	.008	2.55
	Battle deaths in international war/pre-war populations of combatant nations	.048	.002	.000
UNDER WAY	Nation months of international war	.445	.198	.415
	Nation months of international war/no. of nations in interstate system	.102	.010	.002
	Nation months of international war/no. of combatant nations	.241	.058	.119

larger, bloodier, or more intense. In other words, if we ignore the frequencies in war over time and the intervals between them and just look at them in sequence as they unfold, we may discover a trend upward or downward in the magnitude, severity, or intensity of the wars themselves. The results of that approach, based on the data available in Chapter 5, are presented in 7.6, where we show the rank order correlation (Spearman rho) between the recency of the interstate wars and their rank position on battle deaths, battle deaths per capita, nation months, and nation months normalized by the system size at the onset of the war.

7.6   Rank Correlations Between War Date and Severity and Magnitude of Interstate Wars

Variable	Coefficient with War Onset Date (rho)	Statistical Significance (N = 64)
Nation months	−.24	n.s. at .05
Nation months/no. of nations in interstate system	−.27	sig. at .05
Nation months/no. of combatant nations	−.39	sig. at .05
Battle deaths	.11	n.s. at .05
Battle deaths/pre-war populations of combatant nations	−.11	n.s. at .05

The results indicate that the unit of analysis (year or war) makes little difference. That is, if we look at the non-normalized measures, we find that the correlation between the recency of interstate war and the war's severity in battle deaths yields a very weak coefficient of .11. The correlation between the recency of interstate war and magnitude in nation months also indicates no upward trend at all, with a coefficient of −.24. This is further reinforced when we examine the extent to which the normalized indicators correlate with war recency. The rank order coefficient of the wars' recency versus their battle death per capita scores is only −.11, while that for nation months per system member at the time of the war's outbreak is a bit stronger at −.27. The negative correlation results, of course, from the fact that the system size increases at a rapid rate (from 23 to 155 in 165 years).

TRENDS IN THE INTENSITY OF WAR

Although the evidence is fairly strong that we have only a slight upward trend in the incidence of war during the past century and a half (and that trend being in its severity), nevertheless it will be instructive to examine one other aspect of this phenomenon. That is, even if war is not becoming any more or less frequent, or increasing in magnitude, has it perhaps become more intense? Are there, for example, more battle deaths per nation month of war or per capita in the latter decades of the period under study than in the earlier ones?

Rather than approach the question from the point of view of fixed time intervals, however, let us employ the analysis used in the previous section and examine this question in terms of the wars themselves. We do this because we have already ascertained that there is no significant increase in the frequency of war and because intensity is essentially a characteristic of individual wars rather than of years or decades. Furthermore, we again restrict our inquiry to interstate wars only, on the grounds that battle death figures for the non-member entities in extra-systemic wars have not been gathered, thus reducing the usefulness of intensity ratios in these imperial and colonial wars.

For this analysis we will use two different indicators. The first is that of battle deaths per nation month of interstate war, and the second is that of battle deaths per capita based on the pre-war size of the belligerents' total populations. In order to make the visual presentation more manageable, we bring in the outlying high-intensity cases (such as the Russo-Turkish War of 1877-1878, the Chaco War of 1932-1935, and the world wars) by transforming the battle death per capita scores into $\log_e$ form. Since the data are found in 4.2, they need not be reproduced here; rather, we summarize them in graphic form via the scattergram in 7.7 and 7.8.

It should be pointed out that this method of searching for secular trends is different from the rank order correlation method utilized in the previous section. There we compared the rank order of wars on four measures of severity and magnitude with the rank order of war on recency; in other words, we determined the extent to which the observed ranking of wars on magnitude and severity is the same as a hypothetical ranking in which the rank position of a war is determined by its recency in time. In this section, we employ a linear regression type of analysis as we plot the intensities of the interstate wars against their actual chronological occurrences (that is, not ranked), and determine the regression line that best describes the trend in intensity across time.

As with our frequency, magnitude, and severity measures, we again find a highly erratic and fluctuating pattern. And when we fit regression lines to the two different sets of plotted data, it is evident

7.7   Interstate War Intensities (BD/NM)

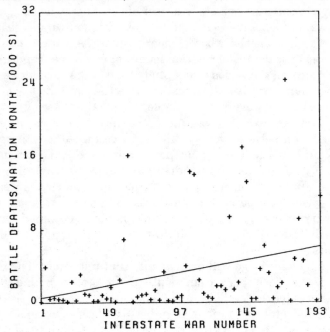

7.8   Interstate War Intensities (BD/POP)

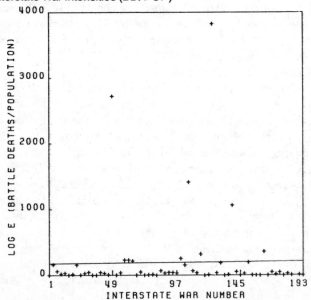

that, as before, any trend is more apparent than real. The regression coefficient for the battle deaths per nation month ratio is .03; a look at the points on the scattergram confirms the poor fit of the regression line, as indicated by a correlation coefficient of .11. What seemed to be a trend was largely the effect of six post-1900 wars: Second Balkan (1913), World War I (1914), Sino-Japanese (1937), World War II (1939), Russo-Finnish (1939), and Russo-Hungarian (1956). On the other hand, the regression coefficient for the battle deaths per population ratio is only .18; its correlation (.0) is even lower than that for battle deaths per nation month. This correlation would be higher if we did not use the $\log_e$ values, as the transformation minimized the very high raw scores.

SUMMARY

Is war on the increase, as many scholars as well as laymen of our generation have been inclined to believe? The answer would seem to be an unambiguous negative. Whether we look at the number of wars, their severity, or their magnitude, there is no significant trend upward or down over the past 165 years. Even if we examine their intensities, we find that later wars are by and large no different from those of earlier periods. Likewise, even if we differentiate among different types of war, there seems to be no appreciable change in their frequency, when we control for their statistical probability as a function of the number of national units available to fight in these types of war. That is, the number of interstate wars per decade has risen no faster than the number of nations in the interstate system, and the number of extra-systemic wars has declined no faster than the number of extra-systemic nations in the world.

At first glance, our findings seem to run counter to other trend analyses such as that reported by Weiss (1963b). Using data from Wright, Richardson, and Sorokin, he discerned a clear upward trend in the *severity* (battle deaths) of war from 1820 to 1949. But he did not normalize for system size and did not differentiate between interstate and extra-systemic wars; more important, when he looked at *frequency,* he found only a very modest upward trend. Moreover, in the analyses by Moyal (1949) and Richardson (1960a: 137-142, 157-167) no trend scores—either up or down—that could not have occurred by sheer chance were uncovered.

What might account, then, for the widespread belief that war *is* on the rise? Four factors come to mind. First, modern communications make every war, in any part of the globe, known to us all in short order; we can no longer be oblivious to the violence and slaughter beyond our borders. Second, the two world wars are a part of the memory of many of us, and their magnitudes and severities (as well as political consequences) remain all too salient. Third, the decades since World War II have seen not only their normal share of war but an allocation of resources and attention to the *preparation* for (some might say *prevention* of) war that certainly exceeds that of any earlier period. Finally, this section does not deal with that type of war that is apparently on the rise: civil war. Moreover, given the ideological, economic, and racial divisions that now mark the global system and its sub-systems, the indications are that intra-national violence will be with us well into the future.

Whether these widely expected disasters will be concentrated within the next several years and then decline or continue indefinitely is difficult to predict. If the historical record of interstate, imperial, and colonial wars is any guide, however, and if, we fail to learn from that record, the optimistic may at least take hope from the fact that those wars have come and gone in a rather fluctuating fashion. The nature of that particular pattern constitutes our major concern in the next chapter.

CHAPTER 8

Cycles and Periodicity in the Incidence of War

As widely held as the belief that war is on the increase is the belief that war comes and goes in some clear and recurrent cyclical pattern. This latter belief, while more difficult to put to the test, is equally in keeping with the scientific mode that reflects the assumption of a high degree of order and pattern in both the physical and social worlds. Thus, in addition to the search for cyclical fluctuations in a wide range of *other* domains, there has been a consistent scholarly interest in the periodicity of war.

For those of us interested in ascertaining the causes of war, the periodicity problem is particularly critical. If, for example, there are no cyclical regularities in the incidence of war, we can safely assume that war is not caused by any single phenomenon with known periodicity. Conversely, if we do indeed find a cyclical pattern, two interesting consequences follow. First, some might conclude that war is inherent in the great ebbs and flows of human activity and is therefore not susceptible to rational intervention. But others, including ourselves, would be strengthened in the conviction that where there is regularity there is likely to be recurrent causation, and that once that causal pattern has been identified, our prospects for the control and elimination of war are considerably improved (Singer and Cusack, 1981).

Perhaps the best-known investigation of the question is that conducted by Sorokin as part of his ambitious study of social and cultural dynamics, reported in the third volume of *Fluctuations of Social Relationships, War and Revolution* (1937). Neither he nor Richardson (1960a: 129-131), who worked with better data but a shorter period, were able to find any strong evidence for such regularities. On the other hand, in secondary analyses of the Sorokin and Richardson data, as well as those of Wright, several researchers (for example,

Denton, 1966; and Denton and Phillips, 1968) concluded that there is indeed an upswing in the incidence of war about every 30 years since 1680. Similarly, in a series of secondary analyses of Wheeler's estimates (1951), Dewey (1964) claims to find a number of discernible periodicities going back to 600 B.C. Another long-range study is Lee's (1931) analysis of Chinese internal wars from 221 B.C. to 1929; finding a recurrent cycle of about 800 years, with shorter cycles within, he fully anticipated the violence of the decades that followed.

In this search for regular fluctuations in the incidence of war, we will follow two separate approaches. In one, we will focus on the recurrent *outbreaks* of war in the various systems under investigation, remaining indifferent to other attributes of these wars such as their durations and the rate at which new participants enter and old participants leave them. These data on the frequency of war will be examined via two different statistical techniques: One will test for goodness of fit between the *observed* intervals of their onsets and the intervals that might be *expected* if they were quite random; the other will subject these intervals to a form of Fourier analysis known as spectral analysis. After analyzing these intervals between each successive war's beginning, we will shift to an approach more appropriate to phenomena that have a beginning and which last long enough to show interesting fluctuations during their entire existence. There we will apply the spectral analysis technique to the amount of war *under way*, year by year, for the entire 165 years.

FLUCTUATIONS IN THE ANNUAL AMOUNT OF WAR BEGUN

We begin here with an inquiry into the regularity of inter-war intervals in a variety of empirical settings. To what extent are the intervals between the beginnings of our international wars equal in length? And if not equal, how nearly random is their distribution? If these intervals are indeed random, they should fit closely to the exponential Poisson density function $\phi(X) = \lambda e^{-\lambda X}$ (where $\lambda = 1/\overline{X}$, and $\overline{X}$ is the mean of the distribution of all intervals); thus the probability of any given interval falling between t_1 and t_2 is equal to $\lambda \int_{t1}^{t2} e^{-\lambda X}$. How close are the observed intervals to those predicted by the null model and found in such phenomena as the movement of vehicles past a given point (in moderate density traffic) or the emission of radioactive particles from a given source?

As 8.1 indicates, the intervals between the *onsets* of war come very close to the distribution predicted by the equation. That is, if we cate-

8.1 Predicted and Observed Distributions of Inter-War Intervals

Length of Interval in Six Month Units	ALL INTERNATIONAL WARS		INTERSTATE WARS ONLY	
	Predicted	Observed	Predicted	Observed
0	.302	.000	.192	.000
1	.223	.265	.158	.197
2	.165	.282	.131	.182
3	.122	.094	.108	.091
4	.090	.111	.089	.121
5	.067	.103	.073	.151
6	.049	.017	.061	.030
7	.036	.060	.050	.030
8	.027	.008	.041	.030
9	.020	.034	.034	.015
10	.015	.008	.028	.015
11	.011	.000	.023	.015
12	.008	.008	.019	.030
13	.006	.000	.015	.015
14	.004	.000	.013	.015
15	.003	.000	.010	.015
16	.002	.000	.009	.000
17	.002	.000	.007	.000
18	.001	.008	.006	.000
19	–	–	.005	.015
21	–	–	.003	.015
29	–	–	.001	.015
	N=118		N=67	

Chi Square = 56.7;   Chi Square = 50.4;
$p > .05$ $p > .05$

gorize our intervals on the basis of half-year units (with a half-year or less as the shortest, 9 years as the longest interval between any two wars of *any* type, and 14.5 as the longest observed interval between the onset of any two *interstate* wars), we find that the observed distribution gives a very good fit to that predicted by the Poisson model. Using the chi-square test, we confirmed the randomness hypothesis in both cases at well above the critical .05 level of significance. Because an exponential Poisson distribution of intervals is always associated with a pure Poisson density distribution in the frequency of events per unit of time, these results fit nicely wth Richardson's finding of a Poisson distribution in the number of wars occurring in each of the 110 years between 1820 and 1929. They also seem to be borne out visually in 8.2.

We can also determine whether fluctuations in the amount of war occur in a cyclical fashion by correlating the amount of war beginning at each observation with the amount that began k observations earlier. Varying the lag factor, k, over a range of values from 1 to m would yield the autocorrelation or autocovariance function. These values

8.2   Annual Amount of International War Begun, 1816–1980

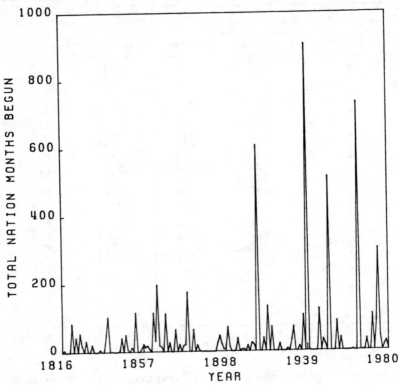

would themselves be instructive as to the presence of periodicity in the series. However, any given autocorrelation coefficient will reflect the concurrent impact of several cycles in the series. If a given time series had known periodicities of 3, 4, and 6 years, we would find that the series exhibited a significant amount of autocorrelation at lag 12, although the apparent 12-year cycle was merely the result of the concurrence of the shorter cycles. Each autocorrelation coefficient may reflect many cycles in the original series. What is needed is a method of decomposing these coefficients in such a way as to reveal the underlying cycles that produce them.

Spectral analysis is such a method, and it may be used to decompose or account for either the autocorrelation function or autocovariance function; in either case, the substantive interpretation is the same. An analogy may be useful at this point to illustrate the utility of spectral analysis. If we sought to determine the color of a beam of light, we would want to know the relative amounts of energy associated with different wavelengths of the electromagnetic spectrum. If we plotted the energy levels observed for an infinite number of wave-lengths, the resulting continuous curve would be the spectral density function. The area under the curve would be equal to the total amount of energy emitted by the light source.

If the light were blue, we would tend to find a sizable proportion of the energy concentrated within a wavelength range of approximately 450 to 500 nanometers. This would be reflected as a peak in the spectral density function. In reality, however, we can make only a finite number of measurements for a relatively small number of wave-lengths within a given band width (such as the visible portion of the spectrum) and estimate the function on the basis of these.

In the case of war, we are trying to assess the impact of various cyclical factors of different frequencies on the variation in war. By taking measurements on a finite number of frequencies (in crests per century), we can estimate and plot the spectral density function of war. The area under this hypothetical density curve will be proportional to the variance in the war series, and the general shape of the curve will reveal whether any particular frequencies dominate the variation in that series.

A perfectly flat spectral density "curve" would indicate that all frequencies within the range investigated account for an approximately equal amount of variation in the series. The existence of a peak, however, indicates that some frequencies account for a disproportionate amount of the variance. The objective of spectral analysis is not to determine the strength of any *particular* cycle, but rather to estimate the *general* shape of the spectral density function underlying the autocovariance function. With these thoughts in mind, let us now turn to consideration of the international war *begun* series.

To meet the assumption of stationarity that is implicit in spectral analysis, it is necessary to (a) normalize the series given in 8.1 by the size of the international system in each year, and (b) to detrend the series. When we subject this normalized series to spectral analysis with the longest cycle (excluding that for infinity) set at about 84 years (equivalent to a frequency of 1.2 crests per century) and the shortest at 2 years (equivalent to 50 on the frequency scale in crests per century), we produce the estimates shown in 8.3. If there were any discernible peaks, their location would suggest which frequencies, and thus which interwar intervals, were most prominent, but the flatness and raggedness of the "curve" indicate that all cycles within the frequency band account for approximately the same amount of variance. The null hypothesis—that the true spectrum is indeed flat—could not be rejected at the .05 level of significance, indicating that

8.3 Power Spectral Estimates of Various Frequencies for Normalized Nation Months of International War Begun

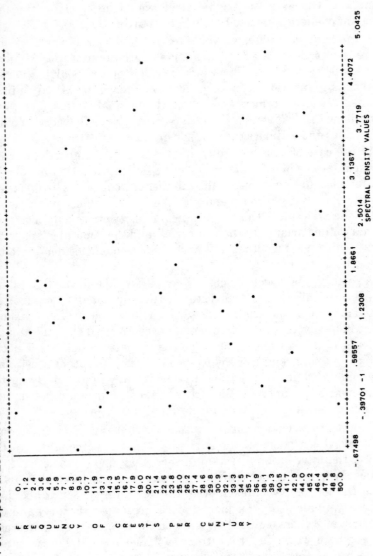

there does not appear to be any periodicity of 50 years or less in international war begun.

Having so far found, via the exponential Poisson and the spectral analysis just described, no evidence for the existence of periodicity in the incidence of war, can we safely conclude that such periodicity is merely a figment of the imagination of those who see pattern and regularity everywhere? Or have we overlooked some important point? As we indicated in introducing this section, one may look not only at data representing the annual amount of war *begun* but also at the amount *under way,* and it is to those data that we must now turn before rejecting the hypothesis of periodicity in the incidence of war.

FLUCTUATIONS IN THE ANNUAL AMOUNT OF WAR UNDER WAY

Any search for periodicity in the incidence of war is likely to be informed by some theoretical framework that seeks to account for the hypothesized or observed periodicity. That framework is, in turn, quite likely to concern itself more with the amount of war that the system (or sub-system or nation) experienced during *each* of a series of years than with the amount that began at some fixed prior date. This, then, is one of the reasons for having computed and presented our war data in the underway as well as the onset form; it permits us to search for the existence of any fairly constant intervals from crest to crest and valley to valley in the longitudinal profile.

In this spectral analysis, we will again use the magnitude (nation month) rather than the severity (battle-connected death) figures; this is because they are readily and accurately normalized for system size, and because—as is evident from the earlier chapters—they correlate very strongly with the battle death figures.

We begin 8.4 with a graph similar to that in 8.2, but this time we show number of nation months of international war *under way* rather than *begun.* It is immediately apparent that we have a rather different longitudinal profile here. Instead of very sharp vertical crests and valleys followed by long flat sections at the base line (for those years in which no war began), we have a profile of more continual fluctuations. This follows, of course, from the fact that while there were 80 years in which no wars began, there were only 20 years in which there was no war under way. In 8.5 we present, using data from Chapter 6, the nation months of war under way (divided by system size for each year) for the amounts of international, interstate, and central system war.

8.4   Annual Amount of International War Under Way, 1816–1980

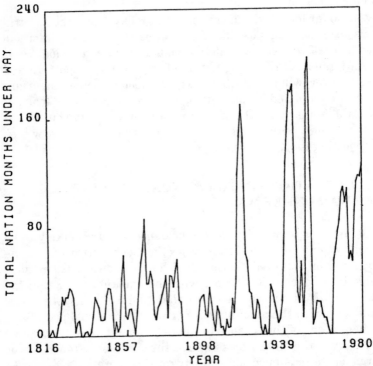

When these underway data are subjected to the spectral analysis procedures outlined above, the results turn out to be somewhat different from those emerging from the onset data. As 8.6 reveals, the spectral density curve is skewed toward the longer cycles (lower frequencies). The higher density values (that is, greater than 10) for 2.4, 3.6, and 8.3 indicate the existence of some moderately clear periodicities at the inter-crest intervals of about 42, 28, and 12 years; that for 3.6, with a density value greater than 14, suggests that the 28 year inter-crest interval is the dominant one. When we smoothed the series, using both the Parzen and the Bartlett functions, the 20-30-year range remained the dominant one. Worth noting in 8.6, however, is the fact that the peaks of war under way during the two world wars (1917 and 1943) are just 26 years apart, and because they are the highest, these two "outlier" cases may be unduly affecting the periodicity values. With that possible artifact in mind, we recalculated the spectral densities with the world wars omitted. Not surprisingly, the 28-year cycle all but disappeared, leaving three moderately strong regularities, with inter-crest intervals of 14, 17, and 21 years. This

8.5 Annual Nation Months of War Under Way, Normalized by System Size

Year	All International Wars	Interstate Wars	Central System Wars
1816	0	0	0
1817	.08	0	.08
1818	.22	0	.22
1819	0	0	0
1820	0	0	0
1821	.40	0	.40
1822	.52	0	.52
1823	1.29	.63	1.29
1824	1.04	0	1.04
1825	1.22	0	1.22
1826	1.16	0	1.16
1827	1.44	0	1.44
1828	1.31	.63	1.31
1829	1.11	.65	1.11
1830	.11	0	.11
1831	.36	0	.36
1832	.40	0	.40
1833	0	0	0
1834	0	0	0
1835	.10	0	0
1836	.13	0	0
1837	0	0	0
1838	.10	0	.10
1839	.45	0	.45
1840	.91	0	.91
1841	.74	0	.71
1842	.61	0	.61
1843	.33	0	.33
1844	.33	0	.33
1845	.35	0	.35
1846	.80	.41	.40
1847	.94	.63	.32
1848	.90	.74	.87
1849	.61	.34	.63
1850	0	0	0
1851	.26	.26	0
1852	.08	.05	.02
1853	.17	.11	.17
1854	1.00	1.00	1.03
1855	1.36	1.36	1.39
1856	.33	.33	.34
1857	.29	.11	.29

(continued)

8.5 (Continued)

Year	All International Wars	Interstate Wars	Central System Wars
1858	.45	0	.46
1859	.45	.26	.46
1860	.25	.25	.26
1861	.03	.03	.03
1862	.40	.40	.41
1863	.91	.59	.91
1864	1.28	.91	1.24
1865	1.50	1.48	.72
1866	2.06	2.06	1.23
1867	.96	.96	.06
1868	1.05	.97	.08
1869	1.30	.97	.33
1870	1.12	.79	.98
1871	.47	.11	.47
1872	.36	0	.36
1873	.64	0	.64
1874	.73	0	.73
1875	.88	0	.88
1876	1.03	0	1.03
1877	1.28	.49	1.28
1878	.35	.01	.35
1879	1.20	.81	.39
1880	1.19	.97	.22
1881	1.00	1.00	0
1882	1.33	1.00	.33
1883	1.57	.90	.67
1884	.72	.24	.72
1885	.69	.33	.66
1886	0	0	0
1887	0	0	0
1888	0	0	0
1889	0	0	0
1890	0	0	0
1891	0	0	0
1892	0	0	0
1893	0	0	0
1894	.27	.26	.02
1895	.67	.15	.51
1896	.74	0	.74
1897	.78	.16	.78
1898	.38	.19	.38
1899	.33	0	.33

8.5   (Continued)

Year	All International Wars	Interstate Wars	Central System Wars
1900	.85	.27	.85
1901	.57	0	.57
1902	.26	0	.26
1903	.07	0	.07
1904	.50	.50	.50
1905	.39	.39	.39
1906	.13	.13	0
1907	.15	.15	0
1908	0	0	0
1909	.26	.26	.26
1910	.12	.12	.12
1911	.14	.14	.14
1912	.63	.63	.63
1913	.38	.38	.38
1914	.94	.94	.94
1915	2.68	2.68	2.68
1916	3.40	3.40	3.40
1917	4.04	4.02	4.04
1918	3.15	2.89	3.15
1919	1.22	.97	1.22
1920	.93	.73	.93
1921	.53	.40	.53
1922	.50	.31	.50
1923	.20	0	.20
1924	.20	0	.20
1925	.42	0	.42
1926	.35	0	.35
1927	.08	0	.08
1928	0	0	0
1929	.11	.11	.11
1930	0	0	0
1931	.01	.01	.01
1932	.57	.57	.57
1933	.50	.50	.50
1934	.36	.36	.36
1935	.25	.25	.25
1936	.13	.13	.13
1937	.18	.18	.18
1938	.38	.38	.38
1939	1.03	1.03	1.03
1940	2.03	2.03	2.03
1941	2.76	2.76	2.76

(continued)

8.5   (Continued)

Year	All International Wars	Interstate Wars	Central System Wars
1942	3.40	3.40	3.40
1943	3.43	3.43	3.43
1944	3.23	3.23	3.18
1945	1.53	1.46	1.51
1946	.47	0	.46
1947	.34	0	.34
1948	.75	.26	.74
1949	.17	.01	.16
1950	.59	.43	.57
1951	2.57	2.41	2.50
1952	2.65	2.49	2.58
1953	1.56	1.41	1.52
1954	.09	0	.08
1955	.14	0	.14
1956	.28	.03	.28
1957	.27	0	.26
1958	.27	0	.26
1959	.17	0	.16
1960	.11	0	.11
1961	.11	0	.11
1962	.04	.02	.04
1963	0	0	0
1964	0	0	0
1965	.44	.44	.43
1966	.49	.49	.48
1967	.58	.58	.57
1968	.63	.63	.62
1969	.78	.78	.77
1970	.81	.81	.80
1971	.70	.70	.69
1972	.77	.69	.76
1973	.39	.30	.38
1974	.43	.26	.43
1975	.36	.18	.36
1976	.60	.16	.60
1977	.74	.16	.74
1978	.76	.20	.76
1979	.75	.23	.75
1980	.82	.33	.80

8.6   Power Spectral Estimates of Various Frequencies for Normalized Nation Months of International War Under Way

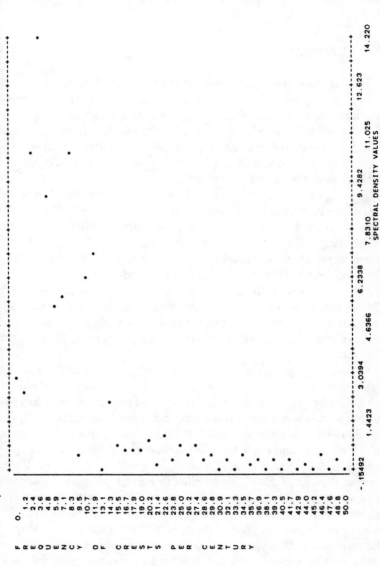

range of 14-21 years is, of course, often treated as the interval be-tween political generations, lending some modest support to certain inter-generational hypotheses built around age, learning, and forget-ting.

SUMMARY

The data and analyses presented in this chapter show that we have only begun to scratch the surface of this fascinating and complex problem. As we indicated earlier, periodicity is one of the most impor-tant forms of regularity associated with the incidence of interna-tional violence, and one whose presence has important implications for its understanding and ultimate elimination. What have we found in this limited inquiry?

Looking at the larger international system first, the findings are far from consistent. There seems to be no uniformity in the intervals between the beginnings of successive wars during these 165 years; to the contrary, their distribution fits closely to that predicted by the exponential Poisson model. But when we shift from the annual amount of war beginning to the amount under way, a modest perio-dicity emerges with the dominant peaks about 15 to 20 years apart. This suggests not so much that discrete wars come and go with some regularity, but that, with *some* level of such violence almost always present, there may be certain periodic fluctuations in the amount of that violence.

At least two possible sets of factors might account for even this weakly observed regularity. One, which would suggest that the find-ing might be artifactual, is that the system size could have increased in sharp and clear steps, rather than more gradually. That is, if large numbers of new nations qualified for system membership at about the same time, and these bunchings occurred at intervals of approxi-mately 15 to 20 years, that factor might possibly account for the pat-tern we discerned. But if we go back to 2.1, we see that the accretion rate, while far from smooth, shows no such periodicity. A second, and more plausible, element might be the interaction effect resulting from systematic changes in (a) the size of wartime partnerships, (b) the duration of the wars, and (c) the intervals between their onsets. Thus, even if none of these three factors shows any individual perio-dicity, it is nevertheless possible that the frequency distributions of all three could well account for the periodicity in the amount of war under way. In a later paper, we hope to investigate this and similar relationships, but to do so now is beyond the task at hand.

One possible inference we can draw from these analyses is that we are no closer to getting at the causes or preconditions of war than before. We may only be closer to understanding the tempo of wars once they have begun. Our interpretation falls somewhere between these two views. That is, even though our periodicity pattern is largely a function of the fluctuations in the amount of war *under way* (in normalized nation months), this figure is also, by definition, partly dependent on fluctuations in the *onset* of war as well; wars must begin before they can produce high magnitude and severity levels. Furthermore, in the absence of evidence to the contrary, it seems prudent to assume that—despite certain obvious differences—the ecological and behavioral phenomena that produce the escalation and termination of war are essentially similar to those that produce its onset.

As we had done in the first edition, in this study we searched for the presence of cycles in individual *national war* experiences. We found no particularly strong evidence of periodicity. Following the reasoning suggested in that context earlier, we take this—along with our other findings—as tentative evidence in support of the proposition that there is some underlying regularity in the incidence of war *in the system,* and that the identity of the specific states experiencing that war is of minor consequence. But we must conclude this chapter on a highly tentative note, not only because the evidence is far from conclusive, but because of the inherently close connection between periodicity and fuller understanding of the causes of these wars.

CHAPTER 9

Seasonal Distributions in the Incidence of War

The importance of weather as a determinant of victory and defeat is well established in the folklore of military history. We are told that the Russian winter, for example, did as much to put Napoleon and Hitler to rout as the legions of the czar and of Stalin. Similarly, once the northern Russian ports were frozen during the autumn of 1918, it was too late for the American expeditionary force to withdraw, with consequences for Soviet-American relations that continue to haunt us even now.

Or consider the fact than many of Europe's statesmen were on vacation, avoiding the summer heat, when Archduke Franz Ferdinand was assassinated in June of 1914; to what extent could war have been averted had they been present in their capitals as the incident escalated into a crisis? Would the history of the twentieth century have been different had Gavrilo Princip fired the fatal shot in another month, instead of when British diplomats were at Ascot and the Kaiser was at Keil for the yacht races? And even if the chancellories had been properly staffed, the fact that July was a major harvesting month in Europe might well have played an inhibitory role.

Our concern here, then, is with the extent to which climate and season have determined the outcome of particular campaigns or wars and how these variables may have influenced the timing, or even the occurrence, of wars. More specifically, we seek in this chapter to ascertain regularities in the onset of war that might be accounted for by season, climate, and the consequences of these considerations in national decision making. What might these considerations be?

First, before considering specific battlefield conditions, strategists pay attention to schedules for the planting and harvesting of crops. In the northern hemisphere for much of our period, we can expect to find considerable reluctance to take men out of the fields and put them

into combat if spring planting or fall harvesting (especially the latter) season is imminent. If the expectation was for a short war, decision makers might well have delayed the final confrontations until
after a given seasonal activity is completed, hoping that most of the
men will not only survive but will return home in time for the next
upsurge in the need for manpower. Even if the hostilities were expected to continue for a year or more, the incentive to complete a final
planting or harvesting could have been quite powerful. These agri-
cultural considerations will, of course, apply differentially across nations and across time, depending on the nature of the economy, demographic resources, the state of technology, and the potency of the
military and political factors of the moment. Then there are the
myriad ways in which seasonal fluctuations may affect political and
diplomatic activities. The willingness to move toward or away from
war might well be affected by such seasonally determined factors as
fiscal years, elections, inaugurations, legislative recesses, and the
like.

Second, there are strategic and tactical considerations of war itself.
Even in the twentieth century, variables such as temperature, pre-
cipitation, visibility, and atmospheric disturbance of communications can markedly affect the success of a campaign. Just as rainfall
made the flintlock almost impossible to fire, the monsoon season in
Vietnam imposed serious (if asymmetric) constraints on the warring
parties. We think, likewise, of the closing of northern ports during
European winters; the importance of fog in many coastwise naval
operations (even after radar's invention); the use of cloud cover for (or
against) aerial activities; the crossing of ice-covered rivers and lakes;
the bogging down of men, horses, and weaponry in mud; and the varying effect of darkness on guerrilla versus conventional forces.

In this volume, however, we cannot examine any specific hypotheses regarding the impact of seasonal phenomena on the incidence of
war. They are too many, too complex, and too interrelated to examine
in detail here. What we can do, however, is provide that body of data
without which they could not be examined: the seasons which, over
different periods, have seen the most and least war begin.

As to coding procedures and format, a few preliminary comments
are in order. First, in order to treat the northern and southern hemispheres together, we have converted all the latter's months into their
equivalents in the former; thus July in the southern hemisphere is
treated as if it were January, August becomes February, and so on.
Three wars were fought in and by southern hemisphere nations exclusively, and dates were converted: Peruvian-Bolivian (1841), La
Plata (1851-1852), and Lopez (1864-1870). However, four wars in-

volve nations of both hemispheres: World War II, Korean, Ecuadorian-Colombian, and Spanish-Chilean. We decided to treat all four as northern hemisphere wars to minimize the number of data conversions. Since World War II and the Korean War were largely fought in and by northern hemisphere nations, our decision requires little explanation, but the other two were more complicated. Ecuador and Colombia straddle the equator, with parts of each in both hemispheres; we left the dates for Colombia (lying mostly in the northern hemisphere) unchanged, but converted the dates for Ecuador (which lies mostly south of the equator). The Spanish-Chilean War, which was fought in the southern hemisphere, involved both Peru and Chile from that region, against Spain from the northern hemisphere. Our decision to call the war a northern hemisphere war (therefore converting dates for Peru and Chile) was based on the fact that Spain initiated the war and was, from our viewpoint, a member of the more active and powerful sub-set of nations, the central system.

In adopting this strategy we do not mean to suggest that winter in Brazil from June through September is exactly the same as winter in England from December to March. Nor do we insist that there is much difference between January and June in either equatorial or arctic climes. But since most of the war participants inhabit the northern and southern *temperate* zones, we believe there is enough similarity between respective winters and summers to justify the comparison.

A second point regarding seasons concerns the dates used to mark the breaks between them. We follow the conventional mode and define them as follows: winter, December 22-March 21; spring, March 22-June 21; summer, June 22-September 21; and autumn, September 22-December 21.

Third, since a major assumption in this seasonal inquiry is that technological innovation in the fields of transport and weaponry particularly may gradually erode the importance of weather, geography, and distance, we define three different technological periods of approximately a half-century each. Thus, our onset figures are presented separately for these periods: 1816-1871, 1872-1919, and 1920-1980.

Fourth, the reader should be alerted to the special coding problem created by the wars that were interrupted by truces that occasionally extended across given months and seasons. Whereas we did not include periods of interrupted combat that lasted for more than a month when computing each war's duration and magnitude, we deviate partially from that rule. That is, we still treat each war as a single episode, but we are indifferent to the length of any truce that may interrupt it when computing our seasonal distributions. Of course, a more detailed inquiry into the effects of seasonal phenomena might well want to take special note of the timing and duration of such interruptions of hostilities. Thus, the Austro-Sardinian and Schleswig-Holstein wars of 1848-1849 are both treated as single wars with only one onset and one termination date, despite seven month truces; similarly, the Second Syrian War of 1839-1840 (an extrasystemic war), despite a 14-month truce, is treated as a single episode. Three other briefer interruptions should also be noted: Second Schleswig-Holstein, 1864 (two months); Second British-Afghan, 1878-1880 (four months); and Palestine, 1948-1949 (three months).

In our earlier volume, we included tabulations for monthly distributions, war termination, and individual nations. Here we concentrate on seasonal distributions in the *onset* of war, the analysis that produced the most interesting results in the first volume.

SEASONAL DISTRIBUTIONS IN THE ONSET OF WAR

As a first important step in the search for any seasonal concentrations in the onset of war, we look at the most general and summary picture. In 9.1 the number of international wars begun in each of the four seasons is shown, plus the number of nation months and battle deaths (in thousands) resulting from those wars. The simple frequency counts are given first, since, on balance, they offer the most valid and useful indicator here. That is, our main concern is the number of times decisions regarding war, in which seasonal considerations might have played a part, were taken. Following the rows in which the figures for our entire 165-year span are given, we show how they differ in each of the three sub-periods (1816-1871, 1872-1919, and 1920-1980).

Looking at the seasonal distributions in the onset of the three classes of war in terms of frequency, magnitude, and severity, what kind of pattern emerges? In terms of the sheer frequency of war, and ignoring severity and magnitude, it is clear that the spring and autumn months are the ones which see the heaviest concentration of war beginnings. That pattern seems to hold most strongly for the earliest period (18 in autumn and 15 in spring, and only 4 each in winter and summer) but does not show up in the second period; the most modern of the periods, however, shows a strong trend toward autumn, with 17 of the 42 wars between 1920 and 1980 beginning in that season.

9.1 Seasonal Distributions in Onset of International War

	Winter 22 Dec-21 Mar	Spring 22 Mar-21 June	Summer 22 June-21 Sept	Fall 22 Sept-21 Dec	MEAN	TOTAL
Number of international wars begun, 1816-1980						
1816-1980	19	31	25	43	29.5	118
1816-1871	4	15	4	18	10.3	41
1872-1919	8	10	9	8	8.8	35
1920-1980	7	6	12	17	10.5	42
Nation months of international war begun, 1816-1980						
1816-1980	1408.5	1074.8	2467.7	1118.4	1517.3	6069.4
1816-1871	46.5	578.2	95.6	516.3	309.1	1236.6
1872-1919	344.1	248.1	728.5	155.2	369.0	1475.9
1920-1980	1017.9	248.5	1643.6	446.9	839.2	3356.9
Battle deaths from international war begun, 1816-1980						
1816-1980	1658660	1035113	27080363	1131131	7726316.8	30905267
1816-1871	25800	586210	263000	462200	334302.5	1337210
1872-1919	305000	373503	8688900	195000	2390600.8	9562403
1920-1980	1327860	75400	18128463	473931	5001413.5	20005654
Battle deaths excluding World Wars and Korean War	1658660	1035113	1461226	1131131	1321532.5	5286130

Does the spring and autumn concentration hold when we shift from the frequency of war to the number of *nation months* begun? Here we find a much less clear picture, with summer leading as the season for the beginning of wars of large magnitude. On the other hand, this deviation is largely accounted for by the more than 1500 nation months resulting from the world wars and the Korean War.

As to the number of *battle deaths* incurred during the wars that began in each of the four seasons, we find a more even distribution, especially when we eliminate the more than 23 million deaths resulting from the world wars and Korea. If, however, we return to the earliest of our three periods, we find that spring and autumn again show the heaviest concentration.

Despite the ambiguous information presented in 9.1, the *number* of wars begun, pehaps our most significant variable, suggests that weather may play an important role in the decision-making process that leads to war. This pattern is especially noticeable in the data presented for the onset of war during the period from 1816 to 1871.

SUMMARY

We find in Wright's *Study of War* that 98 percent of the battles of the Middle Ages, 87 percent of those in the seventeenth and eighteenth centuries, and 78 percent in the last two centuries occurred during spring and summer. Do our data reflect the same seasonal concentrations? If specific battles were as important in more recent periods as they were in determining the outcome of earlier wars, we might be able to compare our findings with those of Wright; but even without such data, some useful generalizations are possible.

Two patterns seem to stand out and therefore merit further investigation. First, in sheer number of joint decisions to go to war over the period of 165 years, spring and fall are clearly the preferred seasons. Second, the passage of time and associated developments in the technology of war, communications, and agriculture seem to have exercised little impact on seasonal concentrations; modest concentrations that appear in the 1816-1871 period, for example, disappear in the middle period, and then begin to show up again in the post-1920 decades. None of the other patterns noted in our earlier volume is sufficiently strong and clear to merit recapitulation here. As a matter of fact, a quick analysis of the months, as well as days of the week, on which wars began also shows an essentially random distribution.

On the other hand, this absence of many strong patterns hardly justifies a turning away from the subject. Rather, what seems to be required next is a more detailed analysis of both the aggregate data presented here and the specific cases on which the figures are originally based. As we move into those specific cases—as well as the other cases of conflict that did *not* eventuate in war—it is likely that seasonal factors will have been far from negligible in decisions to enter, leave, or avoid war.

CHAPTER 10

The War-Proneness of the Nations

Up to this point, our major concern has been with war as a *systemic* phenomenon; we have examined the incidence of various types of war in the international system and its several sub-systems and presented our best estimates of its fluctuations and distributions. For many researchers that may be the most useful orientation, but we hope to make this volume equally valuable to scholars who concentrate not on the larger systemic setting but on a particular geographic region, a given pair of nations, or even a single such entity. In this chapter, therefore, we shift our level of analysis and offer a wide range of war data showing the war experienced by each individual *nation* during its membership in the system.

The literature of international politics fairly brims over with hunches, hypotheses, propositions, and allegations about which particular nations, or classes of nations, are most war-prone. Sometimes the argument is based on the geographical locus or resources of the nations, sometimes on the type of political system or style of leadership, and not infrequently on some putative innate characteristic of the people. While much of this literature is often stronger on rhetoric than on evidence, the general question—why some nations are more war-prone than others—merits investigation. We insist, however, on a considerable broadening of the inquiry and urge that a wide range of attributes be examined and that as much attention be paid to those characteristics that change and fluctuate as to those of a relatively enduring nature.

Thus, any search for correlations between the attributes of the nations and their war-proneness during all or part of their tenure in the system might well look at both the more stable and the more erratic aspects of their physical, structural, and cultural attributes. Among the *physical* attributes to which one might turn as possible predictors of national war-proneness are population, birth and death rates, ethnic composition and homogeneity, basic geography, natural resources, industrial production, military capability, and so forth. Some of the *structural* attributes worth investigating might be governmental organization, party number and strength, economic patterns and wealth distribution, educational facilities, religious institutions, mass media circulation, and, of course, rates of change therein. As to the *cultural* dimensions possibly meriting investigation, there might be national character, military and diplomatic traditions, religiosity, and family orientations, in addition to the direction and rates of change in such elite and mass phenomena as xenophobia, future-orientedness, or propensity for risk-taking.

Regardless of the national attribute or attributes selected for possible analysis, however, no satisfactory results are possible unless we know precisely which nations, during which periods, experienced what amounts of war. Thus, the first table arranges the nations geographically and shows a variety of indicators of national war experience, the second brings the nations together for rank order comparisons, and the third shows the correlations among the various indicators used.

TOTAL AND AVERAGE WAR EXPERIENCE OF THE NATIONS

The nations are listed in 10.1 within their regions in order of the nations' three-digit code numbers. The first column shows the duration of the nation's membership in the total system, thus providing the basis for normalizing the later columns. The next two (columns 2 and 3) show the total number of wars—interstate and extra-systemic —in which the nation fought, and the total number of battle deaths resulting from those wars. Next (column 4) we give the nation's total war months. The following three columns, in which we control for length of system membership, show the nation's battle deaths per year of membership in the total system (column 5); the number of wars per year of tenure (column 6); and its war months per year of membership in the system (column 7). In the final set of columns are three figures that are the result of controlling for the number of wars experienced. We compute the following *war averages*: average length of the nation's participation in war, or its nation months per war (column 8); average number of battle-connected deaths per war (column 9); and the average number of such deaths for each war month (column 10).

Once these three sets of figures are presented for each nation in a given continental region, we compute regional sums and regional means, which permit a modest comparison among the separate regions. For each region we first show, under the totals columns, the
(text continued page 174)

10.1 National War Experience Totaled, Averaged, and Normalized

Code No.	Nation Name	Total Years in System 1	No. of Wars 2	Total Battle Deaths (000's) 3	Total War Months 4	Battle Deaths (000's) per Year 5	Wars per Year 6	War Months per Year 7	Months per War 8	Battle Deaths (000's) per War 9	Battle Deaths (000's) per Month 10
					WESTERN HEMISPHERE						
2	UNITED STATES OF AMERICA	165	8	664.82	262.3	4.029	.048	1.59	32.79	83.10	2.535
20	CANADA	61	2	39.61	102.3	.649	.033	1.68	51.15	19.80	.387
31	BAHAMAS	8	0	0	0	0	0	0	0	0	0
40	CUBA	76	1	1.00	13.5	.013	.013	.18	13.50	1.00	.074
41	HAITI	103	0	0	0	0	0	0	0	0	0
42	DOMINICAN REPUBLIC	81	0	0	0	0	0	0	0	0	0
51	JAMAICA	19	0	0	0	0	0	0	0	0	0
52	TRINIDAD	19	0	0	0	0	0	0	0	0	0
53	BARBADOS	15	0	0	0	0	0	0	0	0	0
54	DOMINICANA	3	0	0	0	0	0	0	0	0	0
55	GRENADA	7	0	0	0	0	0	0	0	0	0
56	SAINT LUCIA	2	0	0	0	0	0	0	0	0	0
70	MEXICO	150	3	19.00	84.8	.127	.020	.57	28.27	6.33	.224
90	GUATEMALA	132	3	1.20	2.2	.009	.015	.02	1.10	.60	.545
91	HONDURAS	82	2	1.80	3.8	.022	.037	.05	1.27	.60	.474
92	EL SALVADOR	106	4	1.50	4.3	.014	.038	.04	1.07	.38	.349
93	NICARAGUA	81	1	.40	2.0	.005	.012	.02	2.00	.40	.200
94	COSTA RICA	61	0	0	0	0	0	0	0	0	0
95	PANAMA	61	0	0	0	0	0	0	0	0	0
100	COLOMBIA	150	2	.44	26.1	.003	.013	.17	13.05	.22	.017
101	VENEZUELA	140	0	0	0	0	0	0	0	0	0
110	GUYANA	15	0	0	0	0	0	0	0	0	0
115	SURINAM	6	0	0	0	0	0	0	0	0	0
130	ECUADOR	127	1	.70	.5	.006	.008	.00	.50	.70	1.400
135	PERU	140	3	11.60	59.2	.083	.021	.42	19.73	3.87	.196
140	BRAZIL	155	3	101.50	80.0	.655	.019	.52	26.67	33.83	1.269
145	BOLIVIA	133	2	81.00	93.6	.609	.015	.70	46.80	40.50	.865
150	PARAGUAY	129	2	250.00	99.3	1.938	.016	.77	49.65	125.00	2.518
155	CHILE	142	2	3.10	64.3	.022	.014	.45	32.15	1.55	.048
160	ARGENTINA	140	2	10.80	66.3	.077	.014	.47	33.15	5.40	.163
165	URUGUAY	99	0	0	0	0	0	0	0	0	0
					REGIONAL SUMMARY						
	31 NATIONS	2608	41	1188.47	964.5	8.261	.337	7.65	352.85	323.29	11.264

(continued)

167

10.1 (Continued)

EUROPE

Code No.	Nation Name	Total Years in System 1	No. of Wars 2	Total Battle Deaths (000's) 3	Total War Months 4	Battle Deaths (000's) per Year 5	Wars per Year 6	War Months per Year 7	Months per War 8	Battle Deaths (000's) per War 9	Battle Deaths (000's) per Month 10
200	UNITED KINGDOM	165	19	1295.23	409.8	7.850	.115	2.48	21.57	68.17	3.161
205	IRELAND	59	0	0	0	0	0	0	0	0	0
210	NETHERLANDS	160	5	27.71	162.5	.173	.031	1.02	32.50	5.54	.171
211	BELGIUM	146	3	97.20	81.8	.666	.021	.56	27.27	32.40	1.188
212	LUXEMBURG	57	0	0	0	0	0	0	0	0	0
220	FRANCE	163	22	1965.12	604.1	12.056	.135	3.71	27.46	89.32	3.253
225	SWITZERLAND	165	0	0	0	0	0	0	0	0	0
230	SPAIN	165	10	195.90	276.3	1.187	.061	1.67	27.63	19.59	.709
235	PORTUGAL	165	1	7.00	32.3	.042	.006	.20	32.30	7.00	.217
240	HANOVER	29	1	.50	.5	.017	.034	.02	.50	.50	1.000
245	BAVARIA	56	2	6.00	5.1	.107	.036	.09	2.55	3.00	1.176
255	GERMANY/PRUSSIA	130	6	5353.50	139.4	41.181	.046	1.07	23.23	892.25	38.404
260	GERMAN FEDERAL REPUBLIC	26	0	0	0	0	0	0	0	0	0
265	GERMAN DEMOCRATIC REP	27	0	0	0	0	0	0	0	0	0
267	BADEN	55	2	1.10	5.4	.020	.036	.10	2.70	.55	.204
269	SAXONY	52	1	.60	1.3	.012	.019	.02	1.30	.60	.462
271	WUERTTEMBURG	55	2	1.10	5.5	.020	.036	.10	2.75	.55	.200
273	HESSE ELECTORAL	51	1	.10	1.3	.002	.020	.03	1.30	.10	.077
275	HESSE GRAND DUCAL	52	1	.10	1.3	.002	.019	.02	1.30	.10	.077
280	MECKLENBURG SCHWERIN	25	1	.10	1.3	.004	.040	.05	1.30	.10	.077
290	POLAND	56	2	360.00	20.8	6.429	.036	.37	10.40	180.00	17.308
300	AUSTRIA-HUNGARY	103	8	1287.20	77.7	12.497	.078	.75	9.71	160.90	16.566
305	AUSTRIA	45	0	0	0	0	0	0	0	0	0
310	HUNGARY	62	3	48.50	46.9	.782	.048	.76	15.63	16.17	1.034

Code No. 1	Nation Name 2	Total Years in System 1	No. of Wars 2	Total Battle Deaths (000's) 3	Total War Months 4	Battle Deaths (000's) per Year 5	Wars per Year 6	War Months per Year 7	Months per War 8	Battle Deaths (000's) per War 9	Battle Deaths (000's) per Month 10
						EUROPE					
315	CZECHOSLOVAKIA	57	1	2.00	3.5	.035	.018	.06	3.50	2.00	.571
325	ITALY/SARDINIA	165	12	759.50	154.7	4.603	.073	.94	12.89	63.29	4.910
327	PAPAL STATES	45	2	2.10	2.2	.047	.044	.05	1.10	1.05	.955
329	TWO SICILIES	46	2	.50	4.8	.011	.043	.10	2.40	.25	.104
332	MODENA	19	1	.10	4.0	.005	.053	.21	4.00	.10	.025
335	PARMA	10	0	0	0	0	0	0	0	0	0
337	TUSCANY	45	1	.10	4.3	.002	.022	.10	4.30	.10	.023
338	MALTA	17	0	0	0	0	0	0	0	0	0
339	ALBANIA	62	0	0	0	0	0	0	0	0	0
345	YUGOSLAVIA/SERBIA	100	5	88.50	57.9	.885	.050	.58	11.58	17.70	1.528
350	GREECE	149	7	53.27	103.6	.358	.047	.70	14.80	7.61	.514
352	CYPRUS	21	1	.50	.3	.024	.048	.01	.30	.50	1.667
355	BULGARIA	73	5	74.00	81.1	1.014	.068	1.11	16.22	14.80	.912
360	RUMANIA	103	5	639.50	65.2	6.209	.049	.63	13.04	127.90	9.808
365	USSR (RUSSIA)	165	19	9731.20	285.8	58.977	.115	1.73	15.04	512.17	34.049
366	ESTONIA	23	0	0	0	0	0	0	0	0	0
367	LATVIA	23	0	0	0	0	0	0	0	0	0
368	LITHUANIA	23	0	0	0	0	0	0	0	0	0
375	FINLAND	62	2	82.00	42.1	1.323	.032	.68	21.05	41.00	1.948
380	SWEDEN	165	0	0	0	0	0	0	0	0	0
385	NORWAY	71	1	2.00	2.0	.028	.014	.03	2.00	2.00	1.000
390	DENMARK	160	2	6.50	11.5	.041	.012	.07	5.75	3.25	.565
395	ICELAND	37	0	0	0	0	0	0	0	0	0
						REGIONAL SUMMARY					
	47 NATIONS	3710	156	22088.74	2696.3	156.607	1.506	20.03	369.38	2270.56	143.863

(continued)

10.1 (Continued)

Code No.	Nation Name	Total Years in System 1	No. of Wars 2	Total Battle Deaths (000's) 3	Total War Months 4	Battle Deaths (000's) per Year 5	Wars per Year 6	War Months per Year 7	Months per War 8	Battle Deaths (000's) per War 9	Battle Deaths (000's) per Month 10
					AFRICA						
402	CAPE VERDE	6	0	0	0	0	0	0	0	0	0
403	SAO TOME PRINCIPE	6	0	0	0	0	0	0	0	0	0
404	GUINEA-BISSAU	7	0	0	0	0	0	0	0	0	0
411	EQUATORIAL GUINEA	13	0	0	0	0	0	0	0	0	0
420	GAMBIA	16	0	0	0	0	0	0	0	0	0
432	MALI	21	0	0	0	0	0	0	0	0	0
433	SENEGAL	21	0	0	0	0	0	0	0	0	0
434	BENIN/DAHOMEY	21	0	0	0	0	0	0	0	0	0
435	MAURITANIA	21	1	2.00	43.7	.095	.048	2.08	43.70	2.00	.046
436	NIGER	21	0	0	0	0	0	0	0	0	0
437	IVORY COAST	21	0	0	0	0	0	0	0	0	0
438	GUINEA	23	0	0	0	0	0	0	0	0	0
439	UPPER VOLTA	21	0	0	0	0	0	0	0	0	0
450	LIBERIA	61	0	0	0	0	0	0	0	0	0
451	SIERRA LEONE	20	0	0	0	0	0	0	0	0	0
452	GHANA	24	0	0	0	0	0	0	0	0	0
461	TOGO	21	0	0	0	0	0	0	0	0	0
471	CAMEROUN	21	0	0	0	0	0	0	0	0	0
475	NIGERIA	21	0	0	0	0	0	0	0	0	0
481	GABON	21	0	0	0	0	0	0	0	0	0
482	CENTRAL AFRICAN REPUBLIC	21	0	0	0	0	0	0	0	0	0
483	CHAD	21	0	0	0	0	0	0	0	0	0
484	CONGO	21	0	0	0	0	0	0	0	0	0
490	ZAIRE (CONGO,KINSHASA)	21	0	0	0	0	0	0	0	0	0

Code No.	Nation Name	Total Years In System 1	No. of Wars 2	Total Battle Deaths (000's) 3	Total War Months 4	Battle Deaths (000's) per Year 5	Wars per Year 6	War Months per Year 7	Months per War 8	Battle Deaths (000's) per War 9	Battle Deaths (000's) per Month 10
					AFRICA						
500	UGANDA	19	1	1.50	5.4	.079	.053	.28	5.40	1.50	.278
501	KENYA	18	0	0	0	0	0	0	0	0	0
510	TANZANIA/TANGANYIKA	20	1	1.00	5.4	.050	.050	.27	5.40	1.00	.185
511	ZANZIBAR	2	0	0	0	0	0	0	0	0	0
516	BURUNDI	19	0	0	0	0	0	0	0	0	0
517	RWANDA	19	0	0	0	0	0	0	0	0	0
520	SOMALIA	21	1	5.00	7.4	.238	.048	.35	7.40	5.00	.676
522	DJIBOUTI	4	0	0	0	0	0	0	0	0	0
530	ETHIOPIA	78	5	61.12	143.4	.784	.064	1.84	28.68	12.22	.426
540	ANGOLA	6	0	0	0	0	0	0	0	0	0
541	MOZAMBIQUE	6	0	0	0	0	0	0	0	0	0
551	ZAMBIA	17	0	0	0	0	0	0	0	0	0
552	ZIMBABWE (RHODESIA)	15	0	0	0	0	0	0	0	0	0
553	MALAWI	17	0	0	0	0	0	0	0	0	0
560	SOUTH AFRICA	61	1	8.70	71.2	.143	.016	1.17	71.20	8.70	.122
570	LESOTHO	15	0	0	0	0	0	0	0	0	0
571	BOTSWANA	15	0	0	0	0	0	0	0	0	0
572	SWAZILAND	13	0	0	0	0	0	0	0	0	0
580	MALAGASY	21	0	0	0	0	0	0	0	0	0
581	COMOROS	6	0	0	0	0	0	0	0	0	0
590	MAURITIUS	13	0	0	0	0	0	0	0	0	0
591	SEYCHELLES	5	0	0	0	0	0	0	0	0	0
				REGIONAL SUMMARY							
	46 NATIONS	901	10	79.32	276.5	1.388	.278	5.99	161.78	30.42	1.733

(continued)

10.1 (Continued)

Code No.	Nation Name	Total Years in System 1	No. of Wars 2	Total Battle Deaths (000's) 3	Total War Months 4	Battle Deaths (000's) per Year 5	Wars per Year 6	War Months per Year 7	Months per War 8	Battle Deaths (000's) per War 9	Battle Deaths (000's) per Month 10
	MIDDLE EAST										
600	MOROCCO	89	3	19.00	74.2	.213	.034	.83	24.73	6.33	.256
615	ALGERIA	19	0	0	0	0	0	0	0	0	0
616	TUNISIA	81	0	0	0	0	0	0	0	0	0
620	LIBYA	29	1	.50	5.4	.017	.034	.19	5.40	.50	.093
625	SUDAN	25	0	0	0	0	0	0	0	0	0
630	IRAN (PERSIA)	126	2	5.50	7.8	.044	.016	.06	3.90	2.75	.705
640	TURKEY/OTTOMAN EMPIRE	165	18	757.12	340.8	4.589	.109	2.07	18.93	42.06	2.222
645	IRAQ	49	3	3.78	6.3	.077	.061	.13	2.10	1.26	.600
651	EGYPT/UAR	71	5	25.00	22.6	.352	.070	.32	4.52	5.00	1.106
652	SYRIA	32	3	11.50	3.1	.359	.094	.10	1.03	3.83	3.710
660	LEBANON	35	1	.50	2.5	.014	.029	.07	2.50	.50	.200
663	JORDAN	35	3	7.12	3.1	.204	.086	.09	1.03	2.37	.298
666	ISRAEL	33	5	7.57	22.6	.229	.152	.68	4.52	1.51	.335
670	SAUDI ARABIA	54	1	.10	.5	.002	.019	.01	.50	.10	.200
678	YEMEN ARAB REPUBLIC	55	0	0	0	0	0	0	0	0	0
680	YEMEN PEOPLES REPUBLIC	14	0	0	0	0	0	0	0	0	0
690	KUWAIT	20	0	0	0	0	0	0	0	0	0
692	BAHREIN	10	0	0	0	0	0	0	0	0	0
694	QATAR	10	0	0	0	0	0	0	0	0	0
696	UNITED ARAB EMIRATES	10	0	0	0	0	0	0	0	0	0
698	OMAN	10	0	0	0	0	0	0	0	0	0
	REGIONAL SUMMARY										
	21 NATIONS	972	45	837.69	488.9	6.101	.703	4.55	69.17	66.23	11.724

		Total Years in System	No. of Wars	Total Battle Deaths (000's)	Total War Months	Battle Deaths (000's) per Year	Wars per Year	War Months per Year	Months per War	Battle Deaths (000's) per War	Battle Deaths (000's) per Month
Code No.	Nation Name	1	2	3	4	5	6	7	8	9	10
					ASIA						
700	AFGHANISTAN	61	1	8.00	12.3	.131	.016	.20	12.30	8.00	.650
710	CHINA	121	11	3128.50	207.9	25.855	.091	1.72	18.90	284.41	15.048
712	MONGOLIA	60	2	6.00	4.2	.100	.033	.07	2.10	3.00	1.429
713	TAIWAN	32	0	0	0	0	0	0	0	0	0
730	KOREA	18	0	0	0	0	0	0	0	0	0
731	KOREA, DEM PEOPLE'S REP	33	1	520.00	37.0	15.758	.030	1.12	37.00	520.00	14.054
732	KOREA, REPUBLIC OF	32	2	420.00	129.8	13.125	.063	4.06	64.90	210.00	3.236
740	JAPAN	114	9	1371.45	197.9	12.030	.079	1.74	21.99	152.38	6.930
750	INDIA	34	5	14.00	17.3	.412	.147	.51	3.46	2.80	.809
760	BHUTAN	10	0	0	0	0	0	0	0	0	0
770	PAKISTAN	34	2	6.80	2.0	.200	.059	.06	1.00	3.40	3.400
771	BANGLADESH	8	0	0	0	0	0	0	0	0	0
775	BURMA	33	0	0	0	0	0	0	0	0	0
781	MALDIVE ISLANDS	16	0	0	0	0	0	0	0	0	0
780	SRI LANKA (CEYLON)	33	0	0	0	0	0	0	0	0	0
790	NEPAL	61	0	0	0	0	0	0	0	0	0
800	THAILAND	94	3	1.81	95.5	.019	.032	1.02	31.83	.60	.019
811	KAMPUCHEA (CAMBODIA)	28	2	7.50	129.4	.268	.071	4.62	64.70	3.75	.058
812	LAOS	27	0	0	0	0	0	0	0	0	0
816	VIETNAM. DEMOCRATIC REP	28	3	511.00	191.3	18.250	.107	6.83	63.77	170.33	2.671
817	VIETNAM. REPUBLIC OF	22	1	650.00	122.6	29.545	.045	5.57	122.60	650.00	5.302
820	MALAYSIA	24	0	0	0	0	0	0	0	0	0
830	SINGAPORE	16	0	0	0	0	0	0	0	0	0
840	PHILIPPINES	35	3	11.09	218.0	.317	.086	6.23	72.67	3.70	.051
850	INDONESIA	32	1	10.00	60.7	.313	.031	1.90	60.70	10.00	.165
900	AUSTRALIA	61	3	34.60	197.1	.567	.049	3.23	65.70	11.53	.176
910	PAPUA NEW GUINEA	6	0	0	0	0	0	0	0	0	0
920	NEW ZEALAND	61	1	17.30	71.3	.284	.016	1.17	71.30	17.30	.243
940	SOLOMON ISLANDS	3	0	0	0	0	0	0	0	0	0
950	FIJI	11	0	0	0	0	0	0	0	0	0
990	WESTERN SAMOA	5	0	0	0	0	0	0	0	0	0
					REGIONAL SUMMARY						
	31 NATIONS	1152	50	6718.05	1694.3	117.850	.961	40.29	714.92	2051.21	54.240

total number of years in which that region's nations have been system members, and then (column 2) the number of national war experiences for that region. It should be noted that the latter is strictly an arithmetical sum of nation wars and takes no account of the fact that many of these will have been the same wars. Thus, it is *not* the number of discrete wars fought by the nations of that region, but a larger number: it reflects nation wars rather than region wars. Likewise, the war month figure (column 4) shows the summation of the war months experienced by each nation of that region, despite the fact that many of these will have been "shared" war months. The column 3 total (if we may skip around here for emphasis) is also a sum—total battle-connected deaths of all nations in the region—but in this case, there is no danger of misinterpretation. As emphasized earlier, a given war can be "shared," as can a war month, but a battle fatality may be assigned to only a single nation. Therefore, that figure would be the same whether we merely summed all nations' battle-connected deaths or computed the battle deaths of all of the wars in which these nations fought, regardless of how many of them participated.

Shifting from the columns devoted to sums (1 to 4) to those covering averages (5 to 7 and 8 to 10), we have computed only the regional means, but there is still some chance of misinterpreting these figures. Under averages we add up the separate national average figures and divide them by the number of nations constituting the region. That is, we present only an arithmetic mean here, not the annual war average for the regions qua regions. Thus, for battle deaths, wars, and war months per year we compute the mean of all the region members' annual war experience averages; all of the averages are added together and divided by the number of nations in the region. In the final set of columns (8 to 10), the regional means of national war averages are exactly that: months per war and battle deaths per war and per war month are designed only to show the mean figure for all the nations in the region, not to show the war experiences of the region as a single unit.

RANKING THE NATIONS BY WAR EXPERIENCE

In the first section, we have provided the basic data by which the major empirical question of this chapter may be answered: Which nations (and regions) have been most war-prone during the period under investigation? The next step is to rearrange these data so as to offer precise evidence for that answer. Clearly, the war-proneness of a nation, and therefore its rank order among other nations, may be measured in a variety of ways; our intention is to use several such criteria and thus provide a variety of rank order hierarchies.

In 10.2, the six measures we consider most useful are offered; for each measure of war-proneness, each nation's rank position and raw score are shown. Of the possible measures permitted by our data, we believe that the "best" all-around index of a nation's war-proneness since the Congress of Vienna is the number of battle-connected deaths resulting from all of its international (that is, extra-systemic as well as interstate) wars. Thus, we present this set of figures first (columns 1 and 2) and list the 82 nations with any war experience at all according to their rank on this measure. In contrast to 10.1, we dispense with the regional breakdowns and deal with the population of the system as a whole.

Since the total number of battle deaths might not be a particularly valid index of a nation's war-proneness because it disregards the time span covered, we next control for length of tenure in the system and list the rank order and battle deaths per year figures for all members of the system in columns 3 and 4. Some might argue that, for the reasons we adduced in Chapter 3, war months experienced provides a better index of war-proneness; thus, each nation's rank and raw score on that measure are shown next (columns 5 and 6), followed by the average war months per war (columns 7 and 8).

Whereas the first eight columns reflect *severity* and *magnitude* of national war experience, the remaining four reflect national equivalents of its *intensity*. For each nation we show the average of battle deaths per war (columns 9 and 10) and an index based on battle deaths per war months in columns 11 and 12. Each of these indices is nothing more than a statistical mean of the intensity scores of each nation's experience in each of its wars. With these alternative measures of war-proneness many different theoretical viewpoints may be accommodated, but only within certain limits, as the final section of this chapter, focusing on the intercorrelations among these six indicators, will make clear.

CORRELATIONS AMONG WAR EXPERIENCE INDICATORS

Having presented nine alternative indicators of national war experience, along with the rank orders based on six of them, it might now be useful to ascertain the extent to which these various measures tap the same basic phenomenon. In 10.3 are shown the Kendall's tau

10.2 Rank Order of Nations on War Experience Indicators

Code No.	Nation Name	SEVERITY				MAGNITUDE				INTENSITY			
		Rank (1)	Battle Deaths (2)	Rank (3)	Battle Deaths per Year (4)	Rank (5)	War Months (6)	Rank (7)	War Months per War (8)	Rank (9)	Battle Deaths per War (10)	Rank (11)	Battle Deaths per War Month (12)
365	USSR (RUSSIA)	1.0	9731.20	1.0	58.977	4.0	285.8	32.0	15.04	4.0	512.17	2.0	34.049
255	GERMANY/PRUSSIA	2.0	5353.50	2.0	41.181	15.0	139.4	23.0	23.23	1.0	892.25	1.0	38.404
710	CHINA	3.0	3128.50	4.0	25.855	8.0	207.9	29.0	18.90	5.0	284.41	5.0	15.048
220	FRANCE	4.0	1965.12	9.0	12.056	1.0	604.1	19.0	27.46	13.0	89.32	12.0	3.253
740	JAPAN	5.0	1371.45	10.0	12.030	9.0	197.9	24.0	21.99	10.0	152.38	8.0	6.930
200	UNITED KINGDOM	6.0	1295.23	11.0	7.850	2.0	409.8	25.0	21.57	15.0	68.17	14.0	3.161
300	AUSTRIA-HUNGARY	7.0	1287.20	8.0	12.497	26.0	77.7	38.0	9.71	9.0	160.90	4.0	16.566
325	ITALY/SARDINIA	8.0	759.50	14.0	4.603	13.0	154.7	35.0	12.89	16.0	63.29	10.0	4.910
640	TURKEY/OTTOMAN EMPIRE	9.0	757.12	15.0	4.589	3.0	340.8	28.0	18.93	17.0	42.06	18.0	2.222
2	UNITED STATES OF AMERICA	10.0	664.82	16.0	4.029	6.0	262.3	14.0	32.79	14.0	83.10	16.0	2.535
817	VIETNAM, REPUBLIC OF	11.0	650.00	3.0	29.545	17.0	122.6	1.0	122.60	2.0	650.00	9.0	5.302
360	RUMANIA	12.0	639.50	13.0	6.209	31.0	65.2	34.0	13.04	11.0	127.90	7.0	9.808
731	KOREA, DEM. PEOPLE'S REP	13.0	520.00	6.0	15.758	37.0	37.0	12.0	37.00	3.0	520.00	6.0	14.054
816	VIETNAM, DEMOCRATIC REP.	14.0	511.00	5.0	18.926	11.0	191.3	7.0	63.77	8.0	170.33	15.0	2.671
732	KOREA, REPUBLIC OF	15.0	420.00	7.0	13.125	16.0	129.8	6.0	64.90	6.0	210.00	13.0	3.236
290	POLAND	16.0	360.00	12.0	6.429	39.0	20.8	37.0	10.40	7.0	180.00	3.0	17.308
150	PARAGUAY	17.0	250.00	17.0	1.938	20.0	99.3	10.0	49.65	12.0	125.00	17.0	2.518
230	SPAIN	18.0	195.90	19.0	1.187	5.0	276.3	18.0	27.63	23.0	19.59	28.0	.709
140	BRAZIL	19.0	101.50	25.0	.655	25.0	80.0	21.0	26.67	20.0	33.83	21.0	1.269
211	BELGIUM	20.0	97.20	24.0	.666	23.0	81.8	20.0	27.27	21.0	32.40	22.0	1.188
345	YUGOSLAVIA/SERBIA	21.0	88.50	21.0	.885	34.0	57.9	36.0	11.58	24.0	17.70	20.0	1.528
375	FINLAND	22.0	82.00	18.0	1.323	36.0	42.1	26.0	21.05	18.0	41.00	19.0	1.948
145	BOLIVIA	23.0	81.00	27.0	.609	21.0	93.6	11.0	46.80	19.0	40.50	26.0	.865
355	BULGARIA	24.0	74.00	20.0	1.014	24.0	81.1	30.0	16.22	27.0	14.80	25.0	.912
530	ETHIOPIA	25.0	61.12	22.0	.784	14.0	143.4	16.0	28.68	28.0	12.22	30.0	.426
350	GREECE	26.0	53.27	31.0	.358	18.0	103.6	33.0	14.80	33.0	7.61	29.0	.514
310	HUNGARY	27.0	48.50	23.0	.782	35.0	46.9	31.0	15.63	26.0	16.17	24.0	1.034
20	CANADA	28.0	39.61	26.0	.649	19.0	102.3	9.0	51.15	22.0	19.80	31.0	.387
900	AUSTRALIA	29.0	34.60	28.0	.567	10.0	197.1	5.0	65.70	29.0	11.53	36.0	.176
210	NETHERLANDS	30.0	27.71	37.0	.173	12.0	162.5	15.0	32.50	35.0	5.54	37.0	.171
651	EGYPT/UAR	31.5	19.00	32.0	.352	38.0	22.6	39.0	4.52	37.0	5.00	23.0	1.106
70	MEXICO	31.5	19.00	39.0	.127	22.0	84.8	17.0	28.27	34.0	6.33	34.0	.224
600	MOROCCO	33.0	17.30	36.0	.213	27.0	74.2	22.0	24.73	25.0	17.30	32.0	.256
920	NEW ZEALAND	34.0	14.00	35.0	.284	28.0	71.3	3.0	71.30	41.0	2.80	33.0	.243
750	INDIA	35.0	11.60	29.0	.412	40.0	17.3	40.0	3.46	38.0	3.87	27.0	.809
135	PERU	36.0	11.50	40.0	.083	33.0	59.2	27.0	19.73	39.0	3.83	35.0	.196
652	SYRIA	37.0	11.09	30.0	.359	41.0	3.1	41.0	1.03	40.0	3.70	11.0	3.710
840	PHILIPPINES	38.0	10.80	33.0	.317	7.0	218.0	2.0	72.67	36.0	5.40	41.0	.051
160	ARGENTINA	39.5	10.00	41.0	.077	30.0	66.3	13.0	33.15	30.5	10.00	39.0	.163
850	INDONESIA	39.5	10.00	34.0	.313	32.0	60.7	8.0	60.70	30.5	10.00	38.0	.165
560	SOUTH AFRICA	41.0	8.70	38.0	.143	29.0	71.2	4.0	71.20	32.0	8.70	40.0	.122

Code No.	Nation Name	SEVERITY				MAGNITUDE				INTENSITY			
		Rank 1	Battle Deaths 2	Rank 3	Battle Deaths per Year 4	Rank 5	War Months 6	Rank 7	War Months per War 8	Rank 9	Battle Deaths per War Month 10	Rank 11	Battle Deaths per War Month 12
700	AFGHANISTAN	42.0	8.00	44.0	.131	49.0	12.3	43.0	12.30	32.0	8.00	40.0	.650
666	ISRAEL	43.0	7.57	38.0	.229	44.5	22.6	52.5	4.52	56.0	1.51	51.0	.335
811	KAMPUCHEA (CAMBODIA)	44.0	7.50	36.0	.268	17.0	129.4	7.0	64.70	43.0	3.75	75.0	.058
663	JORDAN	45.0	7.12	40.0	.204	67.5	3.1	76.5	1.03	51.0	2.37	19.0	2.298
235	PORTUGAL	46.0	7.00	56.0	.042	42.0	32.3	18.0	32.30	34.0	7.00	56.0	.217
770	PAKISTAN	47.0	6.80	41.0	.073	50.0	2.0	78.0	1.00	45.0	3.40	12.0	3.400
390	DENMARK	48.0	6.50	57.0	.041	50.0	11.5	48.0	5.75	46.0	3.25	43.0	.565
245	BAVARIA	49.5	6.50	46.0	.107	50.0	5.1	61.0	2.55	47.5	3.00	28.0	1.176
712	MONGOLIA	49.5	6.00	47.0	.100	63.0	4.2	64.5	2.10	47.5	3.00	24.0	1.429
630	IRAN (PERSIA)	51.0	5.50	55.0	.044	51.0	7.8	56.5	3.90	50.0	2.75	38.0	.705
520	SOMALIA	52.0	5.00	37.0	.238	52.0	7.4	47.0	3.70	39.5	5.00	39.0	.676
645	IRAQ	53.0	3.78	52.0	.077	53.0	6.3	64.5	2.10	58.0	1.26	41.0	.600
155	CHILE	54.0	3.10	62.0	.022	34.0	64.3	19.0	32.15	55.0	1.55	77.0	.048
327	PAPAL STATES	55.0	2.10	54.0	.047	70.5	2.2	73.5	1.10	59.0	1.05	33.0	.955
315	CZECHOSLOVAKIA	57.0	2.00	58.0	.035	66.0	3.5	57.0	3.50	53.0	2.00	42.0	.571
385	NORWAY	57.0	2.00	59.0	.028	73.0	2.0	66.5	2.00	53.0	2.00	31.5	1.000
435	MAURITANIA	57.0	2.00	48.0	.095	39.0	43.7	13.0	43.70	53.0	2.00	78.0	.046
800	THAILAND	59.0	1.81	65.0	.019	22.0	95.5	20.0	31.83	63.0	.60	81.0	.019
91	HONDURAS	60.0	1.80	61.0	.022	65.0	3.8	72.0	1.27	66.0	.60	46.0	.474
92	EL SALVADOR	61.5	1.50	69.0	.014	61.5	4.3	75.0	1.07	74.0	.38	50.0	.349
500	UGANDA	61.5	1.50	50.0	.079	56.0	5.4	50.0	5.40	57.0	1.50	52.0	.278
90	GUATEMALA	63.0	1.20	73.0	.009	70.5	2.2	73.5	1.10	65.0	.60	44.0	.545
267	BADEN	64.5	1.10	63.5	.020	58.0	5.4	59.0	2.70	67.5	.55	57.0	.204
271	WUERTTEMBURG	64.5	1.10	63.5	.020	54.0	5.5	59.0	2.75	67.5	.55	60.5	.200
40	CUBA	66.5	1.00	70.0	.013	48.0	13.5	39.0	13.50	60.5	1.00	74.0	.074
510	TANZANIA/TANGANYIKA	66.5	1.00	53.0	.050	56.0	5.4	50.0	5.40	60.5	1.00	63.0	.185
130	ECUADOR	68.0	.70	74.0	.006	80.0	1.3	80.0	.50	62.0	.70	25.0	1.400
269	SAXONY	69.0	.60	71.0	.007	76.5	1.3	69.5	1.30	64.0	.60	47.0	.462
240	HANOVER	72.0	.50	66.5	.011	80.0	1.3	69.5	1.30	70.5	.50	31.5	1.000
329	TWO SICILIES	72.0	.50	72.0	.010	80.0	1.3	80.0	.50	70.5	.50	69.0	.104
352	CYPRUS	72.0	.50	66.5	.011	82.0	4.8	63.0	2.40	70.5	.25	22.0	1.667
620	LIBYA	72.0	.50	68.0	.014	56.0	5.4	62.0	2.50	70.5	.50	70.0	.093
660	LEBANON	75.0	.44	78.0	.003	69.0	2.5	62.0	2.50	70.5	.50	58.5	.200
100	COLOMBIA	76.0	.40	76.0	.005	73.0	26.1	40.0	13.05	73.0	.22	82.0	.017
93	NICARAGUA	79.5	.10	80.0	.002	76.5	2.0	66.5	2.00	76.0	.40	58.5	.200
273	HESSE ELECTORAL	79.5	.10	81.0	.002	76.5	1.3	69.5	1.30	79.5	.10	72.0	.077
275	HESSE GRAND DUCAL	79.5	.10	77.0	.004	76.5	1.3	69.5	1.30	79.5	.10	72.0	.077
280	MECKLENBURG SCHWERIN	79.5	.10	75.0	.005	64.0	4.0	55.0	4.00	79.5	.10	72.0	.077
332	MODENA	79.5	.10	79.0	.002	61.5	4.3	54.0	4.30	79.5	.10	79.0	.025
337	TUSCANY	79.5	.10	79.0	.002	80.0	4.5	80.0	4.30	79.5	.10	80.5	.023
670	SAUDI ARABIA	79.5	.10	82.0	.002	80.0	4.5	80.0	.50	79.5	.10	60.5	.200

10.3 Rank Order Correlations Among National War Experience Indicators

	BD	BD/YR	WM	WM/Year	BD/War	BD/WM
Battle deaths	1.00					
Battle deaths per year	.85	1.00				
War months	.64	.58	1.00			
War months per year	.57	.59	.76	1.00		
Battle deaths per war	.86	.83	.58	.56	1.00	
Battle deaths per war month	.55	.56	.19	.16	.55	1.00

N = 82

rank order coefficients among the six indicators by which we ranked the nations in 10.2. A brief glance at the results shows that the only three fairly high correlations are among the indicators based on battle deaths: battle deaths versus battle deaths per year, battle deaths versus battle deaths per war, and battle deaths per year versus battle deaths per war. The only other coefficient above .70 is that between war months and war months per year. Using the Z-test (tau ÷ s.d. of rank orders), we did find, however, that all the coefficients are significant at the .01 level or better.

SUMMARY

Having computed the amounts of war experienced by each nation during the years in which it was a system member, and rearranged these figures into rank orderings, we can now summarize our findings. In doing so, we might again emphasize that war-proneness need not be thought of primarily as a function of a nation's attributes or behavior; it should also be examined in light of the geographical, temporal, and political setting in which it is found. Here, then, we report only on the dependent variable and suggest the need for further inquiry along the lines set out at the beginning of the chapter.

In sheer number of wars, France leads the field with 22 wars, followed by England and Russia with 19, Turkey with 18, and Italy—including its predecessor, Sardinia—with 12. Each of these was a charter member of our interstate system, as were Spain, which participated in 10 international wars, followed by the United States with 8. For those with a shorter tenure, China was in 11 wars, Japan in 9, Austria-Hungary in 8, Greece in 7, and Germany (including its predecessor, Prussia) was in 6. Another way of putting this, on the basis of column 6 in 10.2, is that five nations were involved in an average of more than one war per decade: France, England, Turkey, Russia, and Israel—the last is an exceptional case, having been in the system for only 33 of the years under study but having fought in five wars.

Do the same nations stand out on the more refined measures of war experience? As 10.2 makes clear, essentially the same nations sustained the most battle deaths: Russia, Germany, China, France, Japan, England, Austria-Hungary, Italy, and Turkey, in that order. All had more than 750,000 battle deaths, and all but the last two had over a million such losses. On total war months experienced (but not controlling for duration of system membership), we find the following at the top of the list: France, England, Turkey, Spain, Russia, the United States, China, and Japan.

We can summarize these results by saying that most of the war in the system has been accounted for by a small fraction of the nations, most of which would be found near the top of any hierarchy based on diplomatic status, military-industrial capability, or related indicators. It is not surprising that every one of the nations cited so far was a member of what we defined as the central system. Further, of the highly war-prone nations, only Turkey, Spain, and Greece at one time or another were not major powers. Thus, even though we urge a distinction between war-proneness and military aggressiveness, one may nevertheless conclude that the top-ranked nations were compelled to fight often and at length either to maintain their position or to achieve it. In Chapter 11, we will examine this pattern in greater detail, looking at the frequency with which these nations were the initiators or defenders, as well as their respective performances on the battlefield.

CHAPTER 11

Victory, Defeat, and Battle Deaths

Depending on one's point of view and theoretical interpretation of the evidence, those who guide the destinies of nations are seen as entering into war for a multitude of reasons and with a degree of choice ranging from great to infinitesimal. But regardless of the model preferred, almost all points of view recognize that the decision makers are partly influenced by their estimate of the consequences of going into or, when possible, postponing or avoiding the commitment to war. Whether the anticipated consequences of combat weigh more or less heavily than those associated with a nonwar option is, of course, an empirical question, and despite many case studies and a few multicase analyses, the evidence is far from complete. In principle, at least, these decisions (if and when they can be called that) could be more rational if some of the consequences of the prowar strategy were more readily estimated. That is, if those who decide for their nations were in a better positon to predict not only who the "winner" will be but the losses *all* must expect, there might be a reduced propensity toward war all around. Despite the discontinuities between past and future, owing to sweeping changes in everything from weapons technology to command and control procedures, it may well be that history has something to teach us, especially when we are at the brink of war.

In addition to providing statistical regularities in battle deaths and nation months of the interstate wars over the past century and a half, these data may also have some practical relevance for those cases in which war was not successfully avoided. As we pointed out in Chapter 1, one of the major motives behind the Klingberg study (1966) for the U.S. War Department in World War II was the possibility that casualty figures of the past might give some clue as to the point at which Japan might sue for peace. Klingberg's failure to find strong regularities and patterns might have been the result of the often incomplete and incomparable casualty estimates with which he worked. Given the better quality of the data and the greater similarity of the types of war presented here, the inquiry might profitably be conducted anew, and thus we deal here with three general questions.

First, when gross battle deaths reach a given level, does the losing side tend to sue for peace? Conversely, is there a battle death threshold at which the winning side tends to reduce its "war objectives" and entertain peace negotiations short of total victory or some other inflated set of aspirations? Second, are these thresholds to be found, not in absolute fatality figures, but in such normalized (or intensity) figures as battle deaths per month or per capita? Third, and perhaps most interesting, does the critical figure lie in some ratio between combat fatalities of the victor and those of the vanquished?

Concerning the distinction between victor and vanquished, two possible weaknesses should be noted. First, we treat every nation that qualified as an active participant on the victorious side as a "victor," regardless of its contribution to that victory or the costs it sustained; the same holds for all those that fought on the vanquished side in these interstate wars. On occasion, some of the nations we labeled victors suffered far more than the vanquished. Pyrrhic victors like Poland and Belgium in World War II were defeated on the field of battle and returned only at war's end as political victors. Despite their total absorption by the "vanquished," we consider them to have been part of the winning coalition that shared in the spoils in 1945.

Second, we offer no operational indicators of our own by which the victorious and defeated sides may be differentiated. We merely follow the consensus among the acknowledged specialists in deciding which side "won" each war. In other words, even if it turns out that there are systematic differences in the fatalities between victor and vanquished, it is not these that provide the basis for discerning winners and losers; in fact, that classification was made before the present body of data had been assembled and analyzed. While we had some difficulties in discerning a true victor in several of the interstate wars, only two were judged to be a draw: the Korean War of 1950-1953 and the Israeli-Egyptian War of Attrition in 1969-1970. We have also eliminated the eight wars still under way at press time from all of our analyses.

COMPARING BATTLE DEATHS OF VANQUISHED AND VICTORIOUS NATIONS

In 11.1 we present two ratios: that which compares (a) the battle deaths sustained by the defeated side with those of the winning side

11.1 Interstate Wars Ranked by Vanquished/Victor Battle Death Ratios

	BATTLE DEATHS				BATTLE DEATHS/POPULATION		
Rank	Ratio	War No.	War Name	Rank	Ratio	War No.	War Name
1.0	18.60	169	SIX DAY	1.0	84.00	25	ANGLO-PERSIAN
2.0	15.00	118	SINO-SOVIET	2.0	75.41	16	ROMAN REPUBLIC
3.0	13.04	157	SINAI	3.0	54.16	157	SINAI
4.0	5.00	121	MANCHURIAN	4.0	39.64	49	LOPEZ
5.0	4.76	67	SINO-FRENCH	5.0	39.04	46	SECOND SCHLESWIG-HOLSTEIN
6.0	4.47	181	YOM KIPPUR	6.0	34.97	142	RUSSO-FINNISH
7.0	4.00	127	ITALO-ETHIOPIAN	7.0	31.92	184	TURCO-CYPRIOT
8.0	4.00	94	SPANISH-MOROCCAN	8.0	17.51	94	SPANISH-MOROCCAN
8.0	4.00	70	CENTRAL AMERICAN	9.0	15.24	34	ITALO-ROMAN
10.0	3.67	64	PACIFIC	10.0	14.03	127	ITALO-ETHIOPIAN
11.5	3.00	25	ANGLO-PERSIAN	11.0	12.06	193	SINO-VIETNAMESE
11.5	3.00	130	SINO-JAPANESE	12.0	11.84	19	LA PLATA
13.0	2.95	58	FRANCO-PRUSSIAN	13.0	9.86	13	FIRST SCHLESWIG-HOLSTEIN
14.0	2.80	16	ROMAN REPUBLIC	14.0	6.74	154	RUSSO-HUNGARIAN
15.0	2.50	136	NOMOHAN	15.0	6.07	43	ECUADORIAN-COLOMBIAN
17.0	2.33	34	ITALO-ROMAN	16.0	6.06	136	NOMOHAN
17.0	2.33	97	ITALO-TURKISH	17.0	4.64	61	RUSSO-TURKISH
17.0	2.33	43	ECUADORIAN-COLOMBIAN	18.0	4.25	118	SINO-SOVIET
19.0	2.28	133	CHANGKUFENG	19.0	4.08	76	GRECO-TURKISH
21.0	2.00	73	SINO-JAPANESE	20.0	3.97	79	SPANISH-AMERICAN
21.0	2.00	190	UGANDAN-TANZANIAN	21.0	3.96	1	FRANCO-SPANISH
21.0	2.00	46	SECOND SCHLESWIG-HOLSTEIN	22.0	3.79	4	RUSSO-TURKISH
23.0	1.99	82	BOXER REBELLION	23.0	3.51	115	GRECO-TURKISH
24.0	1.82	49	LOPEZ	24.0	3.46	112	HUNGARIAN-ALLIES
25.0	1.71	175	FOOTBALL	25.0	3.33	10	AUSTRO-SARDINIAN
26.0	1.67	148	PALESTINE	26.0	3.26	97	ITALO-TURKISH
28.0	1.60	124	CHACO	27.0	3.26	58	FRANCO-PRUSSIAN
28.0	1.60	4	RUSSO-TURKISH	28.0	3.24	103	SECOND BALKAN
28.0	1.60	19	LA PLATA	29.0	3.19	31	SPANISH-MOROCCAN
30.5	1.56	55	SEVEN WEEKS	30.0	2.26	175	FOOTBALL
30.5	1.50	115	GRECO-TURKISH	31.0	2.16	190	UGANDAN-TANZANIAN
33.5	1.50	1	FRANCO-SPANISH	32.0	2.15	70	CENTRAL AMERICAN
33.5	1.50	88	CENTRAL AMERICAN	33.0	2.12	139	WORLD WAR II
33.5	1.50	109	RUSSO-POLISH	34.0	2.07	106	WORLD WAR I
33.5	1.50	91	CENTRAL AMERICAN	35.0	1.88	64	PACIFIC
33.5	1.50	31	SPANISH-MOROCCAN	36.0	1.77	178	BANGLADESH
37.0	1.43	163	VIETNAMESE	37.0	1.60	88	CENTRAL AMERICAN
38.0	1.40	13	FIRST SCHLESWIG-HOLSTEIN	38.0	1.50	55	SEVEN WEEKS
39.0	1.38	61	RUSSO-TURKISH	39.0	1.49	160	SINO-INDIAN
40.0	1.25	28	ITALIAN UNIFICATION	40.0	1.49	7	MEXICAN-AMERICAN

(continued)

183

11.1 (Continued)

	BATTLE DEATHS				BATTLE DEATHS/POPULATION		
Rank	Ratio	War No.	War Name	Rank	Ratio	War No.	War Name
41.0	1.20	112	HUNGARIAN-ALLIES	41.0	1.48	37	ITALO-SICILIAN
43.0	1.00	160	SINO-INDIAN	42.0	1.39	82	BOXER REBELLION
43.0	1.00	145	FRANCO-THAI	43.0	1.38	28	ITALIAN UNIFICATION
43.0	1.00	79	SPANISH-AMERICAN	44.0	1.30	169	SIX DAY
45.0	.80	142	RUSSO-FINNISH	45.0	.91	133	CHANGKUFENG
46.0	.79	166	SECOND KASHMIR	46.0	.86	22	CRIMEAN
47.5	.67	40	FRANCO-MEXICAN	47.0	.80	91	CENTRAL AMERICAN
47.5	.67	37	ITALO-SICILIAN	48.0	.67	121	MANCHURIAN
49.0	.64	10	AUSTRO-SARDINIAN	49.0	.58	124	CHACO
50.0	.64	106	WORLD WAR I	50.0	.46	130	SINO-JAPANESE
51.0	.62	193	SINO-VIETNAMESE	51.0	.39	67	SINO-FRENCH
52.0	.61	22	CRIMEAN	52.0	.36	145	FRANCO-THAI
53.0	.58	100	FIRST BALKAN	53.0	.31	109	RUSSO-POLISH
54.0	.55	7	MEXICAN-AMERICAN	54.0	.26	100	FIRST BALKAN
55.0	.53	85	RUSSO-JAPANESE	55.0	.22	181	YOM KIPPUR
56.0	.50	184	TURCO-CYPRIOT	56.0	.19	166	SECOND KASHMIR
57.0	.48	139	WORLD WAR II	57.0	.17	73	SINO-JAPANESE
58.5	.43	76	GRECO-TURKISH	58.0	.17	85	RUSSO-JAPANESE
58.5	.43	52	SPANISH-CHILEAN	59.0	.16	40	FRANCO-MEXICAN
60.0	.42	103	SECOND BALKAN	60.0	.11	52	SPANISH-CHILEAN
61.0	.38	178	BANGLADESH	61.0	.09	163	VIETNAMESE
62.0	.33	154	RUSSO-HUNGARIAN	62.0	.08	148	PALESTINE

and (b) the losses when we control for population size. The impression one again gains is that the ratios range widely indeed. In sheer battle fatalities, the defeated side lost from almost 19 times the military personnel as the victor to less than half of the latter's, and when we control for total population, the range increases even further. Second, there are quite a few interstate wars (18 of the 62) in which the victorious side actually sustains greater combat losses than the defeated side, as indicated by those ratios that are less than 1.00. Third, whether or not we control for population, there are a good many wars in which the losses of both sides are approximately equal.

Before assuming, however, that there really are no sharp and clear patterns in the ratio of vanquished-victorious battle losses, we should note how disparate this population of wars may be. Not only do the wars differ among themselves in terms of epoch, locale, duration, severity, intensity, and number of participants, but they also differ appreciably in terms of size, capability, organization, tactics, and technology. Therefore, if we were to subdivide the entire set of wars into subsets on the basis of such distinguishing characteristics, we might well find that the original range in the two victor-vanquished ratios becomes much smaller within each of these separate subsets. Thus, in 11.2 we have computed and shown, for both battle death and battle death per capita ratios, the mean, median, range of ratios, standard deviation, and coefficient of variability. This last measure permits more valid comparison of the dispersion in data sets with different means and standard deviations. We then did the same for five specific subsets looking only at battle death ratios. These subsets are as follows: (a) those that involved at least one major power and those that did not; (b) those that occurred in the nineteenth century and in the twentieth century; (c) those with 20,000 battle deaths or more and those with less; (d) those that lasted six months or more and those that were shorter; and (e) those that involved only one qualified participant on each side and those that were multilateral. Other bases of subdividing our population are possible, of course, depending on one's theoretical concerns, but this range should suffice for many needs.

In examining these figures, we must again note that the standard deviation in many of them is sufficiently large to make one question the validity of the ratios. If, however, we concentrate on a few particular subsets, a more consistent pattern emerges. The wars with more than 20,000 battle deaths, those lasting six or more months, and nineteenth-century wars all show small standard deviations (1.2, 1.1, and 2.3), while those that were less severe, shorter, and took place in the twentieth century all show larger spreads. Moreover, those with

11.2 Central Tendency and Dispersion in the Distribution of Vanquished/Victor Battle Death Ratios

	N	Minimum	Maximum	Mean	Standard Deviation	Median	Coefficient of Variability (V): s.d./mean
Interstate wars	62	.33333	18.600	2.3925	3.2493	1.50	1.36
Interstate wars, battle death per capita ratios	62	.07830	84.000	8.6991	17.077	2.1538	1.96
Non-major power wars	28	.37500	18.600	2.2583	3.3995	1.50	1.50
Major power wars	34	.33333	15.000	2.5029	3.1675	1.50	1.26
19th century wars	27	.42857	4.7619	1.7938	1.1396	1.56	.63
20th century wars	35	.33333	18.600	2.8542	4.1767	1.50	1.46
Wars with fewer than 20,000 battle deaths	38	.33333	18.600	2.8835	3.9880	1.60	1.38
Wars with 20,000 or more battle deaths	24	.42353	5.0000	1.6150	1.1780	1.43	.72
Wars of less than 6 months duration	17	.33333	18.600	3.2535	4.9816	1.50	1.53
Wars of 6 months duration or longer	45	.42857	15.000	2.0672	2.2844	1.50	1.10
Bilateral wars	37	.33333	15.000	2.1239	2.5143	1.50	1.18
Multilateral wars	25	.42353	18.600	2.7900	4.1324	1.56	1.48

NOTE: Does not include ties or ongoing wars.

small dispersion around the mean also show a very consistent mean ratio of vanquished to victor battle deaths: 1.4, 1.5, and 1.6.

Another way of interpreting these ratios is to divide the wars into those that had a given range of battle death and battle death per capita ratios. A brief summary reveals even more clearly that few generalizations can be made about the relationship between casualty levels and war outcome.

There were 12 wars in which the vanquished lost three or more times as many military personnel as the victor(s)—that is, the battle death ratios were equal to or greater than 3.00. These 12 were distributed nearly equally between the dichotomies presented in 11.2: longer or shorter than six months, bilateral or multilateral, and so on. However, six of these 12 were major power wars. A closer examination of a slightly larger subset of wars—those with ratios at or above the mean of 2.00—shows that 14 of the 22 wars in this range involved major powers; and of these 14, 11 involved major powers which were victorious over a non-major power, while the other 3 saw a major power with allies defeat an unallied major power. Similarly, with the 13 wars having a battle death per capita vanquished/victor ratio at or above the mean of 9.86, 8 involved major power victors versus non-major powers. There were 22 interstate wars with vanquished/victor battle death ratios ranging from 1.01 to 1.99, and 18 wars in which the victors lost as many or more in battle than the vanquished (ratios of 1.00 or less); these subsets are very evenly distributed between the dichotomies, including that of major versus non-major power.

SUCCESS, FAILURE, AND BATTLE DEATHS IN EXTRA-SYSTEMIC WARS

So far in this chapter we have looked only at interstate wars and have ignored the problem of wars that involved a system member on one side versus an independent political entity that is not a qualified system member, or versus a non-independent entity. Turning to these wars, it will be recalled that battle death figures were not gathered for the non-system members, making it impossible to calculate victor-vanquished comparisons in the sense used above. On the other hand, an equally important question is whether or not the absolute and relative fatality scores of the system members reveal any significant differences between those cases in which they were able more or less to impose their will on their non-member adversaries (that is, "win") and those in which that military effort was largely unsuccessful. By again following the consensus among scholarly specialists, we can arrive at an intuitively satisfactory classification of the imperial and colonial war cases, in order to see whether there is any discernible relationship between a system member's success or failure in these types of wars and the absolute, per war month and per capita battle deaths it sustained. While in most of these extra-systemic conflicts there was indeed consensus among historians regarding the victory or defeat of the system member involved, we believe a special note should be made about the ambiguous Russian Nationalities War of 1917-1921. We classified Russia as the loser in this war, although Russia won on many of the widespread battle fronts.

In 11.3, we first list those 30 extra-systemic wars in which the system member (or members) was, according to consensus among historians, successful in more or less imposing its will on the entity against whose forces it was fighting, and then follow with those 16 cases in which the non-member was able to resist or defeat the system member's forces. For each of these 46 wars we show the war's code number and the name of the system member(s) involved, followed by its battle deaths in that war, its battle deaths per war month, and its battle deaths per million of its own population.

This listing reveals that the colonial powers were fairly successful in both the nineteenth century (winning 23 of 35 wars) and the twentieth century (winning 7 of 11). We see that the *major* powers rarely lost to colonial entities until the twentieth century and that a handful of nations, led by England and Russia, participated in a disproportionate number of extra-systemic wars. Interestingly, although the victors often seem to have paid a greater cost to win their wars than some of the vanquished paid in a losing cause, the mean number of system members' losses (in thousands of battle deaths) is only slightly lower for the victorious enterprises (13.4) than for those wars in which they were defeated (18.6). We also find that the battle death range is quite large. The lack of any consistent pattern in battle loss figures is reflected in 11.4; here we find, as with the interstate wars, a fairly large dispersion around the mean, particularly in the data for the victorious system members.

NATIONAL VICTORY AND DEFEAT TABULATIONS

In Chapter 10, we presented a variety of indicators by which we could rank the nations of the interstate system on the war-proneness dimension. Here, as a by-product of our major concern, we have the

11.3 Battle Deaths of Victorious and Vanquished System Members in Extra-Systemic Wars

War No.	Name of System Member(s)	Battle Deaths (000's)	Battle Deaths per War Month	Battle Deaths per Million Population
		VICTORS (N=30)		
301	UNITED KINGDOM	2.00	294.1	101
307	UNITED KINGDOM	15.00	517.2	691
310	NETHERLANDS	15.00	267.4	2500
313	USSR (RUSSIA)	5.00	294.1	90
316	USSR (RUSSIA)	15.00	1829.3	259
325	UNITED KINGDOM	20.00	414.1	772
328	UNITED KINGDOM	.01	4.0	0
	TURKEY/OTTOMAN EMPIRE	10.00	3333.3	417
	(COMBINED)	10.01	1820.0	198
331	FRANCE	15.00	153.4	442
337	UNITED KINGDOM	1.50	535.7	54
340	AUSTRIA-HUNGARY	45.00	4090.9	1240
	USSR (RUSSIA)	14.50	14500.0	218
	(COMBINED)	59.50	4958.3	579
343	UNITED KINGDOM	1.50	300.0	55
349	UNITED KINGDOM	3.50	153.5	124
355	USSR (RUSSIA)	5.00	337.8	64
361	SPAIN	100.00	892.9	6098
364	NETHERLANDS	6.00	92.2	1622
370	AUSTRIA-HUNGARY	3.50	1750.0	94
373	UNITED KINGDOM	4.00	221.0	118
376	UNITED KINGDOM	4.50	625.0	102
379	FRANCE	6.00	175.8	119
388	FRANCE	6.00	625.0	156
397	SPAIN	2.00	87.0	110
400	UNITED STATES OF AMERICA	4.50	110.3	60
403	UNITED KINGDOM	22.00	698.4	539
406	TURKEY/OTTOMAN EMPIRE	2.00	666.7	83
412	SPAIN	25.00	429.6	1168
	FRANCE	4.00	296.3	99
	(COMBINED)	29.00	404.5	468
415	FRANCE	4.00	179.4	99
424	FRANCE	1.80	89.6	43
427	INDIA	1.50	105.6	4
430	INDIA	1.00	10000.0	3
436	CHINA	40.00	1092.9	65

(continued)

189

11.3 (Continued)

War No.	Name of System Member(s)	Battle Deaths (000's)	Battle Deaths per War Month	Battle Deaths per Million Population
		VANQUISHED (N=16)		
304	TURKEY/OTTOMAN EMPIRE	15.00	176.5	607
319	TURKEY/OTTOMAN EMPIRE	10.00	735.3	433
322	MEXICO	1.00	151.5	149
334	PERU	1.00	1000.0	588
346	TURKEY/OTTOMAN EMPIRE	5.00	1515.2	174
352	TURKEY/OTTOMAN EMPIRE	3.00	234.4	115
358	SPAIN	7.00	466.7	446
367	TURKEY/OTTOMAN EMPIRE	10.00	469.5	355
382	UNITED KINGDOM	20.00	506.3	568
385	YUGOSLAVIA/SERBIA	2.00	1818.2	1053
391	SPAIN	50.00	1344.1	2747
394	ITALY/SARDINIA	9.00	857.1	289
409	USSR (RUSSIA)	50.00	1275.5	309
418	UNITED KINGDOM	1.00	90.1	21
	NETHERLANDS	.40	36.0	46
	(COMBINED)	1.40	63.1	25
421	FRANCE	95.00	931.4	2267
433	FRANCE	18.00	203.4	410

190

11.4 Central Tendency and Dispersion in the Distribution of Extra-Systemic Battle Deaths, Battle Deaths per War Month, and Battle Deaths per Population

	N	Minimum	Maximum	Mean	Standard Deviation	Median	Coefficient of Variability (V): s.d./mean
BATTLE DEATHS (IN THOUSANDS)							
All extrasystemic wars	46	1.000	1000.000	15.233	22.505	5.000	1.48
Wars in which system member was victor	30	1.000	10.000	13.444	20.925	4.500	1.55
Wars in which system member was defeated	16	1.000	95.000	18.588	25.584	9.000	1.38
BATTLE DEATHS PER WAR MONTH							
All extrasystemic wars	46	63.063	10000.	900.85	1600.4	466.7	1.78
Wars in which system member was victor	30	86.957	10000.	989.70	1949.1	337.8	19.69
Wars in which system member was defeated	16	63.063	1818.2	734.25	541.64	506.	3.73
BATTLE DEATHS PER MILLION POPULATION							
All extrasystemic wars	46	.29334	609.76	57.060	104.58	17.136	1.83
Wars in which system member was victor	30	.29334	609.76	52.376	117.75	11.0	2.25
Wars in which system member was defeated	16	2.4561	274.73	65.842	76.693	41.0	1.16

information that permits a rough ranking on the successful-failure dimension. If a sports metaphor may be allowed, the earlier chapter indicated how many games each team played and how rough the several games were. Here we can ascertain how well they did in terms of overall wins and losses, even though we have no intention of going into the kind of diagnostic detail found in Cook's *Percentage Baseball* (1964). As should be evident by now, these performance records are based only on wars that met our various inclusion criteria, and only for the period during which each nation was a qualified system member. For example, even though Bulgaria won the extra-systemic Serbo-Bulgarian War of 1885, this victory is not included, since Bulgaria did not qualify for system membership until 1908. In 11.5, we list every nation that engaged in at least one international war while it was a member of the system and then show its victories, defeats, and ties in all of its international wars, followed by its performance in interstate wars only. France, Italy, Rumania, and Bulgaria, who fought on both sides during World War II, are now considered to have participated in two wars during the 1940-1945 period, one of which they lost and one of which they won.

The nations are listed not by a percentage index, but by the difference between defeats and victories, inasmuch as the number of wars varied considerably from nation to nation. The scheme used here places the United States—which won six, lost one, and tied one—in sixth place behind those five nations that lost some wars but whose won-lost difference is greater than five. Among the several nations whose won-lost differences are the same—one or two,for example—no specific *rank* is implied in our ordering, nor were these "tied" nations listed in any other specific order aside from their nation numbers.

Thanks to their choice of allies and enemies, as well as military skills and capability, most of the major powers have fared quite successfully in the international war league, occupying the first six positions in the overall standings. If we look at the nine nations that at one time or another were in the major power category, we find that they hold 8 of the first 9 positions and that China is the only one that lost more wars than it won. And even this nation, after achieving major power status in 1950, succeeded in winning 3 of its 4 wars, and holding the United States to a stalemate in the Korean conflict. Also of interest is the fact that while Turkey compiled a record as dismal as its reputation for martial prowess, one of the nations most maligned by military historians—Italy—ended up on the winning side in 9 of its 12 wars. Perhaps diplomatic skill and related virtues are, in the last resort, determinants as strong as manpower and hardware in the outcome of these confrontations.

11.5 National Performance in International War

Nation Name	All Wars	Interstate Wars	Nation Name	All Wars	Interstate Wars
UNITED KINGDOM	16 - 2 -	6 - 0 - 1	WUERTTEMBURG	1 - 1 -	1 - 1 -
FRANCE	15 - 6 -	9 - 4 - 1	TWO SICILIES	1 - 1 -	1 - 1 -
USSR(RUSSIA)	13 - 5 -	9 - 4 -	PAKISTAN	1 - 1 -	1 - 1 -
ITALY/SARDINIA	9 - 3 -	9 - 2 -	VIETNAM DEMOCRATIC REP.	1 - 0 -	1 - 0 - 0
JAPAN	7 - 2 -	7 - 2 -	KOREA DEM. PEOPLE'S REP.	2 - 1 - 0	2 - 0 - 0
UNITED STATES OF AMERICA	6 - 1 -	5 - 1 -	BULGARIA	2 - 3 - 1	2 - 3 - 1
ISRAEL	4 - 0 - 1	4 - 0 - 1	MEXICO	1 - 2 -	1 - 2 -
YUGOSLAVIA/SERBIA	4 - 1 -	4 - 1 -	PERU	1 - 1 -	1 - 1 -
RUMANIA	4 - 1 -	4 - 0 -	KOREA REPUBLIC OF	0 -	0 -
BRAZIL	3 - 0 -	3 - 0 -	PHILIPPINES	0 -	0 -
AUSTRIA-HUNGARY	5 - 3 -	3 - 3 -	ECUADOR	0 -	0 -
GREECE	4 - 0 - 1	4 - 0 - 1	HANOVER	0 -	0 -
GERMANY/PRUSSIA	4 - 2 -	4 - 2 -	SAXONY	0 -	0 -
NETHERLANDS	3 - 0 - 1	3 - 0 - 1	HESSE ELECTORAL	0 -	0 -
BELGIUM	2 - 0 -	2 - 0 -	HESSE GRAND DUCAL	0 -	0 -
CHILE	2 - 0 -	2 - 0 -	MODENA	0 -	0 -
POLAND	2 - 0 -	2 - 0 -	TUSCANY	0 -	0 -
MONGOLIA	2 - 0 -	2 - 0 -	CYPRUS	0 -	0 -
INDIA	3 - 2 -	3 - 2 -	UGANDA	0 -	0 -
CANADA	1 - 0 -	1 - 0 -	LIBYA	0 -	0 -
COLOMBIA	1 - 0 -	1 - 0 -	IRAN (PERSIA)	0 -	0 -
NICARAGUA	1 - 0 -	1 - 0 -	LEBANON	0 -	0 -
PORTUGAL	1 - 0 -	1 - 0 -	SAUDI ARABIA	0 -	0 -
MECKLENBURG SCHWERIN	1 - 0 -	1 - 0 -	KAMPUCHEA(CAMBODIA)	0 -	0 -
CZECHOSLOVAKIA	1 - 0 -	1 - 0 -	VIETNAM REPUBLIC OF	1 -	1 -
NORWAY	1 - 0 -	1 - 0 -	CHINA	4 - 6 -	3 - 6 -
TANZANIA/TANGANYIKA	1 - 0 -	1 - 0 -	BOLIVIA	0 - 2 -	0 - 2 -
SOUTH AFRICA	1 - 0 -	1 - 0 -	PAPAL STATES	0 - 2 -	0 - 2 -
NEW ZEALAND	1 - 0 -	1 - 0 -	FINLAND	0 - 2 -	0 - 2 -
SPAIN	5 - 5 -	2 - 3 -	DENMARK	0 - 2 -	0 - 2 -
EL SALVADOR	2 - 2 -	2 - 2 -	MOROCCO	0 - 2 -	0 - 2 -
ETHIOPIA	1 - 1 -	1 - 1 -	IRAQ	7 - 10 - 1	5 - 5 - 1
THAILAND	1 - 1 -	1 - 1 -	TURKEY/OTTOMAN EMPIRE	3 -	3 -
AUSTRALIA	1 - 1 -	1 - 1 -	HONDURAS	0 - 3 -	0 - 3 -
GUATEMALA	1 - 1 -	1 - 1 -	HUNGARY	3 -	3 -
PARAGUAY	1 - 1 -	1 - 1 -	SYRIA	0 - 3 -	0 - 3 -
ARGENTINA	1 - 1 -	1 - 1 -	JORDAN	0 - 3 -	0 - 3 -
BAVARIA	1 - 1 -	1 - 1 -	EGYPT/UAR	4 - 1	0 - 4 - 1
BADEN	1 - 1 - 0	1 - 1 - 0			

This matter of competence leads, in turn, to one of the points raised in the introducton: whether the capacity to predict the consequences of a given war might affect the decision to choose war in the first place. To put it another way, how well do the initiators of war do, compared to their opponents? Let us attempt here, however tentatively, to answer these two questions: (a) To what extent did the initiators of the 62 interstate wars studied here succeed in gaining that "victory" that must have been an important motivation in many, but not all, of the cases? (b) Whether victorious or not, are their battle deaths systematically lower than those whose entry into the war was less voluntary?

In 11.6, we list 62 (omitting the two ties) of the interstate wars by war number, identify the side whose forces were the initiators, identify the opponent(s), indicate whether the initiator was victorious or not, and then compute the extent to which the responding side's battle deaths exceeded those of the initiator, if indeed they did. As our language should make very clear, we are not labeling any government the "aggressor" in these wars, or trying to reach a firm, data-based conclusion as to which participant "caused" the war, whether by action, threat, or other provocation. Our classification (like that of victory and defeat) is as crude as it is tentative, resting solely on historians' consensus as to whose battalions made the first attack in strength on their opponents' armies or territories. Indeed, one of the major objectives in our current investigations is to uncover precisely the sequence of events that converted mere conflict into bloody battle.

Before presenting our classification and results, a number of the particularly ambiguous cases and our tentative coding decisions merit special comment.

(a) *Mexican-American, 1846-1848:* Although General Taylor reported that "American blood was shed on the American soil," the evidence seems to be that his army first moved into an area claimed by Mexico.

(b) *Crimean, 1853-1856:* The Russians may have made certain movements that led the Turkish army to attack (with allied approval), but Turkey must be labeled the military initiator.

(c) *Italian Independence, 1859:* While the Sardinians gave political support to the Italians within Austrian-held territories, and may even have lent some military assistance, our evidence is that Austria-Hungary was the initiator of serious hostilities.

(d) *Second Balkan, 1913:* A contingent of Bulgarians under General Savov violated official policy by crossing a border into enemy territory, thus giving the Serbians and their allies the *casus belli* for which they were looking.

(e) *Korean, 1950-1953:* The North Korean army would probably be identified as the initiator, but because neither side was victorious, we have not included this conflict.

(f) *Sino-Indian, 1962:* Although China is considered the initiator, Indian forces made the first major provocative, but *bloodless,* move into the disputed territory. Several weeks later they were attacked by the Chinese. India could be considered the aggressor, because it had the weakest legal and historical claims to the area and, moreover, spurned Chinese offers to negotiate their differences.

(g) *Second Kashmir, 1965:* We could have coded India as the initiator, but it should be noted that their forces moved to meet pro-Pakistani irregulars who had infiltrated the Indian sphere in Kashmir.

While recognizing that the factors that lead a government to initiate military hostilities are myriad indeed and certainly go beyond some primitive expectation of victory, it is also likely that the relative prospects for—and relative costs of—victory or defeat will play a key role in such a decision. Granting that premise for the moment, how well have the initiators done over the past 165 years? First, the initiating forces emerged victorious in 42 (or 68 percent) of the 62 cases, suffering 20 defeats. This pattern varies little if we subdivide our 165 years into briefer periods. In the period 1816-1871, the initiators won 14 out of 20, or 70 percent; from 1872 to 1919, they won 13 out of 19, or 68 percent; and in the 1920-1980 period, initiators were victorious 15 out of 23 times, or in 65 percent of the wars. Even if we restrict our focus to those in which a major power was the initiator (22 of 30 were victorious, or 73 percent), the picture remains essentially the same. However, certain subsets of these major power wars indicate a different pattern. There were 22 wars initiated by major powers against minor powers, and the majors were successful in all but two, or 91 percent, of the cases. But when a major power initiated war against another major power, the intitiator was victorious in only 3 of 9 such wars, or 33 percent. The 28 wars that were waged exclusively by minor powers again result in a lower percentage of victories for initiators: they were successful in 17 such wars, or 61 percent.

Did the initiators do better or worse than their adversaries in regard to relative battle fatalities? Apparently better—or, more accurately, less badly. In 46 (or 74 percent) of the 62 cases, the initiators lost the same number or fewer men in battle than did their opponents. Shifting from simple battle death ratios to those in which we normalize for national population, we find that the initiators do not do quite as well. Using this measure, we see that their losses are fewer than their adversaries' in only 39 (or 63 percent) of the 62 wars. Finally,

11.6 Initiation, Victory, and Battle Death Ratios in Interstate Wars

War No.	Initiator	Opponent(s)	Initiator Victor?	Battle Death Ratios Opponent/Initiator	
				BD	BD/Pop
1	FRANCE	SPAIN	YES	1.50	3.96
4	USSR (RUSSIA)	TURKEY/OTTOMAN EMPIRE	YES	1.60	3.79
7	UNITED STATES OF AMERICA	MEXICO	YES	.55	1.49
10	ITALY/SARDINIA	AUSTRIA-HUNGARY	NO	1.56	.30
13	GERMANY/PRUSSIA	DENMARK	YES	1.40	9.86
16	FRANCE	PAPAL STATES	YES	2.80	75.41
19	BRAZIL	ARGENTINA	YES	1.60	11.84
22	TURKEY/OTTOMAN EMPIRE	USSR (RUSSIA)	YES	.61	.86
25	UNITED KINGDOM	IRAN (PERSIA)	YES	3.00	84.00
28	AUSTRIA-HUNGARY	ITALY,FRANCE	NO	.80	.72
31	SPAIN	MOROCCO	YES	1.50	3.19
34	ITALY/SARDINIA	PAPAL STATES	YES	2.33	15.24
37	ITALY/SARDINIA	TWO SICILIES	YES	.67	1.48
40	FRANCE	MEXICO	NO	1.50	6.43
43	COLOMBIA	ECUADOR	YES	2.33	6.07
46	GERMANY/PRUSSIA	DENMARK	YES	2.00	39.04
49	PARAGUAY	ARGENTINA	NO	.55	.03
52	SPAIN	CHILE,PERU	NO	2.33	9.11
55	GERMANY/PRUSSIA	A-H,GERMAN ALLIES	YES	1.56	1.50
58	FRANCE	PRUSSIA,etc.	NO	.34	.31
61	USSR (RUSSIA)	TURKEY/OTTOMAN EMPIRE	YES	1.38	4.64
64	CHILE	PERU,BOLIVIA	YES	3.67	1.88
67	FRANCE	CHINA	YES	4.76	.39
70	GUATEMALA	EL SALVADOR	NO	.25	.46
73	JAPAN	CHINA	YES	2.00	.17
76	GREECE	TURKEY/OTTOMAN EMPIRE	NO	2.33	.25
79	UNITED STATES OF AMERICA	SPAIN	YES	1.00	3.97
82	JAPAN,U.K.,RUSSIA,FRANCE,U.S.A.	CHINA	YES	1.99	1.39
85	JAPAN	USSR (RUSSIA)	YES	.53	.17
88	GUATEMALA	HONDURAS,EL SALVADOR	YES	1.50	1.60
91	NICARAGUA	HONDURAS,EL SALVADOR	YES	1.50	.80

War No.	Initiator	Opponent(s)	Initiator Victor?	Battle Death Ratios Opponent/Initiator	
				BD	BD/Pop
94	SPAIN	MOROCCO	YES	4.00	17.51
97	ITALY/SARDINIA	TURKEY/OTTOMAN EMPIRE	YES	2.33	3.26
100	YUGOSLAVIA/SERBIA	TURKEY/OTTOMAN EMPIRE	YES	.58	.26
103	BULGARIA	TURKEY/OTTOMAN EMPIRE	NO	2.36	.31
106	AUSTRIA-HUNGARY	SERBIA,ALLIES	NO	1.56	.48
109	USSR (RUSSIA)	POLAND	NO	.67	3.20
112	RUMANIA,CZECHOSLOVAKIA	HUNGARY	YES	1.20	3.46
115	GREECE	TURKEY/OTTOMAN EMPIRE	NO	.67	.28
118	USSR (RUSSIA)	CHINA	YES	15.00	4.25
121	JAPAN	CHINA	YES	5.00	.67
124	PARAGUAY	BOLIVIA	YES	1.60	.58
127	ITALY/SARDINIA	ETHIOPIA	YES	4.00	14.03
130	JAPAN	CHINA	YES	3.00	.46
133	USSR (RUSSIA)	JAPAN	NO	.44	1.10
136	JAPAN	USSR (RUSSIA)	NO	.40	.17
139	GERMANY/PRUSSIA	POLAND,ALLIES	NO	2.07	.47
142	USSR (RUSSIA)	FINLAND	YES	.80	34.97
145	THAILAND	FRANCE	YES	1.00	.36
148	JORDAN	ISRAEL	NO	.60	12.77
154	USSR (RUSSIA)	HUNGARY	YES	.33	6.74
157	ISRAEL	EGYPT/UAR	YES	13.04	54.16
160	CHINA	INDIA	YES	1.00	1.49
163	UNITED STATES OF AMERICA	VIETNAM DEMOCRATIC REP	NO	.70	11.31
166	INDIA	PAKISTAN	NO	1.27	5.28
169	ISRAEL	EGYPT/UAR	YES	18.60	1.30
175	EL SALVADOR	HONDURAS	YES	1.71	2.26
178	INDIA	PAKISTAN	YES	.38	1.77
181	EGYPT/UAR	ISRAEL	YES	.22	4.46
184	TURKEY/OTTOMAN EMPIRE	CYPRUS	YES	.50	31.92
190	UGANDA	TANZANIA/TANGANYIKA	NO	.50	.46
193	CHINA	VIETNAM DEMOCRATIC REP.	YES	.62	12.06

the mean battle death ratio for the defenders versus the initiators was 2.9, and the mean battle death per population ratio was 13.04, when all cases are considered.

If we compare the relative costs in human life to the initiating nations vis-à-vis their opponents with that of the victorious nations and *their* opponents, we find fairly similar patterns. That is, the vanquished nations lost an average of 2.39 men for each lost by the victors. And they lost more men than the victors in 44 of the cases, whether or not we control for population. The tactical, demographic, and technological factors that may account for these results lie beyond our immediate concern. For some historical battle figures, and a discussion of the advantages and costs to attacker and defender, see Fuller (1961: 105) and O'Neill (1966: 154).

In sum, we can say that the initiation of military hostilities has not been a sure path to painless victory. The nations whose forces appear to have made the first overt military move in strength not only lost the war in nearly one third of the cases but, with about the same frequency, also suffered more battle fatalities than did their putative victims.

SUMMARY

In opening this chapter, we suggested several possible questions of a general nature to which these data might offer partial answers. Three of them have been of concern here: (a) How much more costly is war to the defeated side than to the victor in terms of battle fatalities? (b) How well does the initiator of hostilities do, vis-à-vis the adversary? (c) Is there any constant set of absolute or relative battle death levels at which wars are likely to terminate?

As to the first, we can summarize by saying that, when all of the international wars are examined, there is no discernible pattern. The mean of the vanquished-victor battle death ratios is 2.4, but the dispersion of this ratio is quite high. On the other hand, if we look at nineteenth-century wars that last more than six months or lead to at least 20,000 battle deaths, there is a more constant ratio.

Regarding the second, we find that the initiator-responder ratios are about the same as those for the victor vis-à-vis the vanquished. Those who strike the first blow, despite some of the military folklore, on the average suffer half of the fatalities suffered by their victims. On the other hand, regardless of the period we focus on, the initiating side—if our coding decisions are correct—loses from one-quarter to one-third of the interstate wars in which it becomes involved. These

figures do not lend themselves, at the moment, to any confident interpretations. We not only have some reservations about our win-lose
and initiate-respond classifications, but would need to examine several other indicators in order to make any judgment regarding the
processes leading up to these wars. Is the somewhat disappointing
win-lose score of the initiators a function of incompetence in the game
of realpolitik? If so, was the trouble largely in faulty estimates of
relative capability, erroneous predictions of the adversary's behavior,
misperceptions of Nth power moves, and so on? Or did the initiators
find themselves all too often in escalatory processes that had gotten
beyond their control earlier than expected? To what extent did their
domestic politics create the kind of constraints and pressures that
shut off the most promising avenues of escape from war? Or, as has
happened in more than one case, did other nations put them in such a
position that they were, in the last analysis, driven into war?

One might, of course, look at the won-lost figures and interpret them
as indicative of a fairly high level of success for the initiators. To win 68
percent of the time, one might argue, is not a poor record. From that
viewpoint, it could be urged that foreign policy decision makers are
indeed quite competent in evaluating capabilities, discerning tendencies, and predicting behavior, not to mention in picking their enemies.
Furthermore, treating 42 victories in 62 contests as a strong record,
one might go on to conclude that the pre-war process is indeed a highly
rational one (in the limited, problem-solving sense) rather than one in
which the environmental conditions determine the outcome, or in
which the nations are largely the pawns of random events. Either interpretation is, in our judgment, premature. Neither the limited material presented here nor the many case studies that now exist provide a
sufficient basis for evaluating the processes by which nations move
from peace to war. This is our major current preoccupation.

Turning to the third of our general questions, it seems quite clear
that there is no absolute or relative battle death threshold at which
nations withdraw or at which wars come to an end. When we look at
the raw or the normalized battle losses for either the winning or losing side, the range is wide indeed. We uncover, at least for the more
important interstate and extra-systemic wars, no particular threshold at which either the ultimate victors or the ultimate losers appear
to modify their expectations and their bargaining positions sufficiently to bring hostilities to a close.

Others have, however, reached somewhat different conclusions. In
a pioneering analysis of the Richardson data, Weiss (1963a) proposed
a model that might account for the probability of a war ending at a

given point in time, depending on "the cumulative number of casualties and the time in which they have been incurred" (p. 102). On the basis of severity and duration to date (using our labels), he found a Markov model that generated a frequency distribution very close to that found in Richardson's data. This model (itself an extension of an earlier one in which cumulative casualties alone predicted termination) was later modified by Horvath (1968), who found that the distribution of war durations could be accounted for by the theory of extreme values, ignoring battle death data. Urging that "a theory based on the number of war dead will never be adequately confirmed" (because of the data quality), his model only "assumes that the duration of a conflict is a probabilistic process independent of the number of people involved, and that the observed distribution of durations is a property of the underlying statistical fluctuations" (p. 18). Horvath's model—based on the duration of U.S. labor disputes, as well as Richardson's duration figures—gave a predicted frequency distribution fit close to that reported in *Statistics of Deadly Quarrels*. A third effort (Voevodsky, 1969), built around the five major wars in U.S. history—Civil, World Wars I and II, Korean, and Vietnamese (1961-1964)—returns to battle deaths as a predictor of termination, along with nonfatal casualties, combat troop strength, and time. That study further requires that the data be observed for a fairly large number of regular periods *within* the war, rather than just the total figures for each war. Using incremental changes in (as well as ratios between) fatalities, casualties, and strength, Voevodsky found that all three growth rates show a distinct leveling-off prior to the end of each war. But he also found that this leveling-off prior can be the precursor of radical escalation; hence, his distinction between Vietnam wars I and II, with 1965 marking the beginning of the second phase.

In sum, the relationship between battle deaths and war termination remains blurred. It seems reasonable to expect that these variables are associated, but it also seems clear that additional variables must be considered; perhaps those suggested in the above papers, or those in Calahan (1944), Coffey (1965), or Kecskemeti (1958). A strong model, then, might also need to include such phenomena as sudden changes in battle death ratios, the defeat of a crack military unit, the loss of a key geographical area, accelerating attrition of materiel, a faltering economy, elimination of an ally, high civilian casualties, crumbling popular support at home, and so forth.

Another reason for the poor predictive power of combat losses is that even though they were severe in individual and humanitarian terms, they tended to be negligible from a demographic point of view.

In only 14 of the 110 completed international wars did the battle death figure exceed 100,000. Even the Russian military personnel losses in World War II and those of Paraguay in the Chaco War were as low as 4.4 and 5.6 percent of the pre-war populations, respectively. We seriously doubt whether the inclusion of civilian deaths would have made the costs of war sufficiently greater and the correlation between such losses and the end of war any higher. Finally, if, as Clausewitz has argued, war is a means to political objectives and thus purely instrumental, the cumulative body count would be of infrequent importance in conventional interstate wars, even though—as was apparent in the Vietnam War—it is a fairly important factor in the political maneuvering associated with guerrilla combat. In brief, it would seem to take more than the systematic extinction of human lives to bring national governments to the conference table.

PART II

CIVIL WAR

CHAPTER 12

Identifying Civil Wars
The Inclusion and
Exclusion Problem

PURPOSES AND EXPECTATIONS

For almost twenty years, the Correlates of War Project has been
engaged in developing systematic descriptions of and explanations
for modern international war. In this part we move for the first time
into the area of *internal* war. We took this step not merely as an anti-
quarian gesture to complete the catalogue of large-scale military
combat involving independent nations since the Congress of Vienna,
but also in the hope that this expansion of our domain will make our
studies more useful and relevant to the scholarly and professional
community. Furthermore, civil wars, insurgencies, and foreign interventions have come to dominate the headlines in our generation and

may now play as important a role in the international community as traditional interstate war.

Beyond the intrinsic value of examining such a major manifestation of social pathology, we were especially interested in the relationships between civil and international war. Many scholars have offered suggestive hypotheses relating the levels and types of internal and external violence, and a few have even produced exploratory attempts at testing those hypotheses. However, no one has studied civil wars quantitatively as a long-range historical phenomenon, and no one has developed the detailed longitudinal data base needed to undertake such a project. Although we have already made some tentative beginnings at what must necessarily be a long and painstaking process of integrating international and civil war phenomena into a general explanatory framework, our mission here has been the creation of a comprehensive list that will enhance the systematic and longitudinal study of civil wars for us as well as the rest of the scholarly community.

In pursuit of this goal, we begin with definitions and a typology of internal conflict, and then present the results of a thorough search through historical materials for civil wars that occurred from 1816 through 1980 within the boundaries of each member of the interstate system. We then characterize those wars along a number of dimensions such as their severity, duration, and intensity, to facilitate comparison between civil wars and the international wars identified and described in Part I.

In the process of compiling this catalogue, we found many conflicts that did not quite meet our criteria but which were nonetheless significant or noteworthy. So that this information may not be lost to other researchers, we include in Appendix B all of those candidate cases that failed to make our list, along with the reason for their exclusion.

PRIOR DEFINITIONS AND COMPILATIONS

What is a civil war? Answering this fundamental question was by no means an easy task. We sought an operational definition, developing indicators that could be used to measure and substantiate criteria by which our population of civil wars might be described and compared. Keeping in mind that our eventual goal was to create a data set of civil wars comparable to that for interstate wars, we began with the search for a reasonable verbal definition of civil war in the traditional literature on internal violence, revolution, and civil war.

In that vast body of monographs and articles, we found few guidelines (Orlansky, 1970). Not surprisingly—given our experience with the international war problem—there has never been a standard definition accepted by all who study these events (Salert, 1976: 5), although most scholars of internal war try to distinguish among civil war, revolution, insurrection, and coup d'état.

Most such distinctions are based on the different *purposes or outcomes* of the violent conflict events. For example, in his classic *Anatomy of Revolution* (1938), Brinton offers the distinction between revolution, as change in government with subsequent social, political, and economic change, and coup, as change in top government authority only. Much in the same vein, Lasswell and Kaplan (1950) use the broad categories of political, social, or palace revolution which aim for or result in, respectively, full-scale political, social, and economic, or mere leadership changes. Moving beyond these concepts, Huntington (1962) sees a difference in the degree of change *intended* by a revolution and defines four categories: (a) palace revolution, changing only the holders of the reigns of power; (b) reform coup, changing the structure of government authority as well; (c) revolutionary coup, changing not only the form of government but also some element of society; and (d) internal war, resulting in mass changes in society at large. Rosenau (1964) differentiates among revolutions along similar lines but gives them different names: personnel, authority, and structural wars.

Such taxonomies offer neither exhaustive nor mutually exclusive categories, although an incremental difference of an undefined quality best expressed as scope, or perhaps size or effect, is implied. At the least, however, these authors sense a major continuum along which internal crises and revolutions can be measured: the degree of change accomplished or intended. Not even this slender thread of continuity is evident in Luard's (1972) proposed typology of civil war. He suggests four categories to be applied to post-1945 civil wars: (1) ideological (along cold war divisions), (2) political (but not chiefly Communist-inspired), (3) postcolonial in newly independent states (many of which were, however, Communist-inspired), and (4) protests against oppressive governments that do not have strong ideological tendencies. And while he does not define civil war itself, he suggests types of internal violence that are *not* to be classified as civil wars, including coup d'état.

Although many classificatory schemes use the term "war" as part of the definition, they mention neither violence nor other specific means used to bring about the changes defined. For our own particular set of research goals, we must define war in terms of violence. Not

only is war impossible without violence (except, of course, in the met-
aphorical sense), but we consider the violent taking of human life the
primary and dominant characteristic of war. We view the *goals* of the
protagonists as unimportant in identifying the occurrence of the
event itself and the *results* of a war as a separate and dependent variable to be measured by indicators other than those establishing the
fact of the war itself.

Some authors stipulate that violence has to be present in any definition of war. Eckstein (1964) includes as internal war any resort to
violence within a political order to change constitutions, rules, or policies of a state. He then proceeds to classify types of internal war as
political revolution (full-scale political change), secessionist wars, riots (characterized by unorganized antagonists and a low level of violence), and coups (elite versus elite), thus mixing motive and result as
well as degree of organization and status of participants as classificatory determinants. In an overview of Eckstein and others, Stone
(1966) argues that too broad and inclusive a typology obscures information that differentiates types of revolution. The scheme he offers,
originally formulated by Johnson (1964), includes six categories,
from spontaneous peasant uprisings to militarized mass insurrec-
tions, the latter defined simply as planned and guided revolutionary
wars. Although Eckstein and Stone/Johnson may have introduced
the requirement of violence into the typology, they have become so
involved in defining how revolutions differ that they lose sight of
what else besides violence makes revolutions the same. There are too
many concepts—motive, result, organization, participants, degree of
violence—to provide the criteria for selection of a population of cases.

Several studies do, however, take major steps in the direction of
population identification. For example, Timasheff (1965) defines revolution as the violence of internal disorganized mobs, political
groups, and ethnic and secessionist groups that oppose the regular
army of the national government. Although he reserves the use of the
term "war" for inter-nation violent conflict, he suggests much of the
definitional framework upon which to build a list of internal wars. He
even excludes from his category of revolution, or violent internal conflict, all riots, police actions, pronunciamentos (changes in top elite),
and coups.

In a similar vein, Edmonds (1972) requires civil war to (a) have
violence, not necessarily organized, (b) be illegal (that is, to not be the
established procedure for change), and (c) to involve principally citizens of the state in which it occurs. Further, he says that civil war
must involve civilians, one side must represent the central govern-

ment and the opposing side must challenge the government's authority, and conventional military tactics must be employed to some degree by both sides, thus putting a wholly guerrilla war outside his
definition of civil war. Within this definition, which taps some useful
indicators, Edmonds finds two types of civil war: wars to displace the
government in power and secessionist wars. Outside of the category
of civil war, besides guerrilla war, are events he calls revolutions,
rapid changes in legal political power by the use of violence. Coups
are included in this category, and civilians need not be involved at all.
With the use of the concept of "rapid change," he suggests a duration
factor, but none is specified in the definition.

Before we look at some quantitative social scientists' contributions
to the concept of civil war, we should also mention the complex study
of revolution by Hagopian (1974). While he never defines civil war,
and while we do not necessarily accept all facets of his exhaustive
definition, he does distinguish between internal war and revolution,
a distinction suggested by the word origins themselves: war is a violent physical clash, revolution a turning over, change.

Although most of the aforementioned approaches are thought-pro-
voking, none provides indicators that define war *operationally*. Thus,
we turned to prior research of a quantitative nature. And there, surprisingly perhaps, we also came up empty-handed. Whereas the traditional studies provide no path toward operational description, the
quantitative studies recommend very little in the way of events categories. That is, most of the quantitative efforts have been spent in
describing the *amount of general conflict* exhibited by certain nations
during certain periods, measured by several indicators of conflict—
usually, but not always, including violence. Why this kind of research
has little bearing on ours will be clearer as we describe various quantitative studies of internal conflict.

Deutsch (1964), one of those who early recommended a testing of
the ideas proliferating in the revolution/internal conflict interest
area, suggests looking at such numerical indicators as the number
and type of participants, numbers killed, and duration before con-
structing any typology of internal conflict. Somewhat along these
lines, Tanter and Midlarsky (1967) posit a "theory of revolutions"
that combines the four Huntington categories of revolution with four
variables offered by Deutsch: mass participation, duration, number
of deaths, and intention as measured by degree of change in both
government and society. They construct a matrix with the four types
of revolution as one axis and different levels of the four variables (for
example, low participation, medium duration, few deaths, and total

changes) as the other axis. Unfortunately, no operationalization of this scheme was attempted.

Among those who have employed operational schemes to study internal conflict during specified periods are Rummel (1963), Tanter (1966), and Wilkenfeld (1968, 1969), who count nine types of conflict events in 74 to 83 nations from 1955 to 1960. Events counted and defined include riots (violent demonstrations by more than 100 participants using force), assassinations, demonstrations, strikes, presence of guerrilla warfare (covert terrorist acts aimed at overthrow of government), purges (systematic elimination of the opposition), revolutions (illegal forced change or attempted change in government), secession or attempted secession, and deaths from internal conflict, excluding execution. Subsequent factor analyses of these nine indicators reveal which of the events occurred to what degree in the chosen spatial-temporal domain, but no attempt is made to say that on the basis of particular levels of some type of conflict the phenomenon of internal war is described. Furthermore, one of the main thrusts of these studies is the comparison and correlation of internal and foreign conflict.

Using many of the same indicators, Feierabend and Feierabend (1966) count the occurrences of 12 types of internal conflict events in 84 nations from 1948 to 1962. The definitions of their types are not entirely quantitative, nor are they concerned with delimiting and defining categories of internal conflict. They are interested primarily in trying to explain the patterns of internal violence their coding revealed. This, too, is the goal of Gurr (1967), who defines civil violence as those collective non-governmental attacks on persons or property occurring within the boundaries of a political unit that result in intentional damage. The definition is operationalized by precise measurement of such indicators as casualties (determined by fatalities), duration, and number of participants. Ranges of each indicator are established (for example, "151 or more killed," "one week" duration, "10 to 100 participants"), and elaborate combined measures are constructed to determine the level of civil violence in each country in its spatial-temporal field.

Finally, Hibbs (1973) defines domestic violence as violence that is (a) anti-regime, (b) of immediate political significance, and (c) directly linked to, or sponsored by, collectivities. Under this definition he includes riots, strikes, anti-government demonstrations, armed attacks, political assassinations, and internal wars; excluded are elite actions such as coups, government-incited repression, and clashes between elites and masses in protest situations.

It should be clear that these studies look in a direction other than our own. We are interested primarily in describing and then accounting for outbreaks of particular kinds and levels of internal violence; they, in when and what kinds of acts of internal conflict behavior are exhibited by nations and what the relationship is, if any, between the occurrence of different kinds of internal and foreign conflict events. Such quantitative studies are too broad for our purposes, in that they include much lower levels of conflict, inapplicable to our definition of major civil wars. The immediate opportunities for cross-fertilization between our specific event-oriented study and their broader process-measuring research are therefore limited.

One group of more useful studies were the conflict lists and compendia employed in the international phase of our research. While in all cases we scoured the literature for additional sources and data, we would like to identify again those general lists we examined. Richardson (1960a), the most complete both in number and time span, categorizes internal and external wars by their fatality range and lists all participants, national and non-national. Sorokin (1937), who presents lists of internal conflicts for a few larger nations, does not specify types. In his classic study, Wright (1965) offers a specific definition of civil war as any war that has as its two factions the government and opposing insurgents fighting within the government's legal boundaries. As an additional variable, he identifies aggressor and gives the aggressor's motives as either Communist revolt, self-determination, or "other." Wood (1968) includes in his list of conflicts those that involved a nation's regular armed forces (one side or both) using weapons of war with intent to kill, lasting at least one hour, in the twentieth century. But his list, which covers both internal and external wars, provides no fatality figures.

Finally, we must call attention to three important sources for the post-World War II period. Perhaps the most useful, although limited in its time span, is that of Cady and Prince (1966). This list of conflicts offers precise dates, fatality estimates, as well as source references. Conflicts reported range from coups d'état to civil wars and include categories of insurrection, colonial war, and terrorism. In his widely cited studies, Kende (1971, 1978) requires his post-1945 wars to have regular armed forces on at least one side, both sides to have lethal weapons, and both sides to have organized leadership. His lengthy list, a mix of internal and foreign wars with an emphasis on "imperialist" intervention, offers no casualty estimates. The Bouthoul and Carrère (1976) compilation was also useful as a checklist, as was the "Chronique" of their journal, *Études Polémologiques*. Finally, Duner (1980) offers an interesting comparison of post-1945 civil war lists.

We used these existing lists as springboards for our own compilations. First, we extracted from them all internal wars that had even a remote possibility of qualifying for our list, after which each candidate war was investigated in historical works or contemporary newspaper accounts. We also read short historical outlines of every country in our spatial-temporal domain to ascertain whether we overlooked a war *not* on anyone else's list. There were many of this type, particularly in Latin America and Asia. In fact, we worked hard to eliminate regional biases in these earlier lists, biases that implicitly attached greater significance to wars involving European nations.

To summarize the impact of prior research on this study, although there has been some helpful prior data collection, conceptually the field is a morass. There is neither a unified approach to the task of defining a typology of internal violence nor even a single agreed-upon concept of what civil war is or is not. At best, the earlier attempts of the political philosophers are only moderately well explained, and they often suggest overlapping categories. At worst, they are confusing and internally inconsistent. It became clear to us that we needed to formulate our own definitions to minimize subjective bias and to facilitate the construction of a data set comparable to that presented in the first half of this volume.

THE CRITERIA OF CIVIL WAR

We are not offering here a complete typology of internal conflict but a more limited scheme for describing and measuring those discrete conflict events we conceive of as civil war. We nevertheless have aimed at creating a typology flexible enough so that additional dimensions might be added by those with theoretical interests other than our own. For example, although we are not currently concerned with the intentions or goals, or results, of the antagonists in a civil war, our population of civil wars admits of further subdivision into such classifications. We have left our categories deliberately broad, and in so doing have created a data set which, resting on a few untested theoretical assumptions, is the more useful for testing a wide range of hypotheses.

Our typology is built on three dimensions: internality, types of participants, and the degree of effective resistance. For our study, a civil war is any armed conflict that involves (a) military action internal to the metropole, (b) the active participation of the national government, and (c) effective resistance by both sides. With these criteria, we differentiate civil wars from other types of internal violent conflicts. We will treat in detail each of these three aspects and then deal with the more difficult task of classifying *internationalized* civil war in its various manifestations.

Internality

One basic property of an internal conflict is obviously that it is internal to a state; that is, significant military action occurs between subjects within the boundaries of the metropole. Given this criterion, we had to construct reproducible rules for distinguishing the metropole of a state from its dependencies. Many states find it advantageous to blur this distinction through legal shams in order to demonstrate that its dependencies are integral parts of its territory; the recent Portuguese claim that its African colonies were merely provinces was not unique. A state may also grant metropolitan rights to some portion of the population of its colonies in order to gain allies in the struggle to retain control over the rest of its colonial population, as did France with the Algerian Christians. Consequently, rather than rely on the often disingenuous and inconsistent distinctions of the states themselves, we decided to develop independent criteria for distinguishing between metropoles and dependencies.

After examining the political structure of empires and their dependencies, we decided the key legal difference between these two types of territories was that the subjects of a dependency enjoyed no direct role in the functioning of the central authority, however much they might have been able to participate in the government of their own territory. With this in mind, we developed the following criteria to distinguish an *integrated* or incorporated territory from a *dependency*.

A territory shall be regarded as integrated if all of the following conditions are fulfilled:

(a) There are no constitutional or statutory provisions that deny the subjects of the territory in question—*as* subjects of that territory—the right to participate in the central government in a manner essentially similar to that of all other citizens.

(b) There are no restrictive provisions or institutionalized discriminatory practices based on ethnicity, race, or religion that have the effect of substantially negating these rights. It is understood, in the contrary case, that these provisions are promulgated by the central authority and are territory-specific.

(c) Districts including the national capital or federal district shall be considered as integrated, regardless of the manner in which they are administered.

The second condition requires further comment. What we are trying to get at is the relationship between a geopolitical unit and some central authority. Hence, we want to look only at the relationship between this unit and that authority, not at internal differences that might in some way single it out from other possessions of a central authority. Thus, for example, when Mississippi effectively restricted the franchise to whites, or to the wealthy or literate, while Michigan did not, this did not make Mississippi a dependency, since the difference was in the way the *local* political elite administered its territory, rather than the way it was treated by the *national* government. Furthermore, we are looking at the relation between political units as *political units*. Thus, if laws discriminate against a particular group uniformly throughout the nation but that group happens to be concentrated in a particular district, we would not consider that district a dependency for that reason alone. Such a law establishes a relationship between a central authority and a particular class of citizens, rather than between a central authority and a subordinate political unit. It is often a matter of historical accident that some states have their deprived citizens scattered throughout the population whereas others have them "conveniently" concentrated in territorial blocs. Although the distinction between first- and second-class citizens is an important one, it is not the same as the distinction between integrated and dependent political units.

There are, to be sure, many factors that go into delimiting the boundaries of a metropole, of which political and geographical factors are only two. In particular, cultural and ethnic heterogeneity are often more important than geography in determining whether or not a particular territory should be considered metropolitan. Of course, this is not always the case. Primarily geographical propinquity determined that the Catalans and Basques would remain a part of metropolitan Spain, whereas Spanish Americans, despite their ethnic heritage, would never be considered other than colonists. Similarly, geography maintained the separateness of Canada and the American colonies from a Britain that still encompasses the Welsh and the Scots.

Obviously, it is not always easy to distinguish between a metropole and its dependencies. And this is an especially important problem because of the scores of conflicts engaged in by the Turkish empire and, to a lesser extent, by the Austro-Hungarian, Chinese, and Russian empires. As we have seen earlier, we decided to treat most such conflicts as extra-systemic international wars—wars between a member of the system and a colony, dependency, or protectorate composed of ethnically different people and located at some geographical distance from the given system member's central government. Thus, nineteenth-century wars between Turkey and its province of Bulgaria or between Austria-Hungary and Hungary were not classified as civil wars. For us there is a major difference between the Hungarian Revolution of 1848 and the rebellion in and around Vienna during the same year. Although Austrians and Hungarians were united under the Dual Monarchy, and although, theoretically, the two parts of the kingdom were equal, in practice they were not.

There is no prominent solution to the problem of divining an exact border between extra-systemic and civil wars. We maintain, however, that the aforementioned Hungarian revolution is closer in nature to the Indian revolt against England in 1857, a clear-cut extra-systemic war, than it is to the Viennese Rebellion of 1848, a clear-cut civil war.

Having defined internality, what constitutes an amount of internal military action significant enough to be identified as a major civil war? We could look for a minimum number of combatants, although it is rarely clear who are combatants and who are passive bystanders. We have thus set a combat fatality threshold similar to our threshold for extra-systemic wars. That is, we are interested here only in wars that resulted in at least 1,000 deaths per year. In this case, we count civilian as well as military deaths.

Types of Participants

Our second criterion involves the participants in internal violence. One of the primary actors in any conflict identified as a civil war must be the national government in power at the time hostilities begin. It may, however, often be difficult to determine which factions or elements are in power, as in cases of rival claims for the right to govern all or part of a state. When such claims are advanced, we label as "the government" those forces in de facto control of the nation's institutions, regardless of the legality or illegality of their claim.

On the side of the national government, then, are all those, from national military forces to local police and citizens, who enter the conflict in the name of that government. This coding rule makes practical sense. Histories and other sources often treat the occurrence of internal unrest and even civil wars sketchily, especially for states outside Western Europe. Under these conditions, we could not hope to identify the complete population of all the incidents of internal war that occurred among non-governmental groups, workers, and local police. Further, involvement of the central authority increases not only the seriousness of an internal conflict but the chances of its being recorded by historians. As will be detailed below, the participation of forces fighting for the central government is what distinguishes a civil war from such phenomena as communal violence and regional internal war.

The control of government policy and domestic administration at the outbreak of a war need not extend to the control of the armed forces. Although a government can generally expect its armed forces to defend it, in a civil war the armed forces may turn against the government. The government then must rely on civilian combatants or other branches of the civilian or military infrastructure that remain loyal. Therefore, control of administration and policies does not necessarily mean complete control of armed forces. In fact, loss of the armed forces by the government is often ultimately the key to victory for the rebels (Russell, 1974).

Effective Resistance

Our third criterion is designed to distinguish genuine war situations from massacres, pogroms, purges, and the kind of unopposed slaughter governments occasionally inflict on passive subjects. For us, the concept of war requires that both sides have the ability to inflict death upon each other. This does not mean parity or symmetry, only that the weaker of the antagonists has the means to resist at "some" cost to the stronger force.

Operationalizing this "some" requires the dichotomization of another continuum, always a difficult and arbitrary procedure. An intuitively reasonable ratio seemed at first to be 20 to 1; the stronger forces must sustain at least five percent of the number of fatalities suffered by the weaker forces for us to consider an event to be a war, not a massacre. But in applying this rule, we found cases in which the ratio was higher than 20 to 1 that were qualitatively indistinguishable from wars with a lower ratio. These were cases in which the weaker side was organized to undertake violence and intended to, or did, initiate hostilities but either miscalculated its relative strength so horrendously, or mustered its forces so ineptly, or was answered with such unassailable weaponry (such as aerial bombardment) that it was not able to kill even one of its opponents for every twenty of its own fatalities. In these cases, we felt that the episode should still be identified as a civil war. Reflecting this consideration, we applied the following rule for identifying effective resistance in a civil war: A violent episode of sustained military combat shall be considered a civil war if (a) both sides are initially organized for violent conflict and prepared to resist the attacks of their antagonists, or (b) the weaker side, although initially unprepared, is able to inflict upon the stronger opponents at least five percent of the number of fatalities it sustains.

In reality, such figures are not always readily discernible. In most candidate cases it is clear that the massacred side *did* offer effective resistance, but in some cases we have had to intuit, deduce, or estimate from faint traces in unreliable sources. When we were unable to establish a case for effective resistance, or when there clearly was none, the conflict under consideration was put into the residual category of "massacre."

An important cautionary note is needed in connection with the concepts of massacre and resistance. We identified a number of cases in which a massacre and a civil war were separate but temporally contiguous episodes. Such a situation required the demarcation of the end of war and the onset of a reprisal massacre. While this separation of the events was frequently difficult to determine in terms of specific dates, the conceptual distinction seems unambiguous. When war is over and some kind of cessation of hostilities is formalized or at least recognized, the victorious forces often punctuate their victory with a massacre of the supporters of the vanquished factions. While these massacre victims *individually* put up resistance when possible, the situation is clearly different from the state of war that existed when the vanquished were a military force. Thus, in cases where the reports of internal wars were complete in detailing the scope of large-scale, post-war massacres, we were careful to separate the massacre from the war. But we believed we should retain, as part of the war, the first wave of killing that is an all-too-common reaction to victory.

During the *course* of a civil war, acts of massacre committed by either or both sides are included in the civil war fatality totals because, both for the extinction of the enemy physically and for a kind of psychological warfare, they are an integral part of the war. And even if we wanted to exclude them, acts of terrorism and massacre during a war are not often reported as discrete events, making their separation difficult, or impossible, even if desirable. As testimony to humanity's epidemic violence over the last two centuries, we have kept records of all the massacres we found in the historical works consulted. A partial list of massacres is integrated into the chronological listing of excluded conflicts in Appendix B.

A PROPOSED TYPOLOGY

Using the broad categories discussed above—internality, types of participants, and effective resistance—we proceed to a fuller definition of civil war and other types of internal violence. Our typology is presented in 12.1 in schematic form.

To recapitulate, we define civil war as a sustained military conflict, primarily internal, pitting the central government against an insurgent force capable of effective resistance. The categories "communal violence" and "regional internal war" merit further comment. By the former we mean violent conflict between or among two or more groups, none of which represents governmental authority. "Regional internal war" refers to conflicts confined to a region, state, or province that do not involve military forces of the central government. The action of many "genuine" civil wars may be confined to a specific region in a state or empire where the central government engages rebels; these are, of course, no less civil wars than are conflicts fought in *all* parts of a state's territory. The key criterion here is the participation, or lack thereof, of central government forces.

Before turning to a treatment of internationalized civil wars, we can suggest indicators that would permit further sub-categorization. One potentially interesting sub-category might reflect the degree of organization attained by the rebels in an internal war. Although such divisions would be difficult to determine with precision, the idea of a range of organizational abilities—from the uniformed, trained military to the rake-waving peasant—seems to be suggested, if not always stated, in analyses of civil wars. In other words, if we wanted to distinguish between types of internal war on the basis of the opposition's level of organization, we might apply the *civil war* label to conflict between government forces and organized forces that have their own governmental institutions and effective territorial control. Moving further along the continuum, a government may confront forces that have only a moderately well-organized political and military leadership; this type of war might be called *insurrection,* a label used frequently to describe something "less" (on some unspecified dimension) than civil war. Even further down the scale would be large-scale violence with little or no military organization and minimal organized leadership. This might be called *riot,* particularly if it is contained in a short time span and a relatively small area. The drawbacks in making such divisions are that the data are so unreliable as to make the distinction between highly and poorly organized often mere guesswork; further, many civil wars involve multiple participants with varying degrees of organization.

12.1 A Typology of War

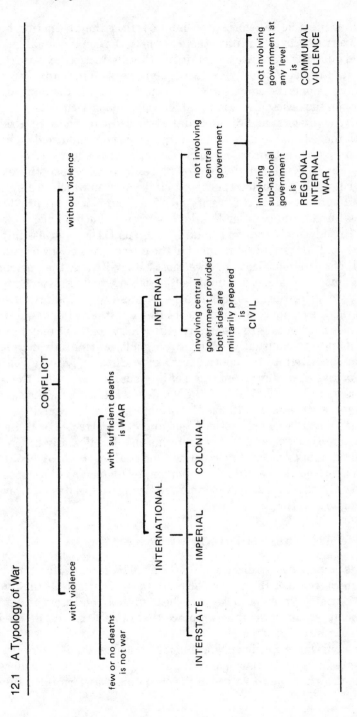

Another possible categorization might reflect the distinction between overt and covert military tactics or between conventional military and guerrilla wars. We do not utilize this distinction because the
categories are not mutually excusive, civil wars often being fought
both ways. Along the same lines, one could subdivide the civil war
category on the bases of weaponry and number of participants.

Finally, civil wars can be, and usually are, defined and categorized
with reference to immediate and long-range purposes and goals. This
procedure has a certain *prima facie* attractiveness but a number of
serious drawbacks as well. In the first place, as we have seen, there is
no consistent body of theory relating to civil war from which we might
derive categories among classes of goals. Since our object is to provide
empirical underpinnings for the development of such a theory, we
thought it advisable to avoid making dubious theoretical assumptions. Second, any simple statement of the purpose of a civil war runs
the risk of oversimplification. In almost all civil wars, the various
participants have a great number of goals, to which is attached a
hierarchy of priorities. The specification of these goals and priorities
is necessarily a complex—and, in most cases, a virtually impossible—
task. Indeed, different groups in a revolutionary coalition may have
different and often mutually incompatible goals, uniting only in their
common opposition to the central authority. Elites may have goals
and priorities that differ from those of the masses who follow them.
(See, for example, Tilly, 1964, on the Vendée in France, as well as his
more general treatment, 1965.) Furthermore, in a brief civil war,
goals may never be clearly articulated, and in a protracted one, they
may undergo serious and frequent mutations. Finally, any scheme
that did attempt to specify the purposes and goals of civil wars would
be open to serious biases, both in reporting by historians and in coding by us. For these reasons, we eschewed trying to classify civil wars
according to goals or purposes.

Internationalized Civil War

To this point, we have discussed civil war in its simplest form, that
of a bilateral conflict. But of the 106 civil wars on our list, 21 involve
outside nations. Because these wars bear directly on international
behavior, it is important that we place them in a carefully defined
niche in our war typology.

When civil war erupts in one nation, it is seldom without interest to
other states in the international community. Frequently one or more
of these states becomes involved in the civil war, transforming it into

an internationalized civil war. Such intervention often leads to an increase in the intensity of the conflict (Pearson, 1974). The indicator we have chosen for involvement, or foreign intervention, is a highly visible (and therefore practical from the coding aspect) form of intervention—direct military participation of such a magnitude that either 1,000 troops are committed to the combat zone or, if the force is smaller or the size unknown, 100 deaths are sustained. By choosing a physical indicator of military participation, we ignore even the most blatant cases of financial and material intervention, but at the same time we are not required to make tenuous judgments about clandestine involvements.

Intervention by foreigners takes many forms (Little, 1975; Ayoob, 1980), but it varies along two principal dimensions: by whom and for whom. With respect to the former, the intervention may be carried out by the official military personnel of a foreign national government, either openly or secretly, or by irregulars or volunteers. This dimension is, as are so many others, a continuum that we must once again dichotomize as "official" or "unofficial" participation. We need to make this distinction to compute the incidence of national participation in civil wars for which only official interventions are counted.

Regarding the other dimension of intervention, the "for whom," an outside force can intervene for the government engaged in the civil war or for its opponents. We regard this distinction as important, especially for the final coding rule discussed below. Our intervention indicator must describe actual participation on the side of, for the *direct* aid and advancement of the cause of, one side or the other.

One final coding rule might be challenged by some. In some instances, the Vietnam War being an obvious example, the international aspect of the war comes to overshadow the internal aspect. It often happens that the arrival of foreign armies, especially on the side of the opponents, means that the internal factions do less of the fighting and the war takes on the combat appearance of an interstate war. When does a civil war end and an interstate war begin? And does an internationalized civil war belong to the interstate or civil category? We studied this matter carefully and finally arrived at a solution that represents a compromise, as many coding decisions must.

First, when the intervention in a civil war is on the side of the government, the war becomes an internationalized civil war but is still considered in the civil war group; it cannot meet our definition of interstate or even extra-systemic war. It is possible, however, as in Vietnam, that a third state might enter the fray on the rebel's side and thus convert the conflict into an interstate war. Thus, the United

States, intervening on the government's side in 1961, made the Vietnam Civil War an internationalized civil war, but when it began bombing North Vietnam in 1965 and when North Vietnam retaliated with increased military infiltration, that war took on the coloration of an interstate war with the bulk of the fighting being done by the United States and North Vietnam, not South Vietnam and the National Liberation Front.

More simply, when the intervener in a civil war comes to the aid of the opponents of the legitimate government, and when that intervener comes to play the dominant role in the war, an internationalized civil war becomes an interstate war. For example, a civil war smouldered in Spain from 1821 through 1823. When the French invaded Spain in 1823 in order to put the Bourbons on the throne, they were launching an interstate war, since their clients were entirely dependent upon the French army for military assistance; there was little native insurrectionary activity by the time the French marched on Madrid.

In one contrary recent case, Afghanistan in 1979, although the Soviet Union came into a civil war on the side of the *government,* its entry also transformed the conflict into an international war because the government in Kabul became, almost at once, a puppet of Moscow and the insurgents a sort of national legitimate authority.

To reiterate this potentially confusing coding rule, an internationalized civil war is still considered a civil war unless an intervener (a) joins the rebel's side and (b) comes to play the dominant role against the legitimate government (and its allies, if any). In that case, the conflict will be coded as a civil war and then become transformed into an interstate war.

SUMMARY

We have presented our basic typology of internal war and defined in detail those wars we label civil and internationalized civil war. We turn now to our list of civil wars since the Congress of Vienna.

CHAPTER 13

The Qualifying Wars and Their Quantitative Attributes

Here we examine the results of our efforts described in the preceding chapter. The basic data presented will be used in all subsequent analyses in this section.

THE BASIC DATA

In 13.1, we present a simple listing of all the civil wars, with three-digit code numbers and their dates, in chronological order; an "I" following the date signifies the intervention of another power. We have chosen not to use the popular names of some of the wars (The War Between the States, The War for the Liberation of ...) because all contenders and historians do not agree on one name for each war. Instead, we have merely listed the name of the country in which the civil war took place. Note that in the case of Argentina in 1841 and China in 1860, the wars began before these nations satisfied our criteria for inclusion in the interstate system.

A more comprehensive table, 13.2 displays our basic data. We show again, in chronological order, the war number, the nation number of the country in which the war was fought, and the name of that nation. Nations that intervened on the government's side are listed, indented, directly below the nation. Nations that intervened on the *insurgents'* side are listed in a comparable fashion below the name of the insurgent. The most common name given to the opposition appears either immediately below the nation name or following the names of those nations that intervened on the government's side.

In column 1, we identify the victor in the war. In four cases—Spain in 1823, Argentina in 1852, Pakistan in 1971, and Vietnam in 1975—the winner was determined only after the war became international. Four of the wars were ongoing as of December 31, 1980: The war in

13.1   Civil Wars Listed Chronologically, with War Number, Name, and
       Years (N = 106)

601.SPAIN (1821-1823)	754.AFGHANISTAN (1924-1925)
604.TURKEY/OTTOMAN EMPIRE (1826)	757.CHINA (1926-1928) I
607.PORTUGAL (1829-1834) I	760.MEXICO (1926-1930)
610.FRANCE (1830)	763.AFGHANISTAN (1928-1929)
613.MEXICO (1832)	766.CHINA (1929-1930)
616.SPAIN (1834-1840) I	769.CHINA (1930-1935)
619.COLOMBIA (1840-1842)	772.BRAZIL (1932)
622.ARGENTINA (1841-1851) I	775.SPAIN (1934)
625.SPAIN (1847-1849)	778.SPAIN (1936-1939) I
628.TWO SICILIES (1848-1849)	781.GREECE (1944-1949) I
631.FRANCE (1848)	784.CHINA (1946-1950)
634.AUSTRIA-HUNGARY (1848)	787.PARAGUAY (1947)
637.CHILE (1851)	790.YEMEN ARAB REPUBLIC (1948)
640.PERU (1853-1855)	793.COSTA RICA (1948)
643.PERU (1856-1858)	796.COLOMBIA (1948)
646.MEXICO (1858-1861)	799.BURMA (1948-1951)
649.VENEZUELA (1859-1863)	802.COLOMBIA (1949-1962)
652.CHINA (1860-1864) I	805.INDONESIA (1950)
653.CHINA (1860-1868)	808.PHILIPPINES (1950-1952)
654.CHINA (1860-1872)	811.BOLIVIA (1952)
655.COLOMBIA (1860-1862)	814.INDONESIA (1953)
658.UNITED STATES OF AMERICA(1861-1865)	817.GUATEMALA (1954)
661.ARGENTINA (1863)	820.ARGENTINA (1955)
664.ARGENTINA (1866-1867)	823.INDONESIA (1956-1960)
667.VENEZUELA (1868-1871)	826.LEBANON (1958) I
670.SPAIN (1868)	829.CUBA (1958-1959)
673.ARGENTINA (1870-1871)	832.IRAQ (1959)
676.FRANCE (1871)	835.VIETNAM, REPUBLIC OF (1960-1965) I
679.SPAIN (1872-1876)	838.ZAIRE (CONGO,KINSHASA) (1960-1965) I
682.COLOMBIA (1876-1877)	841.LAOS (1960-1962)
685.JAPAN (1877)	844.ALGERIA (1962-1963)
688.ARGENTINA (1880)	847.YEMEN ARAB REPUBLIC (1962-1969) I
691.COLOMBIA (1884-1885)	850.LAOS (1963-1973) I
694.CHILE (1891)	853.SUDAN (1963-1972)
697.BRAZIL (1893-1894)	856.RWANDA (1963-1964)
700.BRAZIL (1893-1894)	859.DOMINICAN REPUBLIC (1965) I
703.PERU (1894-1895)	862.UGANDA (1966)
706.BRAZIL (1896-1897)	865.CHINA (1967-1968)
709.COLOMBIA (1899-1903)	868.NIGERIA (1967-1970)
712.URUGUAY (1904)	871.KAMPUCHEA (CAMBODIA) (1970-1975) I
715.USSR (RUSSIA) (1905-1906)	874.JORDAN (1970) I
718.RUMANIA (1907)	877.GUATEMALA (1970-1971)
721.MOROCCO (1907-1908) I	880.PAKISTAN (1971)
724.IRAN (PERSIA) (1908-1909) I	883.SRI LANKA (CEYLON) (1971)
727.MEXICO (1910-1920)	886.BURUNDI (1972)
730.MOROCCO (1911) I	889.PHILIPPINES (1972---)
733.PARAGUAY (1911-1912)	892.ZIMBABWE (RHODESIA) (1972-1979)
736.CHINA (1911)	895.LEBANON (1975-1976) I
739.CHINA (1913)	898.ANGOLA (1975---) I
742.CHINA (1914)	901.AFGHANISTAN (1978-1979)
745.USSR (RUSSIA) (1917-1920) I	904.IRAN (PERSIA) (1978-1979)
748.HUNGARY (1919-1920)	907.NICARAGUA (1978-1979)
751.HONDURAS (1924)	910.EL SALVADOR (1979---)

NOTE: I indicates an internationalized war.

the Philippines that began in 1972, the war in Angola that began in 1975, the war in El Salvador that began in 1979, and the international phase of the war in Afghanistan that began in 1978 and ended its primarily civil phase when the Soviet Union entered the fray on December 22, 1979.

In column 2 we show the dates of the war (with those dates in which we have limited confidence in parentheses), and the dates for interveners. In column 3 is the duration in months, followed by magnitude

(text continued page 233)

13.2 List of Civil Wars with Participants, Duration, Magnitude, Severity, and Intensity

Number and Name of War / Participants and Code Number	Winner (Intervention if any)	Dates of War / National Dates When Different	Duration in Months	Magnitude in Nation Months	Severity in Battle Deaths	Population 1000s pre-war)	Battle Deaths per 1000 Nation Month	Battle Deaths per 1000 Nation Population
601. SPAIN VS. ROYALISTS	OPP+	(12/1)/1821-4/6/1823	16.2	16.2	7000	11498	432.1	.6
604. TURKEY/OTTOMAN EMPIRE VS. JANISSARIES	GOV	6/14/1826-9/(30)/1826	3.6	3.6	6000	31036	1666.7	.2
607. PORTUGAL	GOV	(7/1)/1829-7/5/1834	60.2	96.2	20100	27184	333.9	.7
235. PORTUGAL				60.2	20000	3049	332.2	6.6
200. UNITED KINGDOM	(GOV)	(7/1)/1831-(7/1)/1834		36.0	100	24135	2.8	.0
VS. CONSERVATIVES								
610. FRANCE VS. LIBERALS	OPP	7/25/1830-7/29/1830	.2	.2	1700	32370	8500.0	.1
613. MEXICO VS. LIBERALS	GOV	1/2/1832-12/11/1832	11.3	11.3	4000	6448	354.0	.6
616. SPAIN	GOV	7/(15)/1834-7/(15)/1840	72.0	109.9	32650	74275	453.5	.4
230. SPAIN				72.0	30000	12681	416.7	2.4
200. UNITED KINGDOM	(GOV)	7/10/1835-(9/1)/1837		25.8	2500	25134	96.9	.1
220. FRANCE	(GOV)	10/(31)/1835-7/(1)/1836		8.1	100	33260	12.3	.0
235. PORTUGAL	(GOV)	10/15/1835-2/15/1836		4.0	50	3200	12.5	.0
VS. CARLISTS								
619. COLOMBIA VS. PROGRESSIVES	OPP	7/(15)/1840-7/(15)/1842	24.0	24.0	4000	1887	166.7	2.1
622. *160. ARGENTINA	OPP+	(1/1)/1841-12/6/1842	101.3	198.3	10200	63630	100.7	.2
*160. ARGENTINA		1/(15)/1845-7/18/1851	101.3	101.3	10000	694	98.7	14.4
VS. UNITARIOS								
200. UNITED KINGDOM	(OPP)	1/(15)/1845-7/(15)/1847		30.0	100	27776	3.3	.0
220. FRANCE	(OPP)	1/(15)/1845-8/(15)/1850		67.0	100	35160	1.5	.0
625. SPAIN VS. CARLISTS	GOV	5/(15)/1847-5/(11)/1849	23.6	23.6	3000	13986	127.1	.2

13.2 (Continued)

Number and Name of War / Participants and Code Number	Winner (intervention if any)	Dates of War / National Dates When Different	Duration in Months	Magnitude in Nation Months	Severity in Battle Deaths	Population 1000s pre-war	Battle Deaths per 1000 Nation Month	Battle Deaths per 1000 Population
628. *329 TWO SICILIES VS. LIBERALS	GOV	1/12/1848-1/27/1848 9/3/1848-5/(15)/1849	8.9	8.9	1000	8714	112.4	.1
631. 220 FRANCE VS. REPUBLICANS	OPP	2/22/1848-6/26/1848	4.2	4.2	3000	35520	714.3	.1
634. 300 AUSTRIA-HUNGARY VS. LIBERALS	GOV	3/13/1848-10/31/1848	7.6	7.6	3500	36334	460.5	.1
637. *155 CHILE VS. LIBERALS	GOV	9/(15)/1851-12/(15)/1851	3.0	3.0	3000	1332	1000.0	2.3
640. *135 PERU VS. LIBERALS	GOV	12/21/1853-1/7/1855	12.6	12.6	4000	1960	317.5	2.0
643. *135 PERU VS. CONSERVATIVES	GOV	10/31/1856-3/7/1858	16.3	16.3	3000	2039	184.0	1.5
646. * 70 MEXICO VS. LIBERALS	OPP	2/(15)/1858-1/(1)/1861	34.6	34.6	8000	8515	231.2	.9
649. *101 VENEZUELA VS. LIBERALS	OPP	2/(1)/1859-(12/31)/1863	58.9	58.9	20000	1553	339.6	12.9
652. *710 CHINA *710 CHINA 200 UNITED KINGDOM VS. TAIPINGS	GOV (GOV)	1/1/1860-7/(31)/1864 3/(1)/1862-8/(1)/1862	55.0	60.0 55.0 5.0	2000025 2000000 25	466703 437458 29245	36364.1 36363.6 5.0	4.3 4.6 4.0
653. *710 CHINA VS NIENS	GOV	1/1/1860-8/16/1868	103.5	103.5	75000	437458	724.6	.2
654. *710 CHINA VS MIAOS	GOV	1/1/1860-5/(1)/1872	148.0	148.0	75000	437458	506.8	.2
655. *100 COLOMBIA VS. LIBERALS	GOV	5/(15)/1860-10/(15)/1862	29.0	29.0	2500	2457	86.2	1.0
658. * 2 UNITED STATES OF AMERICA VS CONFEDERACY	GOV	4/10/1861-4/9/1865	48.0	48.0	650000	32194	13541.7	20.2

Number and Name of War Participants and Code Number	Winner (intervention if any)	Dates of War National Dates When Different	Duration in Months	Magnitude in Nation Months	Severity in Battle Deaths	Population in 1000s (pre-war)	Battle Deaths per Nation Month	Battle Deaths per 1000 Population
661. *160 ARGENTINA VS MONTONEROS	GOV	4/2/1863-11/12/1863	7.4	7.4	1000	1568	135.1	.6
664. *160 ARGENTINA VS FEDERALISTS	GOV	12/(15)/1866-10/(15)/1867	10	10.0	1000.0	1741	100.0	.6
667. *101 VENEZUELA VS CONSERVATIVES	OPP	1/11/1868-8/14/1868 8/14/1869-1/7/1871	23.9	23.9	3000	1768	125.5	1.7
670. 230 SPAIN VS LIBERALS	OPP	9/19/1868-9/29/1868	.4	.4	1600	16383	4000.0	.1
673. *160 ARGENTINA VS ENTRE RIOS PROVINCE	GOV	5/20/1870-3/13/1871	9.8	9.8	1500	1916	153.1	.8
676. 220 FRANCE VS COMMUNARDS	GOV	4/2/1871-5/29/1871	1.9	1.9	20000	36190	10526.3	.6
679. 230 SPAIN VS CARLISTS	GOV	4/20/1872-2/20/1876	46.0	46.0	7000	16318	152.2	.4
682. *100 COLOMBIA VS LIBERALS	GOV	11/(15)/1876-(7/1)/1877	7.6	7.6	1000	3034	131.6	.3
685. *740 JAPAN VS SATSUMAS	GOV	1/29/1877-9/24/1877	7.9	7.9	14000	35870	1772.2	.4
688. *160 ARGENTINA VS BUENOS AIRES	GOV	6/(15)/1880-7/21/1880	1.2	1.2	1000	2494	833.3	.4
691. *100 COLOMBIA VS LIBERALS	GOV	11/(15)/1884-8/(15)/1885	9.0	9.0	1000	3372	111.1	.3
694. *155 CHILE VS CONGRESSISTS	OPP	1/7/1891-8/29/1891	7.8	7.8	5000	2636	641.0	1.9
697. *140 BRAZIL VS RIO GRANDE DO SUL	GOV	2/2/1893-(8/31)/1894	19.0	19.0	1500	14982	78.9	.1

(continued)

225

13.2 (Continued)

Number and Name of War / Participants and Code Number	Winner (intervention if any)	Dates of War / National Dates When Different	Duration in Months	Magnitude in Nation Months	Severity in Battle Deaths	Population 1000s (pre-war)	Battle Deaths per Nation Month	Battle Deaths per 1000 Population
700. *140.BRAZIL VS.NAVAL ROYALISTS	GOV	9/6/1893-3/11/1894	6.2	6.2	1000	14982	161.3	.1
703. *135.PERU VS.LIBERALS	OPP	10/(15)/1894-3/19/1895	5.2	5.2	4000	3365	769.2	1.2
706. *140.BRAZIL VS.CANUDOS	GOV	10/(1)/1896-10/5/1897	12.2	12.2	5000	15751	409.8	.3
709. *100.COLOMBIA VS.LIBERALS	GOV	9/(1)/1899-6/(15)/1903	45.5	45.5	100000	4110	2197.8	24.3
712. *165.URUGUAY VS.BLANCOS	GOV	1/1/1904-9/1/1904	8.0	8.0	1000	936	125.0	1.1
715. 365.USSR (RUSSIA) VS.WORKERS/PEASANTS	GOV	1/22/1905-1/(1)/1906	11.4	11.4	1000	147147	87.7	.0
718. 360.RUMANIA VS.PEASANTS	GOV	3/(15)/1907-4/(30)/1907	1.5	1.5	2000	6684	1333.3	.3
721. *600.MOROCCO *600.MOROCCO 220.FRANCE VS.FEZ CAIDS	GOV (GOV)	8/1/1907-8/19/1908 8/7/1907-6/(15)/1908	12.6	22.9 12.6 10.3	1100 1000 100	43949 4628 39321	87.3 79.4 9.7	.0 .2 .0
718. 360.RUMANIA VS.PEASANTS	GOV	3/(15)/1907-4/(30)/1907	1.5	1.5	2000	6684	1333.3	.3

Number and Name of War Participants and Code Number	Winner (intervention if any)	Dates of War National Dates When Different	Duration in Months	Magnitude in Nation Months	Severity in Battle Deaths	Population 1000s pre-war	Battle Deaths per Nation Month	Battle Deaths per 1000 Population
724. *630.IRAN (PERSIA)								
*630.IRAN (PERSIA)	DPP	6/23/1908-7/17/1909	12.9	15.5	1100	164022	85.3	.0
365.USSR (RUSSIA)	(GOV)	4/(30)/1909-7/17/1909		12.9	1000	4663	77.5	.2
VS.CONSTITUTIONALISTS				2.6	100	159359	38.5	.0
727. * 70.MEXICO	DPP	11/20/1910-7/(15)/1914 12/(11)/1914-5/21/1920	109.5	109.5	250000	14850	2283.1	16.8
VS. LIBERALS AND RADICALS								
730. *600.MOROCCO	GOV	1/(15)/1911-6/10/1911	4.9	5.9	1650	44062	336.7	.0
*600.MOROCCO	(GOV)			4.9	1500	4460	306.1	.3
220.FRANCE		5/11/1911-6/10/1911		1.0	150	39602	150.0	.0
VS.FEZ CAIDS								
733. *150.PARAGUAY	DPP	7/(15)/1911-5/11/1912	9.9	9.9	2000	548	202.0	3.6
VS.LIBERALS								
736. 710.CHINA	DPP	10/11/1911-12/(31)/1911	2.7	2.7	1000	495309	370.4	.0
VS.REPUBLICANS								
739. 710.CHINA	GOV	7/12/1913-9/(1)/1913	1.7	1.7	5000	497728	2941.2	.0
VS.REPUBLICANS								
742. 710.CHINA	GOV	3/(15)/1914-9/(15)/1914	6.0	6.0	5000	320650	833.3	.0
VS.PAI-LINGS								
745. 365.USSR (RUSSIA)	GOV	12/9/1917-10/(15)/1920	34.2	118.9	502225	371962	14684.9	1.4
365.USSR (RUSSIA)				34.2	500000	124007	14619.9	4.0
VS.ANTI-BOLSHEVIKS								
200.UNITED KINGDOM	(OPP)	6/23/1918-3/(15)/1920		20.8	350	44439	16.8	.0
220.FRANCE	(OPP)	6/23/1918-9/30/1919		15.3	50	39000	3.3	.0
2.UNITED STATES OF AMERICA	(OPP)	7/(1)/1918-4/20/1920		21.7	275	105710	12.7	.0
740.JAPAN	(OPP)	8/3/1918-10/15/1920		26.4	1500	55473	56.8	.0
375.FINLAND	(OPP)	4/(15)/1919-4/(30)/1919		.5	50	3333	100.0	.0
748. 310.HUNGARY	DPP	3/25/1919-2/(15)/1920	10.7	10.7	4000	7875	373.8	.5
VS.ANTI-COMMUNISTS								
751. 91.HONDURAS	DPP	2/9/1924-3/31/1924	1.8	1.8	1000	815	555.6	1.2
VS.CONSERVATIVES								

(continued)

13.2 (Continued)

	Number and Name of War Participants and Code Number	Winner (Intervention if any)	Dates of War National Dates When Different	Duration in Months	Magnitude in Nation Months	Severity in Battle Deaths	Population 1000s pre-war	Battle Deaths per Nation Month	Battle Deaths per 1000 Population
787.	150 PARAGUAY VS LEFTISTS	GOV	3/7/1947-8/20/1947	5.5	5.5	1000	1305	181.8	.8
790.	678 YEMEN ARAB REPUBLIC VS YAHYA FAMILY	OPP	2/17/1948-3/20/1948	1.1	1.1	4000	3192	3636.4	1.3
793.	94 COSTA RICA VS NATIONAL UNION PARTY	OPP	3/12/1948-4/17/1948	1.2	1.2	2000	756	1666.7	2.6
796.	100 COLOMBIA VS CONSERVATIVES	GOV	4/9/1948-4/12/1948	.1	.1	1400	10845	14000.0	.1
799.	775 BURMA VS KARENS	GOV	9/(15)/1948-(7/31)/1951	34.6	34.6	8000	18015	231.2	.4
802.	100 COLOMBIA VS LIBERALS	GOV	9/(15)/1949-(12/31)/1962	159.6	159.6	300000	11087	1879.7	27.1
805.	850 INDONESIA VS MOLUCCANS	GOV	5/31/1950-11/3/1950	5.1	5.1	5000	76000	980.4	.1
808.	840 PHILIPPINES VS HUKS	GOV	(9/1)/1950-(7/1)/1952	22.0	22.0	9000	20316	409.1	.4
811.	145 BOLIVIA VS LEFTISTS	OPP	4/9/1952-4/11/1952	.1	.1	1500	3070	15000.0	.5
814.	850 INDONESIA VS DARUL ISLAM	GOV	9/20/1953-11/23/1953	2.1	2.1	1000	80451	476.2	.0
817.	90 GUATEMALA VS CONSERVATIVES	OPP	6/8/1954-6/30/1954	.8	.8	1000	3159	1250.0	.3
820.	160 ARGENTINA VS ARMY	OPP	6/(15)/1955-9/19/1955	3.2	3.2	3000	18972	937.5	.2
823.	850 INDONESIA VS LEFTISTS	GOV	12/(15)/1956-(12/31)/1960	48.6	48.6	30000	85654	617.3	.4
826.	660 LEBANON 660 LEBANON 2 UNITED STATES OF AMERICA VS LEFTISTS	GOV (GOV)	5/9/1958-9/(15)/1958 7/16/1958-9/(15)/1958	4.2	6.2 4.2 2.0	1400 1400 0	176318 2082 174236	333.3 333.3 0	.0 .7 .0

Number and Name of War Participants and Code Number	Winner (Intervention if any)	Dates of War National Dates When Different	Duration in Months	Magnitude in Nation Months	Severity in Battle Deaths	Population 1000s pre-war	Battle Deaths per Nation Month	Battle Deaths per 1000 Population
754. 700.AFGHANISTAN VS.ANTI-REFORMISTS	GOV	3/(15)/1924-1/(15)/1925	10.0	10.0	1500	7591	150.0	.2
757. 710.CHINA	OPP	7/(1)/1926-6/(30)/1928	24.0	36.0	10500	497411	437.5	.0
740.JAPAN	(OPP)	6/(1)/1927-6/(1)/1928		24.0	10000	436094	416.7	.0
VS.KUOMINTANG				12.0	500	61317	41.7	.0
760. 70.MEXICO VS.CRISTEROS	GOV	8/(31)/1926-6/(15)/1930	45.5	45.5	10000	15468	219.8	.6
763. 700.AFGHANISTAN VS.ANTI-REFORMISTS	OPP	11/10/1928-10/(15)/1929	11.2	11.2	7500	8131	669.6	.9
766. 710.CHINA VS WAR-LORDS	GOV	3/(1)/1929-10/13/1930	19.4	19.4	75000	478398	3866.0	.2
769. 710.CHINA VS.COMMUNISTS	GOV	11/(15)/1930-10/(15)/1935	59.0	59.0	200000	482048	3389.8	.4
772. 140.BRAZIL VS.PADLISTAS	GOV	6/9/1932-8/31/1932	2.8	2.8	1000	34957	357.1	.0
775. 230.SPAIN VS. ASTURIAS MINERS	GOV	10/4/1934-10/8/1934	.2	.2	1300	24349	6500.0	.1
778. 230.SPAIN	OPP	7/18/1936-3/29/1939	32.4	127.5	658300	142609	20317.9	4.6
VS.FASCISTS				32.4	650000	24810	20061.7	26.2
235.PORTUGAL	(OPP)	8/(1)/1936-3/29/1939		32.0	2000	7300	62.5	.3
255.GERMANY/PRUSSIA	(OPP)	8/27/1936-3/29/1939		31.1	300	67300	9.6	.0
325.ITALY/SARDINIA	(OPP)	7/30/1936-3/29/1939		32.0	6000	43150	187.5	.1
781. 350.GREECE	GOV	12/3/1944-2/12/1945 11/(15)/1946-10/16/1949	37.4	38.6 37.4	160135 160000	56168 7456	4281.7 4278.1	2.9 21.5
350.GREECE 200.UNITED KINGDOM VS.COMMUNISTS	(GOV)	12/5/1944-1/11/1945		1.2	135	48712	112.5	.0
784. 710.CHINA VS.COMMUNISTS	OPP	3/(15)/1946-4/21/1950	49.2	49.2	1000000	455592	20325.2	2.2

(continued)

13.2 (Continued)

	Number and Name of War / Participants and Code Number	Winner (intervention if any)	Dates of War / National Dates When Different	Duration in Months	Magnitude in Nation Months	Severity in Battle Deaths	Population 1000s pre-war	Battle Deaths per Nation Month	Battle Deaths per 1000 Population
829.	40 CUBA VS.CASTROITES	OPP	(6/15)/1958-1/2/1959	6.6	6.6	5000	6523	757.6	.8
832.	645.IRAQ	GOV	3/6/1959-3/10/1959	.2	.2	2000	6952	10000.0	.3
	VS. SHAMMAR TRIBE AND PRO-WESTERN OFFICERS								
835.	817.VIETNAM REPUBLIC OF	OPP+	(1/1)/1960-2/6/1965	61.2	110.4	302000	197842	4934.6	1.5
	817 VIETNAM REPUBLIC OF				61.2	300000	14100	4902.0	21.3
	2 UNITED STATES OF AMERICA	(GOV)	(1/1)/1961-2/6/1965		49.2	2000	183742	40.7	.0
	VS.NLF								
838.	490.ZAIRE (CONGO,KINSHASA)	GOV	7/4/1960-9/(1)/1965	61.9	64.3	100050	23292	1616.3	4.3
	490 ZAIRE (CONGO,KINSHASA)		7/4/1960-9/(1)/1960		61.9	100000	14139	1615.5	7.1
	211.BELGIUM	(GOV)	11/7/1964-11/22/1964		2.4	50	9153	20.8	.0
	VS. KATANGA AND LEFTISTS								
841.	812 LAOS VS PATHET LAO	GOV	10/(15)/1960-7/(15)/1962	21.0	21.0	5000	959	238.1	5.2
844.	615 ALGERIA VS.FORMER REBEL LEADERS	GOV	7/28/1962-1/(15)/1963	5.6	5.6	1500	10920	267.9	.1
847.	678 YEMEN ARAB REPUBLIC	GOV	11/(15)/1962-9/3/1969	81.7	140.3	101000	31900	1236.2	3.2
	678.YEMEN ARAB REPUBLIC				81.7	100000	4640	1224.0	21.6
	651.EGYPT/UAR	(GOV)	(12/15)/1962-(10/31)/1967		58.6	1000	27260	17.1	.0
	VS.ROYALISTS								
850.	812 LAOS	OPP	4/19/1963-2/(15)/1973	117.9	315.5	18500	213340	156.9	.1
	812 LAOS	(GOV)	5/(15)/1964-2/(1)/1973		117.9	15000	2510	127.2	6.0
	2 UNITED STATES OF AMERICA				104.6	500	191830	4.8	.0
	VS PATHET LAO	(OPP)	5/(15)/1965-2/(15)/1973						
	816 VIETNAM DEMOCRATIC REP				93.0	3000	19000	32.3	.2
853.	625 SUDAN VS.ANYA NYA	GOV	10/(1)/1963-2/28/1972	100.9	100.9	250000	12940	2477.7	19.3
856.	517.RWANDA VS.WATUSI	GOV	11/(15)/1963-2/6/1964	2.8	2.8	2500	3060	892.9	.8

No.	Number and Name of War / Participants and Code Number	Winner (Intervention if any)	Dates of War	National Dates When Different	Duration in Months	Magnitude in Nation Months	Severity in Battle Deaths	Population 1000s pre-war	Battle Deaths per Nation Month	Battle Deaths per 1000 Population
859.	42 DOMINICAN REPUBLIC									
	42 DOMINICAN REPUBLIC	GOV	4/25/1965-9/(1)/1965		4.3	8.4	2526	197760	587.4	.0
	2 UNITED STATES OF AMERICA	(GOV)		4/29/1965-9/(1)/1965		4.3	2500	3520	581.4	.7
	VS LEFTISTS					4.1	26	194240	6.3	.0
862.	500 UGANDA	GOV	5/23/1966-6/(1)/1966		.3	.3	2000	8833	6666.7	.2
	VS BUGANDA TRIBE									
865.	710 CHINA	GOV	1/(15)/1967-9/(1)/1968		19.6	19.6	50000	733540	2551.0	.1
	VS RED GUARD									
868.	475 NIGERIA	GOV	7/6/1967-1/12/1970		30.2	30.2	1000000	51120	33112.6	19.6
	VS BIAFRANS									
871.	811 KAMPUCHEA (CAMBODIA)	DPP	3/20/1970-3/(15)/1975		59.9	176.6	156000	250980	2604.3	.6
	811 KAMPUCHEA (CAMBODIA)	(GOV)				59.9	150000	6700	2504.2	22.4
	2 UNITED STATES OF AMERICA	(GOV)		5/1/1970-1/(1)/1973		32.0	500	204800	15.6	.0
	817 VIETNAM REPUBLIC OF	(GOV)		3/27/1970-4/30/1972		25.1	5000	18330	199.2	.3
	VS KHMER ROUGE									
	816 VIETNAM DEMOCRATIC REP	(OPP)	3/30/1970-3/(15)/1975			59.6	500	21150	8.4	.0
874.	663 JORDAN	GOV	9/17/1970-9/24/1970		.3	.4	2100	8560	7000.0	.2
	663 JORDAN			9/20/1970-9/23/1970		.3	2000	2310	6666.7	.9
	VS PALESTINIANS									
	652 SYRIA	(OPP)	9/20/1970-9/23/1970			.1	100	6250	1000.0	.0
877.	90 GUATEMALA	GOV	11/(15)/1970-9/(15)/1971		10.0	10.0	1000	5190	100.0	.2
	VS LEFTISTS									
880.	770 PAKISTAN	DPP+	3/25/1971-12/2/1971		8.3	8.3	500000	116589	60240.9	4.3
	VS BENGALIS									
883.	780 SRI LANKA (CEYLON)	GOV	4/6/1971-5/16/1971		1.3	1.3	2000	13000	1538.5	.2
	VS JANATHA VIMUKTHI PERAMUNA									
886.	516 BURUNDI	GOV	4/30/1972-5/25/1972		.9	.9	50000	3403	55555.5	14.7
	VS HUTU									
889.	840 PHILIPPINES	ON	10/(11)/1972-12/31/1980		99.0	99.0	9000	39040	90.9	.2
	VS NEW PEOPLE'S ARMY									

(continued)

13.2 (Continued)

Number and Name of War / Participants and Code Number	Winner (intervention if any)	Dates of War / National Dates When Different	Duration in Months	Magnitude in Nation Months	Severity in Battle Deaths	Population in 1000s pre-war	Battle Deaths per Nation Month	Battle Deaths per 1000 Population
892. 552 ZIMBABWE (RHODESIA) VS. PATRIOTIC FRONT	OPP	12/28/1972-12/28/1979	84.0	84.0	12000	5512	142.9	2.2
895. 660 LEBANON	GOV	4/13/1975-10/21/1976	18.3	24.7	25000	10185	1366.1	2.5
652 SYRIA	(GOV)	4/9/1976-10/21/1976		18.3	24000	2589	1311.5	9.3
LEFTISTS				6.4	1000	7596	156.3	.1
898. 540 ANGOLA	ON	11/11/1975-12/31/1980	61.7	123.4	9000	15605	145.9	.6
40 CUBA	(GOV)			61.7	7000	6315	113.5	1.1
VS.UNITA				61.7	2000	9290	32.5	.2
901. 700 AFGHANISTAN VS. MOSLEM REBELS	ON+	6/(1)/1978-12/21/1979	18.6	18.6	10000	21050	537.6	.5
904. 630 IRAN (PERSIA) VS. ANTI-SHAH COALITION	OPP	9/3/1978-2/(15)/1979	5.4	5.4	7500	37900	1388.9	.2
907. 93 NICARAGUA VS. SANDINIST NATIONAL LIBERATION FRONT	OPP	10/(1)/1978-7/18/1979	9.5	9.5	35000	2340	3684.2	15.0
910. 92 EL SALVADOR VS. DEMOCRATIC SALVADOREAN FRONT	ON	7/(1)/1979-12/31/1980	18.0	18.0	10000	4714	555.6	2.1

* next to the nation number indicates that the nation was not a member of the central sub-system (1816-1919) at the time war began.
+ after GOV, OPP indicates that GOV or OPP won after the war became interstate.
Dates enclosed in parentheses are uncertain.

in nation months (column 4); severity in battle deaths (column 5); population (column 6); and two intensity measures, battle deaths per nation month (column 7) and battle deaths per capita (column 9). The figures for the ongoing wars reflect estimates as of the end of 1980.

Looking briefly at interesting features of Table 13.2, we found a total of 106 major civil wars from 1816 to 1980. Is it only a coincidence that during the same period we found roughly the same number (118) of interstate wars? That is, we turned up an almost equal number of civil and interstate wars that resulted in at least 1,000 battle deaths in the period under consideration. What, aside from chance, can account for this unexpected outcome, given the belief that civil wars are more easily instigated than interstates?

To some degree, our battle death threshold helped to create the symmetry between the two types of wars. There were several hundred more full-fledged civil than interstate wars resulting in between 100 and 1,000 battle deaths. Indeed, were we to count all civils and interstates in this miniwar category, we would find that civils outnumbered interstates by better than two to one. Nevertheless, since it takes at least two to make an interstate war and only one to make a civil war, we could reasonably expect twice as many civils as interstates. Of course, it might be easier for people to take up arms against foreigners than to fight long and hard against their own countrymen. It must be remembered that we have included as interstate wars those between the metropole and regions on the periphery made up of people from different ethnic backgrounds. Thus, almost all of our civil wars, though they may involve class conflict, were between members of the same ethnic or linguistic family. Should we be more reluctant to slay our own kind than some inferior aliens across the border?

Moreover, we must again point out that the myriads of putches, coups, and palace revolutions that often result in the slaughter of the former leader and his praetorian guard generally (and fortunately) do not involve enough of the civilian and military population to elevate those conflicts to our civil war category. Finally, we have excluded many otherwise qualifying civil wars, especially in Latin America, because they occurred when the independent political entity in question had not yet become an active member of the interstate system.

Despite all of these possible explanations, we are still struck by the similarity between the total number of civil and interstate wars since 1816. Future analyses may reveal whether there is more here than we hazard to explain at this point.

INTERNATIONALIZED CIVIL WARS

Another item that fairly leaps at us from 13.2 is the relatively few cases of large-scale intervention in civil wars. We summarize these interventions in 13.3.

13.3   Interventions in Civil Wars

Nation Number	Nation	Number	War Number*
002	United States	6	745, 826, *835*, 850, 859, *871*
200	England	6	607, 616, 622, 652, 745, 781
220	France	5	616, 622, 721, 730, 745
235	Portugal	2	616, *778*
816	North Vietnam	2	850, 871
740	Japan	2	*745*, 757
652	Syria	2	*874*, 895
211	Belgium	1	838
040	Cuba	1	898
651	Egypt	1	847
375	Finland	1	*745*
255	Germany	1	*778*
325	Italy	1	*778*
365	Russia	1	724
817	South Vietnam	1	*871*

*Support for losing side in italics

Of our 106 civil wars, 21 (20 percent) experienced military intervention by another country that reached serious proportions (at least 1,000 troops committed or 100 battle deaths). And when we examine the battle death figures for those interventions, we see that most were of the limited variety. Although "only" 21 wars involved intervention, there were 33 *cases* of interventions, with several of the wars, such as the Russian Revolution and the Spanish Civil War, involving at least three outside parties. For the most part (67 percent), the interveners supported the side that ultimately won the war. This was not always the government faction, as was the case with North Vietnam's involvement in the Cambodian and Laotian civil wars, and Germany, Italy, and Portugal's assistance to Franco's rebels in Spain.

Of interest is the fact that the United States—which, along with England, leads this exclusive, if infamous, club with interventions—was on the losing side four times: in Russia in 1918, and in Laos, Cambodia, and South Vietnam. We also note that more than half of all the interventions have taken place since 1944.

Well beyond our purview are the scores of interventions that turned the tide but that did not involve either 100 deaths or 1,000 troops committed to combat. One thinks, for example, of the way the United States could make or break revolutions in Central America with the landing of relatively small marine contingents as in Nicaragua in 1912, or the manner in which the British controlled their sphere with a very thin red line in the late nineteenth and earlier twentieth century. As we leave the issue of interventions in civil wars, it should be emphasized that *all analyses in subsequent chapters consider only the nation months and battle deaths for the nation in which the civil war was fought.*

13.4 Victors in Civil Wars

Years	Government	Opposition[2]	Total[3]
1816–1980	66 (65)[1]	36 (35)	102
1816–1899	26 (67)	13 (33)	39
1990–1943	14 (61)	9 (39)	23
1944–1980	26 (65)	14 (35)	40

[1]Percent in ( ).
[2]Opposition totals include four victories gained after war entered interstate phase.
[3]Total excludes four wars (Angola, Philippines, Afghanistan, and El Salvador) that continued beyond December 31, 1980.

Turning to another suggestive bit of information, we discover (13.4) that in the 102 wars that terminated before December 31, 1980, two-thirds were won by the government. This ratio holds throughout several time periods, with the opponents doing slightly better (39-61) during the 1900-1943 period and slightly worse (33-67) during the nineteenth century. This does not mean that violent attempts to overturn governments succeeded one out of three times. As was emphasized above, missing here are the thousands of coups and aborted coups, as well as mini-civil wars, that fell below our battle death threshold. Whether the observed relationship holds for those events as well is an interesting question. The coding problem here would be difficult, if not impossible, if only for the case of a government's triumphant announcement of the execution of an opposition political leader "who was preparing to stage a putsch." How could we score such a claim as an indicator of a civil war won by the regime in power?

We noted earlier that the initiator of an *interstate war* wins about 70 percent of the time, but in civil war the opposition—always, by definition, the initiator—wins only one-third of the time. Of course, in an interstate war, each state is usually adequately armed, whereas in a civil war, most of the fire power and trained armed forces are controlled, at least initially, by the government.

SUMMARY

Visual inspection of the data in 13.2 and 13.4 may yield additional insights. But only by reordering and subjecting them to a variety of statistical tests will we be able to move from speculative insights to reliable findings. We could run an almost infinite series of analyses on these basic data, as we did in the first edition, where we offered 75 tables of analyses. This may have been "overkill" with a vengeance, as we studied different epochs, series with and without world wars, and different systems in an attempt to draw from our data all of the most suggestive patterns. In the first section of this volume we have presented only the most important tables from the original analyses.

We have likewise opted for a more modest presentation in this first pass through our civil war data. For one thing, we deal here with simpler data; most civil wars involve just one country. More practically, space limitations preclude the elaborate and occasionally redundant presentations from the first study. We have therefore selected a handful of some of the more useful analyses and will leave for our creative readers the task of developing the scores of other important analyses to which our data lend themselves.

CHAPTER 14

Ranking the Wars by Severity, Magnitude, and Intensity

In this chapter, we rank the wars on five dimensions and examine more rigorously those patterns suggested by our first pass through the data. Since many of the tables in this chapter replicate those in Chapter 5 in Part I, we need not devote much space to explaining their construction anew.

RANKING CIVIL WARS

In 14.1, we rank all civil wars by severity. This table also shows the rank of each war on the nation months (column 2), population (column 3), battle deaths per nation month (column 4), and battle deaths per capita (column 5) dimensions.

What do these data reveal? First, as we shall discover when we turn to national histories, China's record is an unenviable one. The Taiping rebellion ranks first in severity, the 1946-1950 revolution ranks second, and the earlier phase of that revolution (1930-1935) ranks twelfth. Further, China's figures would be even worse were we to include those deaths suffered in civil wars prior to 1860, the year it entered the international system. Callous observers might note that China's scores are deflated when we take into account its enormous population (column 5). But whether 100,000 people fall in a country with a population of 1 million or in a country of 500 million, we are still dealing with the deaths of a frightening number of human beings as well as the impact of those deaths on thousands and thousands of others.

Moving from countries to trends, we see that of the 14 most severe wars, only 2 took place in the nineteenth century, the aforementioned Taiping Rebellion and the American Civil War. And 8 of those 14 began in the period since World War II, perhaps explaining why we

14.1 Rank Order of All Civil Wars by Severity

War No.	Name of War	Battle Deaths	Nation Months	Popula-tion 3	Battle Deaths per Nation Month 4	Battle Deaths per Capita 5
652	CHINA (1860-1864)	1.0	17.0	8.0	3.0	21.0
784	CHINA (1946-1950)	2.5	18.0	6.0	5.0	28.0
868	NIGERIA (1967-1970)	2.5	29.0	18.0	4.0	9.0
658	UNITED STATES OF AMERICA (1861-1865)	4.5	20.0	26.0	10.0	8.0
778	SPAIN (1936-1939)	4.5	28.0	28.0	6.0	2.0
745	USSR RUSSIA) (1917-1920)	6.5	27.0	13.0	8.0	23.0
880	PAKISTAN (1971)	6.5	60.0	14.0	30.0	22.0
802	COLOMBIA (1949-1962)	8.5	1.0	48.0	17.0	1.0
835	VIETNAM, REPUBLIC OF (1960-1965)	8.5	12.0	42.0	28.0	7.0
727	MEXICO (1910-1920)	10.5	4.0	40.0	27.0	11.0
853	SUDAN (1963-1972)	10.5	7.0	45.0	23.0	10.0
769	CHINA (1930-1935)	12.0	15.0	4.0	18.0	61.0
781	GREECE (1944-1949)	13.0	24.0	57.0	26.0	6.0
871	KAMPUCHEA (CAMBODIA) (1970-1975)	14.0	14.0	59.0	29.0	4.0
709	COLOMBIA (1899-1903)	16.0	22.5	69.0	34.0	3.0
838	ZAIRE (CONGO.KINSHASA) (1960-1965)	16.0	11.0	41.0	40.0	17.0
847	YEMEN ARAB REPUBLIC (1962-1969)	19.0	9.0	66.0	49.0	5.0
653	CHINA (1860-1868)	19.0	5.0	8.0	57.0	80.5
654	CHINA (1860-1872)	19.0	2.0	8.0	20.0	80.5
766	CHINA (1929-1930)	21.5	38.0	5.0	25.0	83.0
865	CHINA (1967-1968)	21.5	37.0	71.0	1.0	92.0
886	BURUNDI (1972)	23.0	99.5	85.0	21.0	13.0
907	NICARAGUA (1978-1979)	24.5	57.0	46.0	61.5	12.0
616	SPAIN (1834-1840)	24.5	10.0	15.0	53.0	26.0
823	INDONESIA (1956-1960)	26.0	19.0	81.0	38.0	64.0
895	LEBANON (1975-1976)	28.0	41.0	78.0	71.0	16.0
607	PORTUGAL (1829-1834)	28.0	13.0	95.0	69.0	18.0
649	VENEZUELA (1859-1863)	28.0	16.0	21.0	11.0	15.0
676	FRANCE (1871)	30.0	86.0	82.0	90.0	54.0
850	LAOS (1963-1973)	31.0	3.0	22.0	31.0	19.0
685	JAPAN (1877)	31.0	62.0	63.0	87.0	63.0
892	ZIMBABWE (RHODESIA) (1972-1979)	32.0	8.0	102.0	98.0	14.0
622	ARGENTINA (1841-1851)	34.5	6.0	10.0	61.5	29.0
757	CHINA (1926-1928)	34.5	31.5	37.0	78.0	98.0
760	MEXICO (1926-1930)	34.5	22.5	30.0	56.0	49.0
901	AFGHANISTAN (1978-1979)	34.5	40.0	31.0	64.0	57.0
808	PHILIPPINES (1950-1952)	37.0	35.0	53.0	76.5	59.0
646	MEXICO (1858-1861)	38.5	25.5	33.0	76.5	40.0
799	BURMA (1948-1951)	38.5	25.5	54.0	51.0	58.0
763	AFGHANISTAN (1928-1929)	40.5	50.0	19.0	36.0	41.0
904	IRAN (PERSIA) (1978-1979)	40.5	72.0	47.0	60.0	76.0
601	SPAIN (1821-1823)	42.5	43.0	35.0	60.0	52.0
679	SPAIN (1872-1876)	42.5	21.0	35.0	85.0	60.0

War No.	Name of War	Battle Deaths 1	Nation Months 2	Population 3	Battle Deaths per Nation Month 4	Battle Deaths per Capita 5
604	TURKEY/OTTOMAN EMPIRE (1826)	44.0	79.0	27.0	32.5	78.0
694	CHILE (1891)	48.0	63.0	80.0	52.0	32.0
706	BRAZIL (1896-1897)	48.0	47.0	36.0	63.0	67.0
739	CHINA (1913)	48.0	88.0	2.0	24.0	101.0
742	CHINA (1914)	48.0	69.0	11.0	45.5	99.0
805	INDONESIA (1950)	48.0	74.0	17.0	42.0	94.0
829	CUBA (1958-1959)	48.0	67.0	61.0	48.0	45.0
841	LAOS (1960-1962)	48.0	36.0	98.0	75.0	20.0
613	MEXICO (1832)	48.5	49.0	62.0	68.0	51.0
619	COLOMBIA (1840-1842)	54.5	31.5	91.0	82.0	30.0
640	PERU (1853-1855)	54.5	45.5	89.0	72.0	31.0
703	PERU (1894-1895)	54.5	73.0	73.0	47.0	37.0
748	HUNGARY (1919-1920)	54.5	51.0	55.0	65.0	55.0
790	YEMEN ARAB REPUBLIC (1948)	54.5	93.0	74.0	22.0	35.0
634	AUSTRIA-HUNGARY (1848)	58.0	64.5	20.0	59.0	90.0
625	SPAIN (1847-1849)	61.5	34.0	43.0	91.0	74.0
631	FRANCE (1848)	61.5	77.5	23.0	50.0	91.0
637	CHILE (1851)	61.5	81.0	96.0	41.0	27.0
643	PERU (1856-1858)	61.5	42.0	88.0	80.0	34.0
667	VENEZUELA (1868-1871)	61.5	33.0	92.0	92.0	33.0
820	ARGENTINA (1955)	61.5	80.0	32.0	43.0	82.0
655	COLOMBIA (1860-1862)	66.0	30.0	84.0	100.0	39.0
856	RWANDA (1963-1964)	66.0	82.5	77.0	44.0	43.0
859	DOMINICAN REPUBLIC (1965)	66.0	76.0	70.0	54.0	47.0
718	RUMANIA (1907)	71.0	89.0	60.0	37.0	69.0
733	PARAGUAY (1911-1912)	71.0	55.0	103.0	79.0	24.0
793	COSTA RICA (1948)	71.0	91.5	101.0	32.5	25.0
832	IRAQ (1959)	71.0	99.5	58.0	12.0	71.0
862	UGANDA (1966)	71.0	96.5	51.0	14.5	72.0
874	JORDAN (1970)	71.0	90.0	86.0	14.5	42.0
883	SRI LANKA (CEYLON) (1971)	75.0	99.5	44.0	35.0	84.0
610	FRANCE (1830)	76.0	95.0	25.0	13.0	96.0
670	SPAIN (1868)	79.5	56.0	34.0	19.0	89.0
673	ARGENTINA (1870-1871)	79.5	39.0	90.0	84.0	44.0
697	BRAZIL (1893-1894)	79.5	75.0	38.5	102.0	88.0
730	MOROCCO (1911)	79.5	53.0	68.0	73.0	65.0
754	AFGHANISTAN (1924-1925)	79.5	102.5	56.0	86.0	77.0
811	BOLIVIA (1952)	79.5	70.0	76.0	7.0	56.0
844	ALGERIA (1962-1963)	79.5	102.5	49.0	74.0	85.0
796	COLOMBIA (1948)	83.5	77.5	50.0	9.0	86.0
826	LEBANON (1958)	83.5	77.5	87.0	70.0	48.0

(continued)

14.1 (Continued)

War No.	Name of War	Battle Deaths 1	Nation Months 2	Population 3	Battle Deaths per Nation Month 4	Battle Deaths per Capita 5
775	SPAIN (1934)	85.0	99.5	29.0	16.0	95.0
628	TWO SICILIES (1848-1849)	94.5	59.0	52.0	94.0	87.0
661	ARGENTINA (1863)	94.5	66.0	94.0	88.0	50.0
664	ARGENTINA (1866-1867)	94.5	53.0	93.0	96.5	53.0
682	COLOMBIA (1876-1877)	94.5	64.5	79.0	89.0	66.0
688	ARGENTINA (1880)	94.5	91.5	83.0	45.5	62.0
691	COLOMBIA (1884-1885)	94.5	58.0	72.0	95.0	70.0
700	BRAZIL (1893-1894)	94.5	68.0	38.5	83.0	93.0
712	URUGUAY (1904)	94.5	61.0	99.0	93.0	38.0
715	USSR (RUSSIA) (1905-1906)	94.5	48.0	12.0	99.0	102.0
721	MOROCCO (1907-1908)	94.5	45.5	67.0	101.0	73.0
724	IRAN (PERSIA) (1908-1909)	94.5	44.0	65.0	103.0	75.0
736	CHINA (1911)	94.5	84.0	3.0	66.0	103.0
751	HONDURAS (1924)	94.5	87.0	100.0	55.0	36.0
772	BRAZIL (1932)	94.5	82.5	24.0	67.0	97.0
787	PARAGUAY (1947)	94.5	71.0	97.0	81.0	46.0
814	INDONESIA (1953)	94.5	85.0	16.0	58.0	100.0
817	GUATEMALA (1954)	94.5	94.0	75.0	39.0	68.0
877	GUATEMALA (1970-1971)	94.5	53.0	64.0	96.5	79.0

think ours is an especially violent age. On the other hand, when we examine the least severe of our wars that resulted in a minimum of 1,000 battle deaths, this picture is altered somewhat. That is, of the 18 wars that share rank position 94.5, over three-fifths (11) occur in the twentieth century. Of course, we will be able to examine these preliminary findings in a more sophisticated fashion when we turn to trends and periodicities in Chapter 16.

The most severe wars are not always the longest, as is apparent in the ranks (column 2) according to nation months of war. The Colombian insurrection of 1949-1962, in place 8.5 on the severity indicator, is first on duration. Actually, the Miao Rebellion in China of 1860-1872 that currently ranks second on the list would be first were we to include the nation months of war experienced from 1855 to 1860, prior to China's entry into the system. The war in Laos, the Mexican Revolution, and the Nien Rebellion in China of 1860-1868 are in third, fourth, and fifth places, respectively. Of the 15 longest civil wars, 10 occurred in the twentieth century, 8 of them since World War II. To some degree, this pattern is counterintuitive; we might expect wars to be briefer in the twentieth than in the nineteenth century. The advent of helicopters, radar, and a host of hardware (and software) innovations should make it easier for governments to search for and destroy the rebels now than in earlier times; of course, recent experiences in Southeast Asia give lie to that kind of analysis.

In many ways, duration figures are not as useful as severity figures, especially since it is not easy to determine when wars begin or terminate in the jungles or mountains of some nation experiencing "disturbances." Perhaps our most revealing measure is the intensity measure—battle deaths per nation month. Short, bloody wars appear to be the most violent of all, with much of the carnage occurring during a brief period. On this indicator (column 4), the 1972 war in Burundi that took 50,000 lives in less than a month ranks first. In second place is the war in Bangladesh of 1971; in third is the Taiping Rebellion; in fourth, the Nigerian Civil War; and in fifth, the Chinese Revolution. Interestingly, after the top-ranking Burundi War, the next 5 are among the most severe as well. Of the 15 most intense wars, 10 are from the twentieth century; 7 of those 10 are from the post-World War II era, perhaps another tribute to the greater lethality of weapons in our time. Such a facile conclusion, however, is not entirely convincing. Many of the wars in the Third World until and including the present era have been fought with weapons not much more lethal than those employed in the nineteenth century. In addition, during earlier periods, one would expect many more battle deaths attributable to wounds and disease than in recent years, given improvements in sanitation and military medicine. Indeed, one of the tactics in putatively more humane wars of today is to devise weapons that wound but do not kill, on the grounds that an army that must carry or tend for its wounded is not as effective as one that can devote all of its attention and cadre to the enemy.

However we explain it, it appears that our period has seen more than its share of bloody and intense civil war. How much more we will discover in succeeding sections. What is clear from 14.1, no matter which indicator we examine, is the overrepresentation of countries in Asia, Latin America, and Africa at the top of the rankings. To be sure, the Russian, Spanish, American, and Greek Civil Wars are among the most severe and intense, but it appears that those who live in the Third World have suffered considerably more—especially the Chinese, whose wars dominate our lists.

But we are still in the preliminary stages of our investigation. Our data have been arrayed in a manner that allows us to make only impressionistic interpretations of the patterns, trends, and participants in civil wars. From this point on, we move to a variety of manipulations that should produce more reliable measures for charting the incidence of civil war in the international system since 1816.

RANK ORDER CORRELATIONS

As with interstate wars, 14.1 suggests a strong positive correlation between the rank orderings of civil wars on indicators of severity, magnitude, and, to some degree, intensity. In 14.2, using the Kendall's tau (B statistic) we show the relationships between our various indicators in a more rigorous manner.

As expected, we find strong associations between nation months and battle deaths—the longer wars also tend to be the most severe. Similarly, it is not surprising to discover that the intensity measure, battle deaths per nation month, is associated with the severity measure but *not* with the magnitude or nation months measure. The strong negative correlation between battle deaths per capita and population was, of course, expected.

FREQUENCY DISTRIBUTIONS

After describing and ranking the civil wars according to several indicators, we move on to more interesting questions concerning the nature of our population. The construction of frequency distributions will allow us to discover the percentages of wars of various sizes and

14.2 Rank Order Correlations Among Several War Indicators, for All Civil Wars

	Pop	Nat-Mos	B-Dths	B-Dths/NM	B-Dths/Cap
Population	1.00				
Nation Months	.08	1.00			
Battle Deaths	.27	.48	1.00		
B-Dths per Nation Month	.28	-.17	.37	1.00	
B-Dths per Capita	-.34	.34	.41	.13	1.00

N = 103

14.3   Frequencies of Civil War by Severity

Log_{10} range	3.0-3.5	3.5-4.5	4.5-5.5	5.5-6.5	
Absolute battle death range	1000-3,100	3,100-31,000	31,000-310,000	310,000-3,100,000	N
All Civil Wars	45	35	16	7	103
Central System Only	27	25	12	5	69
Major Powers Only	4	2	1	1	8

severities as well as whether the distributions produced are randomly distributed or reveal some underlying pattern.

In 14.3 we again use Richardson's log_{10} breakdown to examine the frequency of our 103 (omitting the 3 that are still under way) civil wars according to severity ranges. For all classes of war, we find that the lower ranges account for most of the cases, although 22 percent did result in more than 31,000 battle deaths; this is very close to the 25 percent of *interstate* wars that resulted in more than 31,000 deaths. If one might expect interstate wars to be more bloody because they involve at least two parties, then the relatively sizable number of civils at the most lethal end of the spectrum is a depressing outcome indeed.

The frequencies of civil wars by magnitude (14.4) reveal a comparable pattern. Almost half of the wars ended in less than one year. This figure would be inflated dramatically had we included the thousands of one-day coups and putsches that fall below our battle death threshold and that invariably last less than a week. Nineteen of the wars, however, did last four years or more. Naturally, some of our wars could have been coded as having been longer, as remnants of the losing side often fight on at a low level for years. For example, as late as 1978, we still heard rumors of bands of Vietnamese actively opposing the new regime in Ho Chi Minh City in guerrilla actions not unlike those that flared in that same country in 1958. As discussed earlier, the determination of the beginning and ending of a civil war is even more difficult than that for interstate wars.

Interesting to note is that 7 of the 8 major power civil wars lasted less than one year. Clearly, it would be hard to maintain major power status in the international system while having to contend with insurgents on one's own soil.

14.4   Frequencies of Civil War by Magnitude

Nation months Nation years	12 or less 1 or less	13-48 1-4	49-96 4-8	97-192 8-16	N
All Civil Wars	56	28	12	7	103
Central System Only	40	16	10	3	69
Major Powers Only	7	1	0	0	8

14.5 Observed and Expected Frequencies of Civil War by Magnitude, Natural Logarithmic Transformation—All Civils

	0-.73	.74-1.34	1.35-1.76	1.77-2.15	2.16-2.47	2.48-2.78	2.79-3.18	3.19-3.61	3.20-4.20	4.21+
Interval range-logE	0-.73	.74-1.34	1.35-1.76	1.77-2.15	2.16-2.47	2.48-2.78	2.79-3.18	3.19-3.61	3.20-4.20	4.21+
Interval range-nation months	0-2.1	2.2-3.8	3.9-5.8	5.9-8.6	8.7-11.8	11.9-16.1	16.2-24.1	24.2-37.0	37.1-66.7	66.8+
Expected frequencies	10.3	10.3	10.3	10.3	10.3	10.3	10.3	10.3	10.3	10.3
Observed frequencies	13	9	7	11	13	7	9	10	14	10

mean = 2.59   standard deviation = 1.44

14.6   Cumulative Probability of Civil War Magnitudes

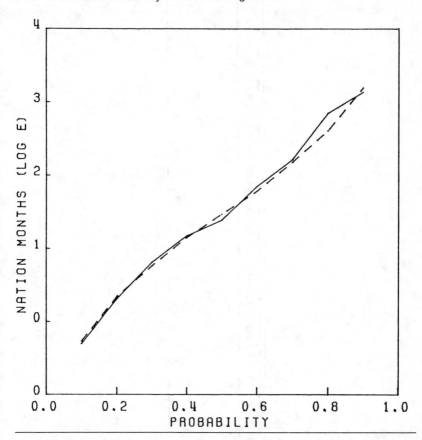

As with 5.5 for interstates, we attempt some modest curve fitting in 14.5. We chose to work with magnitude because the range is more manageable for this exercise than is the range for severity. Our hypothesis is that the distribution is close to a natural logarithmic curve. To test for this, we transform the actual values to more nearly approximate normal curve values and then test the transformed values for normality using the Chi-square.

Following procedures outlined earlier, in 14.5 we present the $\log_e$ intervals for the 103 civil wars, along with the actual, untransformed values for each interval division. The "expected" values—10 percent of the total number of wars of each type in each interval—and the "observed" number of wars whose transformed magnitudes fell into each interval are reported, along with the means and standard deviations used to compute the interval ranges.

14.7 Frequencies of Civil War by Intensity (BD/NM)

Intensity Ratio	0-286	286-1000	1000-3000	3000-8000	8000-22000	22000-60000	60000-160000
All Civil Wars	32	33	16	8	10	2	2
Central System Only	14	22	13	8	9	1	2
Major Powers Only	2	2	0	1	3	0	0

With the values in 14.5, we could compute the similarity between the expected and observed frequencies for each type of war. We used the Chi-square $\Sigma\,(f_{observed} - f_{expected})^2/f_{expected})$, which would be equal to zero if all expected and observed values were identical, and increasingly higher as the differences between the values were greater.

We present in 14.6 a visual representation of the observed and expected frequencies in the form of a cumulative probability graph. The broken line represents the expected frequency at each percentage level given on the horizontal axis; the $\log_e$ scale is given as the vertical axis. The line connecting the heavy dots represents the observed number of wars, each dot showing the actual percentage of the wars included in each successive $\log_e$ range. The distribution tested "fits" the expected distribution at a .05 level of significance, which permits us to say that the distributions of civil war magnitude scores—as with international wars—can be described as natural logarithmic curves.

Finally, the 103 civil wars may be grouped according to their *intensity* ranges, as measured by battle deaths per nation month. As expected, most of the wars show up on the less lethal side of the continuum (14.7).

SUMMARY

Having already summarized the way these wars rank on a variety of dimensions, there is little to add here. It is interesting to note how closely our findings for civil wars compare to those for international wars (Chapter 5). Here we discovered that (a) wars that rank high on severity tend to rank high on magnitude; (b) most of the wars in our population were of the briefer and less lethal variety; (c) major powers have not engaged in many bloody or lengthy civil wars; and (d) there is a close fit between the frequencies observed and those predicted by the log normal distribution.

From the civil wars themselves we now move on to the system and the manner in which they are distributed through time.

CHAPTER 15

Annual Amounts of War Begun and Under Way

We move now from consideration of the civil wars as separate, discrete events to patterns, trends, and cycles during our entire 165-year period. In order to begin this process, we must (as in Chapter 6 for international wars) first present the annual systemic civil war experiences from 1816 through 1980.

Although at first glance it appears that international wars should be more closely related to one another than civil wars in time and place, that is not necessarily the case. We posited earlier that the propensity to wage international war may be affected by the intervals since the last war, as well as economic, demographic, meteorologic, and diplomatic and political factors. All of these, including a contagion effect (Govea and West, 1981), also may affect the propensity to wage internal war. That is, a nation may become involved in civil strife because of economic dislocations, population gains or losses, or the rise of international revolutionary or counterrevolutionary ideologies, among other things. Further, trends in international war might affect trends in civil wars and vice versa. For example, periods of international war could bring with them opportunities for disgruntled citizens to overthrow governments that are pursuing losing causes abroad. Or, conversely, citizens might forget their internecine squabbles and "rally 'round the flag" against a foreign enemy, thus decreasing the likelihood of civil war occurring during a period of intense international martial activity.

Clearly, it makes as much sense to search for trends and cycles in civil war in the international system as it did to search for patterns and cycles in international war. One problem here, however, involves our relative lack of confidence in many of the onset and termination dates for civil wars. Thus, we must look a bit more skeptically at patterns that result from our analyses of the annual indicators.

ANNUAL AMOUNTS OF CIVIL WAR

In 15.1, year by year, is the number of nations in the system (column 1), the number of civil wars begun in each year (column 2), and then our several severity, magnitude, and intensity measures for wars begun—battle deaths (column 3), nation months (column 4), battle deaths per nation months (column 5), battle deaths per hundred population (column 6), and the log of battle deaths per million population (column 7). In the righthand side of the table we move to our war underway measures. After indicating the number of wars under way (column 8), we show the percentage of nations in war (column 9), the nation months under way (column 10), and the percentage of nation months exhausted (column 11). The latter variable is constructed by multiplying the number of nations in the system by 12 and dividing that figure into that for nation months under way. It is possible, as with China in 1860 and Brazil in 1893, for one nation to fight two or more civil wars in the same year or even at the same time, but in almost all cases, as with interstate wars, they have their hands full dealing with one war at a time.

RANKING THE YEARS

The data presented in 15.1 will be reordered in our examination of trends and cycles in Chapter 16. But before we turn to those analyses, we offer in 15.2 and 15.3 the simple rank ordering of the years by the amount of civil wars begun and under way in terms of battle deaths and nation months.

The fact that 1860 is our top-ranked year on battle deaths and that it ranks second on nation months is a statistical artifact. China entered our international system in 1860 at a time when it was fighting three civil wars. None began in 1860, but because of our coding rules, they show up with a January 1, 1860 start date.

Of the 165 years, "only" 75 saw a civil war begin. That is, more than half (90 years) did not experience the onset of a civil war. This does not mean that civil wars were not taking place during those 90 years. As can be seen from 15.3, the rank order of years by the amount of civil war *under way,* only 31 of our years have an unblemished record and experienced neither the onset nor the continuation of civil wars begun in an earlier year.

(text continued page 260)

15.1 Annual Amounts of Civil War

		WAR BEGUN						WAR UNDER WAY			
Year	No. in System 1	No. of Wars Begun 2	Battle Deaths 000's 3	Nation Months 4	Battle Deaths 000's per Nation Month 5	Battle Deaths per Hundred Population 6	Log of Battle Deaths per Million Population 7	No. of Wars Under Way 8	% of Nations in War 9	Nation Months Under Way 10	% of Nation Months Exhausted 11
1816	23	0	0.	0.	0.	0.	0.	0	0.	0.	0.
1817	23	0	0.	0.	0.	0.	0.	0	0.	0.	0.
1818	23	0	0.	0.	0.	0.	0.	0	0.	0.	0.
1819	23	0	0.	0.	0.	0.	0.	0	0.	0.	0.
1820	23	0	0.	0.	0.	0.	0.	0	0.	0.	0.
1821	23	1	7.00	16.2	.43	.06	6.41	1	4.35	1.0	.36
1822	23	0	0.	0.	0.	0.	0.	1	4.35	12.0	4.35
1823	23	0	0.	0.	0.	0.	0.	1	4.35	3.2	1.16
1824	23	0	0.	0.	0.	0.	0.	0	0.	0.	0.
1825	24	0	0.	0.	0.	0.	0.	0	0.	0.	0.
1826	25	1	6.00	3.6	1.67	.02	5.26	1	4.00	3.6	1.19
1827	25	0	0.	0.	0.	0.	0.	0	0.	0.	0.
1828	26	0	0.	0.	0.	0.	0.	0	0.	0.	0.
1829	26	1	20.00	60.2	.33	.66	8.79	1	3.85	6.0	1.92
1830	27	0	1.70	.2	0.	0.	0.	2	7.41	12.0	3.75
1831	29	1	4.00	11.3	.35	.06	6.43	1	3.45	12.0	3.45
1832	29	0	0.	0.	0.	0.	0.	2	6.90	23.0	6.70
1833	29	1	30.00	72.0	.42	.24	7.77	2	6.90	11.7	3.45
1834	29	0	0.	0.	0.	0.	0.	1	3.45	11.7	3.36
1835	29	0	0.	0.	0.	0.	0.	1	3.45	12.0	3.45
1836	29	0	0.	0.	0.	0.	0.	1	3.45	12.0	3.45
1837	29	0	0.	0.	0.	0.	0.	1	3.45	12.0	3.45
1838	31	0	0.	0.	0.	0.	0.	1	3.23	12.0	3.23
1839	32	1	4.00	24.0	.17	.21	7.66	1	3.13	12.0	3.13
1840	32	1	10.00	101.3	.10	1.44	9.58	2	6.25	24.0	3.13
1841	34	0	0.	0.	0.	0.	0.	2	5.88	24.0	5.88
1842	35	0	0.	0.	0.	0.	0.	2	5.71	17.7	4.21
1843	36	0	0.	0.	0.	0.	0.	0	0.	0.	0.
1844	36	0	0.	0.	0.	0.	0.	0	0.	0.	0.
1845	36	0	0.	0.	0.	0.	0.	1	2.63	11.5	2.67
1846	37	0	0.	0.	0.	0.	0.	1	2.63	12.0	2.70
1847	38	1	3.00	23.6	.13	.02	5.37	2	10.26	19.5	4.29
1848	39	3	7.50	20.7	.36	.01	4.53	5	2.50	40.2	8.59
1849	40	0	0.	0.	0.	0.	0.	3	2.50	20.5	4.27
1850	40	1	3.00	3.0	1.00	.23	7.72	1	2.44	12.0	2.50
1851	41	0	0.	0.	0.	0.	0.	2	2.44	9.6	1.95
1852	41	1	0.	3.0	.32	.20	7.62	0	2.44	.4	0.
1853	41	0	4.00	12.6	0.	0.	0.	1	2.44	.4	.07
1854	42	1	0.	0.	0.	0.	0.	1	2.38	12.0	2.38
1855	44	0	0.	0.	0.	0.	0.	1	2.27	.2	.04

		WAR BEGUN						WAR UNDER WAY			
Year	No. in System (1)	No. of Wars Begun (2)	Battle Deaths 000's (3)	Nation Months (4)	Battle Deaths 000's per Nation Month (5)	Battle Deaths per Hundred Population (6)	Log of Battle Deaths per Million Population (7)	No. of Wars Under Way (8)	% of Nations in War (9)	Nation Months Under Way (10)	% of Nation Months Exhausted (11)
1856	44	1	3.00	16.3	.18	.15	7.29	1	2.27	2.0	.38
1857	44	0	0.	0.	0.	0.	0.	1	2.27	12.0	2.27
1858	44	1	8.00	34.6	.23	.09	6.85	2	4.55	12.7	2.41
1859	45	1	20.00	58.9	.34	1.29	9.46	2	4.44	23.0	4.26
1860	47	4	2152.50	335.5	6.42	.16	7.40	6	12.77	67.5	11.98
1861	43	4	650.00	48.0	13.54	2.02	9.91	7	16.28	68.7	13.32
1862	42	0	0.	0.	0.	0.	0.	6	14.29	69.5	13.79
1863	42	1	1.00	7.4	.14	.06	6.46	6	14.29	67.4	13.37
1864	42	0	0.	0.	0.	0.	0.	4	9.52	43.0	8.53
1865	42	0	0.	0.	0.	0.	0.	3	7.14	27.3	5.42
1866	42	1	1.00	10.0	.10	.06	6.35	3	7.14	24.5	4.87
1867	40	0	0.	0.	0.	0.	0.	3	7.50	33.5	6.98
1868	37	2	4.60	24.3	.19	.03	5.54	4	10.81	27.0	6.08
1869	37	0	0.	0.	0.	0.	0.	1	2.70	16.6	3.73
1870	37	1	1.50	9.8	.15	.08	6.66	2	5.41	31.4	7.07
1871	34	1	20.00	1.9	10.53	.06	6.31	3	8.82	16.5	4.06
1872	33	1	7.00	46.0	.15	.04	6.06	2	6.06	12.4	3.13
1873	33	0	0.	0.	0.	0.	0.	1	3.03	12.0	3.03
1874	33	0	0.	0.	0.	0.	0.	1	3.03	12.0	3.03
1875	34	0	0.	0.	0.	0.	0.	1	3.03	12.0	3.03
1876	35	1	1.00	7.6	.13	.03	5.80	1	2.94	12.0	2.94
1877	35	1	14.00	7.9	1.77	.04	5.97	2	5.71	3.2	.77
1878	37	0	0.	0.	0.	0.	0.	2	5.71	13.9	3.32
1879	37	0	0.	0.	0.	0.	0.	0	0.	0.	0.
1880	37	0	0.	0.	0.	0.	0.	0	0.	0.	0.
1881	36	1	1.00	1.2	.83	.04	5.99	1	2.70	1.2	.27
1882	36	0	0.	0.	0.	0.	0.	0	0.	0.	0.
1883	36	0	0.	0.	0.	0.	0.	0	0.	0.	0.
1884	36	1	1.00	9.0	.11	.03	5.69	1	2.78	1.5	.35
1885	36	0	0.	0.	0.	0.	0.	1	2.78	7.5	1.73
1886	36	0	0.	0.	0.	0.	0.	0	0.	0.	0.
1887	38	0	0.	0.	0.	0.	0.	0	0.	0.	0.
1888	39	0	0.	0.	0.	0.	0.	0	0.	0.	0.
1889	38	0	0.	0.	0.	0.	0.	0	0.	0.	0.
1890	38	0	0.	0.	0.	0.	0.	0	0.	0.	0.
1891	38	1	5.00	7.8	.64	.19	7.55	1	2.63	7.7	1.70
1892	39	0	0.	0.	0.	0.	0.	0	0.	0.	0.
1893	39	2	2.50	25.2	.10	.01	4.42	2	5.13	14.8	3.16
1894	39	1	4.00	5.2	.77	.12	7.08	3	7.69	12.9	2.76
1895	39	0	0.	0.	0.	0.	0.	1	2.56	2.6	.56
1896	39	1	5.00	12.2	.41	.03	5.76	1	2.56	3.0	.64

(continued)

15.1 (Continued)

Year	No. in System 1	WAR BEGUN						WAR UNDER WAY			
		No. of Wars Begun 2	Battle Deaths 000's 3	Nation Months 4	Battle Deaths 000's per Nation Month 5	Battle Deaths per Hundred Population 6	Log of Battle Deaths per Million Population 7	No. of Wars Under Way 8	% of Nations in War 9	Nation Months Under Way 10	% of Nation Months Exhausted 11
1897	39	0	0.	0.	0.	0.	0.	1	2.56	9.2	1.96
1898	40	0	0.	0.	0.	0.	0.	0	0.	0.	0.
1899	41	1	100.00	45.5	2.20	2.43	10.10	1	2.44	4.0	.81
1900	42	0	0.	0.	0.	0.	0.	1	2.38	12.0	2.38
1901	42	0	0.	0.	0.	0.	0.	1	2.38	12.0	2.38
1902	43	0	0.	0.	0.	0.	0.	1	2.33	5.5	2.33
1903	43	0	0.	0.	0.	0.	0.	1	2.33	8.0	1.07
1904	44	1	1.00	8.0	.13	.11	6.97	1	2.27	11.3	1.56
1905	44	1	1.00	11.4	.09	.00	1.92	1	2.27	0.	2.14
1906	43	0	0.	0.	0.	0.	0.	1	2.33	6.5	.01
1907	42	2	3.00	14.1	.21	.03	5.58	2	4.76	13.9	1.30
1908	43	1	1.00	12.9	.08	.02	5.37	2	4.65	6.5	2.69
1909	44	0	0.	0.	0.	0.	0.	1	2.27	1.4	1.24
1910	44	1	250.00	109.5	2.28	1.68	9.73	4	9.09	25.1	.26
1911	43	3	4.50	17.5	.26	.00	2.20	2	4.65	16.4	4.76
1912	43	0	0.	0.	0.	0.	0.	2	4.65	13.7	3.17
1913	44	1	5.00	1.7	2.94	.00	2.31	2	4.55	13.5	2.65
1914	44	0	0.	0.	0.	0.	0.	1	2.27	12.0	2.56
1915	43	1	5.00	6.0	.83	.00	2.75	1	2.33	12.0	2.27
1916	42	0	0.	0.	0.	0.	0.	2	4.76	12.7	2.33
1917	46	1	500.00	34.2	14.62	.40	8.30	1	2.17	24.0	2.53
1918	49	0	0.	0.	0.	0.	0.	2	4.08	33.2	4.35
1919	59	1	4.00	10.7	.37	.05	6.23	2	3.39	15.7	5.65
1920	60	0	0.	0.	0.	0.	0.	0	0.	0.	2.22
1921	61	0	0.	0.	0.	0.	0.	0	0.	0.	0.
1922	61	0	0.	0.	0.	0.	0.	0	0.	0.	0.
1923	61	0	0.	0.	0.	0.	0.	0	0.	0.	0.
1924	62	2	2.50	11.8	.21	.03	5.70	2	3.28	11.3	1.54
1925	63	0	0.	0.	0.	0.	0.	1	1.61	.5	.07
1926	64	2	20.00	69.5	.29	.00	3.79	2	3.17	10.0	1.33
1927	64	0	0.	0.	0.	0.	0.	2	3.13	24.0	3.13
1928	64	1	7.50	11.2	.67	.09	6.83	3	4.69	19.7	2.57
1929	64	1	75.00	19.4	3.87	.02	5.05	3	4.69	31.5	4.10
1930	64	1	200.00	59.0	3.39	.04	6.03	3	4.69	16.5	2.14
1931	65	0	0.	0.	0.	0.	0.	1	1.56	12.0	1.56
1932	65	1	1.00	2.8	.36	.00	3.35	2	3.08	14.7	1.89
1933	66	0	0.	0.	0.	0.	0.	1	1.54	12.0	1.54
1934	66	1	1.30	.2	0.	0.	0.	2	3.03	12.2	1.54
1935	66	0	0.	0.	0.	0.	0.	1	1.52	9.5	1.20
1936	66	1	650.00	32.4	20.06	2.62	10.17	1	1.52	5.5	.69
1937	66	0	0.	0.	0.	0.	0.	1	1.52	12.0	1.52

	WAR BEGUN							WAR UNDER WAY			
Year (1)	No. in System (1)	No. of Wars Begun (2)	Battle Deaths 000's (3)	Nation Months (4)	Battle Deaths 000's per Nation Month (5)	Battle Deaths per Hundred Population (6)	Log of Battle Deaths per Million Population (7)	No. of Wars Under Way (8)	% of Nations in War (9)	Nation Months Under Way (10)	% of Nation Months Exhausted (11)
1938	66	0	0.	0.	0.	0.	0.	1	1.52	12.0	1.52
1939	65	0	0.	0.	0.	0.	0.	1	1.54	2.9	.38
1940	62	0	0.	0.	0.	0.	0.	0	0.	0.	0.
1941	55	0	0.	0.	0.	0.	0.	0	0.	0.	0.
1942	53	0	0.	0.	0.	0.	0.	0	0.	0.	0.
1943	52	0	0.	0.	0.	0.	0.	0	0.	0.	0.
1944	57	1	160.00	37.4	4.28	2.15	9.97	1	1.75	.9	.14
1945	64	0	0.	0.	0.	0.	0.	1	1.56	1.4	.19
1946	66	1	1000.00	49.2	20.33	.22	7.69	2	1.52	11.1	1.40
1947	68	1	15.40	5.5	.18	.08	6.64	2	2.94	29.5	3.61
1948	72	4	300.00	37.0	.42	.05	6.15	6	6.94	30.0	3.47
1949	75	1	14.00	159.6	1.88	2.71	10.21	4	4.00	37.0	4.12
1950	75	2	0.	27.1	.52	.01	4.98	5	6.67	36.8	4.09
1951	75	0	1.50	0.	0.	0.	0.	3	3.90	31.0	3.44
1952	77	1	1.00	2.1	.48	.00	2.52	3	2.56	18.1	1.96
1953	78	1	1.00	.8	.94	0.	0.	2	2.44	14.1	1.51
1954	82	1	3.00	3.2	.62	.02	5.06	2	2.38	12.8	1.30
1955	84	1	30.00	48.6	.94	.03	5.86	2	2.30	15.2	1.50
1956	87	0	0.	0.	0.	0.	0.	2	2.25	12.5	1.20
1957	89	2	6.40	10.8	.59	.07	6.61	2	2.44	24.0	2.25
1958	90	0	2.00	.2	0.	0.	0.	4	4.49	34.8	2.22
1959	89	3	405.00	144.1	2.81	1.39	9.54	5	4.67	24.2	2.27
1960	107	2	0.	0.	0.	0.	0.	4	3.60	44.5	3.46
1961	111	0	101.50	87.3	1.16	.65	8.78	5	5.13	48.0	3.60
1962	117	2	267.50	221.6	1.21	1.45	9.58	6	5.88	49.1	3.50
1963	119	3	0.	0.	0.	0.	0.	7	4.92	49.4	3.46
1964	122	0	2.50	4.3	.58	.07	6.57	6	4.84	61.2	4.18
1965	124	1	2.00	.3	0.	0.	0.	6	3.10	49.5	3.33
1966	129	2	1050.00	49.8	21.08	.13	7.20	4	3.85	36.3	2.35
1967	130	2	0.	0.	0.	0.	0.	5	3.76	53.4	3.42
1968	133	0	0.	0.	0.	0.	0.	5	3.01	56.0	3.51
1969	133	0	0.	0.	0.	0.	0.	4	1.48	44.1	2.76
1970	134	3	153.00	70.2	2.18	1.08	9.28	6	4.32	35.6	2.21
1971	139	3	502.00	9.6	52.29	.39	8.26	6	4.32	54.1	3.25
1972	139	3	71.00	183.2	.39	.15	7.30	6	4.32	30.0	1.80
1973	141	0	0.	0.	0.	0.	0.	4	2.84	37.5	2.22
1974	143	2	31.00	80.0	.39	.35	8.16	3	2.10	36.0	2.10
1975	150	0	0.	0.	0.	0.	0.	5	3.33	36.8	2.04
1976	151	0	0.	0.	0.	0.	0.	4	2.65	45.7	2.52
1977	152	3	52.50	33.5	1.57	.09	6.75	3	1.97	36.0	1.97
1978	154	1	52.50	33.5	1.57	.09	2.15	6	3.90	49.9	2.70
1979	155	0	0.	0.	0.	0.	0.	7	4.52	61.7	3.32
1980	155	0	0.	0.	0.	0.	0.	3	1.94	36.0	1.94

15.2 Rank Order of Years by Amount of Civil War Begun

Year	Battle Deaths from Wars Begun (000's)	Rank	Nation Months of War Begun	Rank	Year	Battle Deaths from Wars Begun (000's)	Rank	Nation Months of War Begun	Rank
1860	2152.5	1.0	335.5	1.0	1914	5.0	40.5	6.0	58.0
1967	1050.0	2.0	49.8	16.0	1868	4.6	43.0	24.3	30.0
1946	1000.0	3.0	49.2	17.0	1911	4.5	44.0	17.5	36.0
1961	650.0	4.5	48.0	19.0	1832	4.0	47.0	11.3	45.0
1936	650.0	4.5	32.4	27.0	1840	4.0	47.0	24.0	31.0
1971	502.0	6.0	9.6	51.0	1853	4.0	47.0	12.6	41.0
1917	500.0	7.0	34.2	25.0	1894	4.0	47.0	5.2	60.0
1960	405.0	8.0	144.1	5.0	1919	3.0	52.0	10.7	48.0
1949	300.0	9.0	159.6	4.0	1847	3.0	52.0	23.6	32.0
1963	267.5	10.0	221.6	2.0	1851	3.0	52.0	3.0	64.0
1910	250.0	11.0	109.5	6.0	1856	3.0	52.0	16.3	37.0
1930	200.0	12.0	59.0	14.0	1907	3.0	52.0	14.1	39.0
1944	160.0	13.0	37.4	22.0	1955	2.5	56.0	3.2	63.0
1970	153.0	14.0	70.2	11.0	1893	2.5	56.0	25.2	29.0
1962	101.5	15.0	87.3	8.0	1924	2.5	56.0	11.8	43.0
1899	100.0	16.0	45.5	21.0	1965	2.5	56.0	4.3	61.0
1929	75.0	17.0	19.4	34.0	1959	2.0	58.5	.2	73.0
1972	71.0	18.0	183.2	3.0	1966	1.7	58.5	.3	71.0
1978	52.5	19.0	33.5	26.0	1830	1.5	60.0	.2	73.0
1975	31.0	20.0	80.0	9.0	1870	1.5	61.5	9.8	50.0
1834	30.0	21.5	72.0	10.0	1952	1.3	61.5	.1	75.0
1956	30.0	21.5	48.6	18.0	1934	1.0	63.0	.2	73.0
1829	20.0	24.5	60.2	13.0	1863	1.0	69.5	7.4	57.0
1859	20.0	24.5	58.9	15.0	1866	1.0	69.5	10.0	49.0
1871	20.0	24.5	1.9	67.0	1876	1.0	69.5	7.6	56.0
1926	20.0	24.5	69.5	12.0	1880	1.0	69.5	1.2	69.0
1948	15.4	27.0	37.0	23.0	1884	1.0	69.5	9.0	52.0
1877	14.0	28.5	7.9	54.0	1904	1.0	69.5	8.0	53.0
1950	14.0	28.5	27.1	28.0	1905	1.0	69.5	11.4	44.0
1841	10.0	30.5	101.3	7.0	1908	1.0	69.5	12.9	40.0
1979	10.0	30.5	18.0	35.0	1932	1.0	69.5	2.8	65.0
1858	8.0	32.0	34.6	24.0	1947	1.0	69.5	5.5	59.0
1848	7.5	33.5	20.7	33.0	1953	1.0	69.5	2.1	66.0
1928	7.5	33.5	11.2	46.0	1954	1.0	69.5	.8	70.0
1821	7.0	35.5	16.2	38.0	1816	0.	120.5	0.	120.5
1872	7.0	35.5	46.0	20.0	1817	0.	120.5	0.	120.5
1958	6.4	35.5	10.8	47.0	1818	0.	120.5	0.	120.5
1826	6.0	37.0	3.6	62.0	1819	0.	120.5	0.	120.5
1891	6.0	38.0	7.8	55.0	1820	0.	120.5	0.	120.5
1896	5.0	40.5	12.2	42.0	1822	0.	120.5	0.	120.5
1913	5.0	40.5	1.7	68.0	1823	0.	120.5	0.	120.5

Left half:

Year	Battle Deaths from Wars Begun (000's)	Rank	Nation Months of War Begun	Rank
1824	0.	120.5	0.	120.5
1825	0.	120.5	0.	120.5
1827	0.	120.5	0.	120.5
1828	0.	120.5	0.	120.5
1831	0.	120.5	0.	120.5
1833	0.	120.5	0.	120.5
1835	0.	120.5	0.	120.5
1836	0.	120.5	0.	120.5
1837	0.	120.5	0.	120.5
1838	0.	120.5	0.	120.5
1839	0.	120.5	0.	120.5
1842	0.	120.5	0.	120.5
1843	0.	120.5	0.	120.5
1844	0.	120.5	0.	120.5
1845	0.	120.5	0.	120.5
1846	0.	120.5	0.	120.5
1849	0.	120.5	0.	120.5
1850	0.	120.5	0.	120.5
1852	0.	120.5	0.	120.5
1854	0.	120.5	0.	120.5
1855	0.	120.5	0.	120.5
1857	0.	120.5	0.	120.5
1862	0.	120.5	0.	120.5
1864	0.	120.5	0.	120.5
1865	0.	120.5	0.	120.5
1867	0.	120.5	0.	120.5
1869	0.	120.5	0.	120.5
1873	0.	120.5	0.	120.5
1874	0.	120.5	0.	120.5
1875	0.	120.5	0.	120.5
1878	0.	120.5	0.	120.5
1879	0.	120.5	0.	120.5
1881	0.	120.5	0.	120.5
1882	0.	120.5	0.	120.5
1883	0.	120.5	0.	120.5
1885	0.	120.5	0.	120.5
1886	0.	120.5	0.	120.5
1887	0.	120.5	0.	120.5
1888	0.	120.5	0.	120.5
1889	0.	120.5	0.	120.5
1890	0.	120.5	0.	120.5
1892	0.	120.5	0.	120.5

Right half:

Year	Battle Deaths from Wars Begun (000's)	Rank	Nation Months of War Begun	Rank
1895	0.	120.5	0.	120.5
1897	0.	120.5	0.	120.5
1898	0.	120.5	0.	120.5
1900	0.	120.5	0.	120.5
1901	0.	120.5	0.	120.5
1902	0.	120.5	0.	120.5
1903	0.	120.5	0.	120.5
1906	0.	120.5	0.	120.5
1909	0.	120.5	0.	120.5
1912	0.	120.5	0.	120.5
1915	0.	120.5	0.	120.5
1916	0.	120.5	0.	120.5
1918	0.	120.5	0.	120.5
1920	0.	120.5	0.	120.5
1921	0.	120.5	0.	120.5
1922	0.	120.5	0.	120.5
1923	0.	120.5	0.	120.5
1925	0.	120.5	0.	120.5
1927	0.	120.5	0.	120.5
1931	0.	120.5	0.	120.5
1933	0.	120.5	0.	120.5
1935	0.	120.5	0.	120.5
1937	0.	120.5	0.	120.5
1938	0.	120.5	0.	120.5
1939	0.	120.5	0.	120.5
1940	0.	120.5	0.	120.5
1941	0.	120.5	0.	120.5
1942	0.	120.5	0.	120.5
1943	0.	120.5	0.	120.5
1945	0.	120.5	0.	120.5
1951	0.	120.5	0.	120.5
1957	0.	120.5	0.	120.5
1961	0.	120.5	0.	120.5
1964	0.	120.5	0.	120.5
1968	0.	120.5	0.	120.5
1969	0.	120.5	0.	120.5
1973	0.	120.5	0.	120.5
1974	0.	120.5	0.	120.5
1976	0.	120.5	0.	120.5
1977	0.	120.5	0.	120.5
1980	0.	120.5	0.	120.5

15.3 Rank Order of Years by Amount of Civil War Under Way

Year	Nation Months of War Underway	Rank	% of Possible Nation Months Exhausted	Rank
1862	69.48	1.0	13.79	1.0
1861	68.73	2.0	13.32	3.0
1860	67.55	3.0	11.98	4.0
1863	67.37	4.0	13.37	2.0
1964	61.21	5.0	4.18	22.0
1968	56.03	6.0	3.51	31.0
1979	55.70	7.0	2.99	57.0
1971	54.14	8.0	3.25	46.0
1967	53.39	9.0	3.42	42.0
1978	49.93	10.0	2.70	61.5
1965	49.48	11.0	3.33	44.5
1963	49.42	12.0	3.46	34.5
1962	49.15	13.0	3.50	32.0
1961	48.00	14.0	3.60	30.0
1976	45.68	15.0	2.52	69.0
1960	44.45	16.0	3.46	34.5
1969	44.10	17.0	2.76	59.5
1864	43.00	18.0	8.53	6.0
1848	40.18	19.0	8.59	5.0
1973	37.54	20.0	2.22	82.5
1949	37.05	21.0	4.12	23.0
1950	36.83	22.0	4.09	25.0
1975	36.75	23.0	2.04	88.0
1966	36.32	24.0	2.35	75.0
1974	36.00	25.5	2.10	87.0
1977	36.00	25.5	1.97	89.0
1970	35.57	27.0	2.21	84.0
1958	34.77	28.0	3.22	48.0
1867	33.48	29.0	6.98	8.0
1929	33.23	30.0	5.65	12.0
1919	31.48	31.0	4.10	24.0
1870	31.39	32.0	7.07	7.0
1951	31.00	33.0	3.44	41.0
1972	29.97	34.0	1.80	95.0
1948	29.95	35.0	3.47	33.0
1947	29.45	36.0	3.61	29.0
1865	27.30	37.0	5.42	13.0
1868	27.01	38.0	6.08	10.0
1911	25.11	39.0	4.76	15.0
1866	24.55	40.0	4.87	14.0
1959	24.23	41.0	2.27	79.0
1841	24.00	44.0	5.88	11.0
1918	24.00	44.0	4.35	16.5
1927	24.00	44.0	3.13	52.5
1957	24.00	44.0	2.25	81.0
1980	24.00	47.0	1.29	111.0
1832	23.32	48.0	6.70	9.0
1859	23.00	49.0	4.26	20.0
1849	20.52	50.0	4.27	19.0
1928	19.70	50.0	2.57	66.0
1847	19.55	52.0	4.29	18.0
1952	19.13	53.0	1.96	90.5
1842	18.13	54.0	4.21	21.0
1869	17.68	55.0	3.73	28.0
1871	16.58	56.0	4.06	26.0
1930	16.55	57.0	2.14	85.5
1912	16.45	58.0	3.17	49.0
1920	16.35	59.0	2.22	82.5
1955	15.70	60.0	1.50	106.0
1893	15.17	61.0	3.16	50.0
1932	14.80	62.0	1.89	94.0
1953	14.73	63.0	1.51	105.0
1877	14.13	64.0	3.32	45.0
1908	13.93	65.0	2.69	63.0
1913	13.88	66.0	2.65	65.0
1914	13.68	67.0	2.56	67.0
1894	13.53	68.0	2.76	59.5
1954	12.90	69.0	1.30	109.5
1917	12.77	70.0	2.53	68.0
1858	12.74	71.0	2.41	71.0
1956	12.73	72.0	1.20	113.5
1872	12.55	73.5	3.13	52.5
1830	12.40	73.5	3.75	27.0
1934	12.16	75.0	1.54	101.0
1840	12.03	87.5	3.13	52.5
1822	12.00	87.5	4.35	16.5
1831	12.00	87.5	3.45	38.0
1833	12.00	87.5	3.45	38.0
1835	12.00	87.5	3.45	38.0
1836	12.00	87.5	3.45	38.0
1837	12.00	87.5	3.45	38.0
1838	12.00	87.5	3.23	47.0

Year	Nation Months of War Underway	Rank	% of Possible Nation Months Exhausted	Rank
1839	12.00	87.5	3.13	52.5
1846	12.00	87.5	2.70	61.5
1850	12.00	87.5	2.50	70.0
1854	12.00	87.5	2.38	73.0
1857	12.00	87.5	2.27	79.0
1873	12.00	87.5	3.03	55.5
1874	12.00	87.5	3.03	55.5
1875	12.00	87.5	2.94	58.0
1900	12.00	87.5	2.38	73.0
1901	12.00	87.5	2.38	73.0
1902	12.00	87.5	2.33	76.5
1915	12.00	87.5	2.33	76.5
1916	12.00	87.5	2.27	79.0
1931	12.00	87.5	1.56	98.5
1933	12.00	87.5	1.54	101.0
1937	12.00	87.5	1.52	103.5
1938	12.00	87.5	1.52	103.5
1834	11.71	100.0	3.36	43.0
1845	11.55	101.0	2.67	64.0
1905	11.32	102.0	2.14	85.5
1924	11.26	103.0	1.54	101.0
1946	11.08	104.0	1.40	107.0
1926	10.03	105.0	1.33	108.0
1851	9.60	106.0	1.95	92.0
1935	9.48	107.0	1.20	113.5
1897	9.16	108.0	1.96	90.5
1904	8.03	109.0	1.56	98.5
1891	7.74	110.0	1.70	97.0
1885	7.48	111.0	1.73	96.0
1907	6.55	112.5	1.30	109.5
1909	6.55	112.5	1.24	112.0
1829	6.00	114.0	1.92	93.0
1903	5.50	115.0	1.07	117.0
1936	5.45	116.0	.69	120.0
1899	4.00	117.0	.81	118.0
1826	3.57	118.0	1.19	115.0
1876	3.25	119.0	.77	119.0
1823	3.20	120.0	1.16	116.0
1896	3.00	121.0	.64	121.0
1939	2.93	122.0	.38	123.5
1895	2.61	123.0	.56	122.0
1856	2.03	124.0	.38	123.5
1884	1.53	125.0	.35	126.0
1945	1.43	126.0	.19	129.0
1910	1.37	127.0	.26	128.0
1880	1.21	128.0	.27	127.0
1821	1.00	129.0	.36	125.0
1944	.93	130.0	.14	130.0
1925	.48	131.0	.07	131.5
1853	.35	132.0	.07	131.5
1855	.23	133.0	.04	133.0
1906	.03	134.0	.01	134.0
1816	0.	150.0	0.	150.0
1817	0.	150.0	0.	150.0
1818	0.	150.0	0.	150.0
1819	0.	150.0	0.	150.0
1820	0.	150.0	0.	150.0
1824	0.	150.0	0.	150.0
1825	0.	150.0	0.	150.0
1827	0.	150.0	0.	150.0
1828	0.	150.0	0.	150.0
1843	0.	150.0	0.	150.0
1844	0.	150.0	0.	150.0
1852	0.	150.0	0.	150.0
1878	0.	150.0	0.	150.0
1879	0.	150.0	0.	150.0
1881	0.	150.0	0.	150.0
1882	0.	150.0	0.	150.0
1883	0.	150.0	0.	150.0
1886	0.	150.0	0.	150.0
1887	0.	150.0	0.	150.0
1888	0.	150.0	0.	150.0
1889	0.	150.0	0.	150.0
1890	0.	150.0	0.	150.0
1892	0.	150.0	0.	150.0
1898	0.	150.0	0.	150.0
1921	0.	150.0	0.	150.0
1922	0.	150.0	0.	150.0
1923	0.	150.0	0.	150.0
1940	0.	150.0	0.	150.0
1941	0.	150.0	0.	150.0
1942	0.	150.0	0.	150.0
1943	0.	150.0	0.	150.0

SUMMARY

With the data presented in this chapter, we may launch our investigation of trends and cycles in civil war in the interstate system since 1816. Further, they will be useful in future analyses of the relationship between patterns in international war activity and patterns in civil war activity.

CHAPTER 16

Secular Trends, Cycles, and Seasonality in the Incidence of War

With the data presented in Chapter 15, we can begin our search for patterns in the incidence of civil war during our 165-year period. As with international wars, we search for both trends and cycles. It is possible, as we have seen, to discover cycles without uncovering upward or downward trends in the frequency, magnitude, or severity of civil war.

One might expect to find an upward trend in the incidence of civil war. That is, if civil war is more likely to occur in immature or developing polities, then the increase in the size of the international system, especially since the 1920s, should lead to an increase in the number of civil wars among system members. If, on the other hand, civil wars are related to trends in international war activity, then we should not expect to find trends in civil war activity, since we did not find any for international wars. Or, finally, since the relationship between *systemic* economic, political, and military trends and internal war should be less intimate than that for international war, we should not expect to find much in the way of trends or cycles in civil war throughout the system.

In this chapter, we replicate analyses done in Chapters 7, 8, and 9 for international war to determine the absence or presence of patterns in the way civil wars have occurred in the system.

COMPARING SUCCESSIVE PERIODS FOR AMOUNT OF CIVIL WAR IN THE SYSTEM

Rather than divide our time span into two and five equal periods (as in 7.1 and 7.2), we economize and look here only at a comparison of the amount of civil war begun in 15 successive periods. In 16.1, we have divided our 165-year span into 11-year periods and show for each period the average number of nations in the system, the number of civil wars begun, the number of civil wars begun per nation, the nation months of civil war began during the period, the normalized nation months of civil war (the total nation months over the number of nations in the system), and the total battle deaths resulting from civil wars begun during each of the periods.

Visual inspection suggests very little in the way of trends. It is true that the number of civil wars begun appears to rise over time with 14, 13, and 14 begun during the past three decades, but when these figures are normalized for the number of nations in the system, the trend disappears. A similar trend seems to appear in the figures for nation months of war begun, but it also disappears when we look at the normalized figure. It is clear, however, that the twentieth-century totals for battle deaths are appreciably higher, on the average, than those for the nineteenth century.

Several other items merit attention here. As already noted, all the scores for the 1860s are inflated by China's three large civil wars that began in the 1850s, before that unfortunate nation was a member of our system. Second, the fact that relatively few civil wars began during periods that experienced the world wars suggests that nations engaged in global conflict are much less likely to engage in internal war during those periods. Third, some periods experience appreciably less civil war than others, as can be seen, for example, from 1816 to 1826 and 1882 to 1892. Finally, although the years since World War II have had more than their share of civil wars, the last decade was less bloody than the one that preceded it. While our first pass through the data presented in 16.1 does not reveal any trends in the onset of civil war over time, before we conclude that there have been none in this category of martial activity, we should subject these data to closer statistical analysis.

REGRESSION LINES AS TREND INDICATORS

Employing linear regression, we plot a civil war measure along the vertical axis of a scattergram on which the longitudinal axis represents the successive years. By fitting a straight line that minimizes the square of the distance between that line and all of the data points on the scattergram, we can ascertain how much it departs from the horizontal (no trend) line over the 165 annual observations.

16.1 Comparing the Amount of Civil War Begun in Fifteen Successive Periods

Onset Measure	1816-1826	1827-1837	1838-1848	1849-1859	1860-1870	1871-1881	1882-1892	1893-1903
Avg. No. of Nations (N)	23.3	27.9	35.1	42.4	41.0	34.9	37.3	40.5
Number of Wars	2	4	6	5	10	5	2	5
Wars/Nation	.09	.14	.17	.12	.24	.14	.05	.12
Nation Months	19.8	143.7	169.6	125.4	435.0	64.6	16.8	88.1
Nation Months/Nation	.9	5.1	4.8	3.0	10.9	1.9	.5	2.2
Battle Deaths	13.0	55.7	24.5	38.0	2810.6	43.0	6.0	111.5

Onset Measure	1904-1914	1915-1925	1926-1936	1937-1947	1948-1958	1959-1969	1970-1980	Totals	Means
Avg. No. of Nations (N)	43.4	53.5	64.6	61.6	80.4	119.5	147.2		
Number of Wars	11	4	8	3	14	13	14	106	7.1
Wars/Nation	.25	.07	.12	.05	.17	.11	.10	1.96	.13
Nation Months	181.1	56.7	194.5	92.1	289.3	507.6	394.5	2778.8	185.3
Nation Months/Nation	4.2	1.1	3.0	1.5	3.6	4.2	2.7	49.2	3.3
Battle Deaths	270.5	506.5	954.8	1161.0	372.3	1830.5	819.5	9017.4	601.2

16.2 Regression Lines for Normalized Nation Months of Civil War Under Way
      Annually, 1816–1980

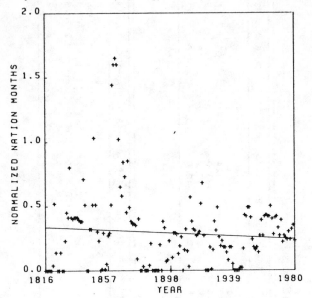

In 16.2, we do this with our normalized nation months of civil war underway indicator. As can be seen, the line that best fits the data departs only slightly from the horizontal. This absence of a trend is clearly reflected by the very low coefficient of determination (r^2) of .01. In 16.2a and 16.2b we divide our period into the two centuries. Again, we find the almost total absence of trends with r^2s of .0 and .04, respectively.

Finally, we present the coefficients for a number of other civil war onset and underway measures in 16.3. As with the previous analyses, we again find no trend, either upward or downward, especially if we control for the size of the system.

CIVIL WAR RANK CORRELATIONS AS TREND INDICATORS

When we employed the year as our unit of analysis, we discerned no trends in civil war experience in the international system; however, we can search for trends in the wars themselves. That is, if we ignore frequencies and the intervals between them and merely examine the wars in sequence as they unfold, we may discover trends in their magnitude, severity, or intensity. Using the data from Chapter 15, we

16.2a   Repression Lines for Normalized Nation Months of Civil War Under
        Way: Nineteenth Century

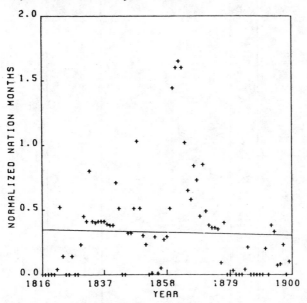

16.2b   Regression Lines for Normalized Nation Months of Civil War Under
        Way: Twentieth Century

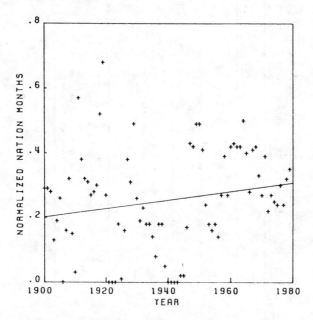

16.3 Linear Trend Statistics for Annual Amounts of Civil War Begun and Under Way (N = 165 Annual Observations)

Type of Measure	Variable	Correlation Coefficient with Time (r)	Coefficient of Determination (r^2)	Regression Coefficient (b)	Significance
	Nation months of civil war	.146	.021	.127	.061
	Nation months of civil war/no. of nations in interstate system	.048	.002	-.001	.538
BEGUN	Battle deaths in civil war	.109	.012	.506	.165
	Battle deaths in civil war/pre-war populations of combatant nations	.122	.015	.001	.118
UNDER WAY	Nation months of civil war	.414	.171	.026	.000
	Nation months of civil war/no. of nations in interstate system	.092	.008	-.001	.238

show in 16.4 the rank order correlation (Spearman rho) between the recency of civil wars and their rank position on several nation months and battle deaths indicators.

As with interstate wars, the results reveal that the unit of analysis (year or war) makes little difference. The correlations for recency of war and nation months ($-.11$), recency and battle deaths. ($.15$), and recency and battle deaths per capita. ($.12$) all suggest the absence of any trends. The correlations for recency and nation months divided by the number of nations in the system, a somewhat more robust $-.23$, relates to the very rapid rate of increase in the size of the system during our period.

TRENDS IN THE INTENSITY OF CIVIL WAR

Despite the absence of trends in our most important (normalized) indicators of civil war activity, it is possible that the wars themselves have become more intense over time. There may be, hidden in our earlier analyses, a trend revealing more battle deaths per nation month of war as we move from the nineteenth to the twentieth century. Leaving the fixed time intervals used in the previous analysis (16.4), we return to the scattergram mode. In 16.5, we plot the intensity of civil wars (battle death/nation months) along the vertical axis on which the longitudinal axis represents the successive years, and then determine the regression line that best describes the trend in intensity over time. A glance at the regression line as well as the regression coefficient itself ($.04$) reveals, once again, the absence of a trend.

Obviously, our inability to turn up trends in the frequency, magnitude, and intensity of civil war over time was biased by our preference for normalized figures. As we have seen, more civil wars resulting in more nation months and more battle deaths have been fought in recent periods than in earlier ones. Nevertheless, this trend should be expected given the ever-increasing opportunities available for civil war as the system expanded from 23 members in 1816 to 155 in 1980. Or, to put it another way, is there a greater likelihood of civil war breaking out in any single nation today than in that same nation 165, 100, or 50 years ago? As with interstate wars, the answer is a clear negative, given the increase in war opportunities resulting from the much larger system. Of course, our analysis of trends does not exhaust the search for patterns in civil wars through time. It might well be that, as with interstate wars, the absence of trends does not also mean the absence of cycles.

16.4   Rank Correlations Between Civil War Date and Severity and Magnitude

Variable	Coefficient with War Onset Date (rho)	Statistical Significance (N = 103)
Nation months	-.11	n.s. at .05
Nation months/no. of nations in interstate system	-.23	sig. at .05
Battle deaths	.15	n.s. at .05
Battle deaths/pre-war populations of combatant nations	.12	n.s. at .05

CYCLES AND PERIODICITIES IN THE INCIDENCE OF WAR

We launch our search for cycles in the incidence of civil wars in the international system with an examination of the regularity, or lack thereof, of inter-war intervals. Here, as in 8.1, we determine the extent to which the intervals between the beginnings of our civil wars are equal in length, and if they are not equal, how nearly random their distribution might be. We test for randomness using the Poisson density function explained in Chapter 8.

16.5   Civil War Intensities: Battle Deaths/Nation Months

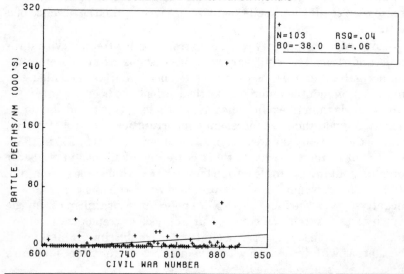

FLUCTUATIONS IN THE ANNUAL AMOUNT OF CIVIL WAR BEGUN

The intervals between the onsets of war revealed in 16.6 come close to the distribution predicted by the equation. Using half-year units with the shortest at six months and the longest eight and one-half years, we find the observed distribution gives a good fit to that predicted; the randomness hypothesis is confirmed above the .05 level of significance.

16.6   Predicted and Observed Distributions of Inter-War Intervals

Length of Interval in Six Month Units	ALL CIVIL WARS	
	Predicted	Observed
0	.283	.028
1	.213	.266
2	.161	.266
3	.121	.143
4	.091	.104
5	.069	.066
6	.052	.057
7	.039	.028
8	.029	.019
9	.022	.019
10	.017	.028
11	.012	.000
12	.009	.000
13	.007	.028
14	.005	.000
15	.004	.000
16	.003	.000
17	.002	.010
	N=106	

Chi square = 42.0; p>.05

Persuaded as we are of the need to go beyond the goodness-of-fit test for periodicity, we once more turn to the spectral analysis option. Beginning with the begun (or onset) data, 16.7 suggests neither the presence nor absence of a recurrent cycle, and when we subjected these data to spectral analysis, we found the same random pattern that appeared vis-à-vis the onset of international war. But given the differences between onset and underway results there, it now behooves us to examine the civil war *underway* data.

16.7   Annual Amounts of Civil War Begun, 1816–1980

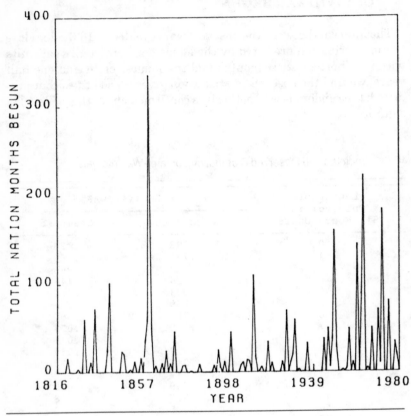

FLUCTUATIONS IN THE ANNUAL AMOUNTS
OF CIVIL WAR UNDER WAY

In this spectral analysis, we again use the magnitude (nation months) rather than severity (battle-connected death) figures because nation months are more readily normalized and, of course, correlate strongly with battle deaths. Looking at 16.8, the annual amount of civil war *under way,* we notice immediately a difference between this profile and that shown in 16.7. We find here more continuous fluctuation with more pronounced peaks and fewer long, relatively flat, sections.

16.8   Annual Amounts of Civil War Under Way, 1816–1980

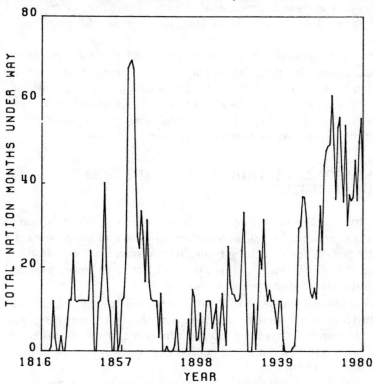

As with international wars, fewer years saw civil wars begun than experienced civil wars under way. While civil wars began in only 75 of our 165 years, they were under way in 134 of those years.

After normalizing these underway data for system size (nation months divided by number of nations in the system each year), we present in 16.9 the results of our spectral analysis. Here we see statistically significant peaks at the 84, 42, and 28 year intervals, indicating a crest in the spectral density function in the frequencies from 1.2 to 3.6 crests per century. The 84-year cycle most likely is a statistical artifact that should not be taken seriously. On the other hand, the 28-year cycle, and perhaps the longer 42-year cycle, are worth considering. The former is especially interesting, in that it conforms closely to the cycle in international war under way that we discerned in Chapter 8—at least until the outlying world wars were omitted.

Does this suggest that cycles in civil war under way are related to cycles in international war under way? We are tempted to turn to that question here but have eschewed, in this volume, all analyses concerning the relationship between international and civil wars. Suffice to say that the results of our spectral analysis suggest a host of intriguing hypotheses to which we will turn in the near future.

SEASONAL DISTRIBUTIONS IN THE ONSET OF CIVIL WAR

One final search for patterns involves the seasonal distribution of civil war over time. As was seen earlier, autumn and spring were the favorite periods for launching international war. Civil war data are presented in 16.10 in a format similar to 9.1, which showed seasonal distributions for international wars.

At first glance, it appears that we have turned up an amazing counterintuitive trend. The season that experiences by far more civil war onsets than any other is the winter; contrary to the interstate experience, fall sees the least amount of civil war, with a very low number (1) for the period 1816-1871.

The first finding, the dominance of winter among the seasons, can be attributed to a statistical artifact. As noted earlier, civil wars are much harder to date accurately than international wars, and thus we often arbitrarily chose January 1 as the onset date (and December 31 as the termination date). Thus, the seeming "popularity" of the inclement winter period as a time to start civil wars must be looked at quite skeptically.

As for the relative paucity of civil wars beginning in the fall, perhaps this outcome is related to the "popularity" of that season for launching *interstate* wars. We are assuming here that nations do not start civil and interstate wars at the same time, but that facile assumption will be examined in the future as we relate international war variables to civil war variables.

In any event, the data for seasonal distributions, which must be taken with a very large dose of salt because of our coding problems, do not contribute much to our search for patterns in civil war since 1816.

16.9   Power Spectral Estimates of Various Frequencies for Normalized Nation Months of Civil War Under Way

16.10 Seasonal Distributions in Onset of Civil War

	Winter 22 Dec-21 Mar	Spring 22 Mar-21 June	Summer 22 June-21 Sept	Fall 22 Sept-21 Dec	Mean	Total
Number of Civil Wars						
Begun, 1816-1980	41	28	20	17	26.5	106
1816-1871	14	8	5	1	7.0	28
1872-1919	11	4	4	5	6.0	24
1920-1980	16	16	11	11	13.5	54
Nation Months of Civil War						
Begun, 1816-1980	1049.7	464.3	607.1	657.7	694.7	2778.8
1816-1871	582.8	139.6	156.8	16.2	223.8	895.4
1872-1919	83.8	74.1	72.7	163.0	98.4	393.6
1920-1980	383.1	250.6	377.6	478.5	372.4	1489.8
Battle Deaths from Civil War						
Begun, 1816-1980	3949000.0	867300.0	2172300.0	1558800.0	2136850.0	8547400.0
1816-1871	2210500.0	687000.0	57300.0	7000.0	740450.0	2961800.0
1872-1919	35000.0	20000.0	107000.0	753000.0	228750.0	915000.0
1920-1980	1703500.0	160300.0	2008000.0	798800.0	1167650.0	4670600.0

SUMMARY

In many ways, much of what we have turned up in this chapter conforms to patterns in international war revealed in Chapters 7 through 9. As with international war, we discovered no trends in the frequency, magnitude, severity, or intensity of civil war since 1816. Of course, we have experienced more and bloodier wars in the more recent period than in most other periods, but when we normalize for system size, these trends disappear. That is, given the increasing opportunities available within the system for civil wars to begin (because of the constant growth in size of the system), we must conclude that citizens of the 155 nations in the system in 1980 did not stand any greater chance of experiencing civil wars in their countries than did citizens of a much smaller system 100 years ago.

When we turned to periodicities, however, we found a different story. To be sure, as with international wars begun, we discovered no cyclical patterns in civil war begun. However, when we looked at civil wars under way, we noted a 28-year cycle, and perhaps a 42-year cycle, with the former bearing an uncanny resemblance to the cycle for international wars under way. Definitive confirmation of these tentative results must await a more complete and thorough search for cycles in both sets of war experiences.

The main area where patterns examined in this chapter differed from those in Chapters 7 through 9 was in the seasonal concentrations of civil wars begun. Despite an apparent tendency for civil wars to begin in the winter, we concluded that, unlike international wars, there does not appear to be any one season that is favored by those who launch civil wars.

With these very preliminary analyses of our data, we leave the system level and turn to the nations themselves as we compare and contrast various national experiences in civil war.

CHAPTER 17

The Civil War-Proneness of the Nations and Regions

As we saw earlier, all nations have not participated equally in international wars. The major powers, plus Turkey, Spain, and a few others, dominated the rankings, while many smaller states, including those in allegedly volatile regions such as Africa, have been able to escape this scourge. Do the nations share more equally in participation in civil wars? One would not expect so, since civil wars allegedly occur in most cases in unstable, developing polities. Images of Latin Americans and Asians engaging in constant internecine strife, ranging from palace revolutions to full-scale jungle and even urban guerrilla war, abound in our scholarly and popular literature. Further, it stands to reason that the nations that participate most in international wars, the major powers, could not long maintain their status were they racked by the kind of civil strife associated with nations in the "tropics."

We tend also to expect civil war in nations with undemocratic political systems. The venerable democracies of Western Europe, the United States, and the British Commonwealth are said to have produced a system that has solved the often difficult succession problem.

How well do these notions about the civil war propensities of nations hold up? By reaggregating the data and moving from the systemic to the national level of analysis, we can address that question in this chapter.

TOTAL AND AVERAGE CIVIL WAR EXPERIENCE OF THE NATIONS

In 17.1, we list by region the civil war experiences of all nations that have been members of the international system since 1816. Following the nation number and name we show the total number of

276

years the nation has been in the system (column 1), an important figure that is used for normalization purposes. We then present the number of wars (column 2), total battle deaths in those wars (column 3), and total war months (column 4). Then follow a series of normalized measures beginning with battle deaths per year in the system (column 5), wars per year (column 6), war months per year (column 7), war months per war (column 8), battle deaths per war (column 9), and battle deaths per month (column 10). These figures can be compared to those in 10.1, the identical table for international war. *However, 17.1 does not include battle deaths and nation months for interveners in other nations' civil wars*. Thus, the United States is shown as having experienced one civil war during its 165-year tenure in the system even though it intervened in several other nations' civil wars.

Summaries provided at the end of each regional table represent the sums of all the individual scores, including the *sums* of the normalized or averaged scores. They are not to be confused with the more meaningful regional aggregations presented in 17.4.

Before moving on to the ranking of nations on these variables, we must comment on one result that is not readily apparent in the table. The total number of wars per region does not reflect the distribution of those wars throughout the region. Thus, in the western hemisphere, although 41 civil wars have been fought in a sub-system that contained 31 nations, only 18 (or 58 percent) of those nations experienced a civil war.

In some regions, much of the war is accounted for by only a handful of nations. In this respect, civil war is more widely spread in the western hemisphere than the other regions. Throughout the rest of the system, 43 percent of the Middle Eastern nations, 36 percent of the Asian nations, 19 percent of the European nations, and only 15 percent of the African nations have experienced a civil war that resulted in at least 1,000 battle deaths per year.

RANKING THE NATIONS BY CIVIL WAR EXPERIENCE

As can be seen in 17.1, civil war experience, like international war experience, has not been shared evenly among all members of the system. In 17.2, we show the rank order of those nations with some civil war experience on severity, magnitude, and intensity indicators. The nations are listed according to their rank on the battle death indicator (column 1). Following the rank is the total number of battle deaths (column 2), the rank on battle deaths per year in the system

(text continued page 287)

17.1 National Civil War Experience Totaled, Averaged, and Normalized

Code No.	Nation Name	Total Years in System 1	No. of Wars 2	Total Battle Deaths (000's) 3	Total War Months 4	Battle Deaths (000's) per Year 5	Wars per Year 6	War Months per Year 7	Months per War 8	Battle Deaths (000's) per War 9	Battle Deaths (000's) per Month 10
	WESTERN HEMISPHERE										
2	UNITED STATES OF AMERICA	165	1	650.00	48.0	3.939	.006	.29	48.00	650.00	13.542
20	CANADA	61	0	0	0	0	0	0	0	0	0
31	BAHAMAS	8	0	0	0	0	0	0	0	0	0
40	CUBA	76	1	5.00	6.6	.066	.013	.09	6.60	5.00	.758
41	HAITI	103	0	0	0	0	0	0	0	0	0
42	DOMINICAN REPUBLIC	81	1	2.50	4.3	.031	.012	.05	4.30	2.50	.581
51	JAMAICA	19	0	0	0	0	0	0	0	0	0
52	TRINIDAD	19	0	0	0	0	0	0	0	0	0
53	BARBADOS	15	0	0	0	0	0	0	0	0	0
54	DOMINICANA	3	0	0	0	0	0	0	0	0	0
55	GRENADA	7	0	0	0	0	0	0	0	0	0
56	SAINT LUCIA	2	0	0	0	0	0	0	0	0	0
70	MEXICO	150	4	272.00	200.9	1.813	.027	1.34	50.22	68.00	1.354
90	GUATEMALA	132	2	2.00	10.8	.015	.015	.08	5.40	1.00	.185
91	HONDURAS	82	1	1.00	1.8	.012	.012	.02	1.80	1.00	.556
92	EL SALVADOR	106	1	10.00	18.0	.094	.009	.17	18.00	10.00	.556
93	NICARAGUA	81	1	35.00	9.5	.432	.012	.12	9.50	35.00	3.684
94	COSTA RICA	61	1	2.00	1.2	.033	.016	.02	1.20	2.00	1.667
95	PANAMA	61	0	0	0	0	0	0	0	0	0
100	COLOMBIA	150	7	409.90	274.8	2.733	.047	1.83	39.26	58.56	1.492
101	VENEZUELA	140	2	23.00	82.8	.164	.014	.59	41.40	11.50	.278
110	GUYANA	15	0	0	0	0	0	0	0	0	0
115	SURINAM	6	0	0	0	0	0	0	0	0	0
130	ECUADOR	127	0	0	0	0	0	0	0	0	0
135	PERU	140	3	11.00	34.1	.079	.021	.24	11.37	3.67	.323
140	BRAZIL	155	4	8.50	40.2	.055	.026	.26	10.05	2.13	.211
145	BOLIVIA	133	1	1.50	1.4	.011	.008	.00	.10	1.50	15.000
150	PARAGUAY	129	2	3.00	15.4	.023	.016	.12	7.70	1.50	.195
155	CHILE	142	2	8.00	10.8	.056	.014	.08	5.40	4.00	.741
160	ARGENTINA	140	6	17.50	132.9	.125	.043	.95	22.15	2.92	.132
165	URUGUAY	99	1	1.00	8.0	.010	.010	.08	8.00	1.00	.125
	REGIONAL SUMMARY										
	31 NATIONS	2608	41	1462.90	900.2	9.692	.322	6.33	290.45	861.27	41.377

Code No.	Nation Name	Total Years in System 1	No. of Wars 2	Total Battle Deaths (000's) 3	Total War Months 4	Battle Deaths (000's) per Year 5	Wars per Year 6	War Months per Year 7	War Months per War 8	Battle Deaths (000's) per War 9	Battle Deaths (000's) per Month 10
	EUROPE										
200	UNITED KINGDOM	165	0	0	0	0	0	0	0	0	0
205	IRELAND	59	0	0	0	0	0	0	0	0	0
210	NETHERLANDS	160	0	0	0	0	0	0	0	0	0
211	BELGIUM	146	0	0	0	0	0	0	0	0	0
212	LUXEMBURG	57	0	0	0	0	0	0	0	0	0
220	FRANCE	163	3	24.70	6.3	.152	.018	.04	2.10	8.23	3.921
225	SWITZERLAND	165	0	0	0	0	0	0	0	0	0
230	SPAIN	165	7	699.90	190.8	4.242	.042	1.16	27.26	99.99	3.668
235	PORTUGAL	165	1	20.00	60.2	.121	.006	.36	60.20	20.00	.332
240	HANOVER	29	0	0	0	0	0	0	0	0	0
245	BAVARIA	56	0	0	0	0	0	0	0	0	0
255	GERMANY/PRUSSIA	130	0	0	0	0	0	0	0	0	0
260	GERMAN FEDERAL REPUBLIC	26	0	0	0	0	0	0	0	0	0
265	GERMAN DEMOCRATIC REP.	27	0	0	0	0	0	0	0	0	0
267	BADEN	55	0	0	0	0	0	0	0	0	0
269	SAXONY	52	0	0	0	0	0	0	0	0	0
271	WUERTTEMBURG	55	0	0	0	0	0	0	0	0	0
273	HESSE ELECTORAL	51	0	0	0	0	0	0	0	0	0
275	HESSE GRAND DUCAL	52	0	0	0	0	0	0	0	0	0
280	MECKLENBURG SCHWERIN	25	0	0	0	0	0	0	0	0	0
290	POLAND	56	0	0	0	0	0	0	0	0	0
300	AUSTRIA-HUNGARY	103	1	3.50	7.6	.034	.010	.07	7.60	3.50	.461

(continued)

17.1 (Continued)

Code No.	Nation Name	Total Years in System 1	No. of Wars 2	Total Battle Deaths (000's) 3	Total War Months 4	Battle Deaths (000's) per Year 5	Wars per Year 6	War Months per Year 7	Months per War 8	Battle Deaths (000's) per War 9	Battle Deaths (000's) per Month 10
					EUROPE						
305	AUSTRIA	45	0	0	0	0	0	0	0	0	0
310	HUNGARY	62	1	4.00	10.7	.065	.016	.17	10.70	4.00	.374
315	CZECHOSLOVAKIA	57	0	0	0	0	0	0	0	0	0
325	ITALY/SARDINIA	165	0	0	0	0	0	0	0	0	0
327	PAPAL STATES	45	0	0	0	0	0	0	0	0	0
329	TWO SICILIES	46	1	1.00	8.9	.022	.022	.19	8.90	1.00	.112
332	MODENA	19	0	0	0	0	0	0	0	0	0
335	PARMA	10	0	0	0	0	0	0	0	0	0
337	TUSCANY	45	0	0	0	0	0	0	0	0	0
338	MALTA	17	0	0	0	0	0	0	0	0	0
339	ALBANIA	62	0	0	0	0	0	0	0	0	0
345	YUGOSLAVIA/SERBIA	100	1	160.00	37.4	1.074	.007	.25	37.40	160.00	4.278
350	GREECE	149	0	0	0	0	0	0	0	0	0
352	CYPRUS	21	0	0	0	0	0	0	0	0	0
355	BULGARIA	73	0	0	0	0	0	0	0	0	0
360	RUMANIA	103	1	2.00	1.5	.019	.010	.01	1.50	2.00	1.333
365	USSR (RUSSIA)	165	2	501.00	45.6	3.036	.012	.28	22.80	250.50	10.987
366	ESTONIA	23	0	0	0	0	0	0	0	0	0
367	LATVIA	23	0	0	0	0	0	0	0	0	0
368	LITHUANIA	23	0	0	0	0	0	0	0	0	0
375	FINLAND	62	0	0	0	0	0	0	0	0	0
380	SWEDEN	165	0	0	0	0	0	0	0	0	0
385	NORWAY	71	0	0	0	0	0	0	0	0	0
390	DENMARK	160	0	0	0	0	0	0	0	0	0
395	ICELAND	37	0	0	0	0	0	0	0	0	0
					REGIONAL SUMMARY						
	47 NATIONS	3710	18	1416.10	369.0	8.764	.143	2.54	178.46	549.22	25.466

Code No.	Nation Name	Total Years in System	No. of Wars	Total Battle Deaths (000's)	Total War Months	Battle Deaths (000's) per Year	Wars per Year	War Months per Year	Months per War	Battle Deaths (000's) per War	Battle Deaths (000's) per Month
		1	2	3	4	5	6	7	8	9	10
	AFRICA										
402	CAPE VERDE	6	0	0	0	0	0	0	0	0	0
403	SAO TOME PRINCIPE	6	0	0	0	0	0	0	0	0	0
404	GUINEA-BISSAU	7	0	0	0	0	0	0	0	0	0
411	EQUATORIAL GUINEA	13	0	0	0	0	0	0	0	0	0
420	GAMBIA	16	0	0	0	0	0	0	0	0	0
432	MALI	21	0	0	0	0	0	0	0	0	0
433	SENEGAL	21	0	0	0	0	0	0	0	0	0
434	BENIN/DAHOMEY	21	0	0	0	0	0	0	0	0	0
435	MAURITANIA	21	0	0	0	0	0	0	0	0	0
436	NIGER	21	0	0	0	0	0	0	0	0	0
437	IVORY COAST	21	0	0	0	0	0	0	0	0	0
438	GUINEA	23	0	0	0	0	0	0	0	0	0
439	UPPER VOLTA	21	0	0	0	0	0	0	0	0	0
450	LIBERIA	61	0	0	0	0	0	0	0	0	0
451	SIERRA LEONE	20	0	0	0	0	0	0	0	0	0
452	GHANA	24	0	0	0	0	0	0	0	0	0
461	TOGO	21	0	0	0	0	0	0	0	0	0
471	CAMEROUN	21	1	1000.00	30.2	47.619	.048	1.44	30.20	1000.00	33.113
481	GABON	21	0	0	0	0	0	0	0	0	0
482	CENTRAL AFRICAN REPUBLIC	21	0	0	0	0	0	0	0	0	0
483	CHAD	21	0	0	0	0	0	0	0	0	0
484	CONGO	21	0	0	0	0	0	0	0	0	0
490	ZAIRE (CONGO,KINSHASA)	21	1	100.00	61.9	4.762	.048	2.95	61.90	100.00	1.616

(continued)

17.1 (Continued)

Code No.	Nation Name	Total Years in System 1	No. of Wars 2	Total Battle Deaths (000's) 3	Total War Months 4	Battle Deaths (000's) per Year 5	Wars per Year 6	War Months per Year 7	Months per War 8	Battle Deaths (000's) per War 9	Battle Deaths (000's) per Month 10
					AFRICA						
500	UGANDA	19	1	2.00	.3	.105	.053	.02	.30	2.00	6.667
501	KENYA	18	0	0	0	0	0	0	0	0	0
510	TANZANIA/TANGANYIKA	20	0	0	0	0	0	0	0	0	0
511	ZANZIBAR	2	0	0	0	0	0	0	0	0	0
516	BURUNDI	19	1	50.00	.2	2.632	.053	.01	.20	50.00	250.000
517	RWANDA	19	1	2.50	2.8	.132	.053	.15	2.80	2.50	.893
520	SOMALIA	21	0	0	0	0	0	0	0	0	0
522	DJIBOUTI	4	0	0	0	0	0	0	0	0	0
530	ETHIOPIA	78	0	0	0	0	0	0	0	0	0
540	ANGOLA	6	1	7.00	61.7	1.167	.167	10.28	61.70	7.00	.113
541	MOZAMBIQUE	6	0	0	0	0	0	0	0	0	0
551	ZAMBIA	17	0	0	0	0	0	0	0	0	0
552	ZIMBABWE (RHODESIA)	15	1	12.00	84.0	.800	.067	5.60	84.00	12.00	.143
553	MALAWI	17	0	0	0	0	0	0	0	0	0
560	SOUTH AFRICA	61	0	0	0	0	0	0	0	0	0
570	LESOTHO	15	0	0	0	0	0	0	0	0	0
571	BOTSWANA	15	0	0	0	0	0	0	0	0	0
572	SWAZILAND	13	0	0	0	0	0	0	0	0	0
580	MALAGASY	21	0	0	0	0	0	0	0	0	0
581	COMOROS	6	0	0	0	0	0	0	0	0	0
590	MAURITIUS	13	0	0	0	0	0	0	0	0	0
591	SEYCHELLES	5	0	0	0	0	0	0	0	0	0
					REGIONAL SUMMARY						
	46 NATIONS	901	7	1173.50	241.1	57.216	.486	20.44	241.10	1173.50	292.544

Code No.	Nation Name	Total Years in System 1	No. of Wars 2	Total Battle Deaths (000's) 3	Total War Months 4	Battle Deaths (000's) per Year 5	Wars per Year 6	War Months per Year 7	War Months per War 8	Battle Deaths (000's) per War 9	Battle Deaths (000's) per Month 10
	MIDDLE EAST										
600	MOROCCO	89	2	2.50	17.5	.028	.022	.20	8.75	1.25	.143
615	ALGERIA	19	1	1.50	5.6	.079	.053	.29	5.60	1.50	.268
616	TUNISIA	81	0	0	0	0	0	0	0	0	0
620	LIBYA	29	0	0	0	0	0	0	0	0	0
625	SUDAN	25	1	250.00	100.9	10.000	.040	4.04	100.90	250.00	2.478
630	IRAN (PERSIA)	126	2	8.50	18.3	.067	.016	.15	9.15	4.25	.464
640	TURKEY/OTTOMAN EMPIRE	165	1	6.00	3.6	.036	.006	.02	3.60	6.00	1.667
645	IRAQ	49	1	2.00	.2	.041	.020	.00	.20	2.00	10.000
651	EGYPT/UAR	71	0	0	0	0	0	0	0	0	0
652	SYRIA	32	0	0	0	0	0	0	0	0	0
660	LEBANON	35	2	25.40	22.5	.726	.057	.64	11.25	12.70	1.129
663	JORDAN	35	1	2.00	.3	.057	.029	.01	.30	2.00	6.667
666	ISRAEL	33	0	0	0	0	0	0	0	0	0
670	SAUDI ARABIA	54	0	0	0	0	0	0	0	0	0
678	YEMEN ARAB REPUBLIC	55	2	104.00	82.8	1.891	.036	1.51	41.40	52.00	1.256
680	YEMEN PEOPLES REPUBLIC	14	0	0	0	0	0	0	0	0	0
690	KUWAIT	20	0	0	0	0	0	0	0	0	0
692	BAHREIN	10	0	0	0	0	0	0	0	0	0
694	QATAR	10	0	0	0	0	0	0	0	0	0
696	UNITED ARAB EMIRATES	10	0	0	0	0	0	0	0	0	0
698	OMAN	10	0	0	0	0	0	0	0	0	0
	REGIONAL SUMMARY										
	21 NATIONS	972	13	401.90	251.7	12.925	.280	6.86	181.15	331.70	24.071

(continued)

283

17.1 (Continued)

ASIA

Code No. 1	Nation Name	Total Years in System 1	No. of Wars 2	Total Battle Deaths (000's) 3	Total War Months 4	Battle Deaths (000's) per Year 5	Wars per Year 6	War Months per Year 7	War Months per War 8	Battle Deaths (000's) per War 9	Battle Deaths (000's) per Month 10
700	AFGHANISTAN	61	3	19.00	39.8	.311	.049	.65	13.27	6.33	.477
710	CHINA	121	11	3496.00	488.1	28.893	.091	4.03	44.37	317.82	7.162
712	MONGOLIA	60	0	0	0	0	0	0	0	0	0
713	TAIWAN	32	0	0	0	0	0	0	0	0	0
730	KOREA	18	0	0	0	0	0	0	0	0	0
731	KOREA, DEM PEOPLE'S REP.	33	0	0	0	0	0	0	0	0	0
732	KOREA, REPUBLIC OF	32	0	0	0	0	0	0	0	0	0
740	JAPAN	114	1	14.00	7.9	.123	.009	.07	7.90	14.00	1.772
750	INDIA	34	0	0	0	0	0	0	0	0	0
760	BHUTAN	10	0	0	0	0	0	0	0	0	0
770	PAKISTAN	34	1	500.00	8.3	14.706	.029	.24	8.30	500.00	60.241
771	BANGLADESH	8	0	0	0	0	0	0	0	0	0
775	BURMA	33	1	8.00	34.6	.242	.030	1.05	34.60	8.00	.231
780	SRI LANKA (CEYLON)	33	1	2.00	1.3	.061	.030	.04	1.30	2.00	1.538
781	MALDIVE ISLANDS	16	0	0	0	0	0	0	0	0	0
790	NEPAL	61	0	0	0	0	0	0	0	0	0
800	THAILAND	94	0	0	0	0	0	0	0	0	0
811	KAMPUCHEA (CAMBODIA)	28	1	150.00	59.9	5.357	.036	2.14	59.90	150.00	2.504
812	LAOS	27	2	20.00	138.9	.741	.074	5.14	69.45	10.00	.144
816	VIETNAM, DEMOCRATIC REP.	28	0	0	0	0	0	0	0	0	0
817	VIETNAM, REPUBLIC OF	22	1	300.00	61.2	13.636	.045	2.78	61.20	300.00	4.902
820	MALAYSIA	24	0	0	0	0	0	0	0	0	0
830	SINGAPORE	16	0	0	0	0	0	0	0	0	0
840	PHILIPPINES	35	2	18.00	121.0	.514	.057	3.46	60.50	9.00	.149
850	INDONESIA	32	3	36.00	55.8	1.125	.094	1.74	18.60	12.00	.645
900	AUSTRALIA	61	0	0	0	0	0	0	0	0	0
910	PAPUA NEW GUINEA	6	0	0	0	0	0	0	0	0	0
920	NEW ZEALAND	61	0	0	0	0	0	0	0	0	0
940	SOLOMON ISLANDS	3	0	0	0	0	0	0	0	0	0
950	FIJI	11	0	0	0	0	0	0	0	0	0
990	WESTERN SAMOA	5	0	0	0	0	0	0	0	0	0
	REGIONAL SUMMARY										
	31 NATIONS	1152	27	4563.00	1016.8	65.709	.545	21.35	379.39	1329.15	79.767

284

17.2 Rank Order of Nations on Civil War Experience Indicators

Code No.	Nation Name	SEVERITY				MAGNITUDE				INTENSITY			
		Rank	Battle Deaths (000's)	Rank	Battle Deaths (000's) per Year	Rank	War Months	Rank	War Months per War	Rank	Battle Deaths (000's) per War	Rank	Battle Deaths (000's) per War Month
		1	2	3	4	5	6	7	8	9	10	11	12
710	CHINA	1.0	3496.0	2.0	28.9	1.0	488.1	12.0	44.4	4.0	317.8	8.0	7.2
475	NIGERIA	2.0	1000.0	1.0	47.6	25.0	30.2	18.0	30.2	1.0	1000.0	3.0	33.1
230	SPAIN	3.0	699.9	8.0	4.2	4.0	190.8	19.0	27.3	11.0	100.0	15.0	3.7
2	UNITED STATES OF AMERICA	4.0	650.0	9.0	3.9	18.0	48.0	11.0	48.0	2.0	650.0	5.0	13.5
365	USSR (RUSSIA)	5.0	501.0	10.0	3.0	19.0	45.6	20.0	22.8	6.0	250.5	7.0	11.0
770	PAKISTAN	6.0	500.0	3.0	14.7	36.0	8.3	33.0	8.3	3.0	500.0	2.0	60.2
100	COLOMBIA	7.0	409.9	11.0	2.7	2.0	274.8	15.0	39.3	13.0	58.6	23.0	1.5
817	VIETNAM REPUBLIC OF	8.0	300.0	4.0	13.6	14.0	61.2	6.0	61.2	5.0	300.0	11.0	4.9
70	MEXICO	9.0	272.0	14.0	1.8	3.0	200.9	10.0	50.2	12.0	68.0	24.0	1.4
625	SUDAN	10.0	250.0	5.0	10.0	8.0	100.9	1.0	100.9	7.0	250.0	17.0	2.5
350	GREECE	11.0	160.0	17.0	1.1	22.0	37.4	16.0	37.4	8.0	160.0	12.0	4.3
811	KAMPUCHEA (CAMBODIA)	12.0	150.0	6.0	5.4	16.0	59.9	9.0	59.9	9.0	150.0	16.0	2.5
678	YEMEN ARAB REPUBLIC	13.0	104.0	13.0	1.9	10.5	82.8	13.5	41.4	14.0	52.0	26.0	1.3
490	ZAIRE (CONGO,KINSHASA)	14.0	100.0	7.0	4.8	12.0	61.9	4.0	61.9	10.0	100.0	21.0	1.6
516	BURUNDI	15.0	50.0	12.0	2.6	52.5	.2	52.5	.2	15.0	50.0	1.0	250.0
850	INDONESIA	16.0	36.0	16.0	1.1	17.0	55.8	22.0	18.6	20.5	12.0	31.0	.6
93	NICARAGUA	17.0	35.0	22.0	.4	34.0	9.5	29.0	9.5	16.0	35.0	14.0	3.7
660	LEBANON	18.0	25.4	20.0	.7	26.0	22.5	26.0	11.2	19.0	12.7	27.0	1.1
220	FRANCE	19.0	24.7	26.0	.2	41.0	6.3	45.0	2.1	26.0	8.2	13.0	3.9
101	VENEZUELA	20.0	23.0	25.0	.2	10.5	82.8	13.5	41.4	22.0	11.5	41.0	.3
235	PORTUGAL	21.5	20.0	19.0	.7	15.0	60.0	8.0	60.2	17.0	20.0	39.0	.3
812	LAOS	21.5	20.0	23.0	.3	5.0	138.9	3.0	69.4	23.5	10.0	48.0	.1
700	AFGHANISTAN	23.0	19.0	24.0	.3	21.0	39.8	24.0	13.3	29.0	6.3	35.0	.5
840	PHILIPPINES	24.0	18.0	21.0	.5	7.0	121.0	7.0	60.5	25.0	9.0	47.0	.1
160	ARGENTINA	25.0	17.5	28.0	.1	6.0	132.0	21.0	22.1	37.0	2.9	51.0	.1
740	JAPAN	26.0	14.0	29.0	.1	38.0	7.9	35.0	7.9	18.0	14.0	18.0	1.8
552	ZIMBABWE (RHODESIA)	27.0	12.0	18.0	.8	9.0	84.0	2.0	84.0	20.5	12.0	50.0	.1
135	PERU	28.0	11.0	35.0	.1	24.0	34.1	25.0	11.4	35.0	3.7	40.0	.3
92	EL SALVADOR	29.0	10.0	33.0	.1	28.0	18.0	23.0	18.0	23.5	10.0	34.0	.6
140	BRAZIL	30.5	8.5	42.0	.1	20.0	40.2	28.0	10.0	40.0	2.1	44.0	.2

(continued)

17.2 (Continued)

Code No.	Nation Name	SEVERITY				MAGNITUDE				INTENSITY			
		Rank	Battle Deaths (000's)	Rank	Battle Deaths (000's) per Year	Rank	War Months	Rank	War Months per War	Rank	Battle Deaths (000's) per War	Rank	Battle Deaths (000's) per War Month
		1	2	3	4	5	6	7	8	9	10	11	12
630	IRAN (PERSIA)	30.5	8.5	36.0	.1	27.0	18.3	30.0	9.1	32.5	4.3	36.0	.5
155	CHILE	32.5	8.0	41.0	.1	31.5	10.8	40.5	5.4	33.5	4.0	30.0	.7
775	BURMA	32.5	8.0	24.0	.2	23.0	34.6	17.0	34.6	27.0	8.0	43.0	.2
540	ANGOLA	34.0	7.0	15.0	1.2	13.0	61.7	5.0	61.7	28.0	7.0	53.0	.1
640	TURKEY/OTTOMAN EMPIRE	35.0	6.0	45.0	.0	44.0	3.6	43.0	3.6	30.0	6.0	19.5	1.7
40	CUBA	36.0	5.0	37.0	.1	40.0	6.6	38.0	6.6	31.0	5.0	29.0	.8
310	HUNGARY	37.0	4.0	38.0	.1	33.0	10.7	27.0	10.7	33.5	4.0	38.0	.4
300	AUSTRIA HUNGARY	38.0	3.5	46.0	.0	39.0	7.6	37.0	7.6	36.0	3.5	37.0	.5
150	PARAGUAY	39.0	3.0	44.0	.0	30.0	15.4	36.0	7.7	48.0	1.5	45.0	.2
42	DOMINICAN REPUBLIC	41.0	2.5	32.0	.1	43.0	4.3	42.0	4.3	38.5	2.5	32.0	.6
517	RWANDA	41.0	2.5	27.0	.1	45.0	2.8	44.0	2.8	38.5	2.5	28.0	.9
600	MOROCCO	41.0	2.5	48.0	.0	29.0	17.5	32.0	8.7	50.0	1.0	49.0	.1
90	GUATEMALA	46.0	2.0	51.0	.0	31.5	10.8	40.5	5.4	52.5	1.0	46.0	.2
94	COSTA RICA	46.0	2.0	47.0	.0	49.0	1.2	49.0	1.2	43.5	2.0	19.5	1.7
360	RUMANIA	46.0	2.0	50.0	.0	47.0	1.5	47.0	1.5	43.5	2.0	25.0	1.3
500	UGANDA	46.0	2.0	31.0	.1	50.5	.3	50.5	.3	43.5	2.0	9.5	6.7
645	IRAQ	46.0	2.0	43.0	.0	52.5	.2	52.5	.2	43.5	2.0	7.0	10.0
663	JORDAN	46.0	2.0	40.0	.1	50.5	.3	50.5	.3	43.5	2.0	9.5	6.7
780	SRI LANKA (CEYLON)	46.0	2.0	39.0	.1	48.0	1.3	48.0	1.3	43.5	2.0	22.0	1.5
145	BOLIVIA	50.5	1.5	53.0	.0	54.0		54.0		48.0	1.5	4.0	15.0
615	ALGERIA	50.5	1.5	34.0	.1	42.0	5.6	39.0	5.6	52.5	1.0	42.0	.3
91	HONDURAS	53.0	1.0	52.0	.0	46.0	1.8	46.0	1.8	52.5	1.0	33.0	.6
165	URUGUAY	53.0	1.0	54.0	.0	37.0	8.0	34.0	8.0	52.5	1.0	52.0	.6
329	TWO SICILIES	53.0	1.0	49.0	.0	35.0	8.9	31.0	8.9	52.5	1.0	54.0	.1

(column 3), and the figures themselves for that normalized indicator (column 4). In columns 5 and 6 are the rank and raw figures for the war month indicator. Columns 7 through 12 reveal the ranks and raw figures for war months per war, battle deaths per war, and battle deaths per war month.

Whereas 82 of the nations fought in at least one major international war, "only" 54 engaged in a major civil war, and 78 nations, almost half of them the new states in Africa, have not participated in either civil or international war. Of course, absence from the civil war list does not mean that a nation has enjoyed a stable political history. Many that do not appear in the table have experienced dozens of coups and revolutions that did not reach our 1,000 battle death threshold. Haiti, for example, suffered through a score of violent changes of government from the turn of the century through 1915, but none of them involved much more than the deaths of the temporary presidents of that country and their immediate retinue.

As for those nations that do appear in the table, China ranks first on battle deaths and nation months and high on all of the other indicators. Nigeria, Spain, the United States, Russia, Pakistan, Colombia, Vietnam, Mexico, and Sudan round out the top ten on battle deaths in civil war. Five of these states—Nigeria, the United States, Pakistan, Vietnam, and Sudan—achieved their positions because of one very bloody civil war. As for nation months in civil war, after China are Colombia, Mexico, Spain, Laos, Argentina, Sudan, Zimbabwe, Venezuela, and Yemen. Sudan, Zimbabwe, Laos, Zaire, and Vietnam top the war months per war category. Finally, as for the greatest amount of bloodshed in the shortest period of time, Burundi, with its 1972 war, leads this grouping. Among the states not previously mentioned that score high here are Bolivia in fourth place, Iraq in seventh, and Uganda and Sri Lanka tied for tenth.

To some degree, the appearance of many non-Western nations in the higher ranks supports those who believe that the Western world is more stable (if not civilized?) than developing states in the Third World. The presence of China, Colombia, Mexico, Pakistan, Sudan, Nigeria, and others in Asia and Latin America near the top of the lists seems to offer graphic evidence of the bloody national histories of non-Western polities.

But the raw figures in the table tell only part of the story. For one thing, many of the revolutions in the Third World are not caused solely by factors internal to those regimes. Large, more developed neighbors or colonial powers often have fomented and supported revolutions, especially in places like the Caribbean, for their own political and economic well-being. More important, a host of Third World countries, including several in allegedly unstable Latin America and many in Africa, have experienced no large civil wars. If anything, the almost total absence of young African nations from our lists is astonishing considering the manner in which these entities were left when the Europeans slunk back to their continent in the late 1950s and early 1960s.

CORRELATIONS AMONG CIVIL WAR EXPERIENCE INDICATORS

As was seen in 17.2, nations that score high on one of the six indicators tend to score high on the others. In 17.3, we show the rank order correlations for the indicators. As expected, almost all of them are significant.

REGIONAL AGGREGATIONS OF NATIONAL CIVIL WAR EXPERIENCES

In 17.1, we offered regional summaries that were merely the totals of all of the figures, even the average or normalized figures. In 17.4, we examine the regional war experience by region (and not by nation) and offer a variety of measures that reveal where each region ranks on experiences in civil wars. After listing the five regions, we show the total nation years in the system for all nations in the region (column 1), the number of wars (column 2), the total nation months (column 3), and the total battle deaths experienced by nations in that region (column 4). These figures were previously presented in 17.1. In columns 5 through 7 we present new data—the annual averages in each region of nation wars, nation months, and battle deaths. Asia leads all of the regions here. It must be remembered, however, that China has contributed disproportionately to Asia's totals. Despite having produced the third greatest number of wars, Europe ends up in last place in all three normalized categories. Of interest are the low wars per year and nation months per nation year totals for Africa as well as the fact that the "turbulent" Middle East shows up pretty well on all three indicators. A careful analysis of this table, in conjunction with 17.1, allows us to dismiss simple assumptions about civil war in the Third World.

17.3 Rank Order Correlations Among National Civil War Experience Indicators

	BD	BD/YR	WM	WM/year	BD/War	BD/WM
Battle Deaths	1.00					
Battle Deaths per year	.75	1.00				
War months	.52	.45	1.00			
War Months per year	.45	.52	.75	1.00		
Battle Deaths per war	.84	.76	.42	.40	1.00	
Battle Deaths per war month	.31	.29	-.18	-.18	.38	1.00

N = 54

17.4 Regional Aggregations of Civil War Experiences

Regional Group	Total Nation Years in System	No. of Nation-Wars	Nation Months of War	Battle Deaths (000's)	Annual Averages		
					Nation Wars per Nation Year	Nation Months per Nation Year	Battle Deaths (000's) per Nation-Year
WESTERN HEMISPHERE	2608	41	900.2	1462.9	.016	.345	.561
EUROPE	3710	18	369.0	1416.1	.005	.099	.382
AFRICA	901	7	241.1	1173.5	.008	.267	1.301
MIDEAST	972	13	251.7	401.9	.013	.259	.413
ASIA	1152	27	1016.8	4563.0	.023	.882	3.958

SUMMARY

The national and regional totals presented in this chapter allow one to compare national experiences in civil war since the Congress of Vienna. Conclusions drawn from these data must be tentative, since we have ignored thousands of small coups, palace revolutions, assassinations, and putsches that did not result in at least 1,000 battle deaths per year. Further, we have not included revolutions and civil wars in polities that were independent but had not yet qualified for admission to the international system. Nevertheless, when taken with the international war totals presented in Chapter 10, these civil war data shed new light on the martial activities of nations and regions in the international system over the past 165 years.

With this chapter, we end the brief introduction to our new civil war data. Obviously, we have not exhausted all possibilities for the analysis of these data, nor have we begun to relate them systematically to those presented in Part I of the volume. It is to these tasks that we—and we hope our readers and fellow peace researchers—will turn in the years to come as we continue with the investigations outlined in our preface.

CHAPTER 18

Conclusion

Summing up the findings of a study like this is an almost impossible task. Unlike many social science books, there is no dominant theoretical strand, no culminating argument, no recurrent cadenza. We have tested few hypotheses, confirmed no causal models, and completed no critical experiment. All we have done is generated a particular set of data and then refined and systematized it into a variety of potentially useful forms. An enterprise such as this offers little opportunity for creative expression: tedious, frustrating, expensive, and time-consuming, but—one hopes—valuable in the end.

By itself, this enterprise is of no greater scientific usefulness than any other competent piece of systematic description. It is merely a statistical handbook that measures and describes some of the "wages of war" since 1816. Its value is more instrumental than intrinsic, but even that value may turn out to be negligible unless we and others fully exploit the data sets that it brings together. That exploitation can only occur, however, in the context of a particular type of research strategy, and the strategy we have in mind is being embraced, in our view, by too few, too slowly. Before specifying the general nature of that strategy, though, let us devote a few paragraphs to the more immediate payoffs that arise out of a work such as this. More specifically, what do we and our readers know now that we did not know before?

As we indicated at the outset, this is by no means the first serious effort to describe in a systematic fashion the incidence of war within any extended spatial-temporal domain. But we have enjoyed certain advantages denied to Wright, Richardson, and the others and can therefore regard our data with greater confidence. What information do these data convey?

First, they operationally define the fluctuating composition of the interstate system and all of the international and civil wars of any appreciable magnitude and severity in which the members of that system became involved. Second, they give us a variety of indicators by which these wars may be measured and compared: duration, location, participants, pre-war population, battle-connected fatalities, and the identity of the initiators and victors in each. More specifically, the data permit us to speak with some precision regarding the severity, magnitude, and intensity of each of the wars. With each of the wars of the several types scaled, compared, and ranked on these dimensions, we can aggregate the individual war indicators and measure the incidence of war's occurrence at the systemic and national levels of aggregation.

For *international* war we found that, according to our criteria, there were 67 interstate wars and 51 imperial and colonial wars, leading directly to the death of almost 31 million military personnel, exclusive of civilians. There was some kind of international war under way in all but 20 of the 165 years covered, consuming over 6,000 nation months of active combat, with the system ranging in size from 23 to 155 sovereign national states. On the average, an interstate war began every two and a half and an extra-systemic one began every three and one-quarter years. In terms of possible nation months (normalized for system size), 1917 and 1943 were the most warlike years in the period, with 169.8 and 178.5 nation months of war under way, respectively, or 32.2 and 28.6 percent of the maximum possible. And while we could not compute the number of battle deaths sustained on an annual basis, 1914 and 1939 were the bloodiest in terms of military personnel killed during the wars that began in those years, with over 8 million and over 15 million, respectively; were civilian casualties included, these figures would be appreciably greater.

Looking at the entire period, there is no evidence that international war has been on the increase. The number of wars, the battle deaths, and the nation months have fluctuated considerably over time, with the "average" decade seeing 7.9 wars, over 400 nation months of war, and over 2 million battle deaths. Nor have later wars generally been any more intense, in terms of deaths per capita or per nation month. On the other hand, there is some tentative evidence for the general belief in war cycles. Wars do not seem to *begin* according to any cyclical pattern, but there is some suggestion of a 15- to 20-year periodicity between peaks in the amount of war under way at any given time. Shifting from annual to seasonal observations, we discovered that more wars begin in spring and autumn than in winter and summer, and that advances in the technology of war, agriculture, and industry seems to have had only a modest impact on these seasonal propensities.

Looking next at the nations and their regions, we find, to no one's surprise, that the Europeans were by far the most war-prone. The top position goes to France with 22 wars, followed by England and Russia with 19, Turkey with 18, Italy with 12, and China with 11. Essentially the same nations led in battle deaths sustained, with the following all sustaining more than a million battle deaths during their tenure in the system: Russia, Germany, China, France, Japan, England, and Austria-Hungary, in that order. Similarly, of the more than 6,000 nation months of war the system experienced, over 30 percent of them were accounted for by France, England, Turkey, Spain, and Russia.

Finally, our data permit us to say some interesting things about the immediate results of these wars, in terms of victory, defeat, and battle-connected fatalities. Despite the search for some battle death threshold (absolute or relative) at which wars might be expected to end, none was found. Not only do the defeated nations not respond to a given number of losses, but there seems to be almost no constant advantage to the victorious side in terms of battle death ratios. The victors actually lose as many or more men than their enemies in nearly a third of the interstate wars. If the *victors* often do this badly in the immediate costs of the war, how well do those who actually *initiated* these hostilities do? For one thing, the initiators "win" in almost 70 percent of the interstate wars, and they sustain fewer battle deaths than their "victims" in 60 percent of the cases.

As for the major *civil wars* since 1816, members of the system engaged in 106 such wars, resulting in more than 9 million battle deaths and almost 3,000 nation months of war. On the average, each decade experienced 7 civil wars, with the figures rising in recent years along with the increase in system size. The years 1860 (because of China's three massive civil wars), 1967, and 1946 all experienced the onset of civil wars that resulted in at least 1 million battle deaths, while 1860, 1963, and 1972 lead the years in most civil wars under way.

Newspaper headlines to the contrary, civil war has not been on the increase whether we look at begun or underway figures or any of our frequency, magnitude, severity, or intensity dimensions. Of course, there have been more, longer, and bloodier wars in recent years, but when those figures are normalized for system size, the trends disappear.

Although we did not turn up much of interest in terms of seasonal distributions for the onset of civil wars, we did find a suggestion of a 28- (and perhaps 42-) year cycle for civil wars under way in the system. Coupled with an almost identical result for international war under way, this is among our most intriguing findings.

China with 11 and Colombia and Spain with 7 lead the nations in civil war experience. China, Nigeria, Spain, the United States, and Russia rank 1 through 5 on the battle death indicator, and China, Colombia, Mexico, Spain, and Laos dominate the nation months indicator. Less than one-third (N = 54) of the nations experienced civil wars that resulted in an average of 1,000 battle deaths a year.

As might be expected by the frequency with which China engaged in long and bloody civil wars, Asia leads the regions for the most nation months and battle deaths, with the western hemisphere running second. Although European states have engaged in 18 civil wars (as compared to only 6 for Africa, for example), the *normalized* figures for European nation months and battle deaths per year of nation membership in the system place that more politically developed region at the most pacific end of the civil war experience spectrum.

Concluding this brief summary of findings, we were surprised by the number of similarities between our international and civil war lists. Whether we compared the sheer number of such wars or their patterns over time, too many parallels appeared to allow us to conclude that they occurred by chance alone. *Why* the civil wars should be related to the international wars is a question we leave for future analyses.

A final comment in regard to our findings concerns their similarity with the patterns uncovered by Richardson, Sorokin, Wright, and others. Our data base differs in several ways from theirs, and the question is whether that difference affects, in any appreciable way, the statistical regularities that turn up. We can, of course, make only the most tentative response to that question now, given the fact that the present volume is limited in its coverage to the dependent variable only, whereas our three major predecessors report relationships between and among a much larger set of variables. But on this limited basis, there is indeed a surprising degree of consistency, as our several chapter summaries make clear. Whether these consistencies are merely a function of the "law of large numbers," reflecting statistical regularities that are found in a wide variety of social systems, or more significant than that we cannot yet say. Nor can we answer, at this juncture, the more fundamental question as to whether the differing data bases will produce markedly different patterns as we move on to inquire into the correlates, predictors, and causes of international war.

The above comments, then, serve to summarize the data presented in this volume and to indicate the directions we have followed in trying to account for those data. They cannot, of course, do justice either to the richness of these distributions in the incidence of war or to the complexities of the research strategy to which we adhere. But our hope is that both the availability of the new and revised material presented in the preceding chapters and the kind of investigative design outlined in the preface will continue to stimulate a renewed attack on the causes of war problem. Much more in the way of energy, resources, creativity, and rigor will be necessary before we have either diagnosed this deadly disease or put the tools of prevention in the hands of those who have the need for—and will to use—them. Thus, we reiterate the theme of our dedication page, and hope that an applied science of war prevention will be created in time to make unnecessary a *third* edition of this volume.

APPENDIX A

Wars that Are Included
Explanatory Notes and References

In the list that follows, we break down all the wars that are included in this study into three main classes: interstate ($N = 67$), extra-systemic ($N = 51$), and civil ($N = 106$). For each of these we list the sources from which we gathered our basic information, including participants, dates, and fatality estimates. For the wars whose inclusion might not be obvious (given our criteria for inclusion-exclusion) or whose duration, magnitude, or severity may be ambiguous, we also provide a brief explanatory note.

It should be stressed that these references are by no means exhaustive; we began in almost every case with the more obvious monographs and then worked our way through additional ones until we were satisfied that the information we needed was accurate and complete. Moreover, we have not listed all sources consulted, particularly those whose estimates or interpretations we ultimately rejected.

The interstate wars are numbered in chronological order from 1 to 199, the extra-systemic from 301 to 451, and the civil from 601 to 910. We have left two numbers between each war to allow for additions to our lists.

INTERSTATE WARS
1. Franco-Spanish, 1823

Although the French fought on the side of, and at the "request" of, the deposed Spanish Bourbons against the Liberal Government, this war was not considered an internationalized civil war because the Spanish Liberals had controlled the country for three years and had, in effect, won the civil war (see #601).

Hume (1900); Clarke (1906); Phillips (1914); Bodart (1916); Geoffrey de Grandmaison (1928); Artz (1934); Richardson (1960a).

4. Russo-Turkish, 1828-1829

In the Russian van, naturally, were Greeks and other Balkan peoples who made minor contributions to the war effort.

Russell (1877); von Sternegg (1891-1895); von Sax (1913); Crawley (1930); Woodhouse (1952); Florinsky (1953); Allen and Muratoff (1953).

7. Mexican-American, 1846-1848

Wilcox (1892); Smith (1919); Bemis (1936); Morris (1953); Peterson (1957); Singletary (1960).

10. Austro-Sardinian, 1848-1849

Fighting alongside the Sardinian Army were irregulars from several Austrian provinces and duchies in Italy.

Friedjung (1912); Bodart (1916); Sorokin (1937); Urlanis (1960).

13. First Schleswig-Holstein, 1848-1849

von Sternegg (1892-1898); Bodart (1916); Sorokin (1937); Urlanis (1960).

16. Roman Republic, 1849

The Roman Republic was established in 1848, and the Pope was divested of his temporal powers. The subsequent war to overthrow the secular Republic was fought by Austrian, French, and Sicilian troops for the Pope, who had no forces of his own. This war differed from similar uprisings in Venice and Milan in that it involved independent nations on each side (the Allies on one and the Republic—successor to the Papal States—on the other) and resulted in the requisite number of battle deaths. The Milanese and Venetian rebellions do not even qualify as colonial wars in this latter respect.

King (1899); Johnson (1901); Harbottle (1904); Bodart (1916); Berkeley (1932); Sorokin (1937); Pieri (1962).

19. La Plata, 1851-1852

The wars of La Plata began in the late 1830s. Since French and British intervention resulted in few battle deaths, European participation was excluded. During the next decade, fighting continued among and between Uruguayans and Argentinians; but Argentina, the only system member of the two (Uruguay had not crossed the population threshold), did not suffer the requisite number of battle deaths. Brazil's entry into the fray in 1851 finally qualified the conflict as an interstate war. See also #622.

Dawson (1935); Levene (1937); Cady (1950); Best (1960, vol. 2); Calogeras (1963).

22. Crimean, 1853-1856

Russell (1877); Bodart (1916); Dumas and Vedel-Peterson (1923); Sorokin (1937); Allen and Muratoff (1953); Urlanis (1960).

25. Anglo-Persian, 1856-1857

Fortescue (1930, vol. 13); Kelly (1968).

28. Italian Unification, 1859

The Sardinians were aided by Italian nationals from Austrian territories.

King (1899); Bodart (1916); Dumas and Vedel-Peterson (1923); Sorokin (1937); Richardson (1960a); Urlanis (1960).

31. Spanish-Moroccan, 1859-1860

Harbottle (1904); Dumas and Vedel-Peterson (1923); Usborne (1936); Sorokin (1937); Spain, Servicio Historico Militar (1947); Richardson (1960a); Urlanis (1960); Miege (1961).

34. Italo-Roman, 1860

This and the following war (Italo-Sicilian) were part of the struggle for Italian unification. Although Rome and Sicily were in philosophical and political agreement, they resisted the emerging Italian state separately in time and place.

Nolan (1865); King (1899); Harbottle (1904); Thayer (1911).

37. Italo-Sicilian, 1860-1861

Garibaldi's landing in the Kingdom of the Two Sicilies and his celebrated conquest of Naples were not included as part of this interstate war between Victor Emmanuel's armies and the Sicilians.

Same sources as #34.

40. Franco-Mexican, 1862-1867

Some Mexicans fought on the French side. Although Maximilian was Austrian, the Austro-Hungarian government sent no troops. The British and Spanish forces that originally landed with the French in 1861 withdrew before hostilities began.

Niox (1874); Harbottle (1904); Bodart (1916); Dumas and Vedel-Peterson (1923); Dawson (1935); Urlanis (1960); Bock (1966).

43. Ecuadorian-Colombian, 1863

Berthe (1903); Harbottle (1904); Le Gouhir y Rodas (1925); Pattee (1941); Richardson (1960a).

46. Second Schleswig-Holstein 1864

Bodart (1916); Dumas and Vedel-Peterson (1923); Steefel (1932); Clark (1934); Friedjung (1935); Urlanis (1960).

49. Lopez, 1864-1870

Almanach de Gotha (1865); Box (1927); Levene (1937); Warren (1949); Laine (1956); Best (1960, vol. 2); Calogeras (1963); Kolinski (1965).

52. Spanish-Chilean, 1865-1866

Although Bolivia and Ecuador opposed Spain, they did not engage Spanish forces and were not treated as participants in our study.

Galvez (1919); Galdames (1941); Dellepiane (1943); Davis (1950); Encina (1950); Richardson (1960a); Markham (1968).

55. Seven Weeks, 1866

Bodart (1916); Dumas and Vedel-Peterson (1923); Clark (1934); Friedjung (1935); Urlanis (1960).

58. Franco-Prussian, 1870-1871

Baden, Bavaria, and Wuerttemberg, which began the war as independent states, became part of the emerging German Empire by late 1870 and consequently were not included as belligerents after that date. The bloody fighting in and around the Paris Commune was excluded because of its civil nature.

France, Ministry of Foreign Affairs (1915); Bodart (1916); Dumas and Vedel-Peterson (1923); Sorokin (1937); Urlanis (1960).

61. Russo-Turkish, 1877-1878

Russia was again aided by Balkan peoples, but Turkey had defeated most of their forces in engagements from 1875 to 1877 (see #367).

von Sternegg (1866-1889); Hozier (1878); von Sax (1913); Sumner (1937); Seton-Watson (1952); Allen and Muratoff (1953); Richardson (1960a).

64. Pacific, 1879-1883

Markham (1892); Dumas and Vedel-Peterson (1923); Galdames (1941); Dellepiane (1943); Richardson (1960a).

67. Sino-French, 1884-1885

From 1882 to 1884 the French waged an imperial war against the Annamese and the Chinese-supported Black Flag guerrillas of Tonkin (see #379). In the treaty of Hue of 1883, the French protectorate over South Vietnam and part of North Vietnam was established, but fighting continued with guerrillas, at which time irregular Chinese forces engaged the French. A temporary agreement between France and China in 1884 led to misunderstanding and full-scale war (now an interstate war because of China's open participation).

Cordier (1902); Bodart (1916); Kiernan (1929); Khôi (1955); Taboulet (1955); Li (1956); Buttinger (1958); Lancaster (1961); Roberts (1963); Eastman (1967); McAleavy (1968).

70. Central-American, 1885

Burgess (1926); Meza (1935); Richardson (1960a); Karnes (1961).

73. Sino-Japanese, 1894-1895

Koreans were initially involved.

Cordier (1902); Li (1914); Morse (1918); Ono (1922); Richardson (1960a).

76. Greco-Turkish, 1897

Harbottle (1904); Dumas and Vedel-Peterson (1923); Sorokin (1937); Richardson (1960a).

79. Spanish-American, 1898

More than 4000 of the American battle deaths were attributed to disease.

White (1909); Sorokin (1937); Morris (1953).

82. Boxer Rebellion, 1900

This rebellion originally involved an international rescue mission to save Europeans in Peking and other areas from the ravages of the Boxers who were not supported by the government. On June 17, government forces resisted the violation of their territory and even began to work with the Boxer irregulars. From that date to August 16, when the siege of Peking was lifted, the government of China was indeed in military combat with the international armies. After that date, although some foreign military contingents tangled with Chinese official forces, the bulk of the interstate fighting stopped. A preliminary agreement was signed on January 16, 1901 and the final settlement was approved on August 7, 1901. The infamous punitive expeditions that took place from the fall of 1900 through much of 1901 involved primarily German and Russian forces shooting at whatever Chinese they encountered, very few of whom were uniformed Chinese regulars. Austrian, German, and Italian participation in the formal interstate war phase is not counted because none of the three committed 1,000 troops to combat or suffered 100 battle deaths.

Anthouard (1902); *Deutschland in China* (1902); Frey (1904); Tan (1955); Fleming (1959); Purcell (1963); Clements (1967); Lensen (1967).

85. Russo-Japanese, 1904-1905

Dumas and Vedel-Peterson (1923); Ogawa (1923); Akagi (1936); Seton-Watson (1952); Richardson (1960a); Urlanis (1960); Martin (1967).

88. Central American, 1906

This conflict naturally was closely related to the one that followed.

Castellanos (1925); Karnes (1961).

91. Central American, 1907

Castellanos (1925).

94. Spanish-Moroccan, 1909-1910

Usborne (1936); Sorokin (1937).

97. Italo-Turkish, 1911-1912

The Italians continued fighting in Tripoli against Senussi tribesmen until the 1920s, but after the war with Turkey, the number of Italian battle deaths drops below the inclusion threshold.

Beehler (1913); McClure (1913); Sorokin (1937); Askew (1942); Urlanis (1960).

100. First Balkan, 1912-1913

Fried (1914); *Report of International Commission* (1914); Young (1915); Dumas and Vedel-Peterson (1923); Helmreich (1938); Urlanis (1960).

103. Second Balkan, 1913

Report of the International Commission (1914); Young (1915); Helmreich (1938); Richardson (1960a).

106. World War I, 1914-1918

Battle death figures are most likely conservative, since casualty statistics are unreliable for Eastern Europe and Russia.

Dumas and Vedel-Peterson (1923); Fay (1928); Schmitt (1930); Sorokin (1937); Albertini (1952-1957); Falls (1959); Urlanis (1960); Esposito (1964a).

109. Russo-Polish, 1919-1920

Reddaway (1961); Wandycz (1969); Davies (1972).

112. Hungarian-Allies, 1919

Kiritzesco (1934).

115. Greco-Turkish, 1919-1922

Allied participation was limited both in terms of troops actively engaged and battle deaths.
Urlanis (1960).

118. Sino-Soviet, 1929
The forces combatting the Russians in Manchuria were clearly acting for the new central government.
Ho (135); Wei (1956); Chow (1960).

121. Manchurian, 1931-1933
Lei (1932); "Chinese-Japan Truce" (1933); Snow (1933); Richardson (1960a).

124. Chaco, 1932-1935

Ireland (1938); La Foy (1946); Richardson (1960a); Zook (160); Garner (1966).

127. Italo-Ethiopian, 1935-1936

Badoglio (1937); Sandford (1946); Richardson (1960a).

130. Sino-Japanese, 1937-1941

This undeclared war, which started with the Marco Polo Bridge incident, was treated as part of World War II after December 7, 1941.
Esposito (1964b).

133. Chankufeng, 1938

Coox (1977).

136. Nomohan, 1939

Phillips (1942); Friters (1949); Jones (1954); Erickson (1962); Rupen (1964); Coox (1973); Ikuhiko (1976).

139. World War II, 1939-1945

As in World War I, battle death figures are on the conservative side because of unreliable reports from Eastern Europe.

When Germany established de facto control of the governments in such countries as France, Belgium, and Poland, these nations were dropped as participants in the war, even though the Free French, Free Belgian, and other similar military contingents fought with the Allies until the war's end. In the case of Holland, although a sizable Dutch force resisted the Japanese in Indonesia in early 1942, the contingent was, for all intents and purposes, an arm of the Anglo-American command in the Far East, supplied and, indeed, directed by the Allies. Consequently, Dutch participation is said to have ceased when it capitulated to Germany in 1940.

Partisan and underground fighting in France, Yugoslavia, and Greece is not included. Thailand and Mexico, which sent less than 1000 troops into active combat, suffered few battle deaths and were therefore excluded. The Russian invasion of Poland in September 1939 was not included because it was relatively unopposed and resulted in few battle deaths for both sides. Also excluded was the participation of Spain's "volunteer" Blue Legion on the Fascist side against the Soviet Union. The Franco-British combat in 1940-1941 in Syria *was* included.

Chambers et al. (1950); Burt (1956); Aron (1958); *Geschichte des Zweiten Weltkrieges 1939-1945* (1960); Cline (1963); Esposito (1964b); Paxton (1972); Miller (1975).

142. Russo-Finnish, 1939-1940

Brody (1904); Coates (1941); Chew (1971).

145. Franco-Thai 1940-1941

New York Times (1941); Decoux (1949); Paxton (1972).

148. Palestine, 1948-1949

During the last months of British occupation (fall 1947 through May 1948), the British army lost several hundred troops in clashes with both Arab and Jewish forces. Arab-Israeli incidents between 1949 and 1956 and 1957 and 1967 do not reach our battle death threshold.

O'Ballance (1956); Glubb (1957); Israel Office of Information (1960); Kimche (1960); Lorch (1961); Abdel-Kader (1962).

151. Korean, 1950-1953

Given the size of the contingent and the structure of the command, the Chinese "volunteers" have been considered official representatives of the Chinese government in this war.

Keesing's (1952); United Nations Command (1953); Barclay (1954); Leckie (1962); Rees (1964).

154. Russo-Hungarian, 1956

The military history of the Hungarian revolt remains to be written. Completely accurate figures for the size of the "freedom fighter" army, let alone its casualties, probably never will be ascertained. We do not consider this a civil war. Even though the official Hungarian government requested Soviet intervention, very few natives aided the Soviets.

Meray (1959); Vali (1961); Zinner (1962); Ignotus (1972).

157. Sinai, 1956

Bromberger and Bromberger (1957); Henriques (1957); Marshall (1958); Thomas (1967).

160. Sino-Indian, 1962

Early in this war, some Indian sources suggested that their forces had suffered 2500 battle deaths. At war's end, however, this figure, according to Prime Minister Nehru, was around 200, excluding "missing." Unofficial estimates range from 200 to 5,000 for India and a like number for China.

New York Times (1962); *United Asia* (1962); *Communist China,* 1962 (1963); *Facts on File* (1963); *Britannica Book of the Year* (1963); Rouland (1967); Kaul (1967); Maxwell (1970).

163. Vietnamese, 1965-1975

From January 1961 through February 6, 1965, this was considered a civil war. The war became internationalized in January of 1961 when sufficient U.S. "advisors" assisted the Saigon government against the National Liberation Front. On February 7, 1965, after the NLF attack on Pleiku, the United States started to bomb North Vietnam and thus converted the war into an interstate war. New Zealand, which participated on the U.S.-Saigon side, never sent more than 1,000 troops; nor did it suffer the requisite 100 battle deaths.

Pike (1966); Buttinger (1967); Fall (1967); Kahin and Lewis (1969); U.S. Senate (1969); Gettleman (1970); Cooper (1970); Grant (1970); Herring (1979).

166. Second Kashmir, 1965

Facts on File (1965); Lamb (1967).

169. Six Day, 1967

Safran (1969).

172. Israeli-Egyptian, 1969-1970

The constant artillery and air duels along the cease-fire lines of the Six Day War satisfied our definition of an interstate war.

Middle East Record (1969-1970); Whetten (1974); Heikal (1975); Dupuy (1978); Bar-Siman-Tov (1980).

175. Football, 1969

Keesings (1969); *New York Times* (1969).

178. Bangladesh, 1971

Keesings (1971-1972).

181. Yom Kippur, 1973

Although marginal participants, Jordan and Saudi Arabia did commit more than 1,000 troops each to the anti-Israeli effort.

O'Ballance (1978).

184. Turco-Cypriot, 1974

Markides (1977).

187. Vietnamese-Cambodian, 1975—

These two former allies began skirmishing almost immediately after the Khmer Rouge seized control of Pnompenh. Although the Vietnamese eventually launched a successful full-scale invasion and brought their own Cambodian friendlies with them, a war between the Khmer Rouge and the Vietnamese continued in the jungles as of December 1980.

Keesings (1975-1980); *New York Times* (1975-1980).

190. Ugandan-Tanzanian, 1978-1979

Keesings (1978-1979); *New York Times* (1978-1979).

193. Sino-Vietnamese, 1979

The formal outbreak of war in February 1979 was preceded by several large-scale incidents in December 1978 and January 1979.

Keesings (1979); *New York Times* (1979).

196. Russo-Afghan, 1979—

Although the Soviet Union is supported by the Kabul regime that it propped up, we consider this to be an interstate war between Russians and some Afghans and the Afghan people. In some ways, it resembles the Hungarian War of 1956.

Keesings (1980-1981); *New York Times* (1979-1981).

199. Irani-Iraqi, 1980—

Keesings (1980-1981); *New York Times* (1980-1981).

EXTRA-SYSTEMIC WARS

301. British Maharattan, 1817-1818

This was treated as an imperial war because the Maharattan tribes had never been part of the British Raj.

Frazer (1897); Fortescue (1923, vol. ll).

304. Greek, 1821-1828

On October 20, 1827, British, French, and Russian fleets engaged in a one-day naval battle against the Turks in Navarino Bay. The Turks lost 3,000 sailors; the British, 80; the French, 40; and the Russians, 60. Although this incident is directly related to Turkish operations against Greece, we have chosen not to include it in the Greek war data.

Phillips (1897); Crawley (1930); Anderson (1952); Woodhouse (1952).

307. First-Anglo Burmese, 1823-1826

The other two major Anglo-Burmese wars do not meet our battle death criterion.

Fortescue (1923, vol. 11); Harvey (1929); Cady (1958).

310. Javanese, 1825-1830

Klerck (1938); Vlekke (1960).

313. Russo-Persian, 1826-1828

von Schlechta-Wssehrd (1866); Schiemann (1913); Baddeley (1908); Sykes (1951); Atkin (1980).

316. First Polish, 1831

Exaggerated patriotic firsthand accounts such as the first three cited reported that handfuls of courageous Polish freedom fighters slaughtered 100,000 Russian troops. While many Russians did not return to the front, most of the deaths, including that of the commander-in-chief, can be attributed to disease. During much of the nineteenth century, disease was the major killer in wars in Eastern Europe and the Middle East.

Hordynski (1832); Brzozowski (1833); Gnorowski (1839); Puzyrewsky (1893); Schiemann (1913); Grunwald (1955); Leslie (1956); Reddaway (1961); Curtiss (1965).

319. First Syrian, 1831-1832

Mehemet Ali of Egypt asked his Ottoman suzerain for all of Syria as reward for Egypt's aid to Turkey in Greece. When the Porte refused, Ali took Syria and advanced almost to Constantinople. Fearing the Egypt-ians would take the Straits, Russia landed troops on the Asiatic side of the Bosporus and, in effect, stopped the war without firing a shot.

Sabry (1930); Dodwell (1931); Polites (1931); Cattaui and Cattaui (1950).

322. Texan, 1835-1836

Some fighting continued after 1836 until the abortive New Mexican campaign of 1842, but these skirmishes involved only a handful of men.

Bancroft (1885); Stephenson (1921); Callcott (1936); Alessio Robles (1945-1946).

325. First British-Afghan, 1838-1842

Thompson and Garrett (1934); Sykes (1940); Majumdar (1948); Fletcher (1965); Macrory (1966); Norris (1967).

328. Second Syrian, 1839-1840

British and Austrian participation was limited to naval bombardment of the Syrian coast and relatively bloodless occupation of Mehemet Ali's strongholds.

Jochmus (1883); Jordan (1923); Sabry (1930); Dodwell (1931); Polites (1931); Moltke (1935); Cattaui and Cattaui (1950); Anderson (1952); Temperly (1964).

331. Franco-Algerian, 1839-1847

Martin (1963).

334. Peruvian-Bolivian, 1841

Arguedas (1923); Basadre (1940); Dellepiane (1943); Vasquez-Machi-cado, Mesa, and Gisbert (1963).

337. First British-Sikh, 1845-1846

This was treated as an imperial war because the Sikhs had never been a part of the British Raj.

Gough and Innes (1897); Fortescue (1927, vol. 12); Majumdar (1948); Burt (1956); Singh (1966); Bond (1967).

340. Hungarian, 1848-1849

Headley (1852); Bodart (1916); Curtiss (1965).

343. Second British-Sikh, 1848-1849

Same sources as #337.

346. First Turco-Montenegran, 1852-1853

Frilley and Wlahovitj (1876); Gopcevic (1877).

349. Sepoy, 1857-1859

Originally an army mutiny, this conflict reached such proportion as to qualify as an Indian war for liberation from the British.

Collier (1963); Edwardes (1963).

352. Second Turco-Montenegran, 1858-1859

Same sources as #346.

355. Second Polish, 1863-1864

Edwards (1865); Reddaway (1961); Leslie (1963).

358. Spanish-Santo Dominican, 1863-1865

New York Times (1863-1865); Clarke (1906).

361. Ten Years' War, 1868-1878

While fighting continued into the 1880s, the last major rebel force signed a peace agreement with the Spanish in 1878.

Barrios y Carrion (1888-1890); Clarke (1906); Beals (1933); Guerra y Sanchez (1950); Ponte Dominguéz (1958); Payne (1967).

364. Dutch-Achinese, 1873-1878

The Dutch did not completely subdue the Achinese until 1908, but the first and major phase of the conflict ended in 1878. Although Dutch forces suffered 10,000 battle deaths from 1878 to 1908 in incessant border warfare and raiding, the requirement of an average 1000 deaths a year was not met.

Kielstra (1883); Rose (1915); Vlekke (1960).

367. Balkan, 1875-1877

Hozier (1878); Langer (1931); Sumner (1937); Stavrianos (1958); Mackenzie (1967).

370. Bosnian, 1878

Dumas and Vedel-Peterson (1923); Haumant (1930).

373. Second British-Afghan, 1878-1880

Hanna (1910).

376. British-Zulu, 1879

Morris (1965).

379. Franco-Indochinese, 1882-1884

Bodart (1916); Cordier (1920); Kirnan (1939); Khôi (1955); Li (1956); Buttinger (1958); Lancaster (1961); Roberts (1963).

382. Mahdist, 1882-1885

After the Tel-El-Kebir incident in 1882, England seized control of Egyptian affairs. Consequently, losses suffered by Egyptian forces under British command in the Sudan were considered British battle deaths. After the debacle of Gordon's death at Khartoum, the British withdrew from the Sudan and temporarily gave up hopes of reconquest. They resumed the campaign from 1896 to 1899, but the combined Anglo-Egyptian armies suffered surprisingly light casualties.

Churchill (1900); Alford and Sword (1932); Theobald (1951); Shibeika (1952); Holt (1958); Magnus (1958).

385. Serbo-Bulgarian, 1885

Mallat (1902); Mijatovich (1917); Dumas and Vedel-Peterson (1923); MacDermott (1962).

388. Franco-Madagascan, 1894-1895

Resistance continued in the interior for several years. Almost all of the French battle deaths were disease-related.

Bodart (1916); Deschamps (1960); Brown (1979).

391. Cuban, 1895-1898

Clarke (1906); Beals (1933); Portell Vilá (1949); Smith (1965).

394. Italo-Ethiopian, 1895-1896

The several skirmishes that took place before the official declaration of war were not included because they were neither severe nor sustained. Italian forces also engaged Mahdist bands, but these contests resulted in relatively few battle deaths.

Berkeley (1935); Italy, Comitato per la Documentazione Dell'Opera Dell'Italia in Africa (1952); Battaglia (1958).

397. First Philippine, 1896-1898

Although Aguinaldo agreed to a truce in the winter of 1897 and left the islands, several rebel chieftains did not surrender.

Kalaw (1925); Zaide (1954); Agoncilla (1956).

400. Second Philippine, 1899-1902

Heitman (1903); Storey and Lichauco (1926); Grunder and Livezey (1951).

403. Boer, 1899-1902

Dumas and Vedel-Peterson (1923); Pemberton (1964); Belfield (1975).

406. Ilinden

This was a major Macedonian revolt against the Turks.

Anastasoff (1977).

409. Russian Nationalities, 1917-1921

Finns, Ukrainians, Latvians, Estonians, Lithuanians, and others battled the Bolsheviks. The Russian Revolutionary government had a mixed record in these wars. It crushed the independent movement in the Ukraine, Georgia, and other areas of Asian Russia, but it lost to the Finns, Latvians, Estonians, and Lithuanians. Of course, during this period the Soviets were also successfully waging a war against White and foreign troops on several fronts from Siberia to the Black Sea. See also #745.

Doroshenko (1939); Graves (1941); Hrushevsky (1941); Carr (1950-1953); Bilmanis (1951); Reshetar (1952) Ironside (1953); Unterberger (1956); Rauch (1957); Smith (1958); Senn (1959); Page (1959); Sullivant (1962); Jutikkala (1962); Wuorinen (1965).

412. Riffian, 1921-1926

The Spanish were harassed by rebels in Morocco from 1910 through 1921, but they did not suffer sufficient battle deaths until 1921, when the Rifs began an organized rebellion. After the capture of Abd-El-Krim in 1926, desultory fighting continued into the 1930s.

L'Afrique Française (1926); Jacques (1927); Harris (1927); Usborne (1936); Fontaine (1950); Gabrielle (1953); Landau (1956); Payne (1967); Woolman (1968).

415. Druze, 1925-1927

MacCallum (1928); Longrigg (1958).

418. Indonesian, 1945-1946

Only during the brief period of British occupation did the battle deaths of British and Dutch troops reach the appropriate threshold. This first uprising was marked by the bloody battle of Surabaya. During the second phase of the revolt (1946-1949), only the Dutch participated; their battle deaths were insufficient to merit inclusion.

Wehl (1948); Wolf (1948); Gebrandy (1950); Kahin (1952); Woodman (1955).

421. Indochinese, 1945-1954

Keesing's (1954); Fall (1963); O'Ballance (1964).

424. Madagascan, 1947-1948

Deschamps (1960); Thompson and Adloff (1965).

427. First Kashmir, 1947-1949

The official forces of India and Kashmir opposed Pathan tribes, Kashmir rebels, and Pakistani irregulars. The army of Pakistan did participate in a minor way, supplying the Kashmiris and defending strategic points behind the battle lines. Generally the Indians were circumspect in engaging Pakistani troops. Given these considerations, the conflict in the disputed territories was tenuously classified as an imperial war between the Indian government and the people of Kashmir.

India, Ministry of Information (1949); Mellor (1951); Birwood (1954); Korbel (1959); Poplai (1959); Williams (1962); Lamb (1967).

430. Hyderabad, 1948

New York Times (1948).

433. Algerian, 1954-1962

Deadline Data (1957, 1961, 1962); Horne (1977).

436. Tibetan, 1956-1959

Thomas (1959); Patterson (1960); Richardson (1962).

439. Philippine-MNLF, 1972—

Accurate casualty estimates are difficult to come by in this secessionist war between Moslems and the central government.

Keesings (1972-80); Philippines Information Bureau (1974); Suhkre and Noble (1977).

442. Ethiopian-Eritrean, 1974—

Keesings (1974-1980).

445. Timor, 1975—

The Indonesian attempt to incorporate this former Portuguese possession continued at a greatly reduced scale as of the end of 1980.

Keesings (1975-80); Jolliffe (1978); Chomsky (1979).

448. Saharan, 1975—

The War of the Polisario front against Morocco and Mauritania (to 1979) for control of the Spanish Sahara has never involved direct Algerian intervention.

Keesings (1975-1980).

451. Ogaden, 1976—

The exact role of Somalia in this war is clear only for the years 1977-1978. One alternative coding scheme would involve *three* Ogaden wars. From 1976 to 1977, Cuba and Ethiopia fought rebels in the Ogaden in a colonial war. During the middle phase, the war looked like an interstate war. From 1977 to the present, Somalia's participation was too limited to allow labeling the conflict anything other than a colonial war.

Keesings (1975-1980).

CIVIL WARS

601. Spain, 1821-1823

When France intervened to liberate King Ferdinand and to restore his authority, this war was transformed into an interstate war. By that time the Royalist opposition had been crushed.

Sorokin (1937); Richardson (1960a); Urlanis (1960); Campos y Serrano (1961); Smith (1965); Wright (1965); Holt (1967); Menendez Pidal (1968); Gambra (1972).

604. Turkey, 1826

Some historical accounts suggest that the defeat of the Janissaries was a massacre and not a "civil war." However, the Janissaries were well-trained and well-armed military personnel. Thus, we are estimating, with limited documentation, that at least one in twenty deaths involved the Sultan's troops. The Janissaries' fatalities include the loss of their entire families.

Deans (1854); Mathieu (1857); Eversley (1917); Atamian (1955); Richardson (1960a); Dumont (1963).

607. Portugal, 1829-1834

The heaviest fighting occurred after Dom Pedro, emperor of Brazil, arrived in Portugal in 1831 to support the parliamentary-constitutional government of his daughter Donna Maria against his brother Dom Miguel, whose forces were fighting to re-establish the autocratic monarchy.

Bollaert (1870); Richardson (1960a).

610. France, 1830

Bodart (1916); Bertier de Sauvigny (1955); Leys (1955); Beach (1971).

613. Mexico, 1832

Schlarman (1950); Bravo Ugarte (1962).

616. Spain, 1834-1840

The Carlist offensive was announced in October 1833, but the first government action did not occur until July 1834. The British who participated were volunteers with official sanction from their government; 1,850 of their deaths were from disease.

Bollaert (1870); Urlanis (1960); Holt (1967); Harbottle and Bruce (1971).

619. Colombia, 1840-1842

Government, struggling to defeat progressive rebels, was forced to request aid from Ecuador. Ecuador was not yet a member of system.

Henao and Arrubla (1938).

622. Argentina, 1841-1851

This war is enmeshed with a war in Uruguay that fails of inclusion because Uruguay was not a member of the system in 1841. In Uruguay, the Colorados under Rivera were supported by the Argentine Unitarios living in exile in Uruguay. By June 1838, Rivera and the Unitarios had control of all of Uruguay except for Montevideo. Meanwhile, in Argentina, there was no serious internal conflict until after the French blockade of the Argentine coast (March 1838), an act of protest directed against Rosas rather than for his opponents the Unitarios. In September and October, France and Rivera joined to force the flight of Oribe from Montevideo. An anti-Rosas Argentine government was set up in Uruguay, and revolts broke out in the Argentine provinces. Uruguay (Rivera) declared war on Argentina (Rosas) in February 1839. Rosas put down the revolts in his provinces with help from Oribe by 1842; Rivera invaded Argentina and was defeated by Oribe in December 1842. In February 1843, Oribe invaded Uruguay at the head of an Argentine army and put Montevideo under a nine-year siege. In 1845, revolts broke out in the Argentine provinces again; England and France intervened for the rebels, who were defeated by Rosas in November. Finally, in 1851, Argentine General Urquiza united the Argentine provinces with help from Brazil and invaded Uruguay, defeated Oribe, and lifted the seige of Montevideo in October. Then Urquiza, at the head of an allied army of Uruguayans, Argentinians, and Brazilians, defeated Rosas in Argentina in 1852 in an interstate war (#19).

Cady (1929); Kirkpatrick (1931); Acevedo (1934); Munro (1942); Best (1960); Crow (1971).

625. Spain, 1847-1849

Bollaert (1870); Clark (1906); Smith (1965); Holt (1967); Godechot (1971).

628. Two Sicilies, 1848-1849

King (1899); Orsi (1913); Godechot (1971).

631. France, 1848

Cayley (1856); Bodart (1916); Robertson (1952); Godechot (1971).

634. Austria-Hungary, 1848

Cayley (1856); Maurice (1887); Bodart (1916); Sorokin (1937); Droz (1957); Godechot (1971).

637. Chile, 1851

Williams et al. (1955); Richardson (1960a); Bernstein (1965); Davis (1968).

640. Peru, 1853-1855

Basadre (1940); Munro (1942); Pike (1967); Marett (1969).

643. Peru, 1856-1858

Same sources as #640.

646. Mexico, 1858-1861

Jensen (1953); Richardson (1960a); Davis (1968).

649. Venezuela, 1859-1863

Munro (1942); Wise (1951); Williams et al. (1955); Gilmore (1964).

652. China, 1860-1864

This war began in 1851 before China was a member of the system. The T'ai P'ing rebels did not entirely give up their cause after the fall of Nanking in 1864 but joined forces with other rebels (such as the Nien) and bandits and continued to cause trouble, usually at the local provincial level, until 1868. British and French forces were stationed along the China coast to protect their commercial interests. British presence in and around Shanghai had an important deterrent effect on the T'ai P'ings from 1860 to 1864, but their only active fighting was limited to February-August 1862. The French navy did not fight the T'ai P'ings. The "Ever Victorious Army" consisted of Americans, French, British (few in number, at half-pay from the British government) and Chinese volunteers. We have not included as part of this war the French and British forced entry into Peking in 1859-1860.

Lin-le (1866); Wilson (1868); Spielmann (1900); Selby (1948); Michael (1957); Gregory (1959); Teng (1963); Pelissier (1963); Chu (1966); Franke (1970); Jen Yu-wen (1973).

653. China, 1860-1868

Influenced by Taiping victories in the 1850s, Niens in Anhwei and Honan revolted in 1854. On occasion, they fought alongside Taipings. Several foreign gunboats intervened from time to time. The revolt involved two rather separate groups—the eastern and western Niens.

Chiang (1964); Ping (1959); Teng (1961).

654. China, 1860-1872

The Miao revolt in Kweichow, Hunan, Yunnan, Kwangsi, and Szech-
wan that began in 1855 was also tied to the Taiping Rebellion. Three
color-marked armies—white, red, and brown—constituted the major
military army of the Miaos. After the government suppressed the Nien
in 1868, they turned on the Miaos with a fury bordering on genocide.
We have indicated the close relationship between this war and the two
preceding ones by not separating their code numbers in our normal
fashion.

Ping (1959); Teng (1971).

655. Colombia, 1860-1862

Henao and Arrubla (1938); Munro (1942).

658. United States, 1861-1865

Ironically, perhaps, since this celebrated *civil* war involved a secession
movement, it could almost qualify as an extra-systemic war. However,
the lack of ethnic differences between the two sides, as well as the military contention for control of areas near the capital, clearly place the
war in the civil category.

Bodart (1916); Dumas and Vedel-Peterson (1923); Perré (1962); Morris
(1970); Carrère (1972).

661. Argentina, 1863

Kirkpatrick (1931); Best (1960).

664. Argentina, 1866-1867

Same sources as #661.

667. Venezuela, 1868, 1869-171

New York Times (1868-1871); Rondon Marquez (1944); Gilmore (1964).

670. Spain, 1868

Bollaert (1870); Clarke (1906); Sorokin (1937).

673. Argentina 1870-1871

Small rebellion in Entre Rios.
Best (1960).

676. France, 1871

Bodart (1916); Sorokin (1937); Richardson (1960a); Urlanis (1960); Perré (1962); Carrère (1972).

679. Spain, 1872-1876

Sorokin (1937); Clarke (1906); Richardson (1960a); Holt (1967); Harbottle and Bruce (1971).

682. Colombia, 1876-1877

Henao and Arrubla (1938); Richardson (1960a).

685. Japan, 1877

Mounsey (1879); Richardson (1960a).

688. Argentina, 1880

This clash between Buenos Aires and the united provinces was the last of many over the question of Buenos Aires autonomy.

Akers (1930); Richardson (1960a); Langer (1968).

691. Colombia, 1884-1885

Henao and Arrubla (1938); Munro (1942); Richardson (1960a).

694. Chile, 1891

Akers (1930); Richardson (1960a); Bernstein (1965); Blakemore (1965); Harbottle and Bruce (1971).

697. Brazil, 1893-1894

The rebels in Rio Grande do Sul were not fighting for secession, but they did want greater autonomy from the centralist republican government. The fighting spread to Santa Catarina and Parana provinces, and the defeated navy rebels from the war in Rio harbor (#700) helped the Rio Grande Forces.

Bello (1968); Davis (1968); Love (1971).

700. Brazil, 1893-1894

Navy royalists took over Rio harbor and bombarded the city.

Bello (1968); Martin and Lovett (1968); Davis (1968).

703. Peru, 1894-1895

Pike (1967).

706. Brazil, 1896-1897

This revolution in the backlands of Bahia province was led by a religious fanatic who opposed taxation. The first of several government expeditions sent against the settlement was defeated, but in the final siege of the rebel's town, every inhabitant was killed at great cost in lives to the government.

Akers (1930); Cunha (1944); Bello (1966); Davis (1968).

709. Colombia, 1899-1903

Some date the beginning of this war, "The War of 1000 Days," to the day the president was imprisoned by liberal rebels. Certainly the war intensified after this point to become one of the bloodiest in Colombian history.

Henao and Arrubla (1938); Galbraith (1953); Wood (1968); Bergquist (1978).

712. Uruguay, 1903-1904

This rather small war is considered to be the final martial conflict between the Blancos and Colorados, whose antagonism dates from the 1830s.

Acevedo (1934); Rodriguez Herrero (1934).

715. Russia, 1905-1906

Moorehead (1958); Harcave (1964).

718. Rumania, 1907

Beginning in Moldavia as a peasant revolt with anti-Semitic overtones, the rebels later directed their activities against landlords in general.

Stavrianos (1958); Richardson (1960a).

721. Morocco, 1907-1908

Ashmead-Bartlett (1910); Usborne (1936); Richardson (1960a); Freeman-Grenville (1973); Burke (1976).

724. Iran, 1909-1909

The shah's revocation of the constitution sparked this conflict. The Russians arrived with over 6,000 soldiers in March 1909 to help the fast-failing shah. Although the constitutionalists won the war, some Russians remained in Iran until 1910.

Wilbur (1963); Browne (1966).

727. Mexico, 1910-1920

There is not enough space here to recount completely the sweeping governmental and social changes during this period. There were four major changes, with reformers or moderates as presidents in all except the very conservative military regime of Huerta, 1913-1914. The forces that supported the deposed dictator, Porforia Díaz—most of the army and conservatives—fought all the revolutionary regimes. Besides the conservative opposition, revolutionary governments fought Zapata in the south and Villa in the north.

Jensen (1953); McHenry (1962); Wright (1965); Cumberland (1968).

730. Morocco, 1911

Usborne (1936); Richardson (1960a); Burke (1976).

733. Paraguay, 1911-1912

Warren (1949).

736. China, 1911

MacNair (1931); Pritchard (1951); Li (1956); Mende (1961); Clubb (1964); McAleavy (1967); Franke (1970).

739. China, 1913

The "Second Revolution" was a challenge to the newly formed government of Yuan Shih-kai by the Revolutionary Republicans of Sun Yat-sen.

MacNair (1931); Li (1956); Clubb (1964); McAleavy (1967); Franke (1970).

742. China, 1914

While most of Yuan Shih-kai's trouble was in the south, he had to suppress the bandit rebels of Pai-Ling (White Wolf) in the northwest.

Li (1956); Richardson (1960a); Chesneaux (1973).

745. Russia, 1917-1920

This conflict includes simultaneous wars between the Bolshevik government and the several White armies and their foreign supporters. We do not include in this war the interstate war between Russia and Poland, from 1919 to 1920. The Poles did not intervene in the civil war, nor did they ally themselves with any of the government's opponents.

The nations that intervened in the civil war sent sizable contingents, with the Japanese force reaching more than 70,000, but they fought few pitched battles with Bolshevik armies. A good number of the battle deaths among the capitalist interveners involved disease and frostbite. Although Japanese troops stayed in Siberia until 1922, we consider their intervention to have ended with our formal ending of the civil war in October 1920.

Stewart (1933); Yanaga (1949); Urlanis (1960); Brinkley (1966); Bradley (1968); Dupuy and Dupuy (1970); Heflin (1970); Liebman (1970); Silverlight (1970); Barlein (1971).

748. Hungary, 1919-1920

The Communist government's efforts to establish itself in the face of violent conservative opposition was further complicated by the border dispute and war with Rumania and Czechoslovakia. See #112.

Jasci (1969); Heflin (1970); Völgyes (1971).

751. Honduras, 1924

The United States, which landed small contingents of troops to "keep order," played a significant role even though we do not consider it a *formal* intervener.

New York Times (1924).

754. Afghanistan, 1924-1925

Fletcher (1965); Fraser-Tyler (1967); Gregorian (1969).

757. China, 1926-1928

Although China was torn by many regional wars during the period from 1920 through 1926, only when the Nationalists under Chiang Kai-shek challenged the forces that controlled Peking, the officially recognized government, can we say a civil war existed. Japan, in support of Chang Tso-lin of Manchuria, who controlled Peking, intervened to protect its interests in 1927. A serious clash between the Nationalists and Japanese took place at Tsinan in May 1928.

Takeuchi (1935); McAleavy (1967); Chi (1969); Johnson (1976).

760. Mexico, 1926-1930

This rebellion took place in Jalisco, Guanajuato, and Michoacan by "Cristeros," religious-oriented conservatives in opposition to the anti-clerical government.

Munro (1942); Schlarman (1950); Parkes (1966); Cumberland (1972); Bailey (1974).

763. Afghanistan, 1928-1929

Richardson (1961); Fletcher (1965); Fraser-Tyler (1967); Gregorian (1969).

766. China, 1929-1930

Although campaigns against the warlords took place after October 1930, the Nationalists of Chiang Kai-shek engaged in the most serious fighting prior to that date. Instrumental in government victories was the intervention in 1930 of Chang Hsueh-liang, the warlord of autonomous Manchuria. More than a half-million rebels were in the warlord's van of several armies, while the Nationalists fielded comparably massive armies. Casualty estimates for this war are often mixed with those of the simultaneous civil war fought with the Communists (#769).

MacNair (1931); Clubb (1964); McAleavy (1967).

769. China, 1930-1935

Beginning in November 1930, five "Banditry Suppression Campaigns" against the Communists were launched by Chiang, the last one from October 1933 to October 1934, and ending with the Communists' Long March in Shensi and their pursuit by the Nationalist Army, through to October 1935. Although an anti-Japanese alliance between the Communists and Nationalists was not signed until 1937, large-scale fighting between them ended with the Long March.

T'ang (1934); Isaacs (1961); Clubb (1964); McAleavy (1967); Wilson (1971).

772. Brazil, 1932

Richardson (1960a); Bernstein (1965); Bello (1966); Young (1967).

775. Spain, 1934

This revolt of miners and workers in the Asturias region was harshly put down by the Republic.

Ramos-Oliviera (1946); Thomas (1961).

778. Spain, 1936-1939

While forces of the left occasionally fought fratricidally, in most cases, the powerful Spanish Communists fought with the government forces against the Fascists. Although at the time some questioned whether the German and Italian intervention represented the participation of their *governments,* today it is certain that Berlin and Rome approved and organized the intervention. Russian intervention is also cited by many authorities, but their main activity on the scene was to coordinate and supply the multinational volunteers and to provide military advisors. The international Volunteer Brigades, numbering more than 30,000, did not formally represent a system member.

Thomas (1961); Payne (1970); Coverdale (1975).

781. Greece, 1944-1949

Richardson (1960a); Wright (1965); O'Ballance (1966a); Cady and Prince (1968); Wood (1968); Heflin (1970); Taylor and Hudson (1972).

784. China, 1946-1950

Clubb (1964); Wright (1965); Cady and Prince (1966); McAleavy (1967); Kende (1971); Taylor and Hudson (1972).

787. Paraguay, 1947

Cardoza (1949); Warren (1949); Cady and Prince (1966).

790. Yemen, 1948

Ingrams (1963); Cady and Prince (1966); O'Ballance (1970).

793. Costa Rica, 1948

Nicaragua sent troops to occupy a border area but did not participate in the fighting.

Cady and Prince (1966); Bell (1971).

796. Colombia, 1948

Most histories include this as part of a long civil war (#802) which we consider to have begun in 1949. We treat the conflicts as distinct entities, since this war features a different government antagonist and is separate in time.

Cady and Prince (1966); Mydans and Mydans (1968).

799. Burma, 1948-1951

Tinker (1957); Cady (1958); Cady and Prince (1966); Wood (1968); Donnison (1970); Taylor and Hudson (1972).

802. Colombia, 1949-1962

Formal civil war, banditry, and terrorism mark this struggle. There were periods of little violence during this very long conflict, notably 1952 and 1957-1958.

Huntington (1962); Cady and Prince (1966); Mydans and Mydans (1968); Petras (1968); Wood (1968); Kende (1971); Rummel (1972); Taylor and Hudson (1972); Maullin (1973).

805. Indonesia, 1950

The South Molucca Republic, proclaimed on April 26, 1950, was pacified in November.

Kahin (1952); Kosut (1967).

808. Philippines, 1950-1952

Vinacke (1956); Bashore (1962); Hammer (1962); Tirona (1962); Cady and Prince (1966); Wood (1968); Taylor and Hudson (1972); Kerkvliet (1977).

811. Bolivia, 1952

Alexander (1958); Wright (1965); Cady and Prince (1966); Malloy (1970); Taylor and Hudson (1972).

814. Indonesia, 1953

In Atjeh, Darul Islam, a group that wanted to make Islam the official religion of the state, began a terrorist campaign in the summer of 1953.

Cady and Prince (1966); Kosut (1967).

817. Guatemala, 1954

There was no formal American participation in this war, although the CIA armed, trained, and financed the winning rebel force.

Jensen (1955); Bannon and Dunne (1963); Tomasek (1974).

820. Argentina, 1955

Rummel (1972); Taylor and Hudson (1972).

823. Indonesia, 1956-1960

Scattered reports suggest widespread rebellions during this period in Sumatra, Java, the Moluccas, and the Celebes. Although the rebellions were unrelated, we choose to treat them as one, as in the case of the Chinese wars against the warlords.

Feith (1964); Cady and Prince (1966); Kosut (1967); Rummel (1972); Taylor and Hudson (1972).

826. Lebanon, 1958

Nantet (1963); Agwani (1965); Cady and Prince (1966).

829. Cuba, 1958-1959

Although revolt began in 1956 when rebels landed from the *Granma*, Castro's armies did not have 1,000 combatants until July 1958.

Cady and Prince (1966); Mydans and Mydans (1968); Wood (1968); Taylor and Hudson (1972).

832. Iraq, 1959

Shammar (Arab) tribes allied with pro-Western military officers while the Kurds took the side of the year-old leftist government that won handily.

Taylor and Hudson (1972); O'Ballance (1973).

835. South Vietnam, 1960-1965

This war began as a civil war when southern rebels, many of whom had been trained and supplied in North Vietnam, launched a small rebellion in 1958. The war does not cross our severity threshold until 1960, the year in which the rebels took the name "National Liberation Front." In that year, the United States had some 800 advisers in South Vietnam. When, in 1961, the number of advisers began to grow and when they began shooting as well as advising, the war can be said to have entered its international civil war phase. The problems of body count are dealt with in an interesting manner in Herr (1977).

Alcock and Lowe (1969); Bourne (1970); Kende (1971); Chomsky (1971); Baldwin (1972); Carrère and Valat-Morio (1972); *Études Polémologiques* (1972); Taylor and Hudson (1972); Leitenberg and Burns (1973); Turner (1975); Herr (1977).

838. Congo, 1960-1965

Because of our coding rules, we do not count the United Nations' participation.

Cady and Prince (1966); Mydans and Mydans (1968); Lefever (1972); Taylor and Hudson (1972).

841. Laos, 1960-1962

Cady and Prince (1966); Mydans and Mydans (1968); Wood (1968); Adams and McCoy (1970); Gettleman (1970); Langer and Zaslof (1970); Chomsky (1971); Taylor and Hudson (1972).

844. Algeria, 1962-1963

Cady and Prince (1966); Ottaway (1970); Horne (1977).

847. Yemen, 1962-1969

Cady and Prince (1966); Mydans and Mydans (1968); Wood (1968); O'Ballance (1970); *Études Polémologiques* (1972); Taylor and Hudson (1972).

850. Laos, 1963-1973

After the brief cease-fire of July 1962-April 1963, the neutralists and conservatives allied to oppose the Pathet Lao. The war ends with a cease-fire in 1973. The communist takeover in 1975 was affected with little military combat. We have included as "volunteer" foreign participants the U.S.-CIA paid Thai, South Vietnamese, and Nationalist Chinese troops fighting in the Vang Pao Clandestine Army. Our definition of U.S. intervention is limited to official U.S. military forces engaged in combat missions. At the time of the February 1973 cease-fire, only 450 U.S. military personnel were involved in air missions, and 200 other official military forces were present. These figures do not include the paramilitary CIA and Special Forces advisers whose exact number still is not known. Even at the apex of the U.S. bombing, 1968-1970, it is questionable whether there were 1,000 regular troops involved at any one time, although precise figures on the air war are still difficult to obtain. As for the North Vietnamese intervention, figures vary from a low of 500 military advisers to tens of thousands of ground troops. The truth is somewhere in between, with 5,000 a reasonable estimate at the highest, and perhaps fewer than 1,000 at the time of cease-fire.

Wright (1965); Mydans and Mydans (1968); Wood (1968); Adams and McCoy (1970); Gettelman, et al. (1970); Langer and Zasloff (1970); *Keesings* (1970-1974); Chomsky (1971); Taylor and Hudson (1972).

853. Sudan, 1963-1972

Wood (1968); *Études Polémologiques* (1972); Taylor and Hudson (1972); Eprile (1974).

856. Rwanda, 1963-1964

We include this conflict as civil war even though the Watusi (Tutsi) organized and struck from outside Rwanda's borders. They were former residents of Rwanda, however, fighting the Hutu-dominated government for the right to govern Rwanda. Following the Watusi defeat in battle, the Hutus massacred thousands of Watusi still living in Rwanda.

Taylor and Hudson (1972).

859. Dominican Republic, 1965

Cady and Prince (1966); Mydans and Mydans (1968); Wood (1968); Carey (1972); Taylor and Hudson (1972); Gleijeses (1978.

862. Uganda, 1966

Young (1966); Gukiina (1972); Taylor and Hudson (1972).

865. China, 1967-1968

The Red Guard did not get beyond the government's control until December 1966, having begun their cultural revolution in May. The army was sent against them in January 1967.

An (1972); Cheng (1972); Taylor and Hudson (1972).

868. Nigeria, 1967-1970

Clendenen (1972); *Études Polémologiques* (1972); Taylor and Hudson (1972).

871. Cambodia, 1970-1975

The United States did not have 1,000 military personnel engaged in the Cambodian conflict except during the incursion in May of 1970. Furthermore, it is not always clear whom the United States was fighting in Cambodian territory. The government of South Vietnam fought not only South Vietnamese Communists in Cambodia but also Cambodian Communists, but it is very difficult to prepare separate fatality estimates for the two years, particularly since the ARVN troops claim to have fought only North Vietnamese in Cambodian sanctuaries.

Far Eastern Economic Review (1970-1972); *Keesings* (1970-1975); Caldwell and Tan (1973); Indochina Solidarity Committee (1973); Leitenberg and Burns (1973); Indochina Resource Center (1974).

874. Jordan, 1970

Higham (1972); Snow (1972).

877. Guatemala, 1970-1971

Crow (1971); *Keesings* (1971-1972); Taylor and Hudson (1972).

880. Pakistan, 1971

Civil war between east and west Pakistan became an interstate war on December 3, when India intervened to decide the outcome of the conflict and to help establish independent Bangladesh. Many of the fatality estimates include deaths resulting from starvation and exposure in the migrations of non-combatants, as well as deaths by terrorism after the war was officially over. We include in our estimate non-combatant deaths in combat areas, but not the deaths in refugee camps, nor the widespread communal violence in the newly created state of Bangladesh following the treaty and cease-fire. See also #178.

Asian Recorder (1972); Ayoob and Subrahmanyam (1972); *Études Polémologiques* (1972); *Facts on File* (1972); Payne (1973).

883. Sri Lanka, 1971

Keesings (1971-1972).

886. Burundi, 1972

Hutus opposing the Tutsi-dominated government claimed to be the victims of attempted genocide after they tried to overthrow the government in a political coup. There was some involvement by forces of Zaire, especially air support.

Études Polémologiques (1972); Melady (1974); Lemarchand (1975).

889. Philippines, 1972—

It is almost impossible to determine whether this insurrection by the New People's Army has maintained itself since 1972 at the 1,000 battle deaths per year threshold. This civil war is not to be confused with the secessionist colonial war waged by the MNLF against the central government during the same period (#439).

Keesings (1972-1981); *New York Times* (1972-1981).

892. Rhodesia, 1972-1979

The white Rhodesian government's attacks against rebel bases in neighboring countries are not considered here.

New York Times (1972-1980).

895. Lebanon, 1975-1976

Salibi (1976); Meo (1977); Haley and Snider (1979).

898. Angola, 1975—

Keesings (1975-1981); Valdes (1979).

901. Afghanistan, 1978-1979

The civil war became an interstate war when Russia took over Kabul in December 1979.

New York Times (1978-1979).

904. Iran, 1978-1979

New York Times (1978-1979).

907. Nicaragua, 1978-1979

New York Times (1978-1979).

910. El Salvador, 1979—

New York Times (1979-1981).

International and Civil Wars Excluded

Listed below are all the wars cited in major compendia, as well as a score of others discovered in our own investigations, that have not qualified for our study. The excluded wars are presented in chronological order identified by their participants. Wars with only one participant were civil wars; wars with two or more participants were international wars. Almost all of these wars failed of inclusion because they resulted in fewer than 1,000 battle deaths for interstate wars, or an average of 1,000 per year for system members for the other wars. When the primary cause of exclusion was something other than battle deaths, we have so indicated with (M) representing the participants' lack of membership in the interstate system and (Ma) the fact that the encounter was a massacre and not a war. In many of the more celebrated or controversial cases, we have noted the sources that informed our coding decisions.

England-Kandyans, 1818: Powell (1873).

Russia-Georgians and Circassians, 1816-1864: Allen and Muratoff (1908); Baddeley (1908); Seton-Watson (1967).

Argentina, 10/1819-10/1820 (M): Best (1960).

Holland-Sumatrans, 1819-6/1821.

Turkey-Arabs, 1820.

Austria-Hungary-Neapolitan Republics, 1820-3/1821: King (1899); Orsi (1914); Artz (1936); Romani (1950); Godechot (1971).

Turkey-Janina, 1820-1822.

Turkey-Nubians, 1820-1822.

Turkey-Crete, 1/15/1822-4/1825, 1-12/1828: Gordon (1844); Eliade (1933); Great Britain Naval Institute (1945); Smith (1965).

Austria-Hungary-Carbonarists, 3/10-4/8/1821: Orsi (1914); Artz (1936).

Siam-Kedah, 1821 (M).

Turkey-Persia, 8/1821-1822.

England-Ashanti, 4/1821-9/1826: Fortescue (1923, vol. 11).

Khokand-Khojas, 1822-2/1828, 9-11/1830 (M): Bellew (1875); Nalivkine (1889).

Haiti-Santo Domingo, 1823 (M).

Central America, 1823 (M).

England-Burma, 9/1824-1826.

Holland-Bonians, 1825.

Russia, 12/1825.

England-Bharatpur, 12/1825-1/1826: Fortescue (1923, vol. 11).

Argentina and Uruguayans-Brazil, 3/27/1825-9/15/1828 (M).

England-Tasmania, 1825-1830.

Central America, 1827-1829 (M).

France-Algerians, 4/1827-5/1830.

Argentina, 1828-1831 (M).

Mexico-Spain, 1829.

Chile, 1829-4/1830 (M).

Muscat-Zanzibar, 1829-1837 (M).

France-Madagascar, 1829.

Turkey-Herzogovinians, Bosnians, and Albanians, 1830-11/1831.

England, France, and Belgians-Holland, 8/25/1830-1833: Cheminon and Fauvel-Gallais (1902); Blok (1912); Essen (1916); Linden (1920); Cammaerts (1921); Pirenne (1926).

Austria-Hungary-Modena and Parma, 1831.

Central America, 1831-1845 (M).

Greece, 10/31-1/15/1833: Dakin (1973).

Argentina, 4/1833-4/1834 (M): Best (1960).

Portugal-Matahaganans, 1833-1836.

France-Annamese, 1833-1839.

Turkey-Palestinians, 1834.

England, Hottentots, and Boers-Kaffirs, 12/1834-5/1835.

Austria-Hungary-Bosnians and Herzogovinians, 1835-1846.

Brazil, 9/1835-3/1845: Laytano (1936); Love (1966).

Argentina, Bolivia, and Peru-Chile, 7/1836-1/1839 (M).

Turkey-Bosnians, 1836-1837: MacDermott (1962).

Boers-Matabele, 1836-1837.

Ma-Kalanga-Matabele, 1837 (M).

Afghanistan-Persia, 1837-1838 (M).

Austria-Hungary-Montenegro, 1838.

France-Mexico, 1838-1839.

England-Zulus, 2/1838-2/1840.

England-Khelat, 11/13/1839.

Russia-Khiva, 1839-1842: Allworth (1967).

Colombia, 1839.

England and France-China (Opium War), 9/1839-8/1842: Fortescue (1927, vol. 12); Costin (1937).

Matabele-Mashonas, 1840 (M).

Tibet-Dogras, 1841 (M).

Turkey-Bulgaria, 4/6-5/1841; MacDermott (1962).

England-Sind, 1-6/1843: Thompson and Garrett (1934); Huttenback (1962).

Uruguay, 1843-1851 (M): Scarone (1956).

England-Gwalior, 12/1843.

France-Morocco, 1843-1844.

England-Borneo Pirates, 1845.

France-Madagascar, 1845.

Turkey and Maronites-Druzes, 1845.

Austria-Hungary-Poles, 1846: Blum (1948).

Holland-Balinese, 1846-6/1849.

France-Cochin China, 1847.

Switzerland, 7-11/20/1847.

China-Kashagaria, 1847-1/1848 (M): Bellew (1875).

Baden, 3/7-9/19/1848: Cayley (1856); Droz (1957).

Prussia, 3/15-10/17/1848: Cayley (1856); Robertson (1952); Droz (1957); Godechot (1971).

Austria-Hungary-Poles, 1848: Maurice (1887).

Rumania, 1848 (M): Riker (1931); Stavrianos (1968).

Austria-Hungary, 6/1848: Seton-Watson (1965); Bradley (1971).

Modena, 1848-1849: Maurice (1887); King (1899).

Parma, 1848-1849.

Tuscany, 1848-1849.

Central America, 1849-1858.

Turkey-Bosnians, 1849-11/1850.

Saxony, 5/1849: Cayley (1856); Droz (1957).

Turkey-Bulgarians, 6/1-9/1850: MacDermott (1952).

England-Basutos, 12/1850-12/1852.

Russia-Turkestan, 1851-1875: Allworth (1967).

France, 12/1851: Cayley (1856).

Argentina, 9/11/1852-1853: Kirkpatrick (1931); Best (1960).

Dards-Dogras, 1852 (M).

England-Burmese, 4/1852-1/1853.

Turkey-Montenegro, 12/1852-6/1859.

Mexico, 1853-1855: Johnson (1939); Bravo-Ugarte (1949); Bernstein (1965); David (1968).

Colombia, 4-11/1854: Henao and Arrubal (1938); Williams et al. (1955); Bernstein (1965).

England-Bantu, 1854.

China-Triads, 5/1/1854-8/31/1855: Wakeman (1966); Teng (1971).

Spain, 6/28-7/19/1854: Clarke (1906); Kiernan (1966).

British-Santals, 1855: Natrajan (1979).

Haiti-Santo Domingo, 1855-1856 (M).

Nicaragua, 5/1855-5/1857 (M): Munro (1918).

Spain, 7/14-7/23/1856: Clarke (1906); Kiernan (1966).

England and France-China, 10/22/1856-10/24/1860.

China-Khokand, 1857 (M): Bellew (1875).

France-Fulas, 1857.

France-Annam, 1857-1862.

Peru-Ecuador, 1859.

Modena, Parma, Tuscany, 1859-1860: King (1899).

Holland-Boninese, 2/1859-1/1860.

Argentina, 10/1859-9/1861.

Holland-Banjermasinese, 4/1859-1863.

Russia-Circassians, 1859-1864.

France-Arabs, 1860.

Druses and Moslems-Christians, 1860 (Ma): Tibawi (1969); Hitti (1970).

Arabs-Africans, 1860-1869 (M).

Ethiopia, 1861 (M).

France-Cochinchinese, 1861-1862.

Turkey-Herzogovinians, 1861-1862: Miller (1913).

China-Khojas, 1862-1864, 1876-1878: Bellew (1875); Khan (1963); Chu (1966); Michell (1970).

Turkey-Montenegro, 1862.

Turkey-Serbs, 1862.

Italy-Garibaldians, 1862.

Siam-Cambodia, 12/1862-7/1863 (M).

England, France, and Holland-Japan, 8/13/1863-4/17/1869.

Bengal, 1863 (M).

France-China, 1862-1864.

United States-Sioux, 1862-1867.

Central America, 1/23-11/15/1863 (M).

England-Wahabis, 10/18-12/22/1863.

England-Maoris, 4/1863-2/1866.

Uruguay, 1863-1872 (M): Koebel (1915); Akers (1930); Kirkpatrick (1931); Acevedo (1934).

Afghanistan, 1864-1868 (M): Khan (1963).

England-Bhutan, 1865.

England-Jamaicans, 10/11-11/1865.

Boers-Basutos, 1865-1867.

Russia-Bokhara, 12/1865-6/1868.

Japan, 1866-1868.

Spain, 1/3/1866-9/28/1868: Mazade (1869); Bollaert (1870); Strobel (1898); Clarke (1906); Hennessey (1962).

England, France and Greece-Turkey, 9/2/1866-1869.

France and Papal States-Garibaldians, 1867.

Ethiopia, 1867 (M).

England-Ethiopia, 10/1867-5/1868.

Haiti, 1867-1869: Davis (1967).

Japan, 1/3/1868-1869: Mounsey (1879).

Egypt-Zobeir's Army, 1869.

Italy-Papal States, 1870.

France-Algerians, 3/1871-1/1872.

England-Ashanti, 1/1873-2/1874: Ward (1959).

France-Tonkin, 1873-1874.

Egypt-Dafurians, 1873-1874.

Argentina, 10/1873-5/1874: Rennie (1943); Williams et al. (1955).

Egypt-Ethiopia, 9/1875-3/1876.

Turkey, 1876: Miller (1913); Eversley (1917); Stojanovic (1939); Stavrianos (1958).

United States-Sioux, 1876-1877.

England-Kaffirs, 1877-1878.

Russia-Turkomans, 1878-1881: Pierce (1960); Allworth (1967).

Egypt-Slavers, 1878-1879.

Argentina-Patagonians, 1878-1883: Best (1960).

England-Basutos, 1879-1881.

Uganda, 1880 (M).

England-Transvaal, 12/20/1880-8/8/1881: Mansford (1967).

Austria-Hungary-Dalmatians, 1882.

England-Egypt, 1882: Maurice and Arthur (1924).

France-Tunisia, 3/31/1881-4/4/1882.

France-Madagascar, 5/1883-12/1885.

Peru, 10/1883-8/1884: Markham (1968).

Oman, 1883-1884 (M).

France-Hovas, 1883-1885.

England-Italy, 6/1885-1895.

Ethiopia-Egyptians and Suakin Tribes-Sudanese and Darfurians-Shi-
luks, 6/1885-1895 (M).

Russia-Afghanistan, 3/30/1885.

England-Burma, 1885-1889: Scott (1924); Woodman (1955); Cady (1958).

Uganda, 1885-1890 (M).

Siam-Laos, 1885-1893.

England-Arabs and Yaos, 1885-1896.

Italy-Ethopia, 1/1887.

Germany-Arabs and Swahili, 8/1888-1890.

Turkey-Cretans, 1889: *London Times* (1889).

Guatemala-Salvador, 7/23-11/15/1889.

Argentina, 7/1890: Etcheparaborda (1966).

United States-Sioux, 11/1890-1/1891.

France-Senegalese, 1890-1892.

Holland and Sasaks-Balinese, 1891-11/1894.

Argentina, 7/29-9/1893: Etcheparaborda (1966).

Uganda, 1892 (M).

France-Senegalese, 1892-1894.

Belgium and Congolese-Arabs, 10/1892-2/1894: Wack (1905); Martelli
(1962).

France-Sudanese, 1893.

France-Siam, 1893.

Bornu-Raheb's Army, 1893.

Uganda, 1893.

Morocco-Spain, 1893-1894.

France-Morocco, 1893-1894.

France-Tuaregs, 1893-1904.

France-Tonkinese, 1894.

Turkey-Armenians, 1894-1896, 1909, 1919 (Ma).

Germans-Wahemes, 10/1894-7/1898.

England-Masuri, 1895-1896.

Turkey-Cretans, 1895-1897: *London Times* (1895-1897); Dakin (1973).

Turkey-Druzes, 1896: Miller (1913).

England-Mashonas and Matabele, 1896-1899.

England and Egypt-Sudanese, 3/1896-1/1900.

Costa Rica-Nicaragua, 3/20-4/29/1897 (M).

England-Benin, 1/1897.

England-Bunyoro and Buganda, 6/1897.

England-Moslems (India), 1897-1898.

England-Sierra Leone, 1898.

Venezuela, 1898-1899: Moron (1963).

France-Bornu, 1899-1901.

England, Italy, and Ethiopia-Somalians, 1899-1904.

Russia-Manchurians, 1900.

England-Ashanti, 3/1900-9/1903: Fuller (1921).

England, Germany, and Italy-Venezuela, 12/11/1902-2/13/1903.

Turkey-Albanians, 1903-1911: Swire (1930); Anastasoff (1938).

England-Moslems (Nigeria), 1-5/1903.

England-Nigerians, 1903.

Colombia-Panamanians, 1903.

England-Tibet, 1903-1904.

Germany-Herreros and Hottentots, 1903-1908: Germany, Armee Grosser
    Generalstab (1906-1907); Johnston (1913); MacLean (1918); Hintrager
    (1955); First (1963).

United States-Dominican Republic, 1904: Perkins (1941); Callcott (1942);
    Bemis (1943); Munro (1964).

France-Senussi, 1904-1911.

Paraguay, 8/8-12/15/1904: Warren (1980).

England-Nandi, 1905.

Germany-Maji-Maji, 1905-1909: Buell (1908); Johnston (1913); Listowel (1965).

Russia-Jews, 10/1905.

China, 1905-1910: Lee (1970); Chesneaux (1973).

England-Zulus, 3-7/1906.

Cuba, 8-9/29/1906: Chapman (1927); Fitzgibbon (1935); Heinl (1962).

Holland-Venezuela, 1908.

England-Indians, 1908.

Turkey, 1908: Miller (1913).

Portugal, 1910: Wheeler (1978).

Nicaragua, 1911-1912: Perkins (1941); Callcott (1942); Munro (1964).

Cuba, 5/20-6/27/1912: Fitzgibbon (1935).

China, 5/12-6/12/1912: McAleavy (1967).

China-Tibet, 1912-1913: Richardson (1962).

British-Dervishas, 1913-1920.

France and Moroccans-Zaians, 1914-1917.

Haiti-United States, 1915-1920: Callcott (1942); Bemis (1943); Munro (1964).

China, 12/1915-3/1916: MacNair (1913); Li Chien-nung (1956); Franke (1970).

Russia-Turkestan, 1916: Allworth (1960).

Dominican Republic, 1916: Callcott (1942); Munro (1964).

France-Chief Kaossen, 1916-1917.

England-Ireland, 4/24-4/29/1916.

France-Caids, 11/1916-1917.

Cuba, 2/10-6/1917: Fitzgibbon (1935).

Russia, 3/7-11/7/1917: Yaroslavsky and Tovstukha (1946); Liebman (1971).

China-Tibet, 1-7/1918.

Finland, 1918 (M): Smith (1958); Wuorinen (1965); Liebman (1971); Rabinowitch (1976).

Poland-Ukraine, 1-6/1919.

England-Irish, 1919-1922.

England-Punjabis, 6/1919.

Japan-Koreans, 1919.

England-Afghanistan, 5/6-8/8/1919: Fletcher (1965).

Germany, 10/28-11/9/1919: Pinson (1954).

France-Syrians, 1918-1920.

England-Iraquis, 6/1920-1921: Foster (1935); Hasluck (1938); Longrigg (1953).

Lithuania-Poland, 4/8/1920-12/10/1927: Reddaway (1951); Wandycz (1969); Benes (1970).

Italy-Sanusi, 1920-1/1932.

England-Moplahs, 8/1921-1922.

Italy, 3/3-11/15/1922: Schmidt (1938); Cassels (1969).

Ireland, 6/8/1922: Neeson (1966).

France-Tache de Taza, 1923.

Bulgaria, 6/9-6/14/1923 (Ma): Stavrianos (1958).

Japan-Koreans, 10/1923.

Spain, 9/12-9/13/1923.

China, 10/1924: Chi (1969).

Turkey-Kurds, 3-4/1924 (Ma): Eagleton (1963); O'Ballance (1973).

Hejaz-Wehabi, 1924-1925 (M): Glubb (1960).

China, 1926: Chi (1969).

Holland-Javanese, 12/11/1926-1927.

China, 4/1927 (Ma): Sheridan (1975).

United States-Nicaragua, 1927-1933: Macauley (1967).

France-Moroccans, 1929-9/1933.

Brazil, 10/3-10/27/1930.

Argentina, 1930: Hasbrouck (1938).

France-Vietnamese, 1930-1931.

Sinkiang, 1930-1933 (M): Lamb (1969).

Ecuador, 1932.

El Salvador, 1/22/1932 (Ma): White (1973).

Peru, 2-7/1932: Basadre (1968), Marett (1969).

Iraq-Kurds, 8/1933: Eagleton (1963), O'Ballance (1973).

Cuba, 1933-1934: Aguilar (1972).

Saudi Arabia-Yemen, 1934: Wenner (1967).

Germany, 6/30-7/1934 (Ma).

Austria, 2/12-2/16/1934, 7/25-7/30/1934: Gehl (1963); Schuschnigg (1971); Maass (1972).

British-Palestinians, 1934-1939.

China-Mongols, 11/1936-1937: Clubb (1964).

Dominican Republic, 10/1937 (Ma): Rodman (1964).

England-Hindus, 1936-1938.

England-Iraq, 1941: Great Britain Central Office of Information (1948); Khadduri (1960).

England and Russia-Iran, 1941: Lenczowski (1949).

France-Algerians, 5/1945.

India, 7/1-10/30/1946 (M).

Bolivia, 7/18-7/22/1946.

England-Hindus-Moslems, 2/1946-1/18/1948 (M) (Ma).

Russia-Iran, 1946-1948: Lenczowski (1949).

China-Formosans, 2/28-3/21/1947: Kerr (1965).

England-Malayans, 1947-1952: Pye (1956); Short (1958); O'Ballance (1966).

South Korea, 10/20/1948.

England-Burmese, 1948-1954.

China-Tibetans, 1950.

Burma-Chinese, 1950-1953.

Thailand, 6/29-7/1/1951.

France-Tunisians, 1952-1956.

England-Kenyans, 1952-1955: Great Britain Colonial Office (1960); Listowel (1965); Rosberg (1966).

France-Moroccans, 1953-1956.

China-Taiwan, 1954-1956.

England-Cypriots, 1955-1959.

Nicaragua-Costa Rica, 1955.

India-Nagas, 1955-1964: Aram (1974).

France-Cameroons, 1956-1958: Levine (1964).

Yemen-Aden, 1956-1960.

Haiti, 1956-1957.

North Vietnam, 11/2-11/20/1956: Buttinger (1968).

Honduras-Nicaragua, 1957.

Oman, 7/19-8/26/1957 (M).

Venezuela, 1957-1968.

Jordan, 1958.

Rwanda, 11/1959 (M).

Cameroons, 1959-1961 (M).

Holland-West Irian, 1960-1962.

Portugal-India, 1961.

Iraq-Kurds, 1961-1975: Adamson (1965); Vanly (1965); O'Ballance (1973);
    Time (1974).

Cuba-United States, 1961-1963.

Portugal-Angolans, 1961-1975.

France-Tunisia, 7-9/1961.

Burundi-Rwanda, 1962-1964.

Portugal-Guinea Bissau, 1962-1974.

Iraq, 2/8/1963.

Cyprus, 1963-1964.

Egypt-Somalia, 1963-1964.

Algeria-Morocco, 1963-1964.

Tanzania, 1964.

Malaysia-Indonesia, 1964-1966.

Uganda, 1964.

Kenya, 1964.

Gabon, 1964.

Zambia, 5-9/1964.

Portugal-Angolans, 1965-1975.

Brazil, 3/31-4/2/1964: Bello (1966).

Guatemala, 1964: Petras (1968).

Peru, 1965.

Indonesia, 1965-1966 (Ma).

Nigeria, 1-10/1966: Clendenen (1972).

Czechoslovakia-Warsaw Pact, 8/1968.

Chad, 1969: *African Diary* (1965-1970).

South Africa-Namibians, 1966—.

Zaire, 7-11/1966.

China-Russia, 3/1969.

England-Irish, 1969—.

Chile, 9/11-9/18/1973.

Portuguese Timor, 1975 (M).

Portugal, 4/25/1975: Harsgor (1975); Harvey (1978).

Chad, 1976—.

References

Abdel-Kader, A. Razak. LE CONFLIT JUDÉO-ARABE. Paris: François Maspero, 1962.

Acevedo, Eduardo. ANALES HISTORICOS DEL URUGUAY. Montevideo: Barreiro y Ramos, 1934, vols. 3-5.

Adams, N. S. and A. W. McCoy (eds.). LAOS: WAR AND REVOLUTION. New York: Harper, 1970.

Adamson, David G. THE KURDISH WAR. New York: Praeger, 1965.

African Diary 1961-1972.

L'Afrique Française. 36/6 (June, 1926), 327-37.

Agoncilla, Teodoro A. THE REVOLT OF THE MASSES. Quezon City: Univ. of Philippines, 1956.

Aguilar, Luis E. CUBA 1933. Ithaca: Cornell Univ., 1972.

Agwani, M. S. (ed.). THE LEBANON CRISIS, 1958: A DOCUMENTARY STUDY. London: Asia Publishing House, 1965.

Akagi, Roy. JAPAN'S FOREIGN RELATIONS: A SHORT HISTORY 1542-1936. Tokyo: Hokuseido, 1936.

Akers, Charles E. A HISTORY OF SOUTH AMERICA. London: John Murray, 1930.

Albertini, Luigi. THE ORIGINS OF THE WAR OF 1914. 3 vols. (Trans. Isabella Massey.) London: Oxford Univ., 1952-1957.

Albrecht-Carrié, René. A DIPLOMATIC HISTORY OF EUROPE SINCE THE CONGRESS OF VIENNA. New York: Harper, 1958.

Alcock, Norman Z. and Keith Lowe. "The Vietnam War as a Richardson Process," JOURNAL OF PEACE RESEARCH, 7 (1970), 105-12.

Alessio Robles, Vito. COAHUILA Y TEXAS. 2 vols. Mexico City: Antigua Libreroa Robredo, 1945-1946.

Alexander, Robert J. THE BOLIVIAN NATIONAL REVOLUTION. New Brunswick: Rutgers Univ., 1958.

Alford, Henry and W. Denniston Sword. THE EGYPTIAN SUDAN: ITS LOSS AND RECOVERY. London: Macmillan, 1932.

Allen, W. E. D. and Paul Muratoff. CAUCASIAN BATTLEFIELDS. Cambridge: Cambridge Univ., 1953.

Allworth, Edward (ed.). CENTRAL ASIA. New York: Columbia Univ., 1967.

Almanach de Gotha. Gotha: Justus Perthes, 1764-1940.

Amaral, Ignacio M. do. ENSAIO SOBRE A REVOLUCAO BRASILEIRA. Rio de Janeiro: Imprensa Naval, 1963.

Anastasoff, Christ. THE TRAGIC PENINSULA: A HISTORY OF THE MACEDONIAN MOVEMENT FOR INDEPENDENCE SINCE 1878. St. Louis: Blackwell Wiebendy, 1938.

———. THE BULGARIANS. Hicksville: Exposition, 1977.

Anderson, R. C. NAVAL WARS IN THE LEVANT. Princeton: Princeton Univ., 1952.

Anderson, Thomas P., THE WAR OF THE DISPOSSESSED: HONDURAS AND EL SALVADOR. Lincoln: Nebraska Univ., 1981.

Annual of Power and Conflict. London: Institute for the Study of Conflict, 1971-.

Annual Register of World Events. London: Longmans, 1758-.

An Tai Sung. MAO TSE-TUNG'S CULTURAL REVOLUTION. Indianapolis: Bobbs-Merrill, 1972.

Anthouard, Albert F. LES BOXEURS. Paris: Plon-Nourrit, 1902.

Antonius, George. THE ARAB AWAKENING. London: Hamish Hamilton, 1938.

Aram, M. PEACE IN NAGALAND: THE EIGHT YEAR STORY, 1964-1972. New Delhi: Arnold Heinemann, 1974.

Arguedas, Alcides. HISTORIE GÉNÉRALE DE LA BOLIVIE. Paris: Alcan, 1923.

Aron, Robert. THE VICHY REGIME 1940-1944. London: Putnam, 1958.

Artz, Frederick B. REACTION AND REVOLUTION, 1815-1832. New York: Harper, 1936.

Ashmead-Bartlett, Ellis. THE PASSING OF THE SHEREEFIAN EMPIRE. Edinburgh: William Blackwood, 1910.

Asian Record, January 15-21, 1971.

Askew, William C. EUROPE AND ITALY'S ACQUISITION OF LIBYA 1911-1912. Durham, N.C.: Duke Univ., 1942.

Atamian S. THE ARMENIAN COMMUNITY. New York: Philosophical Library, 1955.

Atkin, Muriel. RUSSIA AND IRAN, 1780-1828. Minneapolis: Univ. of Minnesota, 1980.

Averoff-Tossizza, Evangelos. BY FIRE AND AXE: THE COMMUNIST PARTY AND THE CIVIL WAR IN GREECE, 1944-1949. New York: Caratzas Publishers, 1978.

Ayoob, Mohammed (ed.). CONFLICT AND INTERVENTION IN THE THIRD WORLD. New York: St. Martin's 1980.

———. **and K. Subrahmanyam.** THE LIBERATION WAR. New Delhi: S. Chand, 1972.

Baddeley, John F. THE RUSSIAN CONQUEST OF THE CAUCAUSUS. New York: Longmans, Green, 1908.

Badoglio, Pietro. THE WAR IN ABYSSINIA. London: Methuen, 1937.

Baerlein, Henry. SOUTHERN ALBANIA. Chicago: Argonaut, 1968.

———. THE MARCH OF THE SEVENTY THOUSAND. London: Leonard Parsons, 1971.

Bailey, David C. VIVA CRISTO REY! Austin: Univ. of Texas, 1974.

Baldwin, Frank. "Patrolling the Empire: Reflections on the U.S.S. Pueblo." BULLETIN OF CONCERNED ASIAN SCHOLARS, 4/2 (Summer, 1972), 54-74.

Bancroft, Hubert Howe. HISTORY OF MEXICO. San Francisco: A. L. Bancroft, 1885.

Bannon, John F. and Peter Dunne. LATIN AMERICA. Milwaukee: Bruce, 1963.

Barclay, C. N. The First Commonwealth Division. Aldershot, U.K.: Gale and Polden, 1954.

Barrios y Carrion, Leopoldo. SOBRE LA HISTORIA DE LA GUERRA DE CUBA. Barcelona: Revista Cientifico-Militar y Biblioteca Militar, 1888-1890.

Bar-Siman-Tov, Yaacov. THE ISRAELI-EGYPTIAN WAR OF ATTRITION, 1969-1970: A CASE STUDY OF LIMITED WAR. New York: Columbia Univ., 1980.

Basadre, Jorge. HISTORIA DE LA REPUBLICA DEL PERU. Lima: Editorial Cultura Anartica S. A., 1940.

Bashore, Maj. Boyd T., "Dual Strategy for Limited War," in F. Osanka (ed.). MODERN GUERRILLA WARFARE. Glencoe: Free Press, 1962.

Battaglia, Roberto. LA PRIMA GUERRA D'AFRICA. Rome: Einaudi, 1958.

Beach, Vincent W. CHARLES X OF FRANCE. Boulder, Colo: Pruett, 1971.

Beals, Carleton. THE CRIME OF CUBA. Philadelphia: Lippincott, 1933.

Beebe, Gilbert and Michael de Bakey. BATTLE CASUALTIES: INCIDENCE, MORTALITY AND LOGISTIC CONSIDERATIONS. Springfield, Ill.: C.C. Thomas, 1952.

Beehler, William H. THE HISTORY OF THE ITALIAN-TURKISH WAR. Annapolis, Md.: Advertiser-Republican, 1913.

Beer, Francis A. PEACE AGAINST WAR: THE ECOLOGY OF INTERNATIONAL VIOLENCE. San Francisco: W. H. Freeman, 1981.

Belden, Jack. CHINA SHAKES THE WORLD. New York: Monthly Review, 1949.

Belfield, Eversly. THE BOER WAR. Hamden: Archon, 1975.

Bell, John Patrick. CRISIS IN COSTA RICA: THE 1948 REVOLUTION. Austin: University of Texas, 1971.

Bellew, Dr. W. H., "History of Kashghar," in Thomas D. Forsyth, REPORT OF A MISSION TO YARKAND IN 1873. Calcutta: Foreign Department Press, 1875.

Bello, José Maria. A HISTORY OF MODERN BRAZIL, 1889-1964. Stanford: Stanford Univ., 1966.

Bemis, Samuel Flagg. A DIPLOMATIC HISTORY OF THE UNITED STATES. New York: Holt, 1936.

————. THE LATIN AMERICAN POLICY OF THE UNITED STATES. New York: Harcourt, 1943.

Benes, Vaclav L. POLAND. New York: Praeger, 1971.

Benoit, Emile and Harold Lubell. "World Defense Expenditures." JOURNAL OF PEACE RESEARCH, 3 (1966), 97-113.

Bergquist, Charles. COFFEE AND CONFLICT IN COLUMBIA, 1886-1910. Durham, N.C.: Duke Univ., 1978.

Berkeley, George F. H. ITALY IN THE MAKING 1815-1846. Vol. 1. Cambridge: Cambridge Univ., 1932.

————. THE CAMPAIGN OF ADOWA AND THE RISE OF MENELIK. London: Constable, 1935.

Berndt, Otto. DIE ZAHL IM KRIEGE. Vienna: Freytag u. Berndt, 1897.

Bernstein, Harry. MODERN AND CONTEMPORARY LATIN AMERICA. New York: Russell & Russell, 1965.

Berthe, Augustine. GARCIA MORENO. Vol. 1. Paris: Librairie de la "Sainte Famille," 1903.

Bertier de Sauvigny, Guillaume de. LA RESTAURATION. Paris: Flammerion, 1955.

Best, Felix. HISTORIA DE LAS GUERRAS ARGENTINAS. 2 vols. Buenos Aires: Peuser, 1960.

Bilmanis, Alfred. A HISTORY OF LATVIA. Princeton: Princeton Univ., 1951.

Birwood, Christopher. INDIA AND PAKISTAN. New York: Praeger, 1954.

Blackey, Robert. MODERN REVOLUTIONS AND REVOLUTIONISTS: A BIBLIOGRAPHY. Santa Barbara, Ca.: Clio. 1976.

Blainey, Geoffrey. THE CAUSES OF WAR. New York: Macmillan, 1973.

Blakemore, Harold. "The Chilean Revolution of 1891 and its Historiography." HISPANIC AMERICAN HISTORICAL REVIEW, 45 (August, 1965), 393-421.

Blok, Petrus J. A HISTORY OF THE PEOPLE OF THE NETHERLANDS. New York: Putnam, 1912.

Blum, Jerome, NOBLE LANDLORDS AND AGRICULTURE IN AUSTRIA, 1815-1848: A CASE STUDY IN THE ORIGINS OF THE PEASANT EMANCIPATION OF 1848. Baltimore: Johns Hopkins Univ., 1948.

Blumenfeld, Ralph D. "A Hundred Years War of Today." HARPER'S MONTHLY, 103 (August, 1901), 367-74.

Bock, Carl H. PRELUDE TO TRAGEDY. Philadelphia: Univ. of Pennsylvania, 1966.

Bodart, Gaston, MILITAR-HISTORISCHES KRIEGS-LEXIKON (1618-1905). Vienna: C. W. Stern, 1908.

————. LOSSES OF LIFE IN MODERN WARS. Oxford: Clarendon, 1916.

Bogart, Ernest L. DIRECT AND INDIRECT COSTS OF THE GREAT WORLD WAR. New York: Oxford Univ., 1919.

Bollaert, William. THE WARS OF SUCCESSION OF PORTUGAL AND SPAIN FROM 1826 to 1840. 2 vols. London: Edward Stanford, 1870.

Bond, Brian (ed.). VICTORIAN MILITARY CAMPAIGNS. New York: Praeger, 1967.

Bourne, Peter G. MEN, STRESS, AND VIETNAM. Boston: Little Brown, 1970.

Bouthoul, Gaston and Rene Carrère, "Deux Ans D'aggressivité mondiale, 1967-1969." ÉTUDES POLÉMOLOGIQUES 2 (October 1971), 17-108.

————. *Le Défi de la Guerre (1740-1974): Deux Siècles de Guerres et de Révolutions.* Paris: Presses Universitaires de France, 1976.

Box, Pelham Horton. ORIGINS OF THE PARAGUAYAN WAR. Urbana: Univ. of Illinois, 1927.

Bradley, John. ALLIED INTERVENTION IN RUSSIA. New York: Basic, 1963.

Bradley, J. F. N. CZECHOSLOVAKIA. Edinburgh: Edinburgh Univ., 1971.

Bravo Ugarte, Jose. MEXICO INDEPENDIENTE. v. 22, in A. Ballesteros y Beretta (ed.), HISTORIA DE AMERICA. Barcelona: Salvat, 1949.

_____. HISTORIA DE MEXICO. v. 3. Mexico City: Editorial Jus, 1962.

Brinkley, George A. THE VOLUNTEER ARMY AND ALLIED INTERVENTION IN SOUTHERN RUSSIA, 1917-1921. South Bend, Ind.: Univ. of Notre Dame, 1966.

Brinton, Crane. THE ANATOMY OF REVOLUTION. New York: Prentice-Hall, 1938.

BRITANNICA BOOK OF THE YEAR. Chicago: Encyclopaedia Britannica, 1963.

Brody, Alter, et.al. (eds.). WAR AND PEACE IN FINLAND. New York: Soviet Russia Today, 1940.

Bromberger, Merry and Serge. SECRETS OF SUEZ. London: Pan, 1957.

Brown, Mervyn. MADAGASCAR REDISCOVERED. Hamden, Conn.: Archon, 1979.

Browne, Edward G. THE PERSIAN REVOLUTION OF 1905-1909. London: Frank Cass, 1966.

Brzozowski, Marie. LA GUERRE DE POLOGNE EN 1831. Leipzig: Brockhaus, 1833.

Buell, Raymond Leslie. THE NATIVE PROBLEM IN AFRICA. Vol. 1. New York: Macmillan, 1908.

Burgess, Paul. JUSTO RUFFINO BARRIOS. Philadelphia: Dorrance, 1926.

Burke, Edmund. PRELUDE TO PROTECTORATE IN MOROCCO. Chicago: U. of Chicago, 1976.

Burr, Robert N. "The Balance of Power in Nineteenth Century South America: An Exploratory Essay." THE HISPANIC AMERICAN HISTORICAL REVIEW, 25 (February, 1955), 37-60.

Burt, Alfred L. THE EVOLUTION OF THE BRITISH EMPIRE AND COMMON-WEALTH. Boston: Heath, 1956.

Buttinger, Joseph. THE SMALLER DRAGON. New York: Praeger, 1958.

_____. VIETNAM, A DRAGON EMBATTLED. Vol 2. New York: Praeger, 1967.

Cady, John F. FOREIGN INTERVENTION IN THE RIO DEL PLATA 1838-1850. Philadelphia: Univ. of Pennsylvania. 1950.

_____. A HISTORY OF MODERN BURMA. Ithaca: Cornell Univ., 1958.

Cady, Richard H. and William Prince. POLITICAL CONFLICTS, 1944-1966. Ann Arbor, Mich.: Bendix Social Sciences Division, 1966.

Calahan, H. A. WHAT MAKES A WAR END? New York: Vanguard, 1944.

Caldwell, Malcolm and Lek Hor Tan. CAMBODIA IN THE SOUTHEAST ASIAN WAR. New York: Monthly Review, 1973.

Callcott, Wilfred H. SANTA ANNA. Norman: Univ. of Oklahoma, 1936.

_____. THE CARIBBEAN POLICY OF THE UNITED STATES. Baltimore: Johns Hopkins Univ., 1942.

Calogeras, Joao P. A HISTORY OF BRAZIL. (Trans. and ed. Percy A. Martin.) New York: Russell and Russell, 1963.

Cammaerts, Emile. A HISTORY OF BELGIUM. New York: D. Appleton, 1921.

Campos Y Serrano, Martinez de. ESPAÑA BELICA: EL SIGLO XIX. Madrid: Aguilar, 1961.

Cardoza, Efraim, PARAGUAY INDEPENDIENTE, v. 21, in A Ballesteros y Beretta (ed.). HISTORIA DE AMERICA. Barcelona: Salvat, 1949.

Carey, James C. "The Latin American Legacy: The Background for Civil War," in Robin Higham (ed.), CIVIL WARS IN THE TWENTIETH CENTURY. Lexington: Univ. of Kentucky, 1972.

Carmichael, Joel. THE SHAPING OF THE ARABS. New York: Macmillan, 1967.

Carr, Edward H. THE BOLSHEVIK REVOLUTION 1917-1923. 3 vols. London: Macmillan, 1950-1953.

Carrère, Rene, "1870-1871, Guerre ancienne ou guerre moderne?" ÉTUDES POLÉ-MOLOGIQUES, 5 (July, 1972), 23-24.

————. **and Pierre Valat-Morio,** "La violence mondiale, 1970-1971," ÉTUDES PO-LÉMOLOGIQUES, 6 (October, 1972), 16-70.

Carroll, Berenice A. "Germany Disarmed and Rearming, 1925-1935." JOURNAL OF PEACE RESEARCH, 3 (1966), 114-24.

Cassels, Alan. FASCIST ITALY. London: Routledge, 1969.

Castellanos, Pedro Zamora. VIDA MILITAR DE CENTRO AMERICA. Guatemala City, 1925.

Cattaui, René and Georges. MOHAMED ALY ET L'EUROPE. Paris: Libraire Orientaliste, 1950.

Cayley, Edward. THE EUROPEAN REVOLUTIONS OF 1848. 2 vols. London: Smith, Elder, 1856.

Chadwick, H. Munro. THE NATIONALITIES OF EUROPE AND THE GROWTH OF NATIONAL IDEOLOGIES. Cambridge: Cambridge Univ., 1945.

Chaliand, Gerard. REVOLUTION IN THE THIRD WORLD: MYTHS AND PROS-PECTS. New York: Viking, 1977.

Chambers, Frank, Christina Harris, and Charles Bayley. THIS AGE OF CON-FLICT. New York: Harcourt, 1950.

Chapman, Charles E. A HISTORY OF THE CUBAN REPUBLIC. New York: Mac-millan, 1927.

Cheminon, J. and G. Fauvel-Gallais. LES ÉVENEMENTS MILITAIRES EN CHINE. Paris: Chapelot, 1902.

Cheng, Peter. A CHRONOLOGY OF THE PEOPLE'S REPUBLIC OF CHINA. To-towa, N.J.: Rowman and Littlefield, 1972.

Chesneaux, Jean. PEASANT REVOLTS IN CHINA, 1840-1949. London: W. W. Por-ter, 1973.

Chew, Allan. THE WHITE DEATH. East Lansing: Michigan State Univ., 1971.

Chi Hsi-hseng, THE CHINESE WARLORD SYSTEM, 1916-1928. Washington D.C.: 1969.

Chiang Siang-tseh, THE NIEN REBELLION. Seattle: Univ. of Washington, 1954.

Chien Yu-wen. THE TAIPING REVOLUTIONARY MOVEMENT. New Haven: Yale Univ., 1973.

"The Chinese-Japanese Truce of Tangku." LITERARY DIGEST, 115/23 (June 10, 1933), 11.

Chomsky, Noam. "Destroying Laos." NEW YORK REVIEW OF BOOKS, 15/2 (July 23, 1970), 21-33.

————. AT WAR WITH ASIA. London: Fontana, 1971.

————. "East Timor: The Press Coverup." INQUIRY, February 14, 1979, 16-20.

Chow Ro-bin. CHUNG-EH KUAN-HIH SHIH. Taipei: 1960.

Chu Wen-djang. "The Moslem Rebellion in Northwest China, 1862-1878." CENTRAL ASIATIC STUDIES, 5 (1966).

Churchill, Winston S. THE RIVER WAR. 2 vols. London: Longmans, 1900.

Clark, Chester Wells. FRANZ JOSEPH AND BISMARCK: THE DIPLOMACY OF AUSTRIA BEFORE THE WAR OF 1866. Cambridge: Harvard Univ., 1934.

Clarke, Henry Butler. MODERN SPAIN, 1815-1898. Cambridge: Cambridge Univ., 1906.

Clements, Paul H. THE BOXER REBELLION. New York: AMS Press, 1967.

Clendenen, Clarence C. "Tribalism and Humanitarianism: The Nigerian-Biafran Civil War," in Robin Higham (ed.). CIVIL WARS IN THE TWENTIETH CEN-TURY. Lexington: Univ. of Kentucky, 1972.

Cline, Howard. THE UNITED STATES AND MEXICO. New York: Atheneum, 1963.

Clubb, Edmund O. TWENTIETH CENTURY CHINA. New York: Columbia Univ., 1964.

Coates, William P. and Zelda. THE SOVIET FINNISH CAMPAIGN. London: Eldon, 1941.

Coffey, Rosemary K. "The Heart of Deterrence." BULLETIN OF THE ATOMIC SCI-
ENTISTS, 21/4 (April, 1965), 27-29.
Collier, Richard. THE SOUND OF FURY. London: Collins, 1963.
COLLIERS ENCYCLOPEDIA YEARBOOK. 1947.
COMMUNIST CHINA, 1962. Hong Kong: Union Research, 1963.
Cook, Earnshaw. PERCENTAGE BASEBALL. Cambridge: Massachusetts Inst. of
Technology, 1964.
Cooper, Chester. THE LOST CRUSADE. New York: Dodd, Mead, 1970.
Coox, Alvin. "The Forgotten War of 1939." CONFLICT, 5 (June 20, 1973), 4-20.
_____. THE ANATOMY OF A SMALL WAR. Westport, Conn.: Greenwood, 1977.
Cordier, Henri. HISTOIRE DES RELATIONS DE LA CHINE AVEC LES PUIS-
SANCES OCCIDENTALES. Vol. 3. Paris: F. Alcan, 1902.
_____. HISTOIRE GÉNÉRALE DE LA CHINE ET DE SES RELATIONS AVEC LES
PAYS ÉTRANGERS DEPUIS LES TEMPS LES PLUS ANCIENS JUSQU'À LA
CHUTE DE LA DYNASTIE MANDCHOU. Vol. 4. Paris: Geuthner, 1920.
Costin, W.C. GREAT BRITAIN AND CHINA, 1833-1860. London: Oxford Univ.,
1937.
Coverdale, John F. ITALIAN INTERVENTION IN THE SPANISH CIVIL WAR.
Princeton: Princeton Univ., 1975.
Crawley, Charles William. THE QUESTION OF GREEK INDEPENDENCE. Cam-
bridge: Cambridge Univ., 1930.
Crow, John A. THE EPIC OF LATIN AMERICA. Garden City: Doubleday, 1971.
Cumberland, Charles C. MEXICO: THE STRUGGLE FOR MODERNITY. New
York: Oxford Univ., 1968.
_____. THE MEXICAN REVOLUTION: THE CONSTITUTIONALIST YEARS. Aus-
tin: Univ. of Texas, 1972.
Cunha, Euclides da. REBELLION IN THE BACKLANDS (OS SERTOES). Chicago:
Univ. of Chicago, 1944.
Curtiss, John Shelton. THE RUSSIAN ARMY UNDER NICHOLAS I. Durham,
N.C.: Duke Univ., 1965.
Dakin, Douglas, THE GREEK STRUGGLE IN MACEDONIA, 1897-1913. Thessa-
loniki: 1966.
_____. THE UNIFICATION OF GREECE, 1770-1923. New York: St. Martins, 1972.
_____. THE STRUGGLE FOR GREEK INDEPENDENCE, 1821-1833. London: B.T.
Batsford, 1973.
Dallin, David J. SOVIET RUSSIA AND THE FAR EAST. New Haven: Yale Univ.,
1948.
Davies, Norman. WHITE EAGLE, RED STAR: THE POLISH-SOVIET WAR, 1919-
1920. New York: St. Martins, 1972.
Davis, Harold F. HISTORY OF LATIN AMERICA. New York: Ronald Press, 1968.
Davis, H.P. BLACK DEMOCRACY. New York: Biblo and Tannen, 1967.
Davis, William Columbus. THE LAST CONQUISTADORES. Athens: Univ. of Geor-
gia, 1950.
Dawson, Daniel. THE MEXICAN ADVENTURE. London: G. Bell and Sons, 1935.
Deadline Data on World Affairs. New York: Deadline Data (weekly since 1955).
Deans, William. HISTORY OF THE OTTOMAN EMPIRE. London: A. Fullarton,
1854.
Decoux, Jean. A LA BARRE DE L'INDOCHINE. Paris: Hachette, 1949.
Dellepiane, Carlos. HISTORIA MILITAR DEL PERU. Vol. 1. Lima: Imprenta del
Ministero de Guerra, 1943.
Dennis, Lawrence. THE DYNAMICS OF WAR AND REVOLUTION. New York:
Weekly Foreign Letter, 1940.
Denton, Frank H. "Some Regularities in International Conflict, 1820-1949." BACK-
GROUND, 9/4 (February, 1966), 283-96.
_____. and Warren Phillips. "Some Patterns in the History of Violence." JOURNAL
OF CONFLICT RESOLUTION, 12/2 (June, 1968), 182-95.

Deschamps, Hubert. HISTOIRE DE MADAGASCAR. Paris: Berger-Levrault, 1960.
Deutsch, Karl W. "External Involvement in Internal Wars," in H. Eckstein (ed.), INTERNAL WAR. Glencoe: Free Press, 1964.
Deutschland in China, 1900-1901. Dusseldorf: A Bagel, 1902.
Devillers, P., P. Fistie, and Lê Thành Khôi. L'ASIE DU SUD-EST. Paris: Sirey, 1971.
Dewey, Edward R. THE 177-YEAR CYCLE IN WAR, 600 B.C.—A.D. 1957. Pittsburgh: Foundation for the Study of Cycles, 1964.
Djilas, Milovan. WARTIME. New York: Harcourt, 1977.
Dodwell, Henry. THE FOUNDER OF MODERN EGYPT: A STUDY OF MUHAMMAD ALI. Cambridge: Cambridge Univ., 1931.
Donnison, Frank S. V. BURMA. New York: Praeger, 1970.
Dontas, D. N. GREECE AND THE GREAT POWERS. Thessaloniki: Institute for Balkan Studies, 1966.
Doroshenko, Dmitro. HISTORY OF THE UKRAINE. (Trans. and abr. Hanna Chikalenko-Keller.) Edmonton, Alberta: Institute Press, 1939.
Droz. Jacques. LES REVOLUTIONS ALLMANDES DE 1848. Paris: Presses Universitaires de France, 1957.
Dumas, Samuel and Knud Otto Vedel-Peterson. LOSSES OF LIFE CAUSED BY WAR. London: Oxford Univ., 1923.
Dumont, Jean (ed.). LES COUPS D'ÉTAT. Paris: Hachette, 1963.
Duner, Bertil. "Military Involvement: The Escalation of Internal Conflicts." Swedish Institute of International Affairs, 1980.
Dupuy, R. Ernest and William H. Baumer. THE LITTLE WARS OF THE UNITED STATES. New York: Hawthorn, 1968.
_____. and Trevor N. Dupuy. THE ENCYCLOPEDIA OF MILITARY HISTORY. New York: Harper & Row, 1970.
Dupuy, Trevor. ELUSIVE VICTORY. New York: Harper's, 1978.
Eagleton, William, Jr. THE KURDISH REPUBLIC OF 1946. London: Oxford Univ., 1963.
Eastman, Lloyd E. THRONE AND MANDARINS. Cambridge: Harvard Univ., 1967.
Eckstein, Harry (ed.). INTERNAL WAR. Glencoe: Free Press, 1964.
Edmonds, Martin, "Civil War, Internal War, and Intrasocietal Conflict: A Taxonomy and Typology," in Robin Higham (ed.), CIVIL WARS IN THE TWENTIETH CENTURY. Lexington: Univ. of Kentucky, 1972.
Edwardes, Michael. BATTLES OF THE INDIA MUTINY. London: Batsford, 1963.
Edwards, H. Sutherland. THE PRIVATE HISTORY OF A POLISH INSURRECTION. London: Saunders, 1865.
Eggenberger, David. A DICTIONARY OF BATTLES: New York: Crowell, 1967.
Eliade, M. N. CRETE, PAST AND PRESENT. London: 1933.
Ellis, C.H. THE BRITISH "INTERVENTION" IN TRANSCASPIA, 1918-1919. Berkeley: Univ. of California, 1963.
Encina, Francisco Antonio. HISTORIA DE CHILE. Vol. 14. Santiago: Editorial Nascimento, 1950.
Encyclopaedia Britannica. Chicago: Encyclopaedia Britannica, 1967 ed.
Encyclopedia Americana. New York: Americana Corp., 1967 ed.
Eprik, Cecil. WAR AND PEACE IN THE SUDAN: 1955-1972. London: David Charles, 1972.
Erickson, John. THE SOVIET HIGH COMMAND. London: Macmillan, 1962.
Esposito, Vincent J. (ed.). A CONCISE HISTORY OF WORLD WAR I. New York: Praeger, 1964a.
_____. A CONCISE HISTORY OF WORLD WAR II. New York: Praeger, 1964b.
Essen, Leon vander. A SHORT HISTORY OF BELGIUM. Chicago: Univ. of Chicago, 1916.
Etcheparaborda, Roberto. LA REVOLUCION ARGENTINA DEL 90. Buenos Aires: Editorial Universitario de Buenos Aires, 1966.
_____. TRES REVOLUCIONES, 1890-1893-1905. Buenos Aires: Pleamar, 1968.

Etherton, Thomas P. IN THE HEART OF ASIA. London: Constable, 1925.
Études Polémologiques. 1971—.
Evans, Stanley G. A SHORT HISTORY OF BULGARIA. London: Lawrence and Wishart, 1960.
Eversley, Lord George J. S. THE TURKISH EMPIRE FROM 1288 to 1914. London: T. Fisher Unwin, 1917.
Facts on File. New York: Facts on File (weekly since 1940).
Fall, Bernard. STREET WITHOUT JOY. Harrisburg: Stackpole, 1963.
_____. THE TWO VIET-NAMS. New York: Praeger, 1967.
Falls, Cyril. THE GREAT WAR. New York: Putnams, 1959.
FAR EASTERN ECONOMIC REVIEW. ASIA YEARBOOK. Hong Kong: 1970-72, 1974.
Farer, Tom J. WAR CLOUDS ON THE HORN OF AFRICA: THE WIDENING STORM. New York: Carnegie Endowment, 1978.
Fay, Sidney B. THE ORIGINS OF THE WORLD WAR. 2 vols. New York: Macmillan, 1928.
Feierabend, Ivo K. and Rosalind L. Feierabend. "Aggressive Behaviors within Polities, 1948-1962: A Cross-National Study." JOURNAL OF CONFLICT RESOLUTION, 10/3 (September, 1966), 249-71.
Feith, Herbert. "Indonesia," in G. Kahin (ed.). GOVERNMENT AND POLITICS IN SOUTHEAST ASIA. Ithaca: Cornell Univ., 1964.
Field, G. Lowell. COMPARATIVE POLITICAL DEVELOPMENT: THE PRECEDENT OF THE WEST. Ithaca: Cornell Univ., 1967.
Firkins, Peter. THE AUSTRALIANS IN NINE WARS. London: Robert Hale, 1972.
First, Ruth. SOUTH WEST AFRICA. London: Penguin, 1963.
Fisher, Sydney N. THE MIDDLE EAST: A HISTORY. New York: Knopf, 1968.
Fitzgibbon, Russell H. CUBA AND THE UNITED STATES. Menasha, Wis.: George Banta, 1935.
Fleming, Peter. THE SIEGE AT PEKING. London: Hart-Davis, 1959.
Fletcher, Arnold. AFGHANISTAN: HIGHWAY OF CONQUEST. Ithaca: Cornell Univ., 1965.
Florinsky, Michael T. RUSSIA: A HISTORY AND AN INTERPRETATION. Vol. II. New York: Macmillan, 1953.
Fontaine, Pierre. ABD-EL-KRIM. Paris: Le Sept Couleurs, 1950.
Fortescue, Sir John W. HISTORY OF THE BRITISH ARMY. Vols. 11, 12, and 13. London: Macmillan, 1923, 1927, 1930.
Foster, Henry. THE MAKING OF MODERN IRAQ. Norman: Univ. of Oklahoma, 1935.
France, Ministry of Foreign Affairs. LES ORIGINES DIPLOMATIQUES DE LA GUERRE DE 1870-1871. Paris: G. Ficker, 1915.
Franke, Wolfgang. A CENTURY OF CHINESE REVOLUTION, 1851-1949. Oxford: Blackwell, 1970.
Fraser-Tyler, William K. AFGHANISTAN, London: Oxford Univ., 1967.
Frazer, R. W. BRITISH INDIA. New York: Putnams, 1897.
Freeman-Grenville, F. S. P. A CHRONOLOGY OF AFRICAN HISTORY. London: Oxford Univ., 1973.
Frey, H. FRANCAIS ET ALLIES AU PETCHLIHI: CAMPAGNE DE CHINE DE 1900. Paris: Hachette, 1904.
Fried, Alfred H. "A Few Lessons Taught by the Balkan War." INTERNATIONAL CONCILLIATION, 74 (January, 1914).
Friedjung, Heinrich. OSTERREICH VON 1848 BIS 1860. Stuttgart: J. G. Cotta, 1912.
_____. THE STRUGGLE FOR SUPREMACY IN GERMANY 1859-1866. (Trans. A. J. P. Taylor and W. L. McIvee.) London: Macmillan, 1935.
Frilley, G. and Jovan Wlahovitj. LE MONTÉNÉGRO CONTEMPORAIN. Paris: E. Plon, 1876.

Friters, Gerard M. OUTER MONGOLIA AND ITS INTERNATIONAL POSITION. Baltimore: Johns Hopkins Univ., 1949.

Fuller, Francis. A VANISHED DYNASTY: ASHANTI. London: John Murray, 1921.

Fuller, J. F. C. THE CONDUCT OF WAR, 1789-1961. London: Eyre and Spottiswoode, 1961.

Gabrielle, Léon. ABD-EL-KRIM ET LES ÉVÉNEMENT DU RIF. Casablanca: Edition Atlantides, 1953.

Galbraith, W. O. COLUMBIA. London: Royal Inst. of International Affairs, 1953.

Galdames, Luis. A HISTORY OF CHILE. Chapel Hill: Univ. of North Carolina, 1941.

Galvez, Juan Ignacio. EL PERU CONTRA COLOMBIA, ECUADOR Y CHILE. Santiago: Sociedad Imprentalitografia Universo, 1919.

Gambra, Rafael. LA PRIMERA GUERRA CIVIL DE ESPANA (1821-1823). Madrid: Esceliecer, 1972.

Garner, William R. THE CHACO DISPUTE. Washington: Public Affairs Press, 1966.

Gebrandy, P. S. INDONESIA. London: Hutchinson, 1950.

Gehl, Jürgen. AUSTRIA, GERMANY, AND THE ANSCHLUSS, 1931-1938. London: Oxford Univ., 1963.

Geoffroy de Grandmaison, Charles Alexander. L'EXPÉDITION FRANÇAISE D'ESPAGNE EN 1823. Paris: Plon, 1928.

Germany. Armee Grosser General Stab. Kriegsgeschicht Abteilung. DIE KAMPFE DER DEUTSCHEN TRUPPEN IN SUDWEST AFRICA. 2 vols. Berlin: 1906-1907.

Geschichte des Zweiten Weltkrieges 1939-1945. Wurzburg: A. G. Ploetz, 1960.

Gettleman, Marvin (ed.). VIETNAM. New York: Fawcett, 1970.

———. **S. Gettleman, L. Kaplan and C. Kaplan** (eds.). CONFLICT IN INDO-CHINA. New York: Vintage, 1970.

Gilbert, Martin, RECENT HISTORY ATLAS. London: Macmillan, 1966.

Gilmore, Robert L. CAUDILLISM AND MILITARISM IN VENEZUELA, 1810-1910. Athens: Ohio Univ., 1964.

Gleijeses, Piero. THE DOMINICAN CRISIS. Baltimore: Johns Hopkins Univ., 1978.

Glubb, John B. A SOLDIER WITH THE ARABS. London: Hodder and Stoughton, 1957.

———. WAR IN THE DESERT. London: Hodder & Stoughton, 1960.

———.SYRIA, LEBANON, AND JORDAN. London: Thames & Hudson, 1967.

Gnorowski, S. B. INSURRECTION OF POLAND. London: James Ridgeway, 1839.

Godechot, Jacques. LES REVOLUTIONS DE 1848. Paris: Albin Michel, 1971.

Gopcevic, Spiridion. LE MONTÉNÉGRO ET LES MONTÉNÉGRINS. Paris: Plon, 1877.

Gordon, Thomas. HISTORY OF THE GREEK REVOLUTION. London: Blackwood, 1844.

Gough, Charles and Arthur Innes. THE SIKHS AND THE SIKH WARS. London: A. D. Innes, 1897

Gouvea, Rodger M. and Gerald T. West, "Riot Contagion in Latin America, 1949-1963," JOURNAL OF CONFLICT RESOLUTION, 25 (June, 1981), 349-60.

Grant, Jonathan, Jonathan Unger, and Laurane A. G. Moss (eds.). CAMBODIA: THE WIDENING WAR IN INDOCHINA. New York: Simon and Schuster, 1970.

Graves, W. S. AMERICA'S SIBERIAN ADVENTURE, 1918-1920. New York: P. Smith, 1941.

Great Britain. Central Office of Information. PAIFORCE. London: M.S.O., 1948.

Great Britain. Colonial Office. HISTORICAL SURVEY OF THE ORIGINS AND GROWTH OF MAU MAU. London: H.M.S.O., 1960.

Great Britain, Foreign Office. CORRESPONDENCE RELATING TO THE ASIATIC PROVINCES OF TURKEY, 1896, 7. London: 1896.

———. **Naval Intelligence Division.** JUGOSLAVIA. London: 1944.

_____. GREECE. London: 1945.

_____. **Royal Institute of International Affairs.** THE MIDDLE EAST: A POLITI-CAL AND ECONOMIC SURVEY. London: 1950.

Gregorian, Vartan. THE EMERGENCE OF MODERN AFGHANISTAN. Stanford: Stanford Univ., 1969.

Gregory, John S. "British Intervention Against the Taiping Rebellion." JOURNAL OF ASIAN STUDIES, 19 (November, 1959), 11-24.

_____. GREAT BRITAIN AND THE TAIPINGS. London: Routledge and Kegan Paul, 1969.

Gross, Feliks. WORLD POLITICS AND TENSION AREAS. New York: New York Univ., 1966.

Grunder, Garel and William Livezey. THE PHILIPPINES AND THE UNITED STATES, Norman: Univ. of Oklahoma, 1951.

Grunwald, Constantin de. TSAR NICHOLAS I. (Trans. Brigit Patmore.) New York: Macmillan, 1955.

Guerra y Sanchez, Ramiro. GUERRA DE LOS DIEZ AÑOS. 2 vols. Havana: Cultural, 1950.

Gukiina, Peter M. UGANDA: A CASE STUDY IN AFRICAN POLITICAL DEVELOPMENT. Notre Dame: Univ. of Notre Dame, 1972.

Gurr, Ted with Charles Ruttenberg. THE CONDITIONS OF CIVIL VIOLENCE: FIRST TEST OF A CAUSAL MODEL. Princeton, N.J.: Center for International Studies, 1967.

Hagopian, Mark N. THE PHENOMENON OF REVOLUTION. New York: Dodd, Mead, 1974.

Haley, Edward P. and Lewis W. Snider (eds.). LEBANON CRISIS. Syracuse: Syracuse Univ., 1979.

Hall, D. G. E. A HISTORY OF SOUTH EAST ASIA. New York: St. Martin's, 1968.

Hammer, Kenneth M., "Huks in the Philippines," in F. Osanka (ed.), MODERN GUERRILLA WARFARE. Glencoe: Free Press, 1962.

Hanna, Henry B. THE SECOND AFGHAN WAR. Vol. 3. London: Constable, 1910.

Harbottle, Thomas Benfield. DICTIONARY OF BATTLES FROM THE EARLIEST DATE TO THE PRESENT TIME. London: S. Sonneschein, 1904.

_____. **and George Bruce.** DICTIONARY OF BATTLES. New York: Stein and Day, 1971.

Harcave, Sidney. THE RUSSIAN REVOLUTION OF 1905. London: Collier-Macmillan, 1964.

Harris, Walter. FRANCE, SPAIN, AND THE RIF. London: Arnold, 1927.

Harsgor, Michael. PORTUGAL IN REVOLUTION. Beverly Hills, Cal.: Sage, 1976.

Harvey, George E. THE CAMBRIDGE HISTORY OF INDIA. Cambridge: Cambridge Univ., 1929.

Harvey, Robert. PORTUGAL: BIRTH OF DEMOCRACY. New York: St. Martin's 1978.

Hart, B. H. Liddell. THE REAL WAR, 1914-1918. Boston: Little, Brown, 1930.

Hasbrouck, Alfred. "The Argentine Revolution of 1930." HISPANIC AMERICAN HISTORICAL REVIEW, 18 (August, 1938), 285-321.

Haslip, Joan. THE CROWN OF MEXICO. New York: Holt, Rinehart & Winston, 1971.

Hasluck, E. L. FOREIGN AFFAIRS, 1919-1937. New York: Macmillan, 1938.

Haumant, Emile. LA FORMATION DE LA YUGOSLAVIE. Paris: Bossard, 1930.

Headley, P. C. THE LIFE OF LOUIS KOSSUTH. Auburn, N.Y.: Derby and Miller, 1852.

Healy, David F. GUNBOAT DIPLOMACY IN THE WILSON ERA. Madison: Wisconson Univ., 1976.

Heflin, Jean. Unpublished notes about major power conflicts, a memo to R. C. North, January 19, 1970.

Heikal, Mohammed. THE ROAD TO RAMADAN. London: Collins, 1975.

Heinl, Robert. SOLDIERS OF THE SEA. Annapolis: U.S. Naval Institute, 1962.
Heitman, Francis B. HISTORICAL REGISTRY AND DIRECTORY OF THE UNITED STATES ARMY. Vol. 2. Washington, D.C.: G.P.O., 1903.
Helmert, Heinz and Hansjurgen Usczeck, BEWAFFNETE VOLKSKAMPFE IN EUROPA 1848/49. Berlin: Militarverlag der Deutsche Demokratische Republik, 1973.
Helmreich, Ernst Christian. THE DIPLOMACY OF THE BALKAN WARS, 1912-1913. Cambridge: Harvard Univ., 1938.
Henao, J.M. and G. Arrubla. HISTORY OF COLOMBIA. Chapel Hill: Univ. of North Carolina, 1938.
Hennessy, C.A.M. THE FEDERAL REPUBLIC IN SPAIN, 1868-1874. Oxford: Clarendon, 1962.
Henriques, Robert. 100 HOURS TO SUEZ. New York: Viking, 1957.
Heppell, Muriel and Frank Singleton. YUGOSLAVIA. New York: Praeger, 1961.
Herr, Michael. DISPATCHES. New York: Knopf, 1977.
Herring, George. AMERICA'S LONGEST WAR. New York: Wiley, 1979.
Herring, Hubert. A HISTORY OF LATIN AMERICA. New York: Knopf, 1968.
Hibbs, Douglas A. MASS POLITICAL VIOLENCE: A CROSS-NATIONAL CAUSAL ANALYSIS. New York: Wiley, 1973.
Higham, Robin (ed.). CIVIL WARS IN THE TWENTIETH CENTURY. Lexington: Univ. of Kentucky, 1972.
Hintrager, Oskar. SUDWEST AFRIKA IN DER DEUTSCHEN ZEIT. Munich: R. Oldenbourg, 1955.
Hitti, Philip. A HISTORY OF THE ARABS. New York: St. Martin's 1970.
Ho Han-wen. CHUNG-EH WAI-CHIAO SHIH. Shanghai: Chung Hua Book Co., 1935.
Ho Ping-ti. STUDIES ON THE POPULATION OF CHINA, 1368-1952. Cambridge: Harvard Univ., 1959.
Holt, Edgar. THE CARLIST WARS IN SPAIN. Chester Springs, Pa.: Dufour Editions, 1967.
Holt, Peter M. THE MADHIST STATE IN THE SUDAN, 1881-1898. London: Oxford, 1958.
Hordynski, Joseph. HISTORY OF THE LATE POLISH REVOLUTION. Boston: Carter and Hendle, 1832.
Horne, Alastair. A SAVAGE WAR OF PEACE. New York: Viking, 1977.
Horvath, William. "A Statistical Model for the Duration of Wars and Strikes." BEHAVIORAL SCIENCE, 13/1 (January, 1968), 18-28.
_____. **and Caxton C. Foster.** "Stochastic Models of War Alliances." JOURNAL OF CONFLICT RESOLUTION, 7/2 (June, 1963), 110-16.
Hoyt, Edwin P. ARMY WITHOUT A COUNTRY. New York: Macmillan, 1967.
Hozier, Henry Montague. THE RUSSO-TURKISH WAR. 2 vols. London: W. Mackenzie, 1878.
Hrushevsky, Michael. A HISTORY OF THE UKRAINE. New Haven: Yale Univ., 1941.
Hughes, John. THE END OF SUKARNO. London: Angus and Robertson, 1967.
Hume, Martin A.S. MODERN SPAIN. London: Putnams, 1900.
Huntington, Samuel. "Patterns of Violence in World Politics," in S. Hungtington (ed.), CHANGING PATTERNS OF MILITARY POLITICS. New York: Free Press, 1962.
Huttenback, Robert A. BRITISH RELATIONS WITH SIND, 1799-1843. Berkeley: Univ. of California, 1962.
Hyamson, Albert M. PALESTINE UNDER THE MANDATE. London: Methuen, 1950.
Ignotus, Paul. HUNGARY. London: Ernest Benn, 1972.
Ikuhiko, Hata. "The Japanese-Soviet Confrontation," in James W. Morely (ed.), DETERRENT DIPLOMACY. New York: Columbia Univ., 1976.

India. Ministry of Information and Broadcasting. DEFENDING KASHMIR. Dehli: 1949.

INFORMATION PLEASE ALMANAC. 1972.

Ingrams, Harold. THE YEMEN. London: John Murray, 1963.

Institut Français de Polémologie. "Periodicité et Intensité des Actions de Guerre de 1200 a 1945." GUERRE ET PAIX, 2 (1968), 20-32.

Ireland, Gordon. BOUNDARIES, POSSESSIONS AND CONFLICTS IN SOUTH AMERICA. Cambridge: Harvard Univ., 1938.

Ironside, Edmond. ARCHANGEL, 1918-1919. London: Constable, 1953.

Isaacs, Harold R. THE TRAGEDY OF THE CHINESE REVOLUTION. Stanford: Stanford Univ., 1961.

Israel Office of Information. ISRAEL'S STRUGGLE FOR PEACE. New York: Israel Office of Information, 1960.

Italy, Comitato per la Documentazione Dell'Opera Dell'Italia in Africa. ITALIA IN AFRICA. Rome: Istituto Poligrafico Dello Stato, 1952.

Jacques, Hubert. L'AVENTURE RIFFAINE ET SES DESSOUS POLITIQUES. Paris: Bossard, 1927.

Jasci, Oscar. REVOLUTION AND COUNTER-REVOLUTION IN HUNGARY. New York: Howard Fertig, 1969.

Jen Yu-wen. THE TAIPING REVOLUTIONARY MOVEMENT. New Haven: Yale Univ., 1973.

Jenkins, Gwilym M. and J. G. Watts. SPECTRAL ANALYSIS AND ITS APPLICA-TIONS. San Francisco: Holden Day, 1968.

Jensen, Amy Elizabeth. THE MAKERS OF MEXICO. Philadelphia: Dorrance, 1953.

_____. GUATEMALA. New York: Exposition, 1955.

Jochmus, Augustus. THE SYRIAN WAR AND THE DECLINE OF THE OTTOMAN EMPIRE. 2 vols. Berlin: Albert Cohn, 1883.

Johnson, Chalmers. REVOLUTION AND THE SOCIAL SYSTEM. Stanford: Hoover Institution, 1964.

Johnson, Donald. THE NORTHERN EXPEDITION. Honolulu: Hawaii Univ., 1976.

Johnson, Richard A. THE MEXICAN REVOLUTION OF AYUTLA, 1894. Rock Island: Augustana College, 1939.

Johnston, Harry H. A HISTORY OF THE COLONIZATION OF AFRICA BY ALIEN RACES. Cambridge: Cambridge Univ., 1913.

Johnston, Robert. THE ROMAN THEOCRACY AND THE REPUBLIC. London: Macmillan, 1901.

Jolliffe, Jill. EAST TIMOR: NATIONALISM AND COLONIALISM. St. Lucia: Univ. of Queensland, 1978.

Jones, F. C. JAPAN'S NEW ORDER IN EAST ASIA. London: Oxford Univ., 1954.

Jones, Ronald D. "Construct Mapping." Kansas City: Univ. of Missouri, June 1966, mimeo.

Jordan, Karl G. DER AEGYPTISCH-TURKISCHE KRIEG, 1839. Zurich: Borsig, 1923.

Jorga, N. GESHICHTE DES OSMANISCHEN REICHES. 5 vols. Gotha: Justus Perthes, 1913.

Jutikkala, Eino. A HISTORY OF FINLAND. New York: Praeger. 1962.

Kaas, Albert and Fedor De Lazarovics. BOLSHEVISM IN HUNGARY. London: Grant Richards, 1931.

Kahin, George. NATIONALISM AND REVOLUTION IN INDONESIA. Ithaca: Cornell Univ., 1952.

_____. and John Lewis. THE UNITED STATES IN VIETNAM. New York: Dial, 1969.

Kalaw, Teodoro M. THE PHILIPPINE REVOLUTION. Manila: Manila Book Co., 1925.

Kann, Robert A. THE MULTINATIONAL EMPIRE: NATIONALISM AND RE-FORM IN THE HAPSBURG MONARCHY, 1848-1918. New York: Octagon Books, 1970, 2 vols.

Karnes, Thomas L. THE FAILURE OF UNION: CENTRAL AMERICA 1824-1960. Chapel Hill: Univ. of North Carilina, 1961.

Kaul, B. M. THE UNTOLD STORY. Bombay: Allied Publishers, 1967.

Kecskemeti, Paul. STRATEGIC SURRENDER. Stanford: Stanford Univ., 1958.

Keesing's Contemporary Archives. London, 1931—.

Keller, Helen Rex. A DICTIONARY OF DATES. 2 vols. New York: Macmillan, 1934.

Kelly, J. B. BRITAIN AND THE PERSIAN GULF: 1795-1880. Oxford: Oxford Univ., 1968.

Kende, Istvan. "Twenty-Five Years of Local Wars." JOURNAL OF PEACE RE-SEARCH, 8 (1971), 5-22.

———. "Wars of Ten Years (1967-1976)." JOURNAL OF PEACE RESEARCH, 15 (1978), 227-41.

Kerkvliet, Bernard J. THE HUK REBELLION. Berkeley: Univ. of California, 1977.

Kennan, George F. THE DECISION TO INTERVENE. Princeton: Princeton Univ., 1958.

———. RUSSIA AND THE WEST UNDER LENIN AND STALIN. Boston: Little, Brown, 1960.

Kerr, George H. FORMOSA BETRAYED. Boston: Houghton-Mifflin, 1965.

Keyte, J. C. THE PASSING OF THE DRAGON. London: Carey Press, 1925.

Khadduri, Majid. INDEPENDENT IRAQ, 1932-1958. London: Oxford Univ., 1960.

Khan, Mohammed Anwar. ENGLAND, RUSSIA AND CENTRAL ASIA, 1857-1878. Penshawar, Pakistan: University Book Agency, 1963.

Khôi, Lê Thành. LE VIET-NAM. Paris: Editions de Minuit, 1955.

Kielstra, E. B. BESCHRIJVING VAN DEN ATJEH-OORLOG. 3 vols. 's Gravenhage: Van Cleef, 1883.

Kiernan, E. V. BRITISH DIPLOMACY IN CHINA, 1880-1885. Cambridge: Cambridge Univ., 1939.

Kiernan, V. G. THE REVOLUTION OF 1854 IN SPANISH HISTORY. Oxford: Clarendon, 1966.

Kimche, Jon and David. A CLASH OF DESTINIES. New York: Praeger, 1960.

King, Bolton. A HISTORY OF ITALIAN UNITY. vol. 1. London: James Nisbet, 1899.

Kiritzesco, Constantin. LA ROUMANIE DANS LA GUERRE MONDIALE, 1916-1919. Paris: Payot, 1934.

Kirkpatrick, Frederick A. A HISTORY OF THE ARGENTINE REPUBLIC. Cambridge: Cambridge Univ., 1931

———. LATIN AMERICA, New York: Macmillan, 1939.

de Klerck, E. S. HISTORY OF THE NETHERLANDS EAST INDIES. Vol. 2. Rotterdam: Brusse, 1938.

Klingberg, Frank L. HISTORICAL STUDY OF WAR CASUALTIES. Washington, D.C.: United States, Secretary of War Office, 1945.

———. "Predicting the Termination of War: Battle Casualties and Population Losses." JOURNAL OF CONFLICT RESOLUTION, 10/2 (June, 1966), 129-71.

Knatchbull-Hugessen, C. M. THE POLITICAL EVOLUTION OF THE HUNGAR-IAN NATION. London: National Review Office, 1908.

Knightly, Phillip. THE FIRST CASUALTY. New York: Harcourt, 1975.

Koebel, William H. URUGUAY. New York: Scribner's, 1915.

Kolinski, Charles J. INDEPENDENCE OR DEATH. Gainesville: Univ. of Florida, 1965.

Korbel, Josef. DANGER IN KASHMIR. Princeton: Princeton Univ., 1959.

Kosut, Hal (ed.). INDONESIA: THE SUKARNO YEARS. New York: Facts on File, 1967.

La Foy, Margaret. THE CHACO DISPUTE AND THE LEAGUE OF NATIONS. Bryn Mawr, Pa.: Bryn Mawr Press, 1946.

Laine, Philip. PARAGUAY. New Brunswick, N.J.: Scarecrow, 1956.
Lamb, Alastair. THE KASHMIR PROBLEM. New York: Praeger, 1967.
_____. "Sinkiang in the Twentieth Century," in G. Hambly (ed.), CENTRAL ASIA. New York: Delacorte, 1969.
Lancaster, Donald. THE EMANCIPATION OF FRENCH INDOCHINA. London: Oxford Univ., 1961.
Landau, Rom. MOROCCAN DRAMA. San Francisco: American Academy of Asian Studies, 1956.
Langer, Paul F. and Joseph J. Zasloff. NORTH VIETNAM AND LAOS. Cambridge, Mass.: Harvard, 1970.
Langer, William L. EUROPEAN ALLIANCES AND ALIGNMENTS. New York: Knopf, 1931.
_____. (ed.). AN ENCYCLOPEDIA OF WORLD HISTORY. Boston: Houghton-Mifflin, 1948.
_____. POLITICAL AND SOCIAL UPHEAVAL, 1832-1852. New York: Harper, 1969.
Lasswell, Harold and Abraham Kaplan. POWER AND SOCIETY. New Haven: Yale Univ., 1950.
Laytano, Dante de. HISTORIE DA REPUBLICA RIO GRANDENSE. Porto Alegre: Livraria do Globo, 1936.
Leckie, Robert. CONFLICT. New York: Putnams, 1962.
Lee, J.S. "The Periodic Recurrence of Internecine Wars in China." THE CHINA JOURNAL, 14/3 (March, 1931), 111-15, 159-62.
Lee, Ta-ling. FOUNDATIONS OF THE CHINESE REVOLUTION. New York: St. Johns Univ., 1970.
Lefever, Ernest W. "Peacekeeping by Outsiders: The U.N. Congo Expeditionary Force," in Robin Higham (ed.), CIVIL WARS IN THE TWENTIETH CENTURY. Lexington: Univ. of Kentucky, 1972.
Le Gouhir y Rodas, José. HISTORIA DE LA REPUBLIC DEL ECUADOR. Quito: Prensa Católica, 1925.
Lei, K.N. (ed.). INFORMATION AND OPINION CONCERNING THE JAPANESE INVASION OF MANCHURIA AND SHANGHAI FROM SOURCES OTHER THAN CHINESE. Shanghai: Shanghai Bar Association, 1932.
Leitenburg, Milton and Richard Dean Burns (compilers). THE VIETNAM CONFLICT. Santa Barbara, Cal.: Clio, 1973.
Lemarchand, René. "Ethnic Genocide." SOCIETY, 12/2 (January-February, 1975), 50-60.
Lenczowski, Geoge. RUSSIA AND THE WEST IN IRAN. Ithaca: Cornell Univ., 1949.
Lensen, George A. THE RUSSO-CHINESE WAR. Tallahassee: Diplomatic Press, 1967.
Leslie, R.F. POLISH POLITICS AND THE REVOLUTION OF NOVEMBER, 1930. London: London Univ., 1956.
_____. REFORM AND INSURRECTION IN RUSSIAN POLAND. London: London Univ., 1963.
Lettrich, Joseph. HISTORY OF MODERN SLOVAKIA. New York: Praeger, 1955.
Levene, Ricardo. A HISTORY OF ARGENTINA. Chapel Hill: Univ. of North Carolina, 1937.
Levine, Victor T. THE CAMEROONS. Berkeley: Univ. of California, 1964.
Lewis, G.L. TURKEY. New York: Praeger, 1955.
Leys, M.D.R. BETWEEN TWO EMPIRES. London: Longmans Green, 1955.
Li, Chien-nung. THE POLITICAL HISTORY OF CHINA, 1840-1928. Princeton: Van Nostrand, 1956.
Liebman, Marcel. THE RUSSIAN REVOLUTION. New York: Vintage, 1970.
Linden, Herman vander. BELGIUM: THE MAKING OF A NATION. Oxford: Clarendon, 1920.
Lin-le. TI PING TIEN-KWOH: THE HISTORY OF THE TI-PING REVOLUTION. London: Day & Son, 1866.

Listowel, Judith. THE MAKING OF TANGANYIKA. London: Chatto and Windus, 1965.

Littauer, Raphael and Norman Uphoff (eds.). THE AIR WAR IN INDOCHINA. Boston: Beacon, 1972.

Little, Richard. INTERVENTION: EXTERNAL INVOLVEMENT IN CIVIL WARS. Totawa, N.J.: Rowman & Littlefield, 1975.

Li Ung Bing. OUTLINES OF CHINESE HISTORY. Shanghai: Commercial Press, 1914.

Lobanov-Rostovsky, Andrei. RUSSIA AND ASIA. Ann Arbor: Wahr, 1951. *London Times.*

Longrigg, Stephen Hemsley. IRAQ, 1900 TO 1950. London: Oxford Univ., 1953.

————. SYRIA AND LEBANON UNDER FRENCH MANDATE. London: Oxford Univ., 1958.

Lorch, Netanel. THE EDGE OF THE SWORD. New York: Putnams, 1961.

Love, Joseph. RIO GRANDE DO SUL AND BRAZILIAN REGIONALISM, 1882-1930. Stanford: Stanford Univ., 1971.

Luard, Evan (ed.). THE INTERNATIONAL REGULATION OF CIVIL WARS. New York: New York Univ., 1972.

Lyons, Eugene. ASSIGNMENT IN UTOPIA. New York: Harcourt, Brace, 1937.

Maass, Walter B. ASSASSINATION IN VIENNA. New York: Scribner's, 1972.

McAleavy, Henry. BLACK FLAGS IN VIETNAM. New York: Macmillan, 1968.

————. THE MODERN HISTORY OF CHINA. London: Weidenfield and Nicholson, 1900.

MacCallum, Elizabeth. THE NATIONALIST CRUSADE IN SYRIA. New York: Foreign Policy Assn., 1928.

McClure, William K. ITALY IN NORTH AFRICA. London: Constable, 1913.

McCoy, Al and Nina Adams (eds.). LAOS: WAR AND REVOLUTION. New York: Harper & Row, 1970

MacDermott, Marcia. A HISTORY OF BULGARIA. London: Allen and Unwin, 1962.

McGann, Thomas F. ARGENTINA, THE UNITED STATES, AND THE INTER-AMERICAN SYSTEM, 1880-1914. Cambridge: Harvard Univ., 1957.

McHenry, J. Patrick. A SHORT HISTORY OF MEXICO. Garden City: Doubleday, 1962.

Mackenzie, David. THE SERBS AND RUSSIAN PAN-SLAVISM, 1875-1878. Ithaca: Cornell Univ., 1967.

MacLean, Frank. GERMANY'S COLONIAL FAILURE. Boston: Houghton-Mifflin, 1918.

MacNair, Harley F. CHINA IN REVOLUTION. Chicago: Univ. of Chicago, 1931.

Macauley, Neill. THE SANDINO AFFAIR. Chicago: Quadrangle, 1967.

Macrory, Patrick. SIGNAL CATSTROPHE. London: Hodder and Staughton, 1966.

Magnus, Philip. KITCHENER. London: John Murray, 1958.

Majumdar, R.C., H.C. Raychaudhuri, and Kalikinkar Datta. AN ADVANCED HISTORY OF INDIA. London: Macmillan, 1948.

Mallat, Joseph. LA SERBIE CONTEMPORAINE. Vol. 1. Paris: Librarie Orientale et Américaine, 1902.

Malloy, James M. BOLIVIA, THE UNCOMPLETED REVOLUTION. Pittsburgh: Univ. of Pittsburgh, 1970.

Mansford, Oliver. THE BATTLE OF MAJUBA HILL. New York: Crowell, 1967.

Marett, Robert. PERU. New York: Praeger, 1969.

Markham, Clement S. A HISTORY OF PERU. New York: Greenwood, 1968.

Markides, Kyriacos C. THE RISE AND FALL OF THE CYPRUS REPUBLIC. New Haven: Yale Univ., 1977.

Marshall, S.L.A. SINAI VICTORY. New York: William Morrow, 1958.

Martelli, George. LEOPOLD TO LUMUMBA. London: Chapman and Hall, 1962.

Martin, Christopher. THE RUSSO-JAPANESE WAR. New York: Abelard Schulman, 1967.

Martin, Claude. HISTOIRE DE L'ALGERIE FRANÇAISE, 1830-1962. Paris: Editions des 4 Fils Aymon, 1963.

Martin, Michael R. and Gabriel H. Lovett (eds.). ENCYCLOPEDIA OF LATIN AMERICAN HISTORY. Indianapolis: Bobbs-Merrill, 1968.

Marure, Alejandro. BOSQUEJO HISTORICO DE LAS REVOLUCIONES DE CENTRO AMERICA. Guatemala City: El Progreso, 1837.

Mathieu, Henri. LA TURQUIE. Paris: E. Dentu, 1856.

Maullin, Richard L. SOLDIERS, GUERRILLAS AND POLITICS IN COLOMBIA. Lexington: D.C. Heath, 1973.

Maurice, C. Edmund. THE REVOLUTIONARY MOVEMENT OF 1848-49 IN ITALY, AUSTRIA-HUNGARY, AND GERMANY. New York: Putnam, 1887.

Maurice, F. and George Arthur. THE LIFE OF LORD WOLSELEY. Garden City, N.Y.: Doubleday, 1924.

Maurice, John Frederick. HOSTILITIES WITHOUT DECLARATION OF WAR. London: H.M.S.O., 1883.

Maxwell, Neville. INDIA'S CHINA WAR. London: Jonathan Cape, 1970.

Mazade, Charles de. LES REVOLUTIONS DE L'ESPAGNE CONTEMPORAINE. Paris: Didier, 1869.

Melady, Thomas Patrick. BURUNDI: THE TRAGIC YEARS. Maryknoll, N.Y.: Orbis, 1974.

Mellor, Andrew. INDIA SINCE PARTITION. New York: Praeger, 1951.

Mende, Tibor. THE CHINESE REVOLUTION. London: Thames & Hudson, 1961.

Menendez Pidal, Ramon. HISTORIA DE ESPAÑA. v. 26. Madrid: Espasa-Calpe, 1968.

Mentre, François. LES GÉNÉRATION SOCIALES. Paris: Bossard, 1920.

Meo, Leila. "The War in Lebanon," in Astri Suhrke and Lela Garner Nobel (eds.). ETHNIC CONFLICT in INTERNATIONAL RELATIONS. New York: Praeger, 1977.

Meray, Tiboy. THIRTEEN DAYS THAT SHOOK THE KREMLIN. New York: Praeger, 1959.

Meyer, Joan A. THE CRISTERO REBELLION. New York: Cambridge Univ., 1976.

Meza, Rafael. CENTRO AMERICA: CAMPAÑA NATIONAL DE 1885. Guatemala City: Tipográfia Nácional, 1935.

Michael, Franz. "T'ai P'ing T'ien-kuo." JOURNAL OF ASIAN STUDIES, 17/1 (November, 1957), 67-76.

Michell, Robert. EASTERN TURKESTAN AND DZUNGARIA AND THE REBELLION OF THE TUGANS AND TARANCHIS, 1862 TO 1866. Calcutta: Office of Superintendent of Government Printing, 1870.

MIDDLE EAST RECORD. 1969-1970.

Miege, Jean-Louis. LE MARÓC ET L'EUROPE. Vol. II. Paris: Presses Universaires de France, 1961.

Mijatovich, Chedomille. THE MEMOIRS OF A BALKAN DIPLOMAT. London: Cassell, 1917.

Mikus, Joseph. SLOVAKIA. Milwaukee: Marquette Univ., 1963.

Miller, M. E. BULGARIA DURING THE SECOND WORLD WAR. Stanford: Stanford Univ., 1975.

Miller, William. THE OTTOMAN EMPIRE, 1801-1913. Cambridge: Oxford Univ., 1913.

Milstein, Jeffery S. and William C. Mitchell, "Dynamics of the Vietnam Conflict: A Quantitative Analysis and Predictive Computer Simulation." PEACE RESEARCH SOCIETY PAPERS, 10 (1968), 163-213.

von Moltke, Helmuth. DARSTELLUNG DES TURKISCH-AEGYPTISCHEN FELDZUGS IN SOMMER 1839. Berlin: Junker und Dunnhaupt, 1935.

Moore, Harriet L. SOVIET FAR EASTERN POLICY, 1931-1945. Princeton: Princeton Univ., 1945.

Moore, Joel R. et al. THE HISTORY OF THE AMERICAN EXPEDITION FIGHTING THE BOLSHEVIKI. Detroit: Polar Bear, 1921.

Moorehead, Alan. THE RUSSIAN REVOLUTION. New York: Harper, 1958.

Moron, Guillermo. A HISTORY OF VENZUELA. New York: Roy, 1963.

Morris, Donald. WASHING OF THE SPEARS. New York: Simon and Schuster, 1965.

Morris, Richard B. (ed.). ENCYCLOPEDIA OF AMERICAN HISTORY. New York: Harper, 1970.

Morse, Hosea Ballou. THE INTERNATIONAL RELATIONS OF THE CHINESE EMPIRE. Vol. III. London: Longmans, 1918.

Mounsey, Augustus H. THE SATSUMA REBELLION. London: John Murray, 1879.

Moyal, J. E. "The Distribution of Wars in Time." JOURNAL OF THE ROYAL STATISTICAL SOCIETY (Series A), 112/4 (1949), 446-49.

Munro, Dana G. THE FIVE REPUBLICS OF CENTRAL AMERICA. New York: Oxford Univ., 1918.

_____. THE LATIN AMERICAN REPUBLICS. New York: Appleton-Century, 1942.

_____. INTERVENTION AND DOLLAR DIPLOMACY IN THE CARIBBEAN. Princeton: Princeton Univ., 1964.

Mydans, Carl and Shelly Mydans. THE VIOLENT PEACE. New York: Atheneum, 1968.

Mylonis, G. E. THE BALKAN STATES. St. Louis: Eden, 1946.

NAGALAND IS BORN. Kohmia: Government of Nagaland, 1964.

Nalivkine, Vladimir P. HISTOIRE DU KHANAT DE KHOKAND. Paris: Leroux, 1889.

Nantet, Jacques. HISTOIRE DU LIBAN. Paris: Editions de Minuit, 1963.

Natrajan, L. "The Santhal Insurrection," in A. R. Desai (ed.), PEASANT STRUGGLES IN INDIA. Bombay: Oxford, 1979.

Neeson, Eoin. THE CIVIL WAR IN IRELAND. Cork: Mercier, 1966.

New York Times. THE PENTAGON PAPERS. New York: Bantam, 1971.

Niox, Gustave. EXPEDITION DU MEXIQUE 1861-1867. Paris: J. Dumaine, 1874.

Nolan, Edward H. THE LIBERATORS OF ITALY. London: J. S. Virtue, 1865.

Norris. J. A. THE FIRST AFGHAN WAR 1838-1842. Cambridge: Cambridge Univ., 1967.

O'Ballance, Edgar. THE ARAB-ISRAELI WAR. London: Faber and Faber, 1956.

_____. THE INDO-CHINA WAR 1945-1954. London: Faber and Faber, 1964.

_____. THE GREEK CIVIL WAR, 1944-1949. New York: Praeger, 1966a.

_____. THE COMMUNIST-INSURGENT WAR IN MALAYSIA 1948-1960. London: Faber and Faber, 1966b.

_____. THE WAR IN THE YEMEN. London: Faber and Faber, 1970.

_____. THE KURDISH REVOLT: 1961-1970. London: Faber and Faber, 1973.

_____. NO VICTOR, NO VANQUISHED: THE YOM KIPPUR WAR. San Rafael: Presidio, 1978.

Ogawa, Gotaro. EXPENDITURES OF THE RUSSO-JAPANESE WAR. New York: Oxford Univ., 1923.

O'Neill, Robert. "Doctrine and Training in the German Army," in Michael Howard (ed.). THE THEORY AND PRACTICE OF WAR. New York: Praeger. 1966.

Ono, Giichi. EXPENDITURES OF THE SINO-JAPANESE WAR. New York: Oxford Univ., 1922.

Organski, A. F. K. and Jacek Kugler. THE WAR LEDGER. Chicago: Univ. of Chicago, 1980.

Orlansky, Jesse. "The State of Research on Internal War." Institute for Defense Analysis, Research Paper p-565, 1970.

Orsi, Pietro. CAVOUR AND THE MAKING OF MODERN ITALY. New York: Putnams, 1914.

Ottaway, David and Marina Ottaway. ALGERIA: THE POLITICS OF A SOCIALIST REVOLUTION. Berkeley: Univ. of California, 1970.

Page, Stanley. THE FORMATION OF THE BALTIC STATES. Cambridge: Harvard Univ., 1959.

Parkes, Henry B. A HISTORY OF MEXICO. Boston: Houghton-Mifflin, 1966.

Pasdermadjain, P. HISTOIRE DE L'ARMENIE. Paris: Libraire Orientale H. Samuelian, 1964.

Pattee, Richard. GABRIEL GARCIA MORENO Y EL ECUADOR DE SU TIEMPO. Quito: Editorial Ecuatoriana, 1941.

Patterson, George. TIBET IN REVOLT. London: Faber and Faber, 1960.

Paxton, Robert. VICHY FRANCE. New York: Knopf, 1972.

Payne, Robert. THE CIVIL WAR IN SPAIN 1936-1939. New York: Capricorn, 1970.

———. MASSACRE. New York: Macmillan, 1973.

Payne, Stanley. POLITICS AND THE MILITARY IN MODERN SPAIN. Stanford: Stanford Univ., 1967.

Pearson, Frederic S. "Foreign Military Intervention and Domestic Disputes." INTERNATIONAL STUDIES QUARTERLY, 18 (September, 1974), 259-90.

Peckham, Howard (ed.). THE TOLL OF INDEPENDENCE: ENGAGEMENTS AND BATTLE CASUALTIES OF THE AMERICAN REVOLUTION. Chicago: Univ. of Chicago, 1974.

Pelissier, Roger. THE AWAKENING OF CHINA, 1793-1949. London: Secker and Warburg, 1963.

Pemberton, W. Baring. BATTLES OF THE BOER WAR. London: Batsford, 1964.

Perce, Elbert. THE BATTLE ROLL. New York: Mason Bros., 1858.

Perkins, Dexter. HANDS OFF. Boston: Little, Brown, 1941.

———. THE AMERICAN APPROACH TO FOREIGN POLICY. Cambridge: Harvard Univ., 1952.

Perré, Jean Paul. LES MUTATIONS DE LA GUERRE MODERNE. Paris: Payot, 1962.

Peterson, Clarence Stewart. KNOWN MILITARY DEAD DURING MEXICAN WAR, 1846-1848. Baltimore: by author, 1957.

Petras, James. "Revolution and Guerrilla Movements in Latin America: Venezuela, Guatemala, Colombia, and Peru," in J. Petras and M. Zeitlin (eds.), LATIN AMERICA: REFORM OR REVOLUTION? Greenwich, Conn.: Fawcett, 1968.

PHILIPPINES INFORMATION BULLETIN. 2/2 (April, 1974).

Phillips, G.D.R. RUSSIA, JAPAN AND MONGOLIA. London: Frederick Muller, 1942.

Phillips, Walter Alison. THE WAR OF GREEK INDEPENDENCE. London: Smith, Elder. 1897.

———. THE CONFEDERATION OF EUROPE: A STUDY OF THE EUROPEAN ALLIANCE, 1813-1823. London: Longmans, 1914.

Phillipson, Coleman. TERMINATION OF WAR AND TREATIES OF PEACE. London: T. Fisher Unwin, 1916.

Pierce, Richard. RUSSIAN CENTRAL ASIA, 1867-1917, A STUDY IN COLONIAL RULE. Berkeley: Univ. of California, 1960.

Pieri, Piero. STORIA MILITARE DEL RISORGIMENTO. Turin: Giulio Elnaudi, 1962.

Pike, Douglas. VIET CONG. Cambridge: M.I.T., 1966.

Pike, Frederick B. A MODERN HISTORY OF PERU. New York: Praeger, 1967.

Pinson, Koppel. MODERN GERMANY. New York: Macmillan, 1954.

Pirenne, Henri. HISTOIRE DE BELGIQUE, v. 6. Brussels: Lamertin, 1926.

Pohler, Johann. BIBLIOTHECA HISTORICO-MILITARIS. SYSTEMATISCHE ÜBERSICHT D. ERSCHEINUNGEN ALLER SPRACHEN AUF DEM GEBIETE D. GESCHICHTE D. KRIEGE UND KRIEGSWISSENSCHAFT SEIT ERFINDUNG D. BUCHDRUCKERKUNST B. Z. SCHLUSS DES JAHRES 1880. 4 vols. 1880. Vol. 2. New York: Burt Franklin, 1961.

Polites, Athanase G. LE CONFLIT TURKO-EGYPTIEN. Cairo: Institut Française D'Archéologie Oriental du Caire, 1931.

Ponte Dominguéz. Francisco J. HISTORIA DE LA GUERRA DE LOS DIEZ AÑOS. 2 vols. Havana: A. Muñiz, 1958.

Poplai, S.L. INDIA, 1947-1950. Vol. 2. London: Oxford Univ., 1959.

Portell Vilá, Herminio. HISTORIA DE LA GUERRA DE CUBA Y LOS ETADOS UNIDOS CONTRA ESPAÑA. Havana: 1949.

Post, John D. "A Study in Meteorological and Trade Cycle History: The Economic Crisis Following the Napoleonic Wars." JOURNAL OF ECONOMIC HISTORY, 24 (June, 1974), 315-49.

Powell, Geoffrey. THE KANDYAN WARS 1803-1813. London: Leo Cooper, 1973.

Prinzing, Friedrich. EPIDEMICS RESULTING FROM WARS. Oxford: Clarendon, 1916.

Pritchard, Earl H. "Political Ferment in China, 1911-1947." ANNALS, 277 (September, 1951), 1-12.

Purcell, Victor. THE BOXER UPRISING. Cambridge: Cambridge Univ., 1963.

Puzyrewsky, Alexander. DER POLNISCH-RUSSISCHE KRIEG, 1831. 3 vols. Vienna: Kreisel and Gröger, 1893.

Pye, Lucien. GUERILLA COMMUNISM IN MALAYA. Princeton: Princeton Univ., 1956.

Rabinowitch, Alexander. THE BOLSHEVIKS COME TO POWER. New York: Norton, 1976.

Ramos-Oliviera, A. POLITICS, ECONOMICS AND THE MEN OF MODERN SPAIN. London: 1946.

Ranke, Leopold. THE HISTORY OF SERBIA. London: Bohn, 1853.

Rapoport, Anatol. "Lewis F. Richardson's Mathematical Theory of War." JOURNAL OF CONFLICT RESOLUTION, 1/3 (September, 1957), 249-307.

von Rauch, George. A HISTORY OF SOVIET RUSSIA. New York: Praeger, 1957.

Reddaway, W. F. et al. (eds.). THE CAMBRIDGE HISTORY OF POLAND. Cambridge: Cambridge Univ., 1941.

Rees, David. KOREA: THE LIMITED WAR. New York: St. Martin's, 1964.

REPORT OF THE INTERNATIONAL COMMISSION TO INQUIRE INTO THE CAUSES AND CONDUCT OF THE BALKAN WARS. Geneva: Carnegie Endowment for International Peace. 1914.

Rennie, Isabel F. THE ARGENTINE REPUBLIC. New York: Macmillan, 1945.

Reshetar, John S. THE UKRAINIAN REVOLUTION, 1917-1920. Princeton: Princeton Univ., 1952.

Richardson, H. E. TIBET AND ITS HISTORY. London: Oxford Univ., 1962.

Richardson, Lewis F. "Generalized Foreign Politics." BRITISH JOURNAL OF PSYCHOLOGY, Suppl. Monograph 23 (June, 1939), 1-91.

———. "Frequency of Occurrence of Wars and Other Fatal Quarrels." NATURE, 148/3759 (November 15, 1941), 598.

———. "The Distribution of Wars in Time." JOURNAL OF THE ROYAL STATISTICAL SOCIETY, 107 (1945), 242-50.

———. "Variation of the Frequency of Fatal Quarrels with Magnitude." JOURNAL OF THE AMERICAN STATISTICAL SOCIETY, 43 (1948), 523-46.

———. STATISTICS OF DEADLY QUARRELS. Pittsburgh: Boxwood, 1960a.

———. ARMS AND INSECURITY. Pittsburgh: Boxwood, 1960b.

Riker, T. W. THE MAKING OF RUMANIA. London: Oxford Univ., 1931.

Rio Branco, M. EFEMERIDES BRAZILEIRAS. Rio de Janeiro: Ministerio das Relacoes Exteriores, 1946.

Roberts, Stephen H. THE HISTORY OF FRENCH COLONIAL POLICY. Hamden, Conn.: Archon, 1963.

Robertson, Priscilla. REVOLUTIONS OF 1848: A SOCIAL HISTORY. Princeton: Princeton Univ., 1952.

Robertson, W. S. "Foreign Accounts of Rosas." HISPANIC AMERICAN HISTORICAL REVIEW, 10/2 (May, 1930), 124-37.

Rodman, Selden. QUIQUEYA: A HISTORY OF THE DOMINICAN REPUBLIC. Seattle: Univ. of Washington, 1964.

Rodriguez Herrero, Enrique. CAMPAÑA MILITAR DE 1904. Montevideo: 1934.

Romani, George. THE NEAPOLITAN REVOLUTION OF 1820-1821. Evanston: Northwestern Univ., 1950.

Romanovski, Dmitrii Il'ich. NOTES ON THE CENTRAL ASIAN QUESTION. Calcutta: Office of Superintendent of Government Printing, 1870.

Rondon Marquez, R. A. GUZMAN BLANCO. Caracas: Garrido, 1944.

Rosberg, Carl G., Jr. and John Nottingham. THE MYTH OF "MAU MAU": NATIONALISM IN KENYA. New York: Praeger, 1966.

Rose, J. Holland. THE DEVELOPMENT OF EUROPEAN NATIONS 1870-1919. Cambridge: Cambridge Univ., 1915.

Rosenau, James N. (ed.). INTERNATIONAL ASPECTS OF CIVIL STRIFE. Princeton: Princeton Univ., 1964.

Ross, Frank E. "The American Naval Attack on Shimonoseki in 1863." CHINESE SOCIAL AND POLITICAL SCIENCE REVIEW, 18/1 (April, 1934), 146-55.

Rouland, John. A HISTORY OF SINO-INDIAN RELATIONS. Princeton: Van Nostrand, 1967.

Rummel, Rudolph J., "Dimensions of Conflict Behavior Within and Between Nations." GENERAL SYSTEMS YEARBOOK, 8 (1963) 1-50.

_____. "A Field Theory of Social Action with Application to Conflict Within Nations." YEARBOOK OF THE SOCIETY FOR GENERAL SYSTEMS, 10 (1965), 183-211.

_____. THE DIMENSIONALITY OF NATIONS. Beverly Hills, Cal.: Sage, 1972.

Rupen, Robert A. MONGOLS OF THE TWENTIETH CENTURY. Vol. I. Bloomington: Indiana Univ., 1964.

Russell, D. E. H. REBELLION, REVOLUTION, AND ARMED FORCE. New York: Academic Press, 1974.

Russell, Frank S. RUSSIAN WARS WITH TURKEY. London: Henry S. King, 1877.

Russett, Bruce M., TRENDS IN WORLD POLITICS. New York: Macmillan, 1965.

_____. INTERNATIONAL REGIONS AND THE INTERNATIONAL SYSTEM: A STUDY IN POLITICAL ECOLOGY. Chicago: Rand McNally, 1967.

_____. "Delineating International Regions." in J. David Singer (ed.), QUANTITATIVE INTERNATIONAL POLITICS: INSIGHTS AND EVIDENCE. New York: Free Press, 1968.

_____. J. David Singer, and Melvin Small. "National Political Units in the Twentieth Century: A Standardized List." AMERICAN POLITICAL SCIENCE REVIEW, 62/3 (September, 1968), 932-51.

Sabry, M. L'EMPIRE ÉGYPTIEN SOUS MOHAMED-ALI ET LA QUESTION D'ORIENT. Paris: Librairie Orientaliste, 1930.

Safran, Nadev. FROM WAR TO WAR. New York: Pegasus, 1969.

Salert, Barbara. REVOLUTION AND REVOLUTIONARIES. New York, Elsevier, 1976.

Salibi, Kamal S. CROSSROADS TO CIVIL WAR. Delmar, N.Y.: Caravan, 1976.

Sandford, Christine. ETHIOPIA UNDER HAILE SELASSIE. London: J. M. Dent, 1946.

von Sax, Carl Ritter. GESCHICHTE DES MACHTVERFALLS DER TÜRKEI. Vienna: Manziche k. u. k. Hof Verlags und Universitäts Buchhandlung, 1913.

Scarone, Arturo. EFEMERIDES URUGUAYAS. Montevideo: Instituto Historico y Geografico del Uruguay, 1956.

Schiemann, Theodor. GESCHICHTE RUSSLANDS UNTER KAISER NIKOLAUS I. Vol. 3. Berlin: George Reimer, 1913.

Schlarman, Joseph. MEXICO: A LAND OF VOLCANOES. Milwaukee: Bruce, 1950.

von Schlechta-Wssehdr, Ottokar. "Der Letzte Persiche-Russische Krieg." ZEITSCHRIFT DER DEUTSCHEN MORGEN LANDISCHEN GESELLSCHAFT, 2 (1866), 288-305.

Schlesinger, Max. THE WAR IN HUNGARY, 1848-1849. London: Richard Bentley, 1850.

Schmidt, Carl. THE PLOUGH AND THE SWORD. New York: Columbia Univ., 1938.

Schmitt, Bernadotte. COMING OF THE WAR 1914. New York: Scribners, 1930.

Schuschnigg, Kurt von. THE BRUTAL TAKEOVER. New York: Atheneum, 1971.

Scott, J. G. BURMA. New York: Knopf, 1924.

Senn, Alfred E. THE EMERGENCE OF MODERN LITHUANIA. New York: Columbia Univ., 1959.

Seton-Watson, Hugh. THE DECLINE OF IMPERIAL RUSSIA, 1855-1914. London: Methuen, 1952.

———. THE RUSSIAN EMPIRE, 1801-1917. Oxford: Oxford Univ., 1967.

Seton-Watson, Robert William. BRITAIN IN EUROPE 1789-1914. Cambridge: Cambridge Univ., 1938.

———. A HISTORY OF THE CZECHS AND SLOVAKS. Hamden, Conn.: Archon, 1965.

Shaplen, Robert. "Our Involvement in Laos." FOREIGN AFFAIRS, 48/3 (April, 1970), 478-93.

Shah, Surdan Ikbal Ali. THE TRAGEDY OF AMANULLAH. London: Alexander-Ouseley, 1933.

Sheridan, James E. CHINA IN DISINTEGRATION. New York: Free Press, 1975.

Shibeika, Mekki. BRITISH POLICY IN THE SUDAN 1882-1902. London: Oxford, 1952.

Short, Anthony. "Communism and the Emergency." in Gung wu Wang (ed.). MALAYSIA. London: Pall Mall, 1958.

Silverlight, John. THE VICTOR'S DILEMMA. New York: Weybright and Talley, 1970.

Simpson, Bertram L. THE FIGHT FOR THE REPUBLIC OF CHINA. New York: Dodd, Mead, 1917.

Singer, J. David. "The Correlates of War Project: Interim Report." WORLD POLITICS, 24/2 (1972), 243-70.

———. "Accounting for International War: The State of the Discipline." JOURNAL OF PEACE RESEARCH, XVIII, 1 (1981), 1-18.

———. and Thomas Cusack. "Periodicity, Inexorability, and Steersmanship in Major Power War," in Richard Merritt and Bruce Russett (eds.), FROM NATIONAL DEVELOPMENT TO GLOBAL COMMUNITY. Herts, U.K.: Allen and Unwin, 1981, 404-22.

———. and Melvin Small. "The Composition and Status Ordering of the International System. 1815-1940." WORLD POLITICS, 18/2 (January, 1966a), 236-82.

———. THE WAGES OF WAR, 1816-1965: A STATISTICAL HANDBOOK. New York: Wiley, 1972.

Singh, Khushwant. A HISTORY OF THE SIKHS. Vol. 2. Princeton: Princeton Univ., 1966.

Singletary, Otis A. THE MEXICAN WAR. Chicago: Univ. of Chicago, 1960.

SIPRI, YEARBOOK OF WORLD ARMAMENTS AND DISARMAMENT, 1968-69. London: Duckworth, 1970.

Sloan, Stephen. A STUDY IN POLITICAL VIOLENCE. Chicago: Rand McNally, 1971.

Small, Melvin and J. David Singer. "Patterns in International Warfare, 1816-1965." ANNALS, 391 (September, 1970), 145-55.

———. "The Diplomatic Importance of States, 1816-1970: An Extension and Refinement of the Indicator." WORLD POLITICS, 25 (July, 1973), 577-599.

Smith, C. Jay, Jr. FINLAND AND THE RUSSIAN REVOLUTION. Athens: Univ. of Georgia, 1958.

Smith, Justin H. THE WAR WITH MEXICO. 2 vols. New York: Macmillan, 1919.

Smith, Michael Llewellyn. THE GREAT ISLAND: A STUDY OF CRETE. London: Longmans, 1965.

Smith Rhea M. SPAIN: A MODERN HISTORY. Ann Arbor: Univ. of Michigan, 1965.

Snow Edgar. FAR EASTERN FRONT. New York: H. Smith and R. Haas, 1933.

Snow, Peter J. HUSSEIN. Washington, D.C.: Luce, 1972.

Sorokin, Pitirim A. SOCIAL AND CULTURAL DYNAMICS. Vol. 3 (FLUCTUATION OF SOCIAL RELATIONSHIPS, WAR AND REVOLUTION). New York: American Book, 1937.

Spain. Servicio Historico Militar. HISTORIA DE LAS CAMPAÑAS DE MAR-RUECES. Vol. 1. Madrid: Impr. del Servicio Geografico del Ejercito, 1947.

Spielman, Christian. DIE TAIPING-REVOLUTION (1850-1864). Halle-a.-S.: Herman Gsenius, 1900.

STATESMAN'S YEARBOOK.

Stavrianos, Leften. THE BALKANS SINCE 1453. New York: Holt, Rinehart & Winston, 1958.

Stearns, Peter N. 1848: THE REVOLUTIONARY TIDE IN EUROPE. New York: Norton, 1974.

Steefel, Lawrence C. THE SCHLESWIG-HOLSTEIN QUESTION. Cambridge: Harvard Univ., 1932.

Stephenson, Nathaniel W. TEXAS AND THE MEXICAN WAR. New Haven: Yale Univ., 1921.

von Sternegg. J. K. SCHLACTEN-ATLAS DES XIX. JAHRHUNDERTS: DER RUSSISCH-TURKISCHE KRIEG, 1877-1878. Leipzig: P. Bauerle, 1866(?)—1899(?).

————. SCHLACTEN-ATLAS DES XIX. JAHRHUNDERTS: DER RUSSISCH-TURKISCHE KRIEG, 1828-1829. Leipzig: P. Bauerle, 1891(?)—1895(?).

————. SCHLACTEN-ATLAS DES XIX. JAHRHUNDERTS: DER DEUTSCHE-DÄNISCHE KRIEG, 1848-1850. Leipzig: P. Bauerle, 1892—1898(?).

Stevenson, F. S. A HISTORY OF MONTENEGRO. New York: Arno Press, 1971.

Stewart, George. THE WHITE ARMIES OF RUSSIA. New York: Macmillan, 1933.

Stickney, E. P. SOUTHERN ALBANIA AND NORTHERN EPIRUS IN INTERNATIONAL AFFAIRS, 1912-1923. Stanford: Stanford Univ., 1926.

Stojanovic, M. D. THE GREAT POWERS AND THE BALKANS, 1875-1878. Cambridge: Cambridge Univ., 1939.

Stone, Lawrence. "Theories of Revolution." WORLD POLITICS, 18 (January 1966), 159-76.

Storey, Moorfield and Marcial P. Lichauco. THE CONQUEST OF THE PHILIPPINES BY THE UNITED STATES. New York: Putnam, 1926.

Stracey, P. D. NAGALAND NIGHTMARE. Bombay: Allied Publishers Private Ltd., 1968.

Strakhovsky, Leonid I. INTERVENTION AT ARCHANGEL. Princeton: Princeton Univ., 1944.

Strobel, Edward H. THE SPANISH REVOLUTION, 1868-1875. Boston: Small Maynard, 1898.

Suhrke Astri and Lela Garner Nobel (eds.). ETHNIC CONFLICTS IN INTERNATIONAL RELATIONS. New York: Praeger, 1977.

————. "Muslims in the Philippines and Thailand," in Astri Suhrke and Lela Garner Nobel (eds.), ETHNIC CONFLICTS IN INTERNATIONAL RELATIONS. New York: Praeger, 1977b.

Sula, Abdul B. ALBANIA'S STRUGGLE FOR INDEPENDENCE. New York: Family Press, 1967.

Sullivant, Robert S. SOVIET POLITICS AND THE UKRAINE 1917-1957. New York: Columbia Univ., 1962.

Sumner, Benedict H. RUSSIA AND THE BALKANS 1870-1880. Oxford: Oxford Univ., 1937.

Swire, Joseph. ALBANIA: THE RISE OF A KINGDOM. New York: Smith, 1950.

Sykes, Percy Molesworth. A HISTORY OF AFGHANISTAN. London: Macmillan, 1940.

————. A HISTORY OF PERSIA. 2 vols. London: Macmillan. 1951.

Taboulet, Georges (ed.). LA GESTE FRANÇAISE EN INDOCHINE. Paris: Adrien-Maisonneuve, 1955.

Takeuchi, Tutsuni. WAR AND DIPLOMACY IN THE JAPANESE EMPIRE. Garden City: Doubleday. 1935.

Tan, Chester C. THE BOXER CATASTROPHE. New York: Columbia Univ., 1955.

T'ang Leang-li (ed.). SUPPRESSING COMMUNIST BANDITRY IN CHINA. Shanghai: China United Press, 1934.

Tang, Peter S. H. RUSSIA AND SOVIET POLICY IN MANCHURIA AND OUTER MONGOLIA, 1911-1931. Durham: Duke Univ., 1959.

Tanter, Raymond. "Dimensions of Conflict Behavior Within and Between Nations, 1958-1960." JOURNAL OF CONFLICT RESOLUTION, 10 (March, 1966), 41-64.

——. and Manus Midlarsky. "A Theory of Revolutions." JOURNAL OF CONFLICT RESOLUTION, 11 (September, 1967), 264-80.

Taylor, A. J. P. THE STRUGGLE FOR MASTERY IN EUROPE, 1848-1918. Oxford: Clarendon, 1954.

Taylor, Charles Lewis and Michael C. Hudson. WORLD HANDBOOK OF POLITICAL AND SOCIAL INDICATORS. New Haven: Yale Univ., 1972.

Temperly, Harold. ENGLAND AND THE NEAR EAST. Hamden, Conn.: Archon, 1964.

Teng Ssu-yü. THE NIEN ARMY AND THEIR GUERRILLA WARFARE, 1851-1868. The Hague: Mouton, 1961.

——. HISTORIOGRAPHY OF THE TAIPING REBELLION. Cambridge: East Asia Research Center, Harvard Univ., 1963.

——. THE TAIPING REBELLION AND THE WESTERN POWERS. Oxford: Clarendon Press, 1971.

Thayer, William Roscoe. THE LIFE AND TIMES OF CAVOUR. Vol. 2. Boston: Houghton-Mifflin, 1911.

Theobald, A. B. THE MAHDIYA. London: Longmans, 1951.

Thomas, Hugh. THE SPANISH CIVIL WAR. New York: Harper, 1961.

——. SUEZ. New York: Harper, 1967.

——. CUBA: THE PURSUIT OF FREEDOM. New York: Harper, 1971.

Thomas, Lowell. WITH LAWRENCE IN ARABIA. New York: Century, 1924.

——.THE SILENT WAR IN TIBET. Garden City, N.Y.: Doubleday, 1959.

Thompson, Edward John and G. T. Garrett. THE RISE AND FULFILLMENT OF BRITISH RULE IN INDIA. London: Macmillan, 1934.

Thompson, Virginia and B. Richard Adloff. THE MALAGASY REPUBLIC. Stanford: Stanford Univ., 1965.

Tibawi, Abd-al Latif al. A MODERN HISTORY OF SYRIA. London: Macmillan, 1969.

Tilly, Charles. THE VENDÉE. Cambridge: Harvard Univ., 1964.

——. and James Rule. MEASURING POLITICAL UPHEAVAL. Princeton: Center of International Studies, mimeo, 1965.

Timasheff, Nicholas S. WAR AND REVOLUTION. New York: Sheed and Ward, 1965.

TIME. 84/2, July 10, 1964.

Tinker, Hugh. THE UNION OF BURMA. London: Oxford Univ., 1957.

Tirona, Tomas C., "The Philippine Anti-Communist Campaign," in F. Osanka (ed.). MODERN GUERRILLA WARFARE. Glencoe: Free Press, 1962.

Todorov, N., L. Diney, and L. Melnishki. BULGARIA: HISTORICAL AND GEOGRAPHICAL OUTLINE, Sofia: Sofia Press, 1968.

Tomasek, Robert D., "Caribbean Exile Invasions." ORBIS, 17 (Winter, 1974), 1354-1382.

Turner, Robert T. VIETNAMESE COMMUNISM: ITS ORGINS AND DEVELOPMENT. Stanford: Hoover Institution, 1975.

Ullman, Richard. INTERVENTION AND THE WAR. Princeton: Princeton Univ., 1961.

United Asia. 14/12 (December, 1962), 691-708.

United Nations Command. Report to United Nations Secretary General. October 23, 1953.

U.S. Department of the Army. Historical Section. ORDER OF BATTLE OF THE UNITED STATES ARMY FORCES IN THE WORLD WAR. Washington, D.C.: G.P.O., 1937.

U.S. Senate. Committee on Foreign Relations. HEARINGS BEFORE A SUBCOM-
MITTEE ON U.S. SECURITY AGREEMENTS ABROAD. 91st Congress, First
Session Part Two. 20, 21, 22, 28 October 1969.

Unterberger, Betty. AMERICA'S SIBERIAN EXPEDITION 1918-1920. Durham,
N.C.: Duke Univ., 1956.

Urlanis, Boris T. VOINI I NARODO-NACELENIE EVROPI (Wars and the Population of Europe). Moscow: Government Publishing House, 1960.

Usborne, C. V. THE CONQUEST OF MOROCCO. London: Stanley Paul, 1936.

Valdes, Nelson P. "Revolutionary Solidarity in Angola." in Cole Blasier and Carmelo
Mesa-Lago (eds.), CUBA IN THE WORLD. Pittsburgh: Univ. of Pittsburgh, 1979.

Vali, Ferenc A. RIFT AND REVOLT IN HUNGARY. Cambridge: Harvard Univ.,
1961.

Vanly, Ismet Cheriff. THE REVOLUTION OF IRAKI KURDISTAN. Lausanne:
Committee for the Defense of the Kurdish People's Rights, April 1965.

Vásquez-Machicado, Humberto and José de Mesa, and Teresa Gisbert. MAN-
UAL DE HISTORIA DE BOLIVIA. La Paz: Libreroas Editores, 1963.

Vial, Jean. LE MAROC HÉROIQUE. Paris: Hachette, 1938.

Villacorta Calderon, Jose Antonio. HISTORICA DE LA REPUBLICA DE GUATE-
MALA, 1821-1921. Guatemala City: Tipografica Nacional, 1960.

Vlekke, Bernard. NUSANTARA. Chicago: Quadrangle, 1960.

Vinacke, Harold M. FAR EASTERN POLITICS IN THE POST WAR PERIOD. New
York: Appleton-Century-Crofts, 1956.

Voevodsky, John. "Quantitative Behavior of Warring Nations." JOURNAL OF PSY-
CHOLOGY, 72 (July, 1969), 269-92.

Völgyes, Ivan (ed.). HUNGARY IN REVOLUTION, 1918-19: NINE ESSAYS. Lincoln: Univ. of Nebraska, 1971.

Wack, Henry Wellington. THE STORY OF THE CONGO FREE STATE. New York:
Putnams, 1905.

Wakeman, Frederic. STRANGERS AT THE GATE. Berkeley: Univ. of California,
1966.

Wandycz, Piotr S. SOVIET-POLISH RELATIONS, 1917-1921. Cambridge: Harvard
Univ. 1969.

Wan Lo. "Communal Strife in Mid-Nineteenth Century Kwangtung: The Establishment of Ch'ih Ch'i." PAPERS ON CHINA 19 (1965), 85-119. East Asian Research
Center, Cambridge: Harvard Univ.

Ward, W. E. F. A HISTORY OF GHANA. London: Allen and Unwin, 1959.

Warren, Harris Gaylord. PARAGUAY. Norman: Univ. of Oklahoma. 1949.

_____. "The Paraguayan Revolution of 1904." THE AMERICAS, 36 (January, 1980),
365-84.

Washburn, George. FIFTY YEARS IN CONSTANTINOPLE. Boston: Houghton-
Mifflin, 1909.

Wehl, David. THE BIRTH OF INDONESIA. London: Allen and Unwin, 1948.

Wei, Henry. CHINA AND SOVIET RUSSIA. Princeton: Van Nostrand, 1956.

Weiss, Herbert K. "Stochastic Models for the Duration and Magnitude of a Deadly
Quarrel." OPERATIONS RESEARCH, 11/1 (1963a), 101-21.

_____. "Trends in World Involvement in War." Los Angeles: Aerospace Corporation,
mimeo. 1963b.

Wenner, Manfred W. MODERN YEMEN, 1918-1966. Baltimore: Johns Hopkins
Univ., 1967.

Werth, Alexander. RUSSIA AT WAR. New York: E. P. Dutton, 1964.

Wheeler, Douglas. REPUBLICAN PORTUGAL: A POLITICAL HISTORY, 1910-
1926. Madison: Univ. of Wisconsin, 1978.

_____. **and René Pelissier.** ANGOLA. New York: Praeger, 1971.

Wheeler, Geoffrey. MODERN HISTORY OF SOVIET CENTRAL ASIA. London:
Weidenfeld and Nicholson, 1964.

Wheeler, Raymond H. WAR, 599 B.C.—1950 A.D. INDEXES OF INTERNATIONAL AND CIVIL WAR BATTLES OF THE WORLD. Pittsburgh: Foundation for the Study of Cycles, 1951.

Whetten, Lawrence L. THE CANAL WAR: FOUR POWER CONFRONTATION IN THE MIDDLE EAST. Cambridge: M.I.T. Press, 1974.

White, Alistair. EL SALVADOR. New York: Praeger, 1973.

White, George F. A HISTORY OF SPAIN AND PORTUGAL. London: Methuen, 1909.

White, John A. THE SIBERIAN INTERVENTION. Princeton: Princeton Univ., 1950.

Wilbur, Donald N. CONTEMPORARY IRAN. New York: Praeger, 1963.

Wilcox, Cadmus M. HISTORY OF THE MEXICAN WAR. Washington, D.C: Church News, 1892.

Wilkenfeld, Jonathan. "Domestic and Foreign Conflict of Nations." JOURNAL OF PEACE RESEARCH, 1 (1968), 56-69.

_____. "Some Further Findings Regarding the Domestic and Foreign Conflict Behavior of Nations." JOURNAL OF PEACE RESEARCH, 2 (1969), 147-56.

Wilkinson, David. DEADLY QUARRELS: LEWIS F. RICHARDSON AND THE STATISTICAL STUDY OF WAR. Berkeley; Univ. of Calif., 1980.

Williams, C. F. Rushbrook. THE STATE OF PAKISTAN. London: Faber and Faber, 1962.

Williams, Mary W., Ruhl J. Bartlett, and Russell E. Miller. THE PEOPLE AND POLITICS OF LATIN AMERICA. Boston: Ginn, 1955.

Wilson, Andrew, THE "EVER VICTORIOUS ARMY." Edinburgh: Blackwood, 1868.

Wilson, A. Seyalatnam. POLITICS IN SRI LANKA 1947-1973. London: Macmillan, 1974.

Wilson, Dick. THE LONG MARCH: THE EPIC OF CHINESE COMMUNISM'S SURVIVAL 1935. New York: Viking, 1971.

Wilson, John, "Drought Bedevils Brazil's Sertao." NATIONAL GEOGRAPHIC, 142/5 (November 1972), 704-23.

Wise, George S. CAUDILLO: A PORTRAIT OF ANTONIO GUZMAN BLANCO. New York: Columbia Univ., 1951.

Wolf, Charles, Jr. THE INDONESIAN STORY. New York: John Day, 1948.

Wood, David. "Conflict in the Twentieth Century." ADELPHI PAPERS, 48. London: Institute of Strategic Studies, June 1968.

Woodhead, H. G. W. (ed.). CHINA YEAR BOOK 1931. Shanghai: North China Daily News and Herald, 1931.

Woodhouse, C. M. THE GREEK WAR OF INDEPENDENCE. New York: Hutchinson, 1952.

Woodman, Dorothy. THE REPUBLIC OF INDONESIA. New York: Philosophical Library, 1955.

_____. THE MAKING OF BURMA. London: Cresset, 1962.

Woods, Frederick Adams and Alexander Baltzly. IS WAR DIMINISHING? Boston: Houghton-Mifflin, 1915.

Woolman, David. REBELS IN THE RIF. Stanford: Stanford Univ., 1968.

The World Almanac.

Wright, Quincy. "When Does War Exist?" AMERICAN JOURNAL OF INTERNATIONAL LAW, 26/2 (April, 1932),362-68.

_____. A STUDY OF WAR. Chicago: Univ. of Chicago, 1942 (revised edition, 1965).

Wuorinen, John H. A HISTORY OF FINLAND. New York: Columbia Univ., 1965.

Wyckoff, Theodore. "Standardized List of National Political Units in the Twentieth Century: The Russett-Singer-Small List of 1968 Updated." INTERNATIONAL SOCIAL SCIENCE JOURNAL, 32 (1980), 834-46.

Yanaga, Chitoshi. JAPAN SINCE PERRY. New York: McGraw-Hill, 1949.

Yaroslavsky, E. and I. P. Tovstukha. THE GREAT PROLETARIAN REVOLUTION. v. 2 of M. Gorky and S. Kirov (eds.). THE HISTORY OF THE CIVIL WAR IN THE U.S.S.R. Moscow: Foreign Language Publishing House, 1946.

Young, George. NATIONALISM AND WAR IN THE NEAR EAST. Oxford: Clarendon, 1915.

Young, Jordan M. THE BRAZILIAN REVOLUTION OF 1930 AND THE AFTERMATH. New Brunswick: Rutgers Univ., 1967.

Young, M. Crawford. "The Obote Revolution." AFRICAN REPORT. 11 (June, 1966), 8-14.

Zaide, Gregorio F. THE PHILIPPINE REVOLUTION. Manila: Modern Book Co., 1954.

Zinner, Paul E. REVOLUTION IN HUNGARY. New York: Columbia Univ., 1962.

Zook, David. H. THE CONDUCT OF THE CHACO WAR. New York: Bookman, 1960.

Correlates of War Project Bibliography

This project, designed to ascertain the conditions and events that have been associated with the incidence of war since the Congress of Vienna, began in a modest way in 1963. The early work was devoted largely to the acquisition of data on fluctuations in the incidence of war and certain factors that seemed most likely to account for those fluctuations across time and space. As the data base grew in size and quality, we were able to begin a series of analyses ranging from simple bivariate correlations to the testing of more complex models through the construction of computerized representations of the historical regularities and irregularities, and research of all three types continues to the present.

We have published about 75 articles, books, and dissertations that present and/or analyze relatively hard data on the incidence of external war, and they are listed under sections II and III of the bibliography. In section I are listed some of the more relevant articles that spell out the theoretical and methodological foundations of the enterprise, and in IV are a few of the papers that examine the implications of our research for education and foreign policy making.

While we are not yet in a position to offer any book-length set of integrated findings—that is, a data-based multi-factor explanatory theory of war in which we have high confidence—enough has emerged to warrant the publication of three anthologies during 1979 and 1980. The first, *Correlates of War I: Research Origins and Rationale* (New York: Free Press), brings together 15 papers published over the past 20 years, reflecting the ethical, pragmatic, theoretical, and methodological foundations of our work. In *Correlates of War II: Testing Some Realpolitik Models,* we assembled nine hitherto unpublished analyses, resulting largely from doctoral dissertations completed during the period 1974-1977. And in *Explaining War: Selected Papers from the Correlates of War Project* (Beverly Hills: Sage Publications) we make available 13 other papers from the project, all of which had appeared in various Sage journals and annuals during the 1970s.

I. THEORETICAL ORIENTATION AND RESEARCH STRATEGY

"Inter-Nation Influence: A Formal Model," AMERICAN POLITICAL SCIENCE REVIEW 57/2 (June 1963) 420-30 [Singer]. Reprinted in Singer (ed.), CORRELATES OF WAR I: RESEARCH ORIGINS AND RATIONALE. Free Press, 1979, 48-67.

"Multipolar Power Systems and International Stability," WORLD POLITICS 16/3 (April 1964), 390-406 [Karl Deutsch and Singer].

"The Political Matrix of International Conflict," in McNeill (ed.), THE NATURE OF HUMAN CONFLICT. Prentice-Hall, 1965, 139-54 [Singer].

"Escalation and Control in International Conflict: A Simple Feedback Model," GEN-
ERAL SYSTEMS 15 (1970) 163-73 [Singer]. Reprinted in Singer (ed.), CORRE-
LATES OF WAR I: RESEARCH ORIGINS AND RATIONALE. Free Press, 1979,
68-88.
"The Outcome of Arms Races: A Policy Problem and a Research Approach," PRO-
CEEDINGS OF IPRA THIRD GENERAL CONFERENCE Oslo (1970) 137-46
[Singer]. Reprinted in Singer (ed.), CORRELATES OF WAR I: RESEARCH ORI-
GINS AND RATIONALE. Free Press, 1979, 145-54.
"Modern International War: From Conjecture to Explanation," in Lepawsky et al.
(eds.), THE SEARCH FOR WORLD ORDER: ESSAYS IN HONOR OF QUINCY
WRIGHT. Appleton-Century-Crofts, 1971, 47-71 [Singer].
"The Correlates of War Project: Interim Report and Rationale," WORLD POLITICS
24/2 (January 1972), 243-70 [Singer].
"Historiche Tatsachen u. Wissenschaftliche Daten am Beispiel der Erforschung von
Kriegen" (Historical Facts and Scientific Data in the Study of War), in Ludz (ed.,
SOZIOLOGIE UND SOZIALGESCHICHTE ASPEKTE UND PROBLEME.
Westedeutscher, 1973, 221-41 [Melvin Small and Singer].
"The Future of Events Data Marriages: A Question of Compatibility," INTERNA-
TIONAL INTERACTIONS 2 (1975), 45-62 [Russell Leng].
"The Correlates of War Project: Continuity, Diversity, and Convergence," in Hoole and
Zinnes (eds.), QUANTITATIVE INTERNATIONAL POLITICS: AN APPRAISAL.
Praeger, 1976, 21-66 [Singer].
"The Applicability of Quantitative International Politics to Diplomatic History," THE
HISTORIAN 38 (February 1976), 281-304 [Melvin Small].
"The Historical Experiment as a Research Strategy in the Study of World Politics,"
SOCIAL SCIENCE HISTORY 2/1 (1977), 1-22 [Singer]. Reprinted in Singer (ed.),
CORRELATES OF WAR I: RESEARCH ORIGINS AND RATIONALE. Free Press,
1979, 175-96.
"The Behavioral Approach to Diplomatic History," in De Conde (ed.), DICTIONARY
OF THE HISTORY OF AMERICAN FOREIGN POLICY. Scribners, 1978, 66-77
[Singer].
"Variables, Indicators, and Data in Macro-Political Research," SOCIAL SCIENCE
HISTORY, 6 (May, 1982) [Singer].

II. CONSTRUCTING THE INDICATORS
AND GENERATING THE DATA

"The Composition and Status Ordering of the International System: 1815-1940,"
WORLD POLITICS 18/2 (January 1966), 236-82 [Small and Singer].
"Formal Alliances, 1815-1939: A Quantitative Description," JOURNAL OF PEACE
RESEARCH 1 (1966), 1-32 [Singer and Melvin Small].
"National Political Units in the Twentieth Century: A Standardized List," AMERI-
CAN POLITICAL SCIENCE REVIEW 62/3 (September 1968), 932-51 [Bruce Rus-
sett, Singer, and Melvin Small].
"Formal Alliances, 1816-1965: An Extension of the Basic Data," JOURNAL OF
PEACE RESEARCH 3 (1969), 257-82 [Melvin Small and Singer].
"Inter-Governmental Organization in the Global System, 1816-1964: A Quantitative
Description," INTERNATIONAL ORGANIZATION 24 (Spring 1970), 239-87 [Mi-
chael Wallace and Singer].
"Patterns in International Warfare, 1816-1965," ANNALS OF AMERICAN ACAD-
EMY OF POLITICAL AND SOCIAL SCIENCE 391 (September 1970), 145-55
[Melvin Small and Singer].
"A Sociometric Analysis of Diplomatic Bonds, 1817-1940," East Lansing, Mich.:
Events Data Conference, 1971 [Stuart Bremer].

"Formal Alliance Clusters in the Interstate System, 1816-1965." Washington, D.C.: ASPA Meetings, 1972 [Stuart Bremer].

THE WAGES OF WAR, 1816-1965: A STATISTICAL HANDBOOK. Wiley, 1972 [Singer and Melvin Small].

"Measuring the Concentration of Power in the International System," SOCIOLOGICAL METHODS AND RESEARCH 1/4 (May 1973), 403-37 [James Lee Ray and Singer]. Reprinted in Singer (ed.), EXPLAINING WAR: SELECTED PAPERS FROM THE CORRELATES OF WAR PROJECT. Sage, 1979, 273-304.

"Diplomatic Importance of States, 1816-1970: An Extension and Refinement of the Indicator," WORLD POLITICS 25/4 (July 1973), 577-99 [Melvin Small and Singer]. Reprinted in Singer (ed.), CORRELATES OF WAR I: RESEARCH ORIGINS AND RATIONALE. Free Press, 1979, 199-222.

"Measuring Systemic Polarity," JOURNAL OF CONFLICT RESOLUTION 19/2 (June 1975), 187-216 [Bruce Bueno de Mesquita].

"Clusters of Nations in the Global System, 1865-1964," INTERNATIONAL STUDIES QUARTERLY 19/1 (March 1975), 67-110 [Michael Walace]. Reprinted in Singer (ed.), EXPLAINING WAR: SELECTED PAPERS FROM THE CORRELATES OF WAR PROJECT. Sage, 1979, 253-72.

"Toward a Multi-Theoretical Typology of International Behavior," in Bunge, Galtung, and Malitza (eds.), MATHEMATICAL APPROACHES TO INTERNATIONAL RELATIONS. Bucharest: Romanian Academy (1977), 71-93 [Russell Leng and Singer].

"An Attempt to Scale Major Power Disputes, 1816-1965: The Use of a Method to Detect Development Processes," St. Louis, MO: ISA Meetings (1977) [Richard Stoll].

"The Measurement of System Structure," in Singer (ed.), CORRELATES OF WAR II: TESTING SOME REALPOLITIK MODELS. Free Press, 1979, 36-54 [James Lee Ray].

III. TESTING SOME MODELS AND ANALYZING THE DATA

"National Alliance Commitments and War Involvement, 1815-1945," PEACE RESEARCH SOCIETY (INTERNATONAL) PAPERS 5 (1966), 19-40 [Singer and Melvin Small].

"Alliance Aggregation and the Onset of War, 1815-1945," in Singer (ed.), QUANTITATIVE INTERNATIONAL POLITICS: INSIGHTS AND EVIDENCE. Free Press, 1968, 247-86 [Singer and Melvin Small]. Reprinted in Singer (ed.), CORRELATES OF WAR I: RESEARCH ORIGINS AND RATIONALE. Free Press, 1979, 225-64.

"Inter-Governmental Organization and the Preservation of Peace, 1816-1965: Some Bivariate Relationships," INTERNATIONAL ORGANIZATION 24 (Summer 1970), 520-47 [Singer and Michael Wallace].

"Power, Status, and International War," JOURNAL OF PEACE RESEARCH 1 (1971), 23-35 [Michael Wallace].

"Capability Distribution, Uncertainty, and Major Power War, 1820-1965," in Russett (ed.), PEACE, WAR, AND NUMBERS. Sage, 1972, 19-48 [Singer, Stuart Bremer, and John Stuckey]. Reprinted in Singer (ed.), CORRELATES OF WAR I: RESEARCH ORIGINS AND RATIONALE. Free Press, 1979, 265-97; and in Singer (ed.), EXPLAINING WAR: SELECTED PAPERS FROM THE CORRELATES OF WAR PROJECT. Sage, 1979, 159-88.

"Status, Formal Organization, and Arms Levels as Factors Leading to the Onset of War, 1820-1964," in Russett (ed.), PEACE, WAR, AND NUMBERS, Sage, 1972, 49-69 [Michael Wallace].

"Shared Memberships in Intergovernmental Organizations and Dyadic War, 1865-1964," in Fedder (ed.), THE UNITED NATIONS: PROBLEMS AND PROSPECTS, 1972, 31-61 [Kjell Skjelsbaek].

DIMENSIONS HISTORIQUES DE MODELES DYNAMIQUES DE CONFLICT: AP-
PLICATION AUX PROCESSUS DE COURSE AUX ARMEMENTS, 1900-1965.
Geneva: Graduate Institute of International Studies, doctoral thesis, 1972 [Urs
Luterbacher].

"The Impact of Alliances on Industrial Development," East Lansing, Mich.: Michigan
State University mimeo, March 1973 [Bruce Bueno de Mesquita].

"The Population Density and War Proneness of European Nations, 1816-1965," COM-
PARATIVE POLITICAL STUDIES 6/3 (October 1973), 329-48 [Stuart Bremer,
Singer, and Urs Luterbacher]. Reprinted in Singer (ed.), EXPLAINING WAR: SE-
LECTED PAPERS FROM THE CORRELATES OF WAR PROJECT. Sage, 1979,
189-207.

"Alliances, Capabilities, and War: A Review and Synthesis," in Cotter (ed.), POLITI-
CAL SCIENCE ANNUAL 4 (1973), 237-80 [Bruce Bueno de Mesquita and Singer].

"Status Inconsistency and the War Behavior of Major Powers, 1815-1965," Toronto:
Conference on International Relations Theory, December 1973 [Harald von
Riekhoff].

WAR AND RANK AMONG NATIONS, Lexington Books, 1973 [Michael Wallace].

"Alliance Polarization, Cross-Cutting, and International War, 1815-1964: A Measure-
ment Procedure and Some Preliminary Evidence," JOURNAL OF CONFLICT
RESOLUTION 17/4 (December 1973), 575-604 [Michael Wallace]. Reprinted in
Singer (ed.), EXPLAINING WAR: SELECTED PAPERS FROM THE CORRE-
LATES OF WAR PROJECT. Sage, 1979, 83-111.

STATUS INCONSISTENCY AND WAR INVOLVEMENT AMONG EUROPEAN
STATES, 1816-1970, Ann Arbor, Mich.: University of Michigan, doctoral thesis,
1974 [James Lee Ray].

"Status Inconsistency and War Involvement in Europe, 1816-1970," PEACE SCIENCE
SOCIETY (INTERNATIONAL) PAPERS 23 (1974), 69-80 [James Lee Ray].

"Behavioral Indicators of War Proneness in Bilateral Conflicts," in McGowan (ed.),
SAGE INTERNATIONAL YEARBOOK OF FOREIGN POLICY STUDIES II,
1974, 191-226 [Russell Leng and Robert Goodsell]. Reprinted in Singer (ed.), EX-
PLAINING WAR: SELECTED PAPERS FROM THE CORRELATES OF WAR
PROJECT. Sage, 1979, 208-39.

PROBABILITY MODELS OF WAR EXPANSION AND PEACETIME ALLIANCE
FORMATION. Ann Arbor, Mich.: University of Michigan, doctoral thesis, 1974
[Yoshinobu Yamamoto].

"Structural Clarity and International War: Some Tentative Findings," in Murray (ed.),
INTERDISCIPLINARY ASPECTS OF GENERAL SYSTEMS THEORY, 1975,
126-35 [Singer and Sandra Bouxsein].

"Distance and International War 1816-1965," PROCEEDINGS OF THE IPRA FIFTH
GENERAL CONFERENCE Oslo (1975), 481-506 [Nils Petter Gleditsch and
Singer].

"The Incidence of Intervention in Interstate War, 1816-1965," Cambridge, Mass.:
Peace Science Society (International) Meetings, 1975 [Cynthia Cannizzo].

"Military Confrontation and the Likelihood of War: The Major Powers 1820-1970,"
Cambridge, Mass.: Peace Science Society (International) Meetings, 1975 [Charles
Gochman].

STATUS, CONFLICT, AND WAR: THE MAJOR POWERS, 1820-1970, Ann Arbor,
Mich.: University of Michigan, doctoral thesis, 1975 [Charles Gochman].

"From Bosnia to Sarajevo: A Comparative Discussion of Interstate Crises," JOURNAL
OF CONFLICT RESOLUTION 19/1 (March 1975), 3-24 [Alan Sabrosky]. Re-
printed in Singer (ed.), EXPLAINING WAR: SELECTED PAPERS FROM THE
CORRELATES OF WAR PROJECT. Sage, 1979, 139-57.

THE EFFECTS OF WAR ON INDUSTRIAL GROWTH, 1816-1965, Ann Arbor Mich.:
University of Michigan, doctoral thesis, 1975 [Hugh Wheeler].

"Effects of War on Industrial Growth," SOCIETY 12/4 (May/June 1975), 48-52 [Hugh
Wheeler].

CAPABILITIES, COMMITMENTS, AND THE EXPANSION OF INTERSTATE WAR, 1816-1965, Ann Arbor, Mich.: University of Michigan, doctoral thesis, 1976 [Alan Sabrosky].

"The War Proneness of Democratic Regimes," JERUSALEM JOURNAL OF INTERNATIONAL RELATIONS 1/4 (Summer 1976), 49-69 [Melvin Small and Singer].

COSTS OF COMBAT: A STATISTICAL MODEL FOR PREDICTING THE COST AND OUTCOME OF INTERSTATE WAR, 1816-1965, Ann Arbor, Mich.: University of Michigan, doctoral thesis, 1976 [Cynthia Cannizzo].

"Hostilities in the European State System, 1816-1970," PAPERS, PEACE SCIENCE SOCIETY (International) 26 (1976), 100-116 [Michael Mihalka].

INTERSTATE CONFLICT IN THE EUROPEAN STATE SYSTEM, 1816-1970, Ann Arbor, Mich.: University of Michigan, doctoral thesis, 1976 [Michael Mihalka].

"Predicting the Escalation of Serious Disputes to International War: Some Preliminary Findings." Philadelphia: North American Peace Science Society (International) Meetings, 1977 [Richard Stoll and Michael Champion].

"Realpolitik, Arbitrations, and the Use of Force: The European Experience, 1816-1970," PAPERS, PEACE SCIENCE SOCIETY (International) 27 (1977), 77-87 [Michael Mihalka].

"Capability Distribution and Major Power War Experience, 1816-1965," ORBIS (Winter 1978), 947-57 [Cynthia Cannizzo].

THE MAJOR POWERS AND THE PURSUIT OF SECURITY IN THE NINETEENTH AND TWENTIETH CENTURIES, Ann Arbor Mich.: University of Michigan, doctoral thesis, 1978 [Thomas Cusack].

"Does Size Make A Difference? The Martial and Diplomatic Experience of Major and Other Powers, 1816-1977," in Amstrup and Faurby (eds.), STUDIER I DANSK UDENRIGSPOLITIK, Aarhus, Denmark: Forlaget Politica, 1978 [Melvin Small].

"The Costs of Combat: Death, Duration, and Defeat," in Singer (ed.), CORRELATES OF WAR II: TESTING SOME REALPOLITIK MODELS. Free Press, 1979, 233-57 [Cynthia Cannizzo].

"Systemic Polarization and the Occurrence and Duration of War," JOURNAL OF CONFLICT RESOLUTION 22/2 (June 1978), 241-267 [Bruce Bueno de Mesquita]. Reprinted in Singer (ed.), EXPLAINING WAR: SELECTED PAPERS FROM THE CORRELATES OF WAR PROJECT. Sage, 1979, 113-38.

"Conflict in the International System, 1916-1977: Historical Trends and Policy Futures," in Kegley and McGowan (eds.), CHALLENGES TO AMERICA: UNITED STATES FOREIGN POLICY IN THE 1980s, 89-115 [Singer and Melvin Small]. Reprinted in Singer (ed.), EXPLAINING WAR: SELECTED PAPERS FROM THE CORRELATES OF WAR PROJECT. Sage, 1979, 57-82.

"The Trials of Nations: An Improbable Application of Probability Theory," in Singer (ed.), CORRELATES OF WAR II: TESTING SOME REALPOLITIK MODELS. Free Press, 1979, 3-35 [Stuart Bremer].

"National Capabilities and War Proneness," in Singer (ed.), CORRELATES OF WAR II: TESTING SOME REALPOLITIK MODELS. Free Press, 1979, 57-82 [Stuart Bremer].

"Status, Capabilities, and Major Power War," in Singer (ed.), CORRELATES OF WAR II: TESTING SOME REALPOLITIK MODELS. Free Press, 1979, 83-123 [Charles Gochman].

"Influence Strategies and Interstate Conflict," in Singer (ed.), CORRELATES OF WAR II: TESTING SOME REALPOLITIK MODELS. Free Press, 1979, 124-57 [Russell Leng].

"Interstate Alliances: Their Reliability and the Expansion of War," in Singer (ed.), CORRELATES OF WAR II: TESTING SOME REALPOLITIK MODELS. Free Press, 1979, 161-98 [Alan Sabrosky].

"Post-War Industrial Growth," in Singer (ed.), CORRELATES OF WAR II: TESTING SOME REALPOLITIK MODELS. Free Press, 1979, 258-84 [Hugh Wheeler].

"Wider Wars and Restless Nights: Major Power Intervention in Ongoing War," in Singer (ed.), CORRELATES OF WAR II: TESTING SOME REALPOLITIK MODELS. Free Press, 1979, 199-229 [Yoshinobu Yamamoto and Stuart Bremer].

"The Role of Arms in the Escalation of Disputes,' JOURNAL OF CONFLICT RESOLUTION 23/1 (March 1979), 3-16 [Michael Wallace]. Reprinted in Singer (ed.), EXPLAINING WAR: SELECTED PAPERS FROM THE CORRELATES OF WAR PROJECT. Sage, 1979, 240-52.

"Capability Concentration, Alliance Bonding, and Conflict Among the Major Powers," in Sabrosky (ed.), ALLIANCES AND INTERNATIONAL CONFLICT (forthcoming) [Michael Champion and Richard Stoll].

"Periodicity, Inexorability, and Steersmanship in Major Power War," in Merritt and Russett (eds.), FROM NATIONAL DEVELOPMENT TO GLOBAL COMMUNITY. Allen and Unwin, 1981, 404-22. [Singer and Thomas Cusack].

IV. PRACTICAL IMPLICATIONS:
POLICY AND TEACHING

"Knowledge, Practice, and the Social Sciences in International Politics," in Palmer (ed.), A DESIGN FOR INTERNATIONAL RELATIONS RESEARCH, Monograph 10, Philadelphia: American Academy of Political and Social Science (October 1970) 137-49 [Singer].

"Foreign Policy Indicators: Predictors of War in History and in the State of the Union Message," POLICY SCIENCES 5/3 (September 1974), 271-96 [Singer and Melvin Small]. Reprinted in Singer (ed.), CORRELATES OF WAR I: RESEARCH ORIGINS AND RATIONALE. Free Press, 1979, 298-329.

"The Peace Researcher and Foreign Policy Prediction," PEACE SCIENCE SOCIETY (INTERNATIONAL) PAPERS 21 (1974), 1-13 [Singer]. Reprinted in Singer (ed.), CORRELATES OF WAR I: RESEARCH ORIGINS AND RATIONALE. Free Press, 1979, 155-71.

THE SCIENTIFIC STUDY OF WAR, Learning Package Series, Number 14, New York: Consortium for International Studies Education for the ISA, 1975 [Stuart Bremer et al.].

"Early Warning Indicators from The Correlates of War Project," in Singer and Wallace (eds.), TO AUGUR WELL: EARLY WARNING INDICATORS IN WORLD POLITICS. Sage, 1979, 17-35 [Michael Wallace].

About the Authors

MELVIN SMALL is Professor and Chair in the History Department of Wayne State University and co-investigator in the Correlates of War Project. Editor of *Public Opinion and Historians: Interdisciplinary Perspectives* (Wayne State University Press, 1970), author of *Was War Necessary: National Security and U.S. Entry into War* (Sage, 1980), and co-author (with J. David Singer) of *The Wages of War, 1816-1965: A Statistical Handbook* (Wiley, 1972), Small has published articles on diplomatic history and world politics in, among other journals, *The Historian, Journal of Peace Research, Journal of Conflict Resolution, Historical Methods Newsletter, Film and History, The Americas, World Politics,* and *The American Political Science Review.* He was also chair of the board of Wayne State's Center for Peace and Conflict Studies from 1977 to 1979.

J. DAVID SINGER, Professor of Political Science and Research Political Scientist, Mental Health Research Institute, University of Michigan, has taught at New York University, Vassar, and the Naval War College, and has been a visiting scholar at Harvard, and the Universities of Oslo and Geneva. He is on the editorial boards of the *Journal of Conflict Resolution, Journal of Politics,* and the *Political Science Reviewer* and the advisory board, *Advance Bibliography of Contents: Political Science and Government,* and has served as a consultant to various governmental and research agencies. Among his books are *Financing International Organization; Deterrence, Arms Control, and Disarmament; Human Behavior and International Politics; Quantitative International Politics; The Wages of War; Beyond Conjecture in International Politics: Abstracts of Data-Based Research;* and *Correlates of War, Volumes I and II.*